Social Dilemmas

Theoretical Issues
and Research Findings

INTERNATIONAL SERIES IN EXPERIMENTAL SOCIAL PSYCHOLOGY

Series Editor: MICHAEL ARGYLE, *University of Oxford*

Other titles in the series include

HOWITT
The Mass Media and Social Problems

NOLLER
Nonverbal Communication & Marital Interaction

BROWN
Advances in the Psychology of Religion

HOLLIN and TROWER
Handbook of Social Skills Training, Volume 1

HOLLIN and TROWER
Handbook of Social Skills Training, Volume 2

RUTTER
Communicating by Telephone

BULL
Posture and Gesture

FURNHAM
Lay Theories: Everyday Understanding of Problems in the Social Sciences

SCOTT and SCOTT
Adaptation of Immigrants

LIVINGSTONE
Making Sense of Television

REHM and GADENNE
Intuitive Predictions and Professional Forecasts

STRACK, ARGYLE and SCHWARZ
Subjective Well-Being

FORGAS
Emotion and Social Judgments

ALBERT
Genius and Eminence, 2nd Edition

WALKER
The Psychology of Gambling

Social Dilemmas
Theoretical Issues and Research Findings

Edited by

WIM B. G. LIEBRAND

with

David M. Messick

and

Henk A. M. Wilke

PERGAMON PRESS

OXFORD · NEW YORK · SEOUL · TOKYO

UK Pergamon Press Ltd, Headington Hill Hall,
Oxford OX3 0BW, England

USA Pergamon Press Inc, 660 White Plains Road, Tarrytown,
New York 10591–5153, USA

KOREA Pergamon Press Korea, KPO Box 315, Seoul 110–603,
Korea

JAPAN Pergamon Press Japan, Tsunashima Building Annex,
3–20–12 Yushima, Bunkyo-ku, Tokyo 113, Japan

First edition 1992

Library of Congress Cataloging-in-Publication Data
Social dilemmas: theoretical issues and research findings/
edited by Wim B. G. Liebrand, David M. Messick, and Henk
A. M. Wilke.—1st ed.
p. cm. (International series in experimental social
psychology.)
1. Social problems—Congresses. 2. Social conflict—
Congresses. 3. Social psychology—Congresses.
I. Liebrand, Wim B. G. II. Messick, David M. III. Wilke,
H. A. M. IV. Series.
HN3.S56 1992 361.1—dc20 92–16471

ISBN 0 08 037775 0

Printed in Great Britain by BPCC Wheatons Ltd, Exeter

Contents

Preface

SOCIAL dilemmas are societal problems that arise because we often assign higher priority to our own short-term interests than to the interests of others or to longer-term considerations. We do not generally like to ride bicycles during pollution alerts, to reduce our water or energy consumption, or to send money to the public television. However, we would all be better off if we were more inclined to cooperate in such situations.

At the Third International Conference on Social Dilemmas, we decided to prepare a book describing the advances social psychologists from around the world have made. Their insights may contribute to the understanding and resolution of social dilemmas. Each chapter in this book discusses its research findings in the context of a comprehensive view of social dilemmas. In the first two chapters of the book we try to make this comprehensive framework explicit.

We thank the Royal Dutch Academy of Sciences (KNAW), the European Association of Experimental Social Psychology, and the University of Groningen, The Netherlands, for their generous financial support of the Third International Conference on Social Dilemmas. Without their support neither the conference nor the book would have been possible.

Groningen, *March 1991*

WIM B. G. LIEBRAND
DAVID M. MESSICK
HENK A. M. WILKE

Part I

Introduction

1

Introduction and Literature Review

PAUL A. M. VAN LANGE
Free University, Amsterdam, The Netherlands

WIM B. G. LIEBRAND
University of Groningen, The Netherlands

DAVID M. MESSICK
University of California, Santa Barbara, USA

HENK A. M. WILKE
University of Leiden, The Netherlands

Introduction

When we go out to a nice restaurant for dinner and agree in advance to share the bill, we each tend to order things from the menu that are a bit more pricey than we would have ordered had we been alone. After all, we each pay only a fraction of the price of the meal we ordered, plus a fraction of everyone else's meal. Yet we are all shocked when the bill comes. Each of us would like to be able to shave our taxes a bit, but when we all do, our governments fail to collect enough money to pay for the services that we all need. And is there any real need for us to recycle our newspapers? We each read such an infinitesimal amount of the total newsprint produced that what we do individually makes essentially no difference to the big picture. But forests are being depleted to produce newsprint.

The situations described above are examples of what are called social dilemmas. Social dilemmas are characterized as situations in which private interests are at odds with the collective interests. The dilemma arises when all or most members of a group act in accordance with their private interests and do worse for themselves than had they ignored their own interests. My private interest might lead me to decline to pay the membership dues to join a labor union because I know that I will enjoy the benefits provided by that union regardless of whether or not I am a member. However, if everyone declined to join the labor union, there would be no benefit to enjoy and we would all be the worse for it. We have here a social dilemma.

More formally, social dilemmas can be defined as situations in which each decision maker is best off acting in his own self-interest, regardless of what the other persons do. Each self-interested decision, however, creates a negative outcome or cost for the other people who are involved. When a large number of people make the self-interested choice, the costs or negative outcomes accumulate, creating a situation in which everybody would have done better had they decided not to act in their own private interest.

Experimental Games

Game theory, the strategic analysis of conflicts of interest, was introduced on a large scale in the social and behavioral sciences by the important book of Luce and Raiffa (1957). This work laid the foundation for the development of experimental games which can be thought of as empirical research tools that could be used to test the predictive accuracy of the formal theory of games. Game theory and experimental games provided researchers in the social sciences with a promising new methodology to analyze human behavior in situations of interdependence and conflict.

An experimental game is a situation in which each of the participants (or players) has to choose one of several well-defined alternatives. All choices have consequences for the actor as well as for the other players involved, and the players are aware of these consequences.

A famous and important example is the Prisoner's Dilemma Game (PDG) for two persons. This game constitutes a true social dilemma, consistent with the definitions given above.

The following anecdote, taken from Luce and Raiffa (1957), illustrates both the name and the social dilemma properties of the Prisoner's Dilemma. Two individuals, accused of robbing a bank, are taken into custody and separated. The district attorney, unable to prove that they are guilty, confronts each prisoner with two options: either confess to the crime (option D), or not confess to it (option C). If both suspects confess, each will receive a 5-year sentence. If neither suspect confesses, both will be convicted on some minor charge and receive a 1-month sentence. If one confesses and the other does not, the suspect who does not confess will receive a 10-year sentence while the other will be set free. The consequences associated with the four possible combinations of choices

TABLE 1.1 *Prisoner's Dilemma for Two Persons*

		Column player C	Column player D
Row player	C	3,3	1,4
	D	4,1	2,2

are such that they result in the preference orderings depicted in Table 1.1. The ordering for each prisoner is strict, ranging from 1 (worst outcome: 10-year sentence) to 4 (best outcome: free). As appears from the preference orderings, it is to each prisoner's advantage to confess, regardless of the other's choice. However, if both prisoners act in their own interest and confess, they both end up in a worse position (5-year sentence) than in case they do not confess (1-month sentence). The Prisoner's Dilemma is an example of a mixed-motive game: there is a motive to Cooperate (option C), and there is the incompatible motive to Defect (option D). The specific ordering of payoffs as depicted in Table 1.1 results in two important properties of the Prisoner's Dilemma Game. First, each player has a dominating strategy. Second, if both players choose their dominant strategy, which is prescribed by the principle to maximize the payoff or the principle to maximize the minimum payoff (maximum), a deficient outcome results.

It is obvious that in societal problems more than two persons are involved. From a formal point of view, however, the two-person PDG can be easily extended to a PDG for more than two persons. Moreover, especially the various existing N-person generalizations of the two-person PDG are expected to capture the decisional structure of several real-life problems. Examples of these N-person generalizations will be discussed throughout this book. For present purposes it is sufficient to discuss formally the N-person generalization of the two-person PDG.

To represent outcomes in three- or more-person PDGs, it often is more convenient to use graphs. Figure 1.1 illustrates the graphical display of the two-person PDG from Table 1.1 and an N-person generalization of it.

Again the D-option corresponds to the dominating strategy, the C-option to the common interest strategy. The number of persons choosing option C is depicted on the horizontal axis; the two payoff graphs for each game refer to the outcomes for a player choosing either C or D, given a particular number of C-choices. The correspondence between both graphs and between both graphs and Table 1.1 can be seen by comparing the outcome orderings. On the one hand, the outcome orderings are presented by the matrix cell entries; on the other hand, they are presented by points on the payoff graphs. For example, the payoff graph for choosing D includes always the highest possible payoff

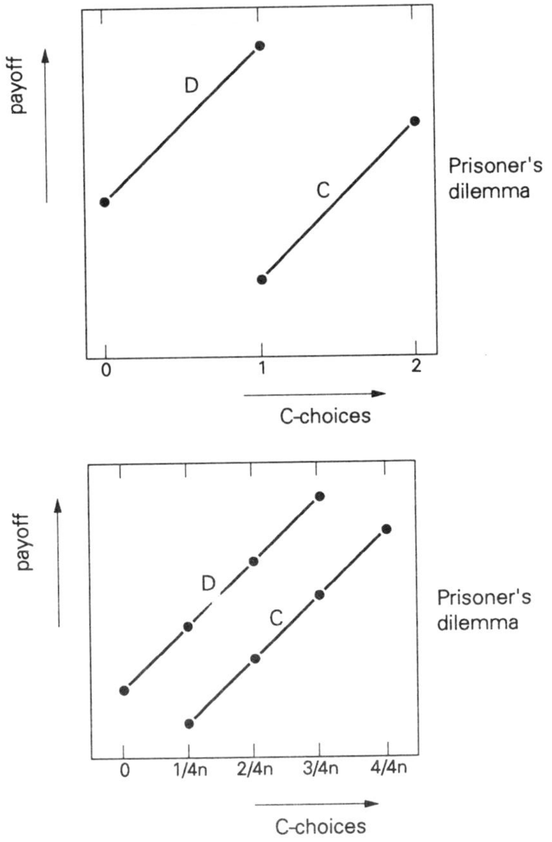

FIG. 1.1

(preference 4, Table 1.1), and lies, for a specific number of C-choices, above the graph for choosing C. However, in case nobody chooses C (left end point), the corresponding payoff for all is less than in case they all had chosen C (right end point of the C-graph is above the left end point of graph D).

An example of the *N*-person PDG is the decision to pollute. Pollution problems can be found at various levels of decision making, ranging from individuals to nations. For example, at the industrial level, no matter what other chemical industries may do to get rid of their chemical waste, it is cheaper to have the waste dumped at some rubbish-dump, or alternatively, in the ocean, than to take care of an adequate decomposition of the waste. The ultimate long-term consequences of this selfish act have to be shared by all individuals. At the individual level the slogan "every litter bit hurts" nicely reflects the negative consequences accompanying the decision to pollute (alternative D). Though all individuals would like to avoid the long-term negative consequences, it remains cheaper and simpler for them to keep polluting as anonymous individuals. The payoff graph for polluting lies for its entire length above the graph indicating the payoff for not polluting.

The use of experimental games as a method of research has several advantages. First, it offers the ability to manipulate the nature of the mutual dependency of the players involved in a simple and precise way, merely by altering the entries in the payoff matrix or manipulating the payoff graphs. Second, it allows one to manipulate other factors which might influence decision making in conflict settings such as the characteristics of the other players involved. Third, it offers a clear operationalization of vague concepts like cooperation and competition. Finally, experimental games can be created that contain the basic elements of complex interpersonal and socio-economical problems. They can contain the fundamental structure of social dilemmas. This book provides numerous examples of such games.

At least partly because of the advantages noted above, the 1960s witnessed a veritable flood of experimental gaming studies. More than 1000 studies have been reported using mainly the two-person PDG. Reviews of this work can be found in Wrightsman, O'Connor, and Baker (1972), Pruitt and Kimmel (1977) and Colman (1982). Although the research effort had great potential, reviewers have been critical of the accomplishments.

According to Pruitt and Kimmel (1977), the two most important problems of the two-person experimental game tradition at that time were the lack of a theoretical basis for generating research questions and the low external validity of the abstract decision tasks for the subjects.

On the theory side, we think that the chapters in this book accurately reflect the growing concern of social dilemma researchers with theoretical concerns from diverse areas of psychology. Research issues stem from such diverse areas as interpersonal relations (Kelley & Thibaut, 1978), intergroup relations (Messick & Mackie, 1989; Rabbie, 1982), equity and fairness (Messick & Cook, 1983), and judgment and decision making (Dawes, 1988). The conceptual underpinnings of much social dilemma work are broader and more intertwined with research in other areas and hence less insular than was previously the case.

The lack of external validity still remains a bit problematic, and will probably always be so to the extent that experimental social dilemmas are evaluated as imitations of those that exist in the world outside the laboratory. Measures have been taken, however, to enhance the representativeness of experimental situations. Different experimental dilemmas are patterned more closely on real problems than was previously the case. For instance, Jerdee and Rosen (1974) and others have developed a class of experimental tasks called resource dilemmas (Messick & Brewer, 1983). These tasks are designed to simulate the shared use of replenishable resources. In resource dilemmas, subjects take resources from a common pool and try to maintain that public good over a series of trials. After each trial the pool replenishes itself at a predetermined rate. Subject's tasks are to use the pool efficiently while trying to do well for themselves individually. The social dilemma structure is reflected by the fact that it is to each person's interest to accumulate as much as possible from the pool, but if each tries to do that the pool will be destroyed.

Another class of games is called public goods games (Messick & Brewer, 1983). These games simulate situations in which members of a group benefit from when a member makes a personally costly act. Others benefit when I join a union or when I pay my taxes. It costs me to do so, but in the long run we are all better off if we all pay the cost and resist the temptation to free-ride on the contributions of others. While public goods games have the same structure as resource dilemmas at a high level of abstraction, the external validity of the research is enhanced to the extent that the experimental paradigm that is used is chosen to mimic as closely as possible the real social dilemma in which the investigator is interested.

Pruitt and Kimmel's (1977) critical review was based mainly on the research addressed to the two-person PDG paradigm, and explicitly was announced to be not a summary of past research, but a diagnosis of a twenty-year tradition. As was implied before, experimental gaming research has addressed the criticism of their approach both in the 1970s as well as in the 1980s. Before we proceed to discuss the theoretical threads running through contemporary work, it seems to be relevant to discuss previous work in experimental gaming.

Literature Review

Formally, social dilemmas are defined by three properties (e.g., Dawes, 1980; Messick & Brewer, 1983; Yamagishi, 1986): (1) a noncooperative choice (option D) is always more profitable to the actor than a cooperative choice (option C), regardless of the choices made by the others; (2) compared to a cooperative choice, a noncooperative choice is always harmful to the others; and (3) the aggregate amount of harm done to others by a noncooperative choice is greater than the profit to the actor himself. The *social* nature of decisions in social dilemmas is obvious because people have influence on each other's welfare. The decision problem or *dilemma* underlying social dilemmas can be explained by two conflicting definitions of rationality (e.g., Kahan, 1974). Individual or egocentric rationality prescribes noncooperation, because this decision leads to individual outcomes which are always higher than those following from a cooperative decision. Collective rationality prescribes cooperation, because each individual is better off when all people cooperate than when all people do not cooperate. This obtains because the harm done to others by noncooperation is larger than the personal profit to the individual actor.

Social dilemma research has been interesting to social and behavioral scientists for at least two interrelated reasons. First, social dilemma research focuses on the conditions under which people are willing to exercise some personal restraint, or to behave less selfishly. The primary purpose in this regard is to understand selfish and cooperative behaviors, and how these behaviors can be influenced by situational and personality variables. Second, social and behavioral scientists are increasingly aware of the fact that many societal problems are caused, at least in part, by collective selfish behavior. As was noted earlier, the problem of maintaining or providing a clean and healthy environment is caused in part by people's reluctance to give up some of their immediate well-being. So research on social dilemmas may enable scientists to offer recommendations for solutions to such societal problems. While these two objectives usually go hand in hand, most social dilemma research to date has been concerned with basic psychological processes.

The purpose of this section is to review experimental research on cooperation in social dilemmas, and to summarize factors that promote cooperation in social dilemmas. We start, however, with a description of the history of social dilemma research.

The Origins of Social Dilemma Research: Experimental Games

Historically, social dilemma research grew out of game theory which is the abstract analysis of strategic social interdependence. There are two major goals of game theory (Colman, 1982; Rapoport, 1966). The first is to describe and develop experimental games that are of theoretical interest. The second is to find rational solutions to these games. Such solutions are based upon assumptions about people's values or utilities, and upon the logical analysis of the decisions people should make given their values.

One of the first reviews of experimental gaming studies was published by Rapoport and his associates (Rapoport & Orwant, 1962; Rapoport & Chammah, 1965). They review the earliest experiments on experimental games, most of which were concerned with testing formal properties and assumptions underlying game theory as set forth by Von Neumann and Morgenstern (1944) and Luce and Raiffa (1957). This early research disclosed the relevance of some potentially important psychological variables. For instance, it showed that people's values and utilities are strongly dependent upon a variety of variables (cf. Deutsch, 1960). Such findings could not be accounted for exclusively on the basis of game theory (cf. Colman, 1982). That is, although game theory provides insight into the logical analysis of social interdependence and into rationality given one's values, there was no room for the "psychological make-up of the participants" (cf. Rapoport, 1966, p. 206). Put differently, game theory was not concerned with, or capable of predicting or explaining, the influence of situational and intrapersonal forces on the values themselves.

Consequently, during the mid-sixties social scientists became increasingly interested in demonstrating the need for psychological and social approaches to cooperative behavior, as evidenced by an immense number of experiments (cf. Pruitt & Kimmel, 1977; Wrightsman, O'Connor, & Baker, 1972). This research was characterized by a focus on situational, personality, or attitudinal correlates of cooperative (game) behavior. Indeed, subsequent research has revealed a large number of factors that promote cooperative game behavior (cf. Colman, 1982; Hamburger, 1979). Thus game research provided a substantial empirical contribution to the fields of cooperation and competition.

Despite these contributions, the experimental game paradigm was criticized, most notably by Nemeth (1972) and Pruitt and Kimmel (1977). Their criticisms carried two charges. First, they claimed there was a lack of theory, and, second, insufficient concern for external validity.

With regard to the first charge we will show that social dilemma researchers have become increasingly concerned with describing and explaining the underlying processes of decision making in situations of conflict. When we discuss "current issues" we will discuss contemporary studies that add to our theoretical understanding of the decision making process. In the present section, however, we discuss the external validity of social dilemma studies.

A Lack of Concern for External Validity?

In her critical analysis, Nemeth (1972) argued that the external validity of the experimental gaming paradigm was in strong need of improvement because the paradigm is very abstract and ambiguous. In real-life situations, she argued, people often are able to exchange information or to communicate about one another's goals or motives, they usually know each other, and this "psychological richness" is often not reflected in the minimal social situation constituted by experimental games. In terms of Aronson and Carlsmith (1969), Nemeth is questioning the *mundane realism* of experimental gaming research; that is, the degree to which the paradigm is superficially similar to everyday situations.

During the past two decades, however, social dilemma researchers have increased mundane realism by developing different types of social dilemmas, as well as different experimental contexts in which such social dilemmas can be studied. That is, there have been more and more attempts to distinguish relevant properties of social dilemmas both in terms of how they occur in daily life situations and in terms of how they can be examined in experimentally controlled situations (cf. Messick & Brewer, 1983).

Some distinctions that have been made about social dilemmas include the following: (1) the number of people (supposedly) involved, ranging from 2 to *N*; (2) whether the participants are individuals (e.g., Dawes, McTavish, & Shaklee, 1977) or groups (e.g. McCallum *et al.*, 1985; Rabbie, Visser, & Van Oostrum, 1982); (3) single-trial versus iterated or sequential social dilemmas: in single-trial social dilemmas people make only one choice, whereas in iterated or sequential social dilemmas people make more than one choice, usually allowing them to respond to (the knowledge of) each other's previous choices; (4) symmetric versus asymmetric social dilemmas: symmetric social dilemmas are situations in which each participant has the same personal resources, and in which the consequences of their own choices are identical to the choices of each participant, whereas asymmetric social dilemmas require either differences in personal resources or consequences of choices (e.g., McClintock, Messick, Kuhlman, & Campos, 1973; Rapoport, Bornstein, & Erev, 1989; Wit & Wilke, 1989); (5) two-choice versus *N*-choice social dilemmas: in two-choice social dilemmas subjects are faced with a cooperative and a noncooperative choice, whereas in *N*-choice, or expanded, social dilemmas subjects are faced with more choices, usually examining thereby the degree of cooperative behavior; and (6) game theoretical differences. These are thoroughly discussed by Colman (1982), Hamburger (1979), Kelley and Thibaut (1978), Liebrand (1983) and Rapoport and Chammah (1965).

In addition to the distinctions among social dilemmas, new research paradigms have been developed in an attempt to increase mundane realism. Two of these paradigms have received considerable experimental attention, the *resource dilemma paradigm* and the *public good paradigm*.

The resource dilemma is essentially inspired by Hardin's (1968) description of *the tragedy of the commons*. He describes a situation in which a community exhausted a scarce resource (free grazing land) because each individual failed to consider the potential long-term consequences of the community's resource use pattern. In such situations, people responded for immediate personal gains, but in the long run accrued to considerable social losses. In order to simulate the essential properties of such social dilemmas, Jerdee and Rosen (1974) and others (e.g., Rubenstein, Watzke, Doktor, & Dana, 1975; Brechner, 1977) have developed a *resource management paradigm* in which each subject of a group makes a series of decisions as to how much to use or to take from a common resource. Each subject is better off by taking as much as possible. However, if all take too much, the resource is used up faster than it can be replenished. Collective noncooperation leads to a serious threat of the depletion of future resources. The common resource can also be underused, namely if all take less than the amount that could be replenished. This resource dilemma paradigm has strong similarities with everyday life dilemmas involved in energy conservation and environmental pollution.

Another mundanely realistic paradigm is the so-called *public goods paradigm*. This paradigm, inspired by the theoretical work of Olson (1965), simulates situations in which members of a group have free access to a good regardless of whether they contributed to its provision or maintenance. Thus there is no incentive to pay for the good. Although the public good paradigm is not necessarily different from the resource management paradigm as regards its underlying structure, it is quite different in terms of how people may interpret the dilemma (cf. Brewer & Kramer, 1986). In public good dilemmas people face the decision whether or not to contribute actively to the collective welfare (the corresponding experimental games are also called *give-some games*), whereas in resource dilemmas people face the decision whether or not to actively pursue self-interest by taking from the already existing common resources (*take-some games*).

It should be noted that both the resource dilemmas and the public good dilemmas have strong similarities with social traps-fences distinction drawn by Platt (1973) and Messick and Brewer (1983). This distinction differentiates situations in which people behave in order to obtain short-term positive consequences for themselves (resource management) from those in which people avoid short-term negative consequences for themselves (public good) but in which the long-term consequences of collective actions are negative for the group as well as for the individual.

This growing variety of social dilemma paradigms has increased the mundane realism of contemporary research. In the past fifteen years, numerous social dilemma experiments have been designed with some specific properties of situations in daily life in mind (e.g., Jerdee & Rosen, 1974; Jorgenson & Papciak, 1981; Liebrand, 1984; McCallum *et al.*, 1985; Messick *et al.*, 1983; Samuelson, Messick, Rutte, & Wilke, 1984).

Even if an experiment lacks *mundane realism*, most have what Aronson and Carlsmith (1969) call *experimental realism*. That is, the experiment absorbs and involves its participants, and provides a meaningful situation to the subjects. A vivid bit of support for experimental realism is described by Dawes (1980), who observed, after an experiment was completed, that people yelled at one another, accused one another of immoral behavior, or became tearful. Such emotional reactions are more likely to be exceptions than the rule and to occur when large amounts of actual money are at stake. Nevertheless, they show how strong a subject's involvement can be (cf. Hamburger, 1979). The anecdotal evidence suggests not only that subjects were indeed facing a real dilemma, but also that they were quite involved and motivated to find the "best" solution. There is also evidence that subjects can often provide plausible explanations for their behavior (cf. McClintock, 1972) and other's behaviors (Van Lange,

Liebrand, & Kuhlman, 1990). In this latter study subjects involved in different games were able to offer causal explanations for behavior that were consistent with the underlying theoretical differences among the games. Moreover, content analysis of free communication between subjects (Bonacich, 1972; Dawes, 1980), as well as subject's judgments of cooperative and noncooperative game behavior (e.g., Kelley *et al.*, 1970), support the idea that subjects are involved, and assign meaning to the choices at hand, even if the social dilemma is not a simulation of any everyday life social dilemma (e.g., Caporael, Dawes, Orbell, & Van de Kragt, 1989). Or, as Caporael *et al.* have put it: "subjects *are* in the social dilemma". All together, this evidence strongly indicates that the level of experimental realism is, or can be, fairly high in social dilemma research.

Factors Influencing Cooperation in Social Dilemmas

As mentioned earlier, there is a wide variety of social dilemmas. One important difference is whether the social dilemma involves just two persons, two-person social dilemmas, or more than two persons, *N*-person social dilemmas. According to Dawes (1980), *N*-person social dilemmas differ in at least three distinct ways from two-person social dilemmas. First, in two-person social dilemmas the harm of noncooperation is focused on one other person, rather than spread out over many others. Second, if the social dilemma is iterated, an individual involved in a two-person social dilemma is able to shape the other's behavior by his or her own behavioral strategy. For example, in an iterated two-person social dilemma an individual can play the so-called Tit for Tat strategy (Axelrod, 1984; Oskamp, 1971). This strategy, which starts off with a cooperative choice and subsequently imitates the other's previous choice, has been shown to be very effective in eliciting cooperation from others. Obviously, this type of behavioral control (Kelley & Thibaut, 1978) is not possible in large-scale social dilemmas. Third, unlike social dilemmas involving many people, in two-person social dilemmas it is impossible to make any anonymous choice. That is, one might assume that individuals in a two-person social dilemma are aware of the fact that the other is going to find out what choice he or she has made.

One can conclude, then, that the two-person social dilemma is quite different from the *N*-person social dilemma. Furthermore, because of these differences, one might argue that the psychological processes underlying choice behavior in two-person social dilemmas may be somewhat different from those underlying choices in *N*-person dilemmas.

Below we will discuss general factors that have been shown to stimulate cooperation in both *N*-person and two-person social dilemmas, as well as factors that are more specifically related to either *N*-person or two-person social dilemmas.

I. General Factors Promoting Cooperation in Social Dilemmas

1. Monetary Payoff Structure

One of the most obvious factors that should promote cooperation in social dilemmas are variations in the specific payoff structure underlying social dilemmas. Specifically, there are two general ways by which cooperation could be influenced, namely to decrease the incentive associated with noncooperative behavior, and to increase the incentive associated with cooperative behavior. Consistent with the findings of a classic study of Kelley and Grzelak (1972), it has been found repeatedly that cooperation is promoted by each of these two variations in payoff (e.g., Bonacich, Shure, Kahan, & Meeker, 1976; Komorita, Sweeney, & Kravitz, 1980). Research has also shown that people are much more likely to cooperate to the extent that interdependent others can benefit more from it (Caldwell, 1976; Komorita, Sweeney, & Kravitz, 1980). This has led Messick and Brewer (1983) to conclude that cooperation is influenced by at least two independent motives, namely a selfish one, the extent to which they themselves can benefit from it, and an altruistic one, the extent to which others can benefit from it. There is also strong support for the generality of the influence of different payoff structures. Using a resource management task, many studies have shown that people are more likely to cooperate if they think that personal restraint is essential or crucial to the maintenance of the shared resource pool (e.g., Jorgenson & Papciak, 1981; Samuelson, Messick, Rutte, & Wilke, 1984). Finally, recent work of Komorita (Komorita & Barth, 1985; Komorita, 1987) has shown that cooperation is promoted when actors believe that interdependent others are able to punish noncooperative behavior and/or to reward cooperative behavior. Although these studies suggest that rewarding cooperation may be in fact more important than punishing noncooperative behavior, it remains to be determined whether this effect is robust across different types of social dilemmas and different types of payoff manipulations.

Generally, the influence of payoff structure has been shown to be strong not only in experimental work on social dilemmas, but also in field studies. Maki, Hoffman, and Berk (1978), for example, found that monetary reward for electricity conservation was one of the most effective means to attaining conservation. A series of studies by Winett and his colleagues (Winett, Kagel, Battalio, & Winkler, 1978; Winett, Kaiser, & Haberkorn, 1978; Winett & Nietzel, 1975) have all shown quite strong effects for monetary rewards, ranging from over 10 to 30 or 40 percent energy conservation.

The effect of variations of payoff structures have also been considered in an attempt to examine the importance of two motives that may lead one to choose noncooperatively, namely fear and greed. Fear is the aversive pressure corresponding to the loss avoided by noncooperation when the others do not cooperate, and greed is the appetitive pressure corresponding to the profit one enjoys by noncooperating when others do cooperate (Coombs, 1973; Rapoport, 1966). The results of this research indicate that both motives are important. People are more likely to cooperate to the extent that they lose less by cooperation when others do not cooperate. Similarly, people are more likely to cooperate to the extent that they gain less by taking advantage of, or free-riding on, the cooperation of others (see also Stroebe & Frey, 1982). Although each motive is important, the findings of previous research are contradictory as to what motive is most important. Some studies have found that greed is more important than fear (Komorita, Sweeney, & Kravitz, 1980; Poppe & Utens, 1985; Simmons, Dawes, & Orbell, 1984), as well as the opposite (Van Lange, Liebrand, & Kuhlman, 1990; Yamagishi & Sato, 1986), or that they are about equally important (Liebrand, Wilke, Vogel, & Wolters, 1986; Bruins, Liebrand, & Wilke, 1989). It is quite likely that the relative importance of each motive depends upon a number of variables, such as whether or not people actually lose money (cf. Van Avermaet & Nieuwkerke, 1989).

2. Communication

One interesting and potentially important way to escape from collective noncooperation is to coordinate the social dilemma in a manner such that people feel committed, or actually promise to contribute, to the collective welfare (cf. Orbell, Van de Kragt, & Dawes, 1988). As mentioned before, there is a collective basis for rational behavior, and communication opportunities may be helpful toward escaping from collectively irrational solutions.

There is evidence that communication enhances cooperation in both two-person (Deutsch, 1960; Radnoff & Weidner, 1966) and N-person social dilemmas (Jerdee & Rosen, 1974; Liebrand, 1984; Jorgenson & Papciak, 1981). However, there are also experiments in which the communication effect was found to be rather weak or virtually absent (Caldwell, 1976; Loomis, 1959). This suggests that communication *per se* may not be sufficient to enhance cooperation. This assertion has been explored and confirmed in a classic study of Dawes, McTavish, and Shaklee (1977). They showed that communication or group discussion promotes cooperation only when the discussion itself is relevant for the decisions that have to be made.

Since the Dawes, McTavish, and Shaklee (1977) study, more attention has been paid to explaining the effect of communication. Although a variety of plausible explanations have been offered (see Messick & Brewer, 1983), two of them seem most important. In addition to the commitment norm described above, the communication effect can be explained by assuming that communication enhances feelings of "we-ness" or group identity, leading individuals to prefer collective welfare more than their own individual welfare. Although it is very difficult to demonstrate which explanation is most important, the commitment norm and feelings of we-ness usually go hand in hand and it is quite likely that each of these mechanisms have an independent effect on cooperation. Orbell, Van de Kragt, and Dawes (1988) reached a very similar conclusion, namely that public commitment through promise-making and group identity have independent effects, and that their combined effect is likely to be larger than the independent effects alone.

3. *Expectations of Others' Cooperation*

Collectively rational solutions to social dilemmas are attainable only if a sufficient number of others are willing to choose cooperatively as well. It is quite likely, then, that people are more likely to cooperate if they expect others to cooperate as well than if they expect the others not to cooperate. In the latter case, it is reasonable not to cooperate in order to protect oneself from being the "sucker." Indeed, across a variety of social dilemmas it has been well established that expectations of others' cooperation and one's own cooperation are strongly interrelated (Dawes, McTavish, & Shaklee, 1977; Messick, Wilke, Brewer, Kramer, Zemke, & Lui, 1983; Schroeder, Jensen, Reed, Sullivan, & Schwab, 1983; Van Lange & Liebrand, 1989).

In addition to the intuitively compelling idea, that expectations influence one's own cooperative behavior because one's willingness to cooperate depends upon what they think others will do (conditional cooperation), a variety of other explanations for the expectation–choice relationship are quite plausible as well. First, this relationship can be explained by assuming that social norms are important to social dilemma, and that people infer social norms from their expectations of others' choice behavior. Second, responsiveness to expectations can be explained by simple conformity. Third, if subjects have little information to base their expectations on, they may base their expectations on their own intended choice ("I cooperate, so others are likely to do the same"). Thus, intended choice is the cause of expectations. Finally, the correlation between choice and expectations may also be explained by *post-hoc* justification or rationalizing one's own cooperative or noncooperative choice by expressing cooperative or noncooperative expectations (Messé & Sivacek, 1979).

Recent work of Kerr (1989) indicates that the relationship between expectations and choice is strong, even if normative or conformity pressures are weak. This suggests that conditional cooperation in combination with assumed consensus or *post-hoc* justification are sufficient to explain the relationship between expectations and choice. It also seems plausible that the relationship between expectations and choice behavior is bidirectional (cf. Abric & Kahan, 1972; Van Lange & Liebrand, 1991). That is expectations may influence choice, as well as the reverse.

4. *The Role of Individual Differences*

Cooperative choice behavior is influenced not only by situational factors, such as the ones described above, but also by pre-existing individual differences. The type of individual differences that have received most attention are social value orientations and trust.

Social value orientations may be defined as preferences for particular distributions of outcomes to oneself and others (Messick & McClintock, 1968; McClintock, 1978). Although a variety of social value orientations can be distinguished, three orientations have received most empirical and theoretical attention. These are (a) cooperation, the orientation to maximize own and others' outcomes; (b) individualism, the orientation to maximize own outcomes; and (c) competition, the orientation to maximize the relative advantage over others. The consistent finding across a variety of social dilemma studies is that cooperators are more likely to exercise personal restraint, or to resist the temptation to choose selfishly, in social dilemmas, than individualists or competitors. The most important conclusion reached by this research is that not everybody is *a priori* inclined to value only their own outcomes, or to see the pursuit of self-interest as rational. Instead, people may transform the payoff matrix, and then maximize the transformed or subjective values (Kelley & Thibaut, 1978). The cooperative (computing the sum of own and others' outcomes) and competitive (computing the difference score in favor of self) transformations lead to choices that are quite different from those flowing from pure self-interest (cf. Kuhlman & Marshello, 1975; McClintock & Liebrand, 1988).

In addition to social value orientations, individual differences in *trust* have received some attention in recent experiments. Specifically, people differ to the extent that they believe that others are honest or dishonest, that trusting others is risky and so on (Yamagishi, 1988). Such individual differences have been found to be related not only to cooperative choice behavior in social dilemmas, but also to the type of solutions they see as most feasible. Specifically, high-trusters are more likely to cooperate than low-trusters, and low-trusters are more willing than high-trusters to contribute to the establishment or maintenance of a sanctioning system that imposes sanctions on noncooperative choices.

In sum, individual differences in social value orientation and trust influence perceptions of social dilemmas, how people approach others, and perhaps most importantly, the way in which social dilemmas can be solved.

5. *Group Size*

The effects of group size were initially studied in relatively small groups. Marwell and Schmitt (1972), for example, found that people cooperated more in two-person social dilemmas than in three-person social dilemmas. Hamburger, Guyer, and Fox (1975) found higher levels of cooperation in three-person groups than in groups of seven persons, and Bonacich, Shure, Kahan, and Meeker (1976) found higher levels of cooperation in six-person groups than nine-person groups. These findings suggest that cooperation declines as groups become larger. However, such differences become smaller or virtually absent when relatively larger groups are compared. For example, Fox and Guyer (1977) replicated the finding that cooperation declines as you move from three-person to seven-person groups, but failed to find differences between seven- and twelve-person groups. Similarly, Liebrand (1984) found no differences between groups of seven and twenty persons. Thus, research suggests that cooperation declines as groups become larger up to about seven or eight persons; if groups become larger than seven or eight persons, then the level of cooperation is not strongly influenced by a further increase in group size.

There are many psychological differences between social dilemmas in which only a few people are involved and those in which many people are involved (see also Olson, 1965). Generally, such differences may include the extent to which one's choice is effective, the extent to which one's choice is visible or one feels identifiable, and the extent to which one feels responsible for the collective welfare. As will be outlined below, these factors are more particularly important in social dilemmas involving many people.

II. Factors Promoting Cooperating in *N*-person Social Dilemmas

1. *Perceived Efficacy*

One factor that may be strongly related to group size is perceived efficacy, or the extent to which one believes that his or her own contributions help to achieve the collective goals. Among the first who recognized the importance of perceived efficacy in relation to group size was Olson (1965) in his book *The Logic of Collective Action*. He argued that the decrease in the perceived efficacy as group size increases forms one of the major explanations for why people fail to cooperate in large groups.

Both laboratory and field studies support the idea that cooperation can be promoted by increasing perceived efficacy. Van de Kragt, Orbell, and Dawes (1983) found evidence that people are willing to cooperate if they think that their choice is critical to the provision of a public good. Although in this study the high level of cooperation can be explained by selfish motives, there is also evidence that people are more willing to contribute if they believe that the group, as opposed to they themselves, will benefit by doing so (cf. Kerr & Bruun, 1983). Finally, efficacy has been directly related to group size. Consistent with Olson (1965), Kerr (1989) found that perceived efficacy declines with group size, even if objective efficacy does not. Efficacy is perceived to be inversely related to group size, and is therefore likely to defer cooperation in large-scale social dilemmas.

2. *Identifiability*

In large groups, people generally are able to "hide in the crowd" or to make a choice believing that nobody will know the choice they made. Bixenstine, Levitt, and Wilson (1966) were among the first to examine the effects of private and public choices, and found higher levels of cooperation when subjects made choices in public than in private, anonymous situations. Subsequent research has confirmed the importance of identifiability as a determinant for cooperative behavior (e.g., Fox & Guyer, 1978; Kahan, 1973).

There have been attempts to examine the psychological processes that mediate the effects of identifiability on cooperation. Using a resource dilemma, Jorgenson and Papciak (1981) found that identifiability had a positive effect on cooperation only when subjects were not able to communicate. Interestingly, in those no-communication conditions, high identifiable subjects reported that they felt more identifiable and more inhibited than low-identifiable subjects, whereas no such differences were found in the communication conditions. It seems likely, then, that identifiability may serve some of the same purposes as communication; namely, to promote feelings of "social control" that encourage people to exercise personal restraint. Finally, it should be noted that the "social control" mechanism may be quite strong in different public situations. It could also account for the effect that people are more willing to work hard under conditions of high visibility than in more anonymous situations (Williams, Harkins, & Latané, 1980).

3. Feelings of Personal Responsibility

Somewhat related to identifiability is the proposition that personal responsibility typically decreases with increasing group size. One of the classic studies showing that people are less helpful when more people are involved was conducted by Latané and Darley (1968). They showed, for example, that smoke pouring into a testing room was more likely to be reported by individuals working alone than by three-person groups. These and similar findings (e.g., Latané & Rodin, 1969; Schwartz & Gottlieb, 1981) can be explained by the idea that there is *diffusion of responsibility*. The problem, of course, is that nobody helps, if everybody denies his or her own responsibility. Similar denials may occur in large social dilemmas. A nice demonstration of responsibility diffusion in a public good paradigm has been provided by Fleishman (1980). He found that feelings of responsibility were enhanced the more others stood to benefit from one's contributions and the greater the collective resources needed to provide the public good. Also feelings of responsibility were positively correlated with contribution size, suggesting that responsibility enhances cooperation. These findings were observed in a public good dilemma in which 100 individuals were said to be involved.

One factor that may influence feelings of personal responsibility is the enhancement of *group identity*. Brewer (1979) and Edney (1980) argued that people would be more likely to contribute to the collective welfare if they felt part of the group, or if collective identity were made salient. In order to test this hypothesis, Kramer and Brewer (1984) examined the effects of group identity on cooperation in a resource dilemma. In one of their experiments, they manipulated group identity by using naturally occurring social categories to make salient either a superordinate (collective) or subordinate (differentiating) group identity. In the superordinate condition, subjects were told that the experiment was concerned with a comparison between university students' behavior and other people's behavior, whereas in the subordinate condition they were told that the experiment was comparing students in psychology to those in economics. They found that people were more likely to exercise personal restraint in the superordinate condition. However, the effect of group identity was strongest when the resource pool was close to being depleted. A possible interpretation of this finding is that group identity leads to feelings of weness and personal responsibility, which enhances self-restraint, especially when it is crucial to do so. A subsequent study of Brewer and Kramer (1986) showed that the effects of group identity in a common resource dilemma were strongest when group size was large. This is consistent with the idea that personal responsibility is more important the larger the group.

A final factor that could influence feelings of personal responsibility is *moralizing*. Dawes (1980) describes evidence that people are more likely to cooperate if groups discuss the morality of cooperation and the immorality of noncooperation. Content analysis of group discussions suggests that subjects often discuss the morality or ethics of cooperation (Dawes, McTavish, & Shaklee, 1977). There is also evidence that individuals who view the social dilemma as a moral issue are the ones who tend to cooperate (Van Lange, Liebrand, & Kuhlman, 1990). If such moral views of social dilemmas are enhanced by an experimenter, then people may be more willing to cooperate. Dawes (1980) describes an experiment in which cooperation was promoted when the experimenter emphasized the ethics of cooperation and the immorality of noncooperation.

III. Factors Promoting Cooperation in Two-person Social Dilemmas

As mentioned before, two-person social dilemmas are quite different from *N*-person social dilemmas. It is not a rarity, however, that two parties (either individuals or groups) are interdependent in a social dilemma structure. For example, should I arrive in time or a little late for an appointment with another person? Should I order a meal a little more expensive when I know that the two of us are going to split the bill? Moreover, groups as well as individuals might find themselves in social dilemmas. For example, IBM and DEC are interdependent in a fashion quite similar to the social dilemma as regards the optimization of their individual profits. Even though each company may increase its own profit (at the expense of the other) by reducing its prices, it is obvious that together they would be better off by maintaining rather high prices.

Numerous experiments have been conducted on two-person social dilemmas, mostly with the Prisoner's Dilemma and related games. Because most of this research has been summarized before (Guyer & Perkel, 1973; Pruitt & Kimmel, 1977; Wrightsman, O'Connor, & Baker, 1972), we will not provide an extensive review of it. Instead, we will discuss recent work that concerns (1) response to others' behavioral strategies, and (2) response to perceived characteristics of others. We will conclude by discussing recent work on how groups may differ from individuals in two-party social dilemmas.

1. *Effects of Others' Strategy*

Participants in a social dilemma do not necessarily understand what their "best" strategy is. They may begin by choosing the more cautious noncooperative option, or by giving the other the benefit of the doubt by playing cooperatively. Research has shown that for the first trial, the percentage of mutual cooperative choices is about 50 percent, which, in the next twenty to thirty trials, declines to about 30 percent. Thereafter, there is a period of recovery, leading ultimately to a stable pattern of about 60 percent cooperative choices. This U-shaped function has been shown by Rapoport and Chammah (1965) and may reflect the fact that people "learn" from experience (see also Pruitt & Kimmel, 1977). Specifically, the decline in cooperation after the first trial could be due to the lack of trust in the other's cooperation, and/or to a tendency to exploit the other's cooperation. Once they have been locked into a mutual noncooperative situation (the so-called DD-lock in effect), people become increasingly aware of the fact that each of them could do better by mutual cooperation. According to Pruitt and Kimmel (1977), people start to realize (1) that their own outcomes are dependent upon the other's behavior, (2) that taking advantage of the other's cooperation is essentially impossible, and (3) that the dilemma boils down to mutual cooperation or mutual noncooperation. This research suggests that people may initially fail to see that collectively rational solutions are in fact rational from a purely self-interested perspective as well in the long run.

There is also a long tradition of research on the effects of others' strategy (cf. Oskamp, 1971). The vast majority of this research has compared the effectiveness of three behavioral strategies, pure cooperation, pure non-cooperation, and the Tit For Tat strategy described earlier. This latter strategy has been found to be more effective than the first two in eliciting cooperation. An important implication of this research is that the Tit For Tat strategy is the most effective strategy if one is motivated to pursue joint welfare as well as own welfare (see Axelrod, 1984). Recent research has also shown that subjects view Tit For Tat as more intelligent than either of the unconditional strategies (McClintock & Liebrand, 1988). It is also seen as a strategy that is fairer than unconditional noncooperation strategy and at least as fair as unconditional cooperation.

The effectiveness of a strategy has been shown to be dependent upon the subjects' own social value orientation. For example, Kuhlman and Marshello (1975) found that people with individualistic and competitive value orientations fail to respond cooperatively to an unconditional cooperative strategy, and that all but competitive people cooperate when the other follows a Tit For Tat strategy. One can increase own and joint benefits but not relative advantage by cooperating with Tit For Tat.

Finally, the work on Osgood's (1962) Graduated and Reciprocated Initiatives in Tension-Reduction (GRIT) indicates that the expression of cooperative intentions, encouraging the other to do so, the announcement of cooperative behavior, and finally, retaliation in case the other does not cooperate (but never making two noncooperative choices in sequence), has been shown to be very effective. Typically, the level of cooperation in response to GRIT is high, usually about 80 percent (Lindskold, 1978; Lindskold, Walters, & Koutsourais, 1983). This research suggests that the verbal strategies, coupled with cooperative behavior, are important determinants of cooperation. This has been found to be especially effective if the intention is repeated and rephrased (Lindskold, Han, & Betz, 1986).

All in all, previous research on the effects of others' strategy has demonstrated that conditional cooperation in which exploitation is impossible and the collectively rational solution attainable is effective in eliciting cooperation. Verbal announcements have also been shown to be helpful.

2. Perceptions of Others' Characteristics

Another line of research has been concerned with the perceptions of others' characteristics. This research has shown that people tend to cooperate more with another described as cooperative than with another described as competitive (Wrightsman, Baxter, Bilsky, & Nelson, 1969). In addition, recent research of Van Lange and Liebrand (1989) has examined the effects of perceptions of others' morality or goodness. The major finding is that people are much more willing to cooperate when the other is seen as more rather than less moral. Furthermore, this is true for people with all social value orientations. Previous research has also shown that people are more likely to cooperate if they think that the other has similar as opposed to dissimilar attitudes (Kaufman, 1967; Tornatzky & Geiwitz, 1968).

Previous research has also been concerned with the effects of gender. First, although certain stereotypes suggest that females would be more cooperative than males, research has failed to show a systematic relationship between gender and cooperation choice behavior in two-person social dilemmas (e.g., Bixenstine, Potach, & Wilson, 1963), or between gender and social value orientation (McClintock & Liebrand, 1988). In addition, the effects of information about the other's gender has failed to show systematic effects.

Individuals versus Groups

Recent work on two-party social dilemmas has contrasted intergroup and interpersonal processes. Recent experiments indicate that groups tend to be less cooperative and more competitive than individuals (McCallum *et al.*, 1985; Rabbie, Visser, & Van Oostrum, 1982). This so-called *discontinuity effect* (Insko, Schopler, Hoyle, Dardis, & Graetz, 1990) has been found to be especially strong during the first phase of a social dilemma (Lindskold, McElwain, & Wayner, 1977; Pylyshyn, Agnew, & Illingworth, 1966).

Insko *et al.* (1990) have suggested some reasons why groups approach social dilemmas less cooperatively than individuals. First, Insko *et al.*

found evidence that groups are more afraid than individuals of being exploited by the other. That is, groups were found to be more likely than individuals to make "self-protecting" choices, which included the option to withdraw from free game. Insko *et al.* (1990) also found that groups made more noncooperative choices than individuals. These results are consistent with the findings of Hoyle, Pinkley, and Insko (1989). It seems likely that groups are less cooperative than individuals for both aversive (e.g., fear) and appetitive (e.g., greed) reasons. There may be several explanations for this effect and it is up to future research to classify the differences between interpersonal and intergroup behavior.

References

Abric, J. C., & Kahan, J. P. (1972). The effects of representations and behavior in experimental games. *European Journal of Social Psychology*, **2**, 129–144.

Aronson, E., & Carlsmith, J. M. (1969). Experimentation in social psychology. In G. Lindzey & E. Aronson (Eds.), *Handbook of Social Psychology*, Vol. 2. Reading, Mass.: Addison-Wesley.

Axelrod, R. (1984). *The Evolution of Cooperation*. New York: Basic Books.

Bixenstine, V. E., Levitt, C. A., & Wilson, K. R. (1966). Collaboration among six persons in a prisoner's dilemma game. *Journal of Conflict Resolution*, **10**, 488–496.

Bixenstine, V. E., Potach, H. M., & Wilson, K. R. (1963). Effects of level of cooperative choice by the other player on choices in a PDG. *Journal of Abnormal and Social Psychology*, **66**, 308–313.

Bonacich, P. (1972). Norms and cohesion as adaptive responses to political conflict: An experimental study. *Sociometry*, **39**, 200–208.

Bonacich, P., Shure, G. H., Kahan, J. P., & Meeker, R. J. (1976). Cooperation and group size in the *N*-person prisoner's dilemma. *Journal of Conflict Resolution*, **20**, 687–705.

Brechner, K. C. (1977). An experimental analysis of social traps. *Journal of Experimental Social Psychology*, **13**, 552–564.

Brewer, M. B. (1979). In-group bias in the minimal intergroup situation: A cognitive-motivational analysis. *Psychological Bulletin*, **86**, 307–324.

Brewer, M. B., & Kramer, R. M. (1986). Choice behavior in social dilemmas: Effects of social identity, group size, and decision framing. *Journal of Personality and Social Psychology*, **50**, 543–549.

Bruins, J. J., Liebrand, W. B. G., & Wilke, H. A. M. (1989). About the saliency of fear and greed in social dilemmas. *European Journal of Social Psychology*, **19**, 155–161.

Caldwell, M. D. (1976). Communication and sex effects in a five-person prisoner's dilemma game. *Journal of Personality and Social Psychology*, **33**, 272–280.

Caporael, L. R., Dawes, R. M., Orbell, J. M., & Van de Kragt, A. J. C. (1989). Selfishness examined: Cooperation in the absence of egoistic incentives. *Behavioral and Brain Sciences*, **12**, 683–699.

Colman, A. M. (1982). *Game Theory and Experimental Games*. Oxford: Pergamon Press.

Coombs, C. A. (1973). A reparameterization of the prisoner's dilemma game. *Behavioral Science*, **18**, 424–428.

Dawes, R. M. (1980). Social dilemmas. *Annual Review of Psychology*, **31**, 169–193.

Dawes, R. M. (1988). *Rational Choice in an Uncertain World*. New York: Harcourt.

Dawes, R. M., McTavish, J., & Shaklee, H. (1977). Behavior, communication, and assumptions about other people's behavior in a commons dilemma situation. *Journal of Personality and Social Psychology*, **35**, 1–11.

Dawes, R. M., Van de Kragt, A., & Orbell, J. M. (1988). Not me, or thee, but we: The importance of group identity in eliciting cooperation in dilemma situations: Experimental manipulations. *Acta Psychologica*, **68**, 83–98.

Deutsch, M. (1960). The effect of motivational orientation upon trust and suspicion. *Human Relations,* **13**, 122–139.
Edney, J. J. (1980). The commons problem: Alternative perspectives. *American Psychologist,* **35**, 131–150.
Edney, J. J., & Harper, C. (1978). The commons dilemma: A review. *Environmental Management,* **2**, 491–507.
Evans, G. W., & Crumbaugh, C. M. (1966). Payoff schedule, sequence of choice and cooperation in PDG. *Psychonomic Science,* **5**, 87–88.
Fleishman, J. A. (1980). Collective action as helping behavior: Effects of responsibility diffusion on contributions to a public good. *Journal of Personality and Social Psychology,* **38**, 629–637.
Fleishman, J. A. (1988). The effects of decision framing and others' behavior on cooperation in a social dilemma. *Journal of Conflict Resolution,* **32**, 162–180.
Fox, J., & Guyer, M. (1977). Group size and others' strategy in an *N*-person game. *Journal of Conflict Resolution,* **21**, 323–338.
Fox, J., & Guyer, M. (1978). "Public" choice and cooperation in *N*-person prisoner's dilemma. *Journal of Conflict Resolution,* **22**, 469–481.
Guyer, M., & Perkel, B. (1973). Experimental games: A bibliography 1945–1971. Communication, 293. Ann Arbor, Michigan: Mental Health Research Institute.
Hamburger, H. (1974). Take some—A format and family of games. *Behavioral Science,* **19**, 28–34.
Hamburger, H. (1979). *Games as Models of Social Phenomena.* San Francisco: W. H. Freeman and company.
Hamburger, H., Guyer, M., & Fox, J. (1975). Group size and cooperation. *Journal of Conflict Resolution,* **19**, 503–531.
Hardin, R. G. (1968). The tragedy of the commons. *Science,* **162**, 1243–1248.
Hoyle, R. H., Pinkley, R. L., & Insko, C. A. (1989). Perceptions of social behavior: Evidence of differing expectations for interpersonal and intergroup interactions. *Personality and Social Psychology Bulletin,* **15**, 365–376.
Insko, C. A., Schopler, J., Hoyle, R. H., Dardis, G. J., & Graetz, K. A. (1990). Individual-group discontinuity as a function of fear and greed. *Journal of Personality and Social Psychology,* **58**, 68–79.
Jerdee, T. H., & Rosen, B. (1974). Effects of opportunity to communicate and visibility of individual decisions on behavior in the common interest. *Journal of Applied Psychology,* **59**, 712–716.
Jorgenson, D. O., & Papciak, A. S. (1981). The effects of communication, resource feedback, and identifiability on behavior in a simulated commons. *Journal of Experimental Social Psychology,* **17**, 373–385.
Kahan, J. P. (1973). Noninteraction in an anonymous three-person prisoner's dilemma game. *Behavioral Science,* **18**, 124–127.
Kahan, J. P. (1974). Rationality, the prisoner's dilemma, and population. *Journal of Social Issues,* **4**, 189–210.
Kaufman, H. (1967). Similarity and cooperation received as determinants of cooperation rendered. *Psychonomic Science,* **9**, 73–74.
Kelley, H. H. (1983). The situational origins of human tendencies: A further reason for the formal analysis of structures. *Personality and Social Psychology Bulletin,* **9**, 8–30.
Kelley, H. H., & Grzelak, J. L. (1972). Conflict between individual and common interests in an *N*-person relationship. *Journal of Personality and Social Psychology,* **21**, 190–197.
Kelley, H. H., & Stahelski, A. J. (1970). Social interaction basis of cooperators' and competitors' beliefs about others. *Journal of Personality and Social Psychology,* **16**, 66–91.
Kelley, H. H., & Thibaut, J. W. (1978). *Interpersonal Relations: A Theory of Interdependence.* New York: Wiley.
Kelley, H. H., Shure, G. H., Deutsch, M., Faucheux, C., Lanzetta, J. T., Moscovici, S., Nuttin, J. M., Rabbie, J. M., & Thibaut, J. W. (1970). A comparative experimental study of negotiation behavior. *Journal of Personality and Social Psychology,* **16**, 411–438.
Kerr, N. L. (1989). Illusions of efficacy: The effects of group size on perceived efficacy in social dilemmas. *Journal of Experimental Social Psychology,* **25**, 287–313.
Kerr, N. L., & Bruun, S. E. (1983). Dispensability of member effort and group motivation losses: Free-rider effects. *Journal of Personality and Social Psychology,* **44**, 78–94.

Komorita, S. S. (1987). Cooperative choice in decomposed social dilemmas. *Personality and Social Psychology Bulletin*, **13**, 53–63.
Komorita, S. S., & Barth, J. M. (1985). Components of reward in social dilemmas. *Journal of Personality and Social Psychology*, **48**, 364–373.
Komorita, S. S., Sweeney, J., & Kravitz, D. A. (1980). Cooperative choice in the *N*-person dilemma situation. *Journal of Personality and Social Psychology*, **38**, 504–516.
Kramer, R. M., & Brewer, M. B. (1984). Effects of group identity on resource use in a simulated commons dilemma. *Journal of Personality and Social Psychology*, **46**, 1044–1057.
Kuhlman, D. M., & Marshello, A. (1975). Individual differences in game motivation as moderators of preprogrammed strategic effects in prisoner's dilemma. *Journal of Personality and Social Psychology*, **32**, 922–931.
Latané, B., & Darley, J. M. (1968). Group inhibition of bystander intervention in emergencies. *Journal of Personality and Social Psychology*, **10**, 215–221.
Latané, B., & Rodin, J. (1969). A lady in distress: Inhibiting effects of friends and strangers on bystander intervention. *Journal of Experimental Social Psychology*, **5**, 189–202.
Liebrand, W. B. G. (1983). Interpersonal differences in social dilemmas: A game theoretical approach. *Dissertation Abstracts*, **43** (7-b), 2373.
Liebrand, W. B. G. (1984). The effect of social motives, communication and group size on behaviour in a *N*-person multi-stage mixed-motive game. *European Journal of Social Psychology*, **14**, 239–264.
Liebrand, W. B. G., & Van Run, G. J. (1985). The effects of social motives on behavior in social dilemmas in two cultures. *Journal of Experimental Social Psychology*, **21**, 86–102.
Liebrand, W. B. G., Wilke, H. A. M., Vogel, R., & Wolters, F. J. M. (1986). Value orientation and conformity in three types of social dilemma games. *Journal of Conflict Resolution*, **30**, 77–97.
Lindskold, S. (1978). Trust development, the GRIT proposal, and the effects of conciliatory acts on conflict and cooperation. *Psychological Bulletin*, **85**, 107–128.
Lindskold, S., Han, G., & Betz, B. (1986). Repeated persuasion in interpersonal conflict. *Journal of Personality and Social Psychology*, **51**, 1183–1188.
Lindskold, S., McElwin, D. C., & Wayner, M. (1977). Cooperation and the use of coercion by groups and individuals. *Journal of Conflict Resolution*, **21**, 531–550.
Lindskold, S., Walters, P. S., & Koutsourais, H. (1983). Cooperators, competitors, and response to GRIT. *Journal of Conflict Resolution*, **27**, 521–532.
Loomis, J. L. (1959). Communication, the development of trust and cooperative behavior. *Human Relations*, **12**, 305–315.
Luce, R. D., & Raiffa, H. (1957). *Games and Decisions: Introduction and Critical Survey*. London: John Wiley and Sons.
Maki, J. E., Hoffman, D. M., & Berk, R. A. (1978). A time series analysis of the impact of a water conservation campaign. *Evaluation Quarterly*, **2**, 107–118.
Marwell, G., & Schmitt, D. (1972). Cooperation in a three-person prisoner's dilemma. *Journal of Personality and Social Psychology*, **21**, 376–383.
McCallum, D. M., Harring, K., Gilmore, R., Drenan, S., Chase, J. P., Insko, C. A., & Thibaut, J. (1985). Competition and cooperation between groups and individuals. *Journal of Experimental Social Psychology*, **21**, 301–320.
McClintock, C. G. (1972). Social motivation—A set of propositions. *Behavioral Science*, **17**, 438–454.
McClintock, C. G. (1978). Social values: Their definition, measurement, and development. *Journal of Research and Development in Education*, **12**, 121–137.
McClintock, C. G., & Liebrand, W. B. G. (1988). The role of interdependence structure, individual value orientation and other's strategy in social decision making: A transformational analysis. *Journal of Personality and Social Psychology*, **55**, 396–409.
McClintock, C. G., Messick, D. M., Kuhlman, D. M., & Campos, F. T. (1973). Motivational bases of choice in three-choice decomposed games. *Journal of Experimental Social Psychology*, **9**, 572–590.
Messé, L. A., & Sivacek, J. M. (1979). Predictions of others' responses in a mixed-motive game: Self-justification or false consensus? *Journal of Personality and Social Psychology*, **37**, 602–607.
Messick, D. M., & Brewer, M. B. (1983). Solving social dilemmas: A review. In: L. Wheeler

& P. Shaver (Eds.), *Review of Personality and Social Psychology*, vol. 4, pp. 11–44. Beverly Hills: Sage.

Messick, D. M., & Cook, K. S. (1983). *Equity Theory*. New York: Praeger.

Messick, D. M., & Mackie, D. M. (1989). Intergroup relations. *Annual Review of Psychology*, **40**, 45–81.

Messick, D. M., & McClintock, C. G. (1968). Motivational basis of choice in experimental games. *Journal of Experimental Social Psychology*, **4**, 1–25.

Messick, D. M., Wilke, H. A. M., Brewer, M. B., Kramer, R. M., Zemke, P. E., & Lui, L. (1983). Individual adaptations and structural change as solutions to social dilemmas. *Journal of Personality and Social Psychology*, **44**, 294–309.

Mook, D. G. (1983). In defense of external invalidity. *American Psychologist*, **38**, 379–387.

Nemeth, C. (1972). A critical analysis of research utilizing the prisoner's dilemma paradigm for the study of bargaining. In L. Berkowitz (Ed.), *Advances in Experimental Social Psychology*, **6**, 203–234.

Olson, M. (1965). *The Logic of Collective Action*. Cambridge, MA: Harvard University Press.

Orbell, J. M., Van de Kragt, A. J. C., & Dawes, R. M. (1988). Explaining discussion-induced cooperation. *Journal of Personality and Social Psychology*, **54**, 811–819.

Osgood, C. (1962). *An Alternative to War or Surrender*. Urbana: University of Illinois Press.

Oskamp, S. (1971). Effects of programmed strategies on cooperation in the prisoner's dilemma and other mixed-motive games. *Journal of Conflict Resolution*, **15**, 225–259.

Oskamp, S., & Perlman, D. (1965). Factors affecting cooperation in a PDG. *Journal of Conflict Resolution*, **9**, 359–374.

Platt, J. (1973). Social traps. *American Psychologists*, **28**, 641–651.

Poppe, M., & Utens, L. (1985). Effects of greed and fear of being gypped in a social dilemma with changing pool size. *Journal of Economical Psychology*, **7**, 61–73.

Pruitt, D. G. (1967). Reward structure and cooperation: The decomposed prisoner's dilemma game. *Journal of Personality and Social Psychology*, **14**, 21–27.

Pruitt, D. G., & Kimmel, M. J. (1977). Twenty years of experimental gaming: Critique, synthesis, and suggestions for the future. *Annual Review of Psychology*, **28**, 363–392.

Pylyshyn, Z., Agnew, N., & Illingworth, J. (1966). Comparison of individuals and pairs as participants in a mixed-motive game. *Journal of Conflict Resolution*, **10**, 211–220.

Rabbie, J. M. (1982). The effects of intergroup competition and cooperation on intra- and intergroup relationships. In: V. J. Derlage & J. L. Grzelak (Eds.), *Cooperation and Helping Behavior: Theories and Research*. New York: Academic Press.

Rabbie, J. M., Visser, L., & Van Oostrum, J. (1982). Conflict behavior of individuals, dyads and triads in mixed-motive games. In H. Brandstatter, J. Davis, & G. Stocker-Kreichgauer (Eds.), *Group Decision Making* (pp. 315–340). London: Academic Press.

Radnoff, R., & Weidner, M. F. (1966). Unenforced commitments in "cooperative" and "noncooperative" nonconstant-sum games. *Journal of Conflict Resolution*, **10**, 497–505.

Rapoport, A. (1966). *Two-person Game Theory*. Ann Arbor: University of Michigan Press.

Rapoport, A., & Chammah, A. M. (1965). *Prisoner's Dilemma: A Study in Conflict and Cooperation*. Ann Arbor: University of Michigan Press.

Rapoport, A., & Orwant, C. (1962). Experimental games: A review. *Behavioral Science*, **7**, 1–37.

Rapoport, A., Bornstein, G., & Erev, I. (1989). Intergroup competition for public goods: Effects of unequal resources and relative group size. *Journal of Personality and Social Psychology*, **56**, 748–756.

Rijsman, J., & Poppe, M. (1977). Power differences between players and level of matrix as determinants of competition in a MDG. *European Journal of Social Psychology*, **7**, 347–367.

Rubenstein, F. D., Watzke, G., Doktor, R. H., & Dana, J. (1975). The effects of two incentive schemes upon the conservation of a shared resource by five person groups. *Organizational Behavior and Human Performance*, **13**, 330–338.

Samuelson, C. D., Messick, D. M., Rutte, C. G., & Wilke, H. A. M. (1984). Individual and structural solutions to resource dilemmas in two cultures. *Journal of Personality and Social Psychology*, **47**, 94–104.

Schroeder, D. A., Jensen, T. D., Reed, A. J., Sullivan, D. D., & Schwab, M. (1983). The actions of others as determinants of behavior in social trap situations. *Journal of Personality and Social Psychology*, **19**, 522–539.

Schwartz, S. H., & Gottlieb, A. (1981). Participants' postexperimental reactions and the ethics of bystander research. *Journal of Experimental Social Psychology*, **17**, 396–407.

Simmons, R. T., Dawes, R. M., & Orbell, J. M. (1984). *Defection in Social Dilemmas: Is Fear or is Greed the Problem?* Unpublished manuscript. Department of Political Science, University of Oregon.

Stroebe, W., & Frey, B. S. (1982). Self-interest and collective action: The economics and psychology of public goods. *British Journal of Social Psychology*, **21**, 121–137.

Tornatzky, L., & Geiwitz, P. (1968). The effects of threat and attraction on interpersonal bargaining. *Psychonomic Science*, **13**, 125–126.

Van Avermaet, E., & Van Nieuwkerke, S. (1989). Bijdragen of niet bijdragen tot een gemeenschappelijk goed: De rol van hebzucht en vrees nader onderzocht. *Nederlands Tijdschrift voor de Psychologie*, **44**, 217–224.

Van de Kragt, A., Orbell, J., & Dawes, R. M. (1983). The minimal contributing set as a solution to public goods problems. *American Political Science Review*, **77**, 112–122.

Van Lange, P. A. M., & Liebrand, W. B. G. (1989). On perceiving morality and potency: Social values and the effects of person perception in a give-some dilemma. *European Journal of Personality*, **3**, 209–225.

Van Lange, P. A. M., & Liebrand, W. B. G. (1991). Social value orientation and intelligence: A test of the Goal-Prescribes Rationality-Principle. *European Journal of Social Psychology*, **21**, 273–292.

Van Lange, P. A. M., Liebrand, W. B. G., & Kuhlman, D. M. (1990). Causal attribution of choice behavior in three *N*-person prisoner's dilemmas. *Journal of Experimental Social Psychology*, **26**, 34–48.

Von Neumann, J., & Morgenstern, O. (1944). *Theory of Games and Economic Behavior*. Princeton: Princeton University Press.

Williams, K., Harkins, S., & Latané, B. (1980). Identifiability as a deterrent to social loafing: Two cheering experiments. *Journal of Personality and Social Psychology*, **40**, 303–311.

Winett, R. A., & Nietzel, M. (1975). Behavioral ecology: contingency management of residential energy use. *American Journal of Community Psychology*, **3**, 123–133.

Winett, R. A., Kaiser, S., & Haberkorn, E. (1978). The effects of monetary rebates and daily feedback on electricity conservation. *Journal of Environmental Systems*, **5**, 327–338.

Winett, R. A., Kagel, J. H., Battalio, R. C., & Winkler, R. C. (1978). The effects of monetary rebates, feedback, and information on residential energy conservation. *Journal of Applied Psychology*, **63**, 73–80.

Wit, A. P., & Wilke, H. A. M. (1989). Effecten van gemeenschappelijke versus individuele lotsbepaling op coöperatief keuzegedrag in drie soorten sociale dilemma's. In: *Fundamentele Sociale Psychologie* (vol 2), A. Van Knippenberg, M. Poppe, J. Extra, G. J. Kok, & E. Seydel (Eds.). Tilburg University Press.

Wrightsman, L. S., O'Connor, J., & Baker, N. J. (Eds.) (1972). *Cooperation and Competition: Readings on Mixed-Motive Games*. Belmont: Brooks-Cole.

Wrightsman, L. S., Baxter, G. W., Nelson, R. H., & Bilsky, L. (1972). Effects of information about the other player's game behavior upon cooperation in mixed-motive game. In L. S. Wrightsman, J. O'Connor, & N. J. Baker (Eds.), *Cooperation and Competition: Readings on Mixed-Motive Games*. Belmont: Brooks-Cole.

Yamagishi, T. (1986). The structural goal/expectation theory of cooperation in social dilemmas. In E. Lawler (Ed.), *Advances in Group Processes*, **3**, 51–87. Greenwich: JAI.

Yamagishi, T. (1988). The provision of a sanctioning system in the United States and Japan. *Social Psychology Quarterly*, **51**, 264–270.

Yamagishi, T., & Sato, K. (1986). Motivational bases of the public goods problem. *Journal of Personality and Social Psychology*, **50**, 67–73.

2

Current Theoretical Issues

WIM B. G. LIEBRAND
University of Groningen, The Netherlands

DAVID M. MESSICK
University of California, Santa Barbara, USA

HENK A. M. WILKE
University of Leiden, The Netherlands

We have organized the chapters in this book into three broad categories. These categories accurately mirror the prevailing issues that social dilemma researchers are studying. The first of these topics, risk and uncertainty, focuses on decision making in situations characterized by uncertainty about the behavior of other people or about the nature of the environment. The second category, structure and interpretation, features contributions examining the influence of problem structure on behavior. This influence is often mediated by how people interpret, frame, or evaluate the structure, so we include work focused on such interpretation in this section. Social dilemmas are inherently collective problems and their solutions must be collective solutions. Thus the last section is devoted to papers examining ways in which the structure can be changed to solve the dilemma. This section also highlights the complex interplay between individual and group level processes.

Risk and Uncertainty

One central topic in judgment and decision making is the question of how people think about and respond to risk and uncertainty (Kahneman, Slovic, & Tversky, 1982). This problem includes the study of the ways in which people make judgments about frequencies, relative frequencies, or probabilities (see Tversky & Kahneman, 1982); the understanding of people's perception of risk (Fischhoff *et al.*, 1981); and the analysis of people's willingness to engage in behavior with uncertain outcomes (Kahneman & Tversky, 1979; Lopes, 1988). It is hardly surprising, therefore, that these concerns are emerging as important research questions in the study of social dilemmas.

It is easy to understand why these concerns would be of importance in the study of social dilemmas. In many types of social dilemmas there is not only uncertainty about the state of relevant variables, like the amount of water remaining in a reservoir or the amount of money required to provide a public good; there is also uncertainty about crucial social factors like the number of people who are willing to cooperate in a joint enterprise or the proportion of people who support one policy over another. Normatively, these types of uncertainty should be analyzed differently (Messick *et al.*, 1988). It is an empirical question, however, whether people respond to these uncertainties. Loewenstein *et al.* (1989), for instance, provide evidence that people's attitudes toward risk may be very different in social and nonsocial domains owing to the differences between social and nonsocial preferences. The processes involved in making judgments about social and nonsocial uncertainty may be quite different as well. We can use our own behavior as a basis for predicting what others may do (Dawes, 1989), but it is less easy to rely on this source of information for estimating next year's rainfall. Furthermore, we believe that we can influence or control the former more than we can the other.

Several of the chapters in this volume deal either explicitly or implicitly with the concepts of risk and uncertainty. Rapoport *et al.* (Chapter 3) study the behavior of five-person groups in situations where the available amount of a shared resource is randomly determined. The uncertainty in this experiment concerns how much of the resource there will be in a given trial and also how much the other members of the group will request. (If the total request exceeds the amount available, no one receives anything.) It appears that subjects deal with the social uncertainty by requesting roughly one-fifth of the mean amount available, unless maximum value of the resource is very large. Then, subjects tend to take more than an equal share.

In the same vein, De Vries and Wilke (Chapter 5) make a distinction between environmental and social uncertainty, referring to what constitutes an optimal collective harvest and what others will do, respectively. They argue that social uncertainty may be considered minimal because subjects assume that everyone will restrict harvesting to an equal share. However, in a social dilemma situation environmental uncertainty about the size of the collective harvest would give rise to a self-advantageous bias, since on an individual level overharvesting is more attractive than under-harvesting. Results of their two experiments support the idea that in a social dilemma situation indeed one's equal share was overestimated. Whereas Rapoport *et al.* found consistent deviations from equal division only when the range, and hence maximum value, of the resource was great, de Vries and Wilke found such deviations systematically associated with particular payoff structures.

Messick and Rutte (Chapter 6) also proposed that people use a type of equal division rule when deciding whether and how much to donate to a public good. They proposed that people first decide whether or not to make a donation, based, possibly, on whether or not they think the group can succeed in providing the public good. If they decide to contribute, they calculate an equal share and correct it by a "cushion" to allow for their estimate of the proportion of the group who will not contribute. This chapter views the prosocial option of donating to a public good as a risky choice, where one's perception of the likelihood of success depends on one's perception of the number of others who will be willing to contribute.

Interestingly, Klandermans (Chapter 18) notes that for public persuasion campaigns to be effective, one goal they must accomplish is to convince people that enough others will participate in the collective action to make it successful. One of the innovative features of his chapter is the stress on the need for such public persuasion campaigns to influence people's expectations about the behavior of others. In this regard, successful campaigns have a certain self-fulfilling quality: if people believe that enough others will participate to make a collective action successful, enough people will participate to make it successful.

People avoid futile actions, especially if those actions are costly. How can one estimate the impact that one's decision is going to have in achieving a collective goal? Kerr (Chapter 4) proposes that one's perceived efficacy, the probability that one will make a difference, is a crucial factor in determining one's willingness to contribute to a public good. His experiments demonstrate clearly that subjects with greater than average ability to provide a public good do so more often than those who have less leverage.

One way to reduce uncertainty in decision situations is to seek relevant information. Camac (Chapter 9) questions how people seek information about the payoffs in two-person social dilemmas. He reports, among other things, that people are more interested in knowing these payoffs for mutual or own benefit than those stemming from exploitation by the other. Furthermore, cooperators are more interested in mutual than own benefit information, whereas this preference is reversed for noncooperators.

Structure and Interpretation

1. Transformation of Outcomes

A central problem in the study of social dilemmas has been to understand the effects of payoffs and, especially, the possible discrepancies between the experimenter's specification of a situation and the interpretation of that situation by the persons involved. These discrepancies could arise from individual differences in social orientations or from situational factors that lead people to frame outcomes in different ways.

Kelley and Thibaut (1978) were among the first to explore these discrepancies in social situations. They assumed that the reward structure as given to subjects will be transformed into an effective structure according to the values subjects assign to their own and to others' outcomes. The implications of this theory have been investigated by first assessing the subjective weights (w_s and w_o) in the value function:

$$\text{value of outcome} = w_s \star \text{own outcome} + w_o \star \text{others' outcome}$$

and then observing subjects' behavior in one or more experimental social dilemmas.

The many different weight configurations are traditionally classified into a few groups called social values, i.e., cooperators ($w_s = w_o = 1$), individualists ($w_s = 1, w_o = 0$), and competititors ($w_s = 1, w_o = -1$). Such experiments have accumulated ample evidence to support the transformation hypothesis. Subjects who assign equal or higher weights to others' outcome than to own outcomes, transform reward structures into effective ones in which cooperation dominates defection. They also cooperate to a greater extent than subjects for which w_o is smaller than w_s (Kuhlman, Camac, & Cunha, 1986; Kramer, McClintock, & Messick, 1986; Liebrand, 1984; Liebrand & Van Run, 1985; McClintock & Liebrand, 1988). In Chapter 9, Camac once again reports a strong support for the effect of social values on cooperation rates. The major contribution of his study, however, is the finding that people with different social values tend to seek information in the payoff matrix that is supportive of the goal they wish to maximize.

The studies reported in Chapters 7 and 8 extend the research on the effects of interpersonal differences in the transformation of reward structures. Extending the work of Kuhlman and Wimberley (1976) and Liebrand *et al.* (1986), Kuhlman, Brown, and Teta (Chapter 7) demonstrate that the transformational processes are not only applied to the given outcome matrix, but they also apply to the subject's evaluation of cooperative and competitive targets as well as to their expectations of the relative frequency of occurrence in a general population.

Van Lange (Chapter 8) manipulates personality description of the other player and finds "smart" targets elicit cooperation from cooperators and defection from noncooperators. A possible interpretation of his finding is that each subgroup perceives "smart" others to be like themselves (assuming, reasonably, that the college student subjects consider themselves to be "smart"). The greater the similarity, the greater one's ability to predict the response of another from one's own response.

2 *Asymmetric Conflicts*

We have discussed transformational processes which lead to interpersonal differences in game behavior and to differences in the way the dilemma is framed. In all these studies the subjects were considered to be exchangeable in that the given payoff matrix was the same for everybody.

The paper by Connolly, Thorn, and Heminger (Chapter 12) explores payoff dimensions that are associated with withholding or sharing information with other users of a shared database. The levels of contribution to the database declined as the cost of contributing increased and also as asymmetries in costs were introduced. This latter result is especially interesting, suggesting that cooperation in such situations depends on the perception of equality.

The effect of asymmetric reward structures was investigated explicitly by Murnighan and King (Chapter 10) and Wit, Wilke, and Oppewal (Chapter 11). Murnighan and King investigate the effects of asymmetries on the development of alternating strategies that provide higher payoffs to both parties than strategies that do not involve alternation. Asymmetries in this case permit participants to take turns, in either simple or more complicated ways, to mutually exploit the payoff structure. Such strategies can only work in contexts in which decisions are going to be repeated many times.

Wit, Wilke, and Oppewal (Chapter 11) examine asymmetries in a one-time public goods game. How are contributions affected when people have different levels of resources, and when they stand to gain differentially from the provision of a public good? Their results show that people give more if they stand to gain more, but that they tend to give equal proportions of their resources.

Nature of Effective Conflict Setting

1. *Framing and Categorization Processes*

A great deal of progress has been made in the last decade toward understanding the effects of group membership and social categorization on cognition and decision making (Messick & Mackie, 1989). The so-called *ingroup bias*, the tendency to benefit members of one's own group to a greater extent than members of a different one, has been exhaustively studied, and numerous cognitive effects of the mere categorization of people into groups have been discovered. Within the domain of social dilemmas, the effects of social categorization were initially studied by Kramer and Brewer (1984) and Brewer and Kramer (1986). Recent studies by Kramer (1989) and Orbell, Van de Kragt, and Dawes (1988) have highlighted the importance of common group membership in inducing cooperative behavior in social dilemmas. In Kramer's (1989) study, for example, subjects (Stanford University undergraduates) were much more trusting and cooperative interacting with (presumed) Stanford MBA (Masters of Business Administration) students when the experimental instructions emphasized their common group membership as opposed to the difference between undergraduates and MBA students. These and similar results underline the need to understand the relationships among categorization processes, perceptions of similarity, and overt behavior.

The study of Bonacich and Schneider (Chapter 14) supports the importance of perceived identity. They describe an original type of social dilemma, a *communications dilemma*. This situation occurs when it is in an organization's best interest for people to share information that they have, but when it is also in the individuals' best interest to hoard information. Organizational inefficiency will result when information needed by one person or unit is withheld. In the experiments reported in this chapter, the authors analyze the effects of one's position in a communication network on one's willingness to share information in situations in which groups are rewarded for efficient problem solving, but in which the individual in the group who first gets the solution is also rewarded. Moreover, when common group identity was made salient, more information was shared than in a control condition, again testifying to the power of perceived group membership.

Besides the transformation of a reward structure into different effective reward structures, there is ample evidence that behavior is a function not only of payoffs but of how those payoffs are framed. There may be important differences between a decision to contribute part of your own possessions in the hope of receiving more than the original contribution (a give-some situation), and a decision to take some collective shared resources (a take-some situation) even if the objective payoffs in the two situations are identical. There are several competing hypotheses with regard to the effects of this framing transformation on cooperation. Komorita and Carnevale (Chapter 13) investigate these hypotheses in three experiments. The results are partly in line with Pruitt's (1967, 1970) work which indicates that give-some dilemmas may evoke higher level of cooperation because they elicit trust and the motive to help. However, there is also evidence supporting Kahneman and Tversky's hypotheses regarding the appraisal of gains and losses. In their terminology, give-some games might be perceived in terms of losses, which would lead to risk seeking behavior and hence to lower cooperation rates than in take-some games. In this case we clearly see the need for subsequent research to settle this debate. One possible moderator might be found in the different utility functions which result in different effective reward structures.

Bornstein's contribution (Chapter 15) adds a layer of complexity to our thinking about intergroup matters by pointing out that intergroup and intragroup incentive structures are often in conflict. Cooperative intragroup behavior may be called for in the service of intergroup competition. The side with the most cooperators wins! But it is wasteful to have more cooperators than is necessary to win. Situations like this one abound with social uncertainty and communication may, or may not, eliminate it, depending on who is permitted to communicate to whom. Intragroup communication may allow group members to coordinate who will and who will not contribute, and intergroup communication permits the groups to collude on efficient but unstable strategies. But communication at both levels tends to destroy the stability achieved by communication at either one or the other.

Structural Solutions

One of the features that makes the study of social dilemmas so important is the prospect of finding solutions to real social problems. In one of the most cited and influential papers on social dilemmas, Hardin (1968) argued that overpopulation, one of the most critical problems of our age, is easily understood as such a situation. Since that time, numerous social problems have been viewed from the perspective of social dilemmas. Problems of overuse of resources and underuse of strategies to protect the environment seem to be natural examples. Failure to vote in democratic elections has been explained in such a way as have productivity declines in collective workplaces. People's reluctance to take collective actions that could be collectively beneficial (joining labor unions, going out on strike) but personally costly, at least in the short run, are easily understood from the perspective of social dilemmas.

One of the most difficult choices for researchers to make is the choice of the mix of "pure" theory and applied emphasis to blend in a research program. As is evidenced in the chapters in this book, some authors have downplayed external validity while others have emphasized it. The risk that is embodied in downplaying external validity is that laboratory games may have little relevance to behavior in other environments. The experimental game environment is not some "pure" distillation of other "real" environments, of course, it is simply another "real" environment, and one that is not very natural at that. Using social dilemma concepts to solve real problems may likewise be evaluated in terms of the extent to which the efforts succeed. If they do succeed, so much the better. If not, the effort must be judged a failure, unless some lesson was learned from the failure that can be applied to attempts to solve other problems. Theoretically based research, like applied research, is successful to the extent that it produces knowledge that can be used in other situations. Applied research is also successful to the extent that it aids in solving the problem it addresses even if it does not apply to other problems. Thus knowing a lot about how people behave in social dilemmas *in the abstract* may be less useful, theoretically and practically, than knowing little about behavior in real concrete situations.

This concern for studying social dilemmas as real-world phenomena has flavored many of the chapters in this book and is the explicit focus of others. Klandermans (Chapter 18) addresses the question of how a government, agency, or organization can elicit cooperative, socially responsible behavior from multitudes of people. Social dilemmas are, after all, collective problems and their solutions must be on a collective scale. A solution to a social dilemma may penalize violators. However, unless the population to whom the sanction is going to apply accepts the necessity of having the sanction, it may not only be ineffective, it may boomerang. How does an agency persuade a population of the desirability of a sanctioning system? Or of joining a collective effort to solve a collective problem? It is interesting to note that Klandermans' contribution is quite similar in intent to Yamagishi's (Chapter 16) except that Yamagishi discusses conditions that should make people voluntarily want to establish a sanctioning system to reward cooperation relative to defection.

One of the earliest and most influential texts in social psychology distinguishes individual and group levels of analysis (Krech & Crutchfield, 1948). These authors ask, "Can social phenomena be fruitfully investigated on the level of individual behavior? Are there other, equally promising levels of social analysis? What are the appropriate units of analysis at each of these levels? What are the relations among these several levels of analysis?" (p. 14). Providing thoughtful answers to these questions poses an intimidating challenge to social psychology generally and to efforts to understand social dilemmas specifically. Especially pertinent is the goal of understanding the relationships between individual level phenomena, such as individual decision making or cognitive processes, and group level phenomena, such as group decision outcomes (Allison & Messick, 1988) or market behavior. Schelling (1978) has written elegantly about this general problem.

Nowhere is the importance of relating individual to group level phenomena more important than in the study of social dilemmas. The societal problems created by social dilemmas are inherently collective problems. That is to say, the problems usually cannot be solved by the behavior of a single person. The actions of a single person will not clear up a traffic jam, eliminate a water shortage, or enhance the productivity of an organization. Why then do social psychologists study the behavior of single individuals? One answer to this question is that if we understand what causes the behavior of a single individual, we will be able to generalize that understanding to be able to predict the behavior of larger aggregates. This position assumes, however, that there will not be emergent properties of aggregate behavior that simply cannot be predicted from the knowledge of single individuals. This assumption is likely wrong in many cases.

Krech and Crutchfield (1948) use the analogy of the difference between studying the behavior of swarms of ants and studying the behavior of single ants. To what extent could one predict the behavior of swarms from a knowledge of the principles of individual ant behavior? This same issue has been raised recently by entomologists trying to understand how swarms of army ants display intelligent flexibility while individual ants appear rigid and dim (Franks, 1989). Consider the following example. Foraging swarms maintain a standard speed when retrieving prey to the nest. This fact means that traffic jams, the inevitable consequence when individuals in crowds move at different speeds, are avoided. This constancy in retrieval speed is all the more remarkable because of the large variation in size among the ants. It appears to be maintained through the use of a simple, individual level rule. If you are moving in the retrieval stream without prey and encounter a slow moving object, join in and thus speed it up. If no such object is encountered, continue at standard speed. This simple rule assures that potential obstacles will be brought up to speed, but once accomplished, additional energy will not be devoted to them (Franks, 1989, p. 142). The study of the behavior of individual ants outside of their swarms would never have disclosed this relationship between a simple individual behavioral principle and its collective consequences.

Most of the research that social psychologists have done on social dilemmas to date has been at the individual level. However, some investigators, recognizing that collective problems will generally require collective solutions, have begun focusing attention on such solutions. The chapters in this volume attest to the wide variety of processes that are available for achieving collective efficiency. One of the most important of these is communication, a social attribute of army ants that is essential to their behavior coordination. Klandermans (Chapter 18) outlines the problems involved in the use of persuasive communication to bring about collective action. Bornstein's (Chapter 15) contribution complicates the story somewhat by showing that while communication can permit efficient coordination in some cases, in other cases it can have a deleterious impact on coordination.

Collective solutions may be achieved by changing the structure of the social dilemma and the papers by Yamagishi (Chapter 16) and Rutte and Wilke (Chapter 17) illustrate two different approaches of this sort. The general question is this: When will people be willing to change the essential quality of the dilemma and how can that be done? Yamagishi envisions a sanctioning system that will reward cooperative decisions and/or penalize selfish ones. But such sanctioning systems have costs themselves that must be paid. Everyone would like to have such a system since it would elicit cooperative actions from others, but everyone would also prefer to have others pay for it. The provision of the sanctioning system itself is a social dilemma, a problem in providing a public good. Yamagishi's important paper raises the issue of how one can bootstrap a secondary public good in order to facilitate the provision of primary one.

Rutte and Wilke discuss a second way of eliminating the dilemma in social dilemmas, by turning access to a public resource over to an exclusive agent or agency. The tragedy of the commons is solved by closing the commons to public access. In their experiment, subjects have the chance to vote to shield the resource from free access. They find that subjects tend to opt for the structural solution when it appears that others will not cooperate voluntarily, especially in the condition in which cooperation is relatively cheap. Subjects seem willing to risk changing the structure in order to promote responsible use of the shared resource when voluntary efforts to do so seem doomed to fail.

Studying the factors that encourage people to want to change the very structure of social dilemmas, shifts the focus from individual level to aggregate level solutions. As desirable as this direction of movement is, one can focus on an even higher level set of issues. Namely, what are the aggregate level consequences of individual level processes. Aside from Schelling's (1978) book warning that there will be no cheap answers to this question, there is very little work on this problem, probably because the theoretical tools needed to cope with the question have not been available. What is needed is a way of studying the global effects of assumptions made about individual decisions, especially as those decisions depend on decisions made by others in the decision maker's environment.

We can illustrate this need through an example. Samuelson, Messick, Rutte, and Wilke (1984) found evidence that when making decisions about how much of a shared renewable resource to harvest for personal use, subjects were influenced by at least three factors. First, there is the desire to have as much of the resource as feasible; second, subjects did not want to be below average in use, especially if the resource was in abundant supply; and, finally, they did not want to overuse the resource to the point where it might be jeopardized. According to these findings, individual decisions are influenced by the decisions of others as well as the level of the resource, which itself, in any real system, will be influenced by the decisions as well as other factors. If a reasonable model of individual decision making could be constructed that reflected the results of the experiments of Messick *et al.* (1984), it would be possible through computer simulation to explore the consequences for resource availability, for example, of various combinations of parameters relating to the relative weightings of the three factors mentioned above. Such a simulation might be useful in determining whether persuasion campaigns would be more effective by stressing information about the usage of others or information about the level of the resource. Computer programs that permit such simulations have recently become available (e.g., Nowak, Szamrej, & Latané, 1990) and they hold out promise for qualitatively new directions for research, namely the study of the global consequences of individual choice processes in social dilemmas.

References

Allison, S. T., & Messick, D. M. (1988). From individual inputs to group outputs, and back again; group processes and inferences about members. In C. Hendrick (Ed.), *Review of Personality and Social Psychology*, vol. 8, pp. 111-143.

Brewer, M. B., & Kramer, R. M. (1986). Choice behaviour in social dilemmas: Effects of social identity, group size, and decision framing. *Journal of Personality and Social Psychology*, **50**, 543–549.

Colman, A. M. (1982). *Game Theory and Experimental Games*. Oxford: Pergamon Press.

Dawes, R. M. (1988). *Rational Choice in an Uncertain World*. New York: Harcourt.

Dawes, R. M. (1989). Statistical criteria for establishing a truly false consensus effect. *Journal of Experimental Social Psychology*, **25**, 1-17.

Fischhoff, B., Lichtenstein, S., Slovic, P., Derby, S. L., & Keeney, R. L. (1981). *Acceptable Risk*. Cambridge: Cambridge University Press.

Franks, N. R. (1989). Army ants: A collective intelligence. *American Scientist*, **77**, 139–145.

Hardin, R. G. (1968). The tragedy of the commons. *Science*, **162**, 1243–1248.

Jerdee, T. H., & Rosen, B. (1974). Effects of opportunity to communicate and visibility of individual decisions on behavior in the common interest. *Journal of Applied Psychology*, **59**, 712–716.

Kahneman, D., & Tversky, A. (1979). Prospect theory: An analysis of decision under risk. *Econometrica*, **47**, 263–291.

Kahneman, D., Slovic, P., & Tversky, A. (Eds.) (1982). *Judgment Under Uncertainty, Heuristics and Biases*. Cambridge: Cambridge University Press.

Kelley, H. H., & Thibaut, J. W. (1978). *Interpersonal Relations: A Theory of Interdependence*. New York: Wiley.

Kramer, R. M. (1989). Helping the group or helping one's self? Cognitive and motivational determinants of cooperation in resource dilemmas. In David Schroeder (Ed.), *Social Dilemmas*. New York: Praeger.

Kramer, R. M., & Brewer, M. B. (1984). Effects of group identity on resource use in a simulated commons dilemma. *Journal of Personality and Social Psychology*, **46**, 1044–1057.

Kramer, R. M., McClintock, C. G., & Messick, D. M. (1986). Social values and cooperative response to a simulated resource conservation crisis. *Journal of Personality*, **54**, 576–592.

Krech, D., & Crutchfield, R. (1948). *Theory and Problems of Social Psychology*. New York: McGraw-Hill.

Kuhlman, D. M., & Wimberley, D. W. (1976). Expectations of choice behavior held by cooperators, competitors and individualists across four classes of experimental games. *Journal of Personality and Social Psychology*, **34**, 69–81.

Kuhlman, D. M., Camac, C. R., & Cunha, D. A. (1986). Individual differences in social orientation. In H. A. M. Wilke, D. M. Messick, & C. G. Rutte (Eds), *Experimental Social Dilemmas*. Frankfurt: Verlag Peter Lang.

Liebrand, W. B. G. (1984). The effect of social motives, communication and group size on behavior in an *n*-person multi-stage mixed motive game. *European Journal of Social Psychology*, **14**, 239–264.

Liebrand, W. B. G., & Van Run, G. J. (1985). The effects of social motives on behavior in social dilemmas in two cultures. *Journal of Experimental Social Psychology*, **21**, 86–102.

Liebrand, W. B. G., Jansen, R. W. T. L., Rijken, V. M., & Suhre, C. J. M. (1986). Might over morality: social values and the perception of other players in experimental games. *Journal of Experimental and Social Psychology*, **22**, 203–215.

Liebrand, W. B. G., Wilke, H. A. M., Vogel, R., & Wolters, F. J. M. (1986). Value orientation and conformity in three types of social dilemma games. *Journal of Conflict Resolution*, **30**, 77–97.

Loewenstein, G. F., Thompson, L., & Bazerman, M. H. (1989). Social utility and decision making in interpersonal contexts. *Journal of Personality and Social Psychology*, 57, 426–441.

Lopes, L. (1987). Between hope and fear: The psychology of risk. *Advances in Experimental Social Psychology*, vol. 20. New York: Academic Press.

Luce, R. D., & Raiffa, H. (1957). *Games and Decisions: Introduction and Critical Survey*. London: John Wiley and Sons.

McClintock, C. G., & Liebrand, W. B. G. (1988). The role of interdependence structure, individual value orientation, and other's strategy in social decision making: A transformational analysis. *Journal of Personality and Social Psychology*, 55, 396–409.

Messick, D. M. (1973). To join or not to join; An approach to the unionization decision. *Organizational Behavior and Human Performance*, **10**, 145–156.

Messick, D. M., & Brewer, M. B. (1983). Solving social dilemmas: A review. In L. Wheeler and P. Shaver (Eds), *Review of Personality and Social Psychology*, vol. 4, pp. 11–44. Beverly Hills, CA: Sage.

Messick, D. M., & Cook, K. S. (Eds) (1983). *Equity Theory*. New York: Praeger.

Messick, D. M., & Mackie, D. (1989). Intergroup relations. *Annual Review of Psychology*, **40**, 45–81.

Messick, D. M., Allison, S. T., & Samuelson, C. D. (1988). Framing and communication effects on group members' responses to environmental and social uncertainty. In S. Maital (Ed.), *Applied Behavioral Economics*, vol. II. Brighton: Wheatsheaf.

Nowak, A., Szamrej, J., & Latané, B. (1990). From private attitude to public opinion: a dynamic theory of social impact. *Psychological Review*, **97**, 362–376.

Orbell, J. M., Van de Kragt, A. J. C., & Dawes, R. M. (1988). Explaining discussion-induced cooperation. *Journal of Personality and Social Psychology*, **54**, 811–819.

Pruitt, D. G. (1967). Reward structure and cooperation: The decomposed prisoner's dilemma game. *Journal of Personality and Social Psychology*, **14**, 21–27.

Pruitt, D. G. (1970). Motivational processes in the decomposed prisoner's dilemma game. *Journal of Personality and Social Psychology*, **14**, 227–238.

Pruitt, D. G., & Kimmel, M. J. (1977). Twenty years of experimental gaming: Critique, synthesis and suggestions for the future. *Annual Review of Psychology*, **28**, 363–392.

Rabbie, J. H. (1982). The effects of intergroup competition and cooperation on intra- and intergroup relationships. In V. J. Derlage and J. L. Grzelak (Eds), *Cooperation and Helping Behavior: Theories and Research*. New York: Academic Press.

Samuelson, C. D., Messick, D. M., Rutte, C. G., & Wilke, H. A. M. (1984). Individual and structural solutions to resource dilemmas in two cultures. *Journal of Personality and Social Psychology*, **47**, 94–104.

Schelling, T. C. (1978). *Micromotives and Macrobehavior*. New York: Norton.

Tversky, A., & Kahneman, D. (1982). Judgment under uncertainty: heuristics and biases. In D. Kahneman, P. Slovic, & A. Tversky (Eds), *Judgment Under Uncertainty: Heuristics and Biases*. Cambridge: Cambridge University Press.

Wrightsman, L. S., O'Connor, J., & Baker, N. J. (Eds) (1972). *Cooperation and Competition: Readings on Mixed-Motive Games*. Belmont: Brooks-Cole.

Part II

Risk and Uncertainty

3

Social Dilemmas with Uniformly Distributed Resources*

AMNON RAPOPORT, DAVID V. BUDESCU,
RAMZI SULEIMAN and EYTHAN WEG
University of Haifa, Israel

Experimental work on resource dilemmas was instigated by the classical essay of Hardin (1968), who brought the implications of the conflict between short-term self-interest and long-term collective interest to the attention of the scientific community. The tragedy of the commons that Hardin described is by now well known. There is a pasture open to all and a group of herdsmen, each of whom tries to keep as many cattle as possible on the commons. The herdsmen will achieve their goals if the total herd is smaller than the carrying capacity of the land. But when social stability becomes a reality, "the inherent logic of the commons remorselessly generates tragedy" (Hardin, 1968, p. 1244). When comparing the positive utility of adding one more animal to his herd to the disutility of overgrazing created by one more animal, a rational herdsman would conclude that the only sensible course of action is to increment his herd by one more animal. When each and every herdsman sharing the commons reaches this conclusion, the inevitable result will be a social catastrophe.

Our concern in the present paper is with a class of social dilemmas (Dawes, 1980; Messick & Brewer, 1983) called *resource dilemmas*, that have been studied by, among others, Messick, Wilke, Brewer, Kramer, Zemke, and Lui (1983), Samuelson and Messick (1986a, 1986b), Samuelson, Messick, Rutte, and Wilke (1984), and Rutte, Wilke, and

* This research was supported by a Fund for Basic Research Grant of the Israeli National Academy of Science and Humanities.
The paper was completed while the second author was on sabbatical leave at the Department of Social and Decision Sciences at the Carnegie Mellon University.
We would like to thank Ariel Cohen for writing the computer programs for the experiment and Tami Shpigler for assistance in data collection.

Messick (1987). A typical resource dilemma experiment was conducted by Samuelson and Messick (1986a) in which six members of a group were instructed that they would share a resource pool with an initial total of 900 points. Communication within the group was not allowed. Each group member could require or "harvest" from 0 to 30 points on each trial. Once all the group members had stated their requests individually and privately, the total group request was subtracted from the existing pool size, and the remaining number of points was multiplied by a replenishable factor that exceeded unity. The outcome then served as the new pool size for the next trial. Subjects were instructed that they could continue to harvest points from the resource pool as long as the resource was maintained at a level above zero or until the experiment was arbitrarily terminated. The exact pool size on each trial was common knowledge.

In the resource dilemma described above, a conflict exists between the temptation each person has to increase his/her request, thereby enhancing his/her payoff, and the need to tacitly cooperate with other group members in order to prevent depletion of the resource. Many environmental problems (e.g., water and air pollution, energy shortage, deforestation) share the pernicious characteristics of the resource dilemma outlined above. However, in general they do not satisfy the assumption underlying the game described above that the resource pool size is known with certainty by every member of the society. In all real-world resource dilemma situations that we have considered, the precise value of the resource is not known. We do not know exactly how much waste can be dumped into a lake before it is rendered unusable, nor how many trees can be felled before the forest turns into arid land. We contend that *environmental uncertainty* (Suleiman & Rapoport, 1989) regarding the size of the natural resource is found in many other problems that can be modeled appropriately by the resource dilemma paradigm.

Resource Dilemmas with Environmental Uncertainty

The only resource dilemma experiment incorporating environmental uncertainty into its design was conducted by Messick, Allison, and Samuelson (1988). In this experiment, groups of four subjects participated in a single-trial task. In one of the two experimental conditions (the "take-some" condition) each subject was asked to request individually and anonymously any amount of cash up to and including $8. Subjects were told that their requests would be totaled and then an unbiased coin would be flipped. If the group total were $16 or less, each group member would receive his or her request regardless of the outcome of the coin flip. Otherwise, group members would receive their requests if the coin flip resulted in heads, and nothing if it resulted in tails.

Although this paradigm may yield interesting results, the binary mechanism (unbiased coin) that determines the individual payoffs is somewhat unrealistic. Whereas there are various public goods (e.g., lighthouses, bridges) of a discrete nature (Hovi, 1986), one is hard pressed to give examples of Bernoulli distributed natural resources. The first goal of the present study, then, is to investigate the effects of variability in the resource on individual requests and on expectations about the requests of others. To render the task realistic, yet keeping it relatively simple, we use uniform distributions of resource with the same expected value but increasingly larger ranges (and variances). To maintain tractability, we focus on single-trial dilemmas, although generalizations to multistage dilemmas with replenishable resources are straightforward.

Recently, Suleiman and Rapoport (1989) proposed a normative model for individual behavior in resource dilemmas with environmental uncertainty that motivated the present experimental study.

Theory

As noted by Suleiman and Rapoport (1989), the take-some game described above is an instance of a more general dilemma in which group members are instructed that a certain amount of money, x, will be made available to them. Group members have to request individually and anonymously how much money to claim from the common resource. Denote the individual request by r_j ($j = 1, \ldots, n$), the total group request by

$$R = \sum_{j=1}^{n} r_j,$$

and let x be a realization of a random variable X with a known distribution function. If $R < x$, each group member receives his/her request, r_j, but if $R > x$, no requests are satisfied.

If x is fixed and known to all group members and preplay communication is allowed, then the group's best strategy is to request the total amount (i.e., set $R = x$) and find an equitable means of distributing the resource. No obvious solution exists when either of the conditions above is not satisfied. By eliminating the possibility of preplay communication and binding agreements, we introduce *strategic uncertainty* regarding the request of the remaining $n - 1$ members of the group. And by letting x vary in a random fashion, we introduce *environmental uncertainty* regarding the resource. Messick (1984) has shown that even when $n = 1$ (i.e., strategic uncertainty is absent), a random resource alters the optimal policy maximizing expected reward.

When preplay communication is prohibited and the resource is a random variable, the individual is faced simultaneously with strategic and environmental uncertainty. A possible way of modeling his/her behavior is to invoke game-theoretical notions. However, game-theoretical models seem to be of little value in this case. First, there is the problem of multiple equilibria that has remained largely unsolved. Also, there is strong evidence refuting game-theoretical models even in simpler resource dilemma games (Rutte *et al.*, 1987).

An alternative theoretical approach has been proposed by Suleiman and Rapoport (1989). In this approach, the beliefs or opinions each player has about what the other group members are about to request are modeled by a (subjective) probability distribution. The model assumes that the probability distribution of the resource and the subject's probability distribution over the others' total request are independent, and then predicts that the subject will choose his/her request so as to maximize expected utility.

Formally, denote by $r_{n\backslash j}$ the total sum of requests of all n members of the group, excluding member j. Let $f_X(x)$ denote the probability density function of the random resource, and $f_R(\cdot)j$ denote the probability density function of player j's beliefs concerning the total request of the remaining $n-1$ group members. Denote the difference between x and $r_{n\backslash j}$ by y:

$$y = x - r_{n\backslash j}.$$

Then, if the two variables X and R_j are independent of each other, the probability density function of the difference score y is given by

$$f_Y(y) = \int_{-\infty}^{\infty} f_X(y+\xi)\, f_{R_j}(\xi) d\xi.$$

Suleiman and Rapoport (1989) show that the request maximizing expected value is the solution of the equation

$$r_j f_Y(y = r_j) + F_Y(y = r_j) = 1, \qquad (1)$$

where

$$F_Y(y) = \int_{-\infty}^{y} f_Y(\xi) d\xi.$$

The generalization to maximization of expected utility (rather than expected value) is straightforward (see Suleiman & Rapoport, 1989).

Several authors (De Vries & Wilke, 1988; Rutte *et al.*, 1987; Selten, 1987) have argued persuasively that when players are symmetric—as they are in the present study—and preplay communication is prohibited, considerations of equality play an important role in determining decisions. Rutte *et al.* (1987) stated two distinct justifications for this social decision heuristic: "it provides both a rule to facilitate one's own decision making and also a standard to evaluate the behavior of others" (p. 214). De Vries and Wilke (1988) went a step further by claiming that the equal share allocation is "the only logical rule to coordinate the distribution of the resource."

Equality implies the equal division of a known quantity (e.g., the resource in our study) among the n symmetric group members. When the quantity is not known precisely, it must be estimated. In our case, the player's equal share can be estimated in two different ways: on the basis of the subject's estimate of the value of the (random) resource and on the basis of his/her estimate of the behavior of the other group members. Denote by $\hat{S}_j$ and $\hat{R}_j$ player j's estimates of the random resource, x, and the total request, $r_{n\backslash j}$, of the remaining group members, respectively. Then the two versions of the equality model predict

$$r_j(s) = \hat{S}_j/n \quad (2)$$

and

$$r_j(o) = \hat{R}_j/(n - 1). \quad (3)$$

The two predictions coincide if the n players share the same opinions about the resource and social norms of behavior. The models in equations (2) and (3) will subsequently be tested against the expected value model in equation (1).

Method

Subjects

Forty-five graduate and undergraduate students at the University of Haifa volunteered to participate in a group decision making experiment for monetary reward contingent on performance. Subjects participated in groups of five, and no acquaintances were permitted in the same group.

Design

The actual resource on each trial (which was not displayed to the subjects) was drawn randomly from one of five different uniform distributions. These distributions had the same mean but different upper and lower limits, representing increasing levels of environmental uncertainty:

Condition I : mean = 500, range = 0 (500, 500)
Condition II : mean = 500, range = 250 (375, 625)
Condition III : mean = 500, range = 500 (250, 750)
Condition IV : mean = 500, range = 750 (125, 875)
Condition V : mean = 500, range = 1000 (0, 1000)

The numbers in parentheses are the lower and upper bounds of the range of the uniform distribution. As shown above, the range was increased by 250 points from one condition to another, starting at 0 and ending at 1000.

The study used a within-subjects design. Each experimental condition was replicated four times, and each group participated in all five conditions for a total of $5 \times 4 = 20$ trials per group. These trials were presented in a random order to each group. To minimize sequential effects, no feedback was given about individual requests, the actual resource, and the outcome for the trial.

Procedure

A DEC PDP 11/73 computer was employed to conduct the experiment. The computer was connected to five CRT terminals, each located in a private and soundproof booth. Upon arrival at the laboratory, subjects were randomly assigned to the five booths.

The subjects were instructed that a common resource would be made available to them, and that its (unknown) value would vary from one trial to another. Each subject could require any portion of the resource. If the total group request would exceed the resource, individual subjects would get nothing for the trial. Otherwise, each subject would be granted his or her request.

The instructions further specified that only the limits of the resource distribution would be displayed on each trial, that sampling from the distribution would be random, and that no feedback about individual requests or the value of the resource would be given. To enhance motivation, subjects were told that at the end of the experiment three of the twenty trials would be chosen randomly and payment would be determined according to the outcomes of these trials. Thus, in principle, the subjects could complete the experiment with zero payoff. The mean payoff per subject was $4.70.

On ten trials (two per condition), after they made their requests, the subjects were asked to answer several questions that were displayed on the CRT terminals. The first presentation of each dilemma was not followed by questions, so two of the remaining three replications were randomly selected for this task. The subjects were asked to:

1. Estimate the size of the resource on this trial.
2. Estimate the range of the total request of the other four members of your group on this trial.
3. Give your best estimate of the total request of the other four members of your group on this trial.
4. We have divided the range of the total request of the other four group members into 11 classes. The classes are 0–125,

126–250, 251–375, 376–500, 501–625, 626–750, 751–875, 876–1000, 1001–1125, 1126–1250, 1250 or more. Please estimate the likelihood that the total request of the remaining four group members falls in any of these 11 classes. Please do so by using a 0–10 scale, where 0 indicates a very low likelihood and 10 indicates a very high likelihood.

Written instructions further explained the four questions.

Results

A preliminary inspection of the data showed that the responses of four subjects deviated consistently and systematically from those of the remaining forty-one subjects. All four subjects displayed an unconditional and unqualified "greedy" behavior characterized by unusually high requests. Their mean requests (across all twenty trials) were 210, 260, 355 and 378, which identify them as outliers by any statistical criterion (the highest mean request among the remaining forty-one subjects was 167, i.e., 43 points less than the smallest request in this group). Since this small group responded to the experimental situation in a drastically different fashion than the bulk of the subjects, their results were excluded from the following analyses. Unless otherwise specified, all the results below are based on a sample of forty-one subjects.

Harvest Decisions

On half of the trials the subjects were asked to state their expectations regarding the source and the behavior of the remaining players. To determine the effect of these questions on the requests, we subjected the individual requests to a 5 (conditions I, II, III, IV, V) by 2 (trials with or without questions) analysis of variance (ANOVA) with repeated measures on both factors. Only the main effect of the experimental condition was significant ($F_{4,160} = 14.47$, $p < .05$). Consequently, the distinction between the two types of trials is ignored.

In the absence of feedback, no systematic changes of requests over iterations are expected. Table 3.1 presents the mean (and standard deviation) of the requests by condition and iteration. A 5 (conditions) by 4 (iterations) ANOVA replicated the highly significant main effect of the uncertainty regarding the source (i.e., condition), uncovered a significant effect of replication ($F_{3,120} = 2.87$, $p < .05$), and showed a nonsignificant interaction ($F_{12,480} = 1.12$, $p > .05$). The entries in Table 3.1 indicate that, although no intermediate feedback was given, the mean requests decreased over iterations. However, because this effect did not interact significantly with the experimental condition, and none of the pairwise

TABLE 3.1 *Means (and Standard Deviations) of Individual Requests by Condition and Iteration*

Iteration	Condition I	II	III	IV	V	Overall
1	98.0 (26.5)	121.3 (81.9)	123.8 (88.2)	109.2 (56.8)	166.3 (115.8)	123.7 (82.3)
2	101.3 (28.7)	96.4 (29.0)	94.9 (37.7)	102.3 (52.7)	160.9 (159.2)	111.2 (82.1)
3	93.1 (20.1)	101.6 (49.3)	100.8 (53.9)	103.0 (44.0)	126.9 (55.0)	105.9 (47.0)
4	97.9 (24.0)	93.1 (52.0)	105.5 (74.8)	101.9 (44.1)	129.7 (61.3)	105.6 (50.6)
Overall	98.6 (24.0)	103.1 (52.0)	106.2 (66.8)	104.1 (49.3)	145.9 (107.2)	111.6 (67.9)

comparisons between iterations were significant (by Tukey's HSD test), we decided to ignore the iteration effects in all subsequent analyses.

Table 3.1 shows that, under environmental uncertainty, subjects request more from the resource, with the most dramatic increase in the case of extreme uncertainty. This impression is confirmed by Tukey's HSD test indicating that the mean requests in condition V are significantly higher than in all other four conditions. It is also noted that the variability of the requests increases as a function of the variability of the resource. This increase casts doubt on the validity of our ANOVA results. However, when the results are reanalyzed following variance stabilizing transformations (e.g., Smith, 1976), the basic pattern is confirmed. Actually, the effect of iterations becomes insignificant, providing additional justification for our decision to pool data across iterations.

The individual requests from the common resource may also be analyzed from a group perspective by aggregating all five requests on a given trial and comparing the resulting sum with the common mean of all the distributions (500) as the threshold of provision. The percentage of cases in which the group requests were satisfied decreased systematically (54, 46, 43, 39 and 10, respectively, in conditions I through V), and the difference between the groups was significant ($F_{4,24} = 3.81$, $p < .05$).

Questionnaire Data

Table 3.2 summarizes the subjects' judgments regarding the common resource in the four random conditions. The top two rows present the actual ranges and standard deviations of the uniform distributions employed, and the bottom three rows summarize the mean estimated values and the standard deviations of the estimates. An ANOVA of the

TABLE 3.2 *Statistical Characteristics of the Source Distributions and the Subjects' Estimates*

Statistic	Condition[a] II	III	IV	V
Range	250	500	750	1000
Standard deviation	72.2	144.3	216.5	288.7
Mean estimate	499.6	485.3	526.1	589.8
Standard deviation of estimates	66.5	128.2	147.3	217.3
Standard deviation of mean estimates	54.9	113.2	124.8	182.1

[a] In condition I the source was fixed.

estimates resulted in a significant effect due to condition ($F_{3,120} = 9.27$, $p < .05$). Pairwise comparisons (by Tukey's HSD) indicated that all estimates are equal except the one for condition V, which clearly exceeds all the others. The bottom two rows of Table 3.2 show that the subjects' judgments are sensitive to the properties of the generating process—the standard deviations (both across all judgments and across mean judgments within subject) increase more or less proportionally to the real standard deviations.

Table 3.3 summarizes the various judgments provided by the subjects regarding the request of the four remaining members of the group. The estimates of the lower bound of the others' requests are not affected by condition ($F_{4,160} = 1.75$, $p > .05$), but the estimates of the upper bound and the best estimate regarding the others' harvests increase systematically ($F_{4,160} = 5.82$, $p < .05$ and $F_{4,160} = 7.73$, $p < .05$). For both estimates the steepest increase in the estimates is associated again with condition V.

The bottom two rows of Table 3.3 are based on the probability distributions (across eleven intervals) deduced from the subjects' likelihood estimates. Most distributions (92 percent) were single peaked, as expected, and only three subjects had distributions with more than two peaks. The inferred mean request and standard deviation of the request vary across the five conditions ($F_{4,160} = 269.1$, $p < .05$ and $F_{4,160} = 23.4$, $p < .05$) with clear, and statistically significant differences between the fixed case (I), the maximal uncertainty condition (V), and the three intermediate conditions (II, III, and IV). Finally, note that, in general, the variability of the estimates increases with the uncertainty of the resource.

Model Testing

Because utilities were not assessed in the present study, we restricted ourselves to testing the maximization of expected value model that predicts the solution of equation (1). We shall denote this solution, given subject

TABLE 3.3 *Means (and Standard Deviations) of Estimates of the Requests of the Other Players*

Statistic	Condition I	II	III	IV	V
Direct estimates					
Minimal request	310.6	339.6	302.8	290.7	322.5
	(109.2)	(81.1)	(112.1)	(134.4)	(147.4)
Best estimate	398.8	436.4	423.3	457.8	517.2
	(86.0)	(103.5)	(136.5)	(184.5)	(162.8)
Maximal request	460.2	580.2	627.6	619.5	787.4
	(132.2)	(263.8)	(304.3)	(208.0)	(615.0)
Distribution of requests					
Mean	462.1	521.5	511.2	536.2	594.5
	(130.3)	(144.1)	(163.0)	(168.2)	(162.2)
Standard deviation	148.7	174.5	190.6	206.0	219.8
	(84.5)	(68.0)	(61.6)	(62.6)	(52.9)

j's probability density function $f_{R_j}(x)$, by $r_j(v)$. As an estimate of $f_{R_j}(x)$, subject j's two responses to question 4 were averaged for each condition separately, and then the resulting means were normalized. To test equation (2), we derived the predicted request $r_j(s)$ from the subject's estimate of the resource in question 1. And to test equation (3), we derived the predicted request $r_j(o)$ from the subject's best estimate of the total request of others in question 3. In both cases we used the mean estimates over the two replications of each of the two questions.

Three predicted requests were thus derived separately for each subject and each condition: $r_j(v)$, $r_j(s)$, and $r_j(o)$. These predicted values were compared to the mean request, denoted by r_j, computed for each subject and each condition separately across the four replications. A deviation score

$$r_j - r_j(\cdot)$$

was computed separately for each subject, condition, and model. Similarly, an absolute deviation score

$$|r_j - r_j(\cdot)|$$

was also computed. We find it necessary to compute and report both measures of discrepancy to show both the direction of the deviations and their absolute magnitude.

The means of the two deviation scores are presented in Table 3.4. Clearly, the maximization of expected value fares poorly in comparison to the two versions of the equality model. This model clearly overpredicts the observed mean request in all five conditions. According to both measures, the model based on the fair and equal division of the estimated source is the best, and a similar pattern of results was obtained in a

TABLE 3.4 *Mean Deviations and Absolute Deviations of Observed Requests from the Models' Predictions by Experimental Condition*

Model	I	II	Condition III	IV	V	Overall
			Mean Deviation Scores			
$r_j(v)$	−52.5	−48.1	−88.5	−137.7	−124.6	−89.7
$r_j(s)$	−1.4	3.2	9.2	−1.1	27.9	7.6
$r_j(o)$	−1.1	−6.0	0.4	−10.4	16.6	−0.1
			Mean Absolute Deviation Scores			
$r_j(v)$	70.0	54.8	95.1	135.9	128.4	96.8
$r_j(s)$	11.3	21.6	23.9	19.6	34.7	22.2
$r_j(o)$	20.3	29.5	33.2	33.9	35.7	30.5

TABLE 3.5 *Frequency of Best Fitting Models by Condition*

Best fitting models	I	II	Condition III	IV	V	Overall
$r_j(v)$	3	11	5	2	7	28
$r_j(s)$	20	17	24	26	19	106
$r_j(o)$	4	9	12	11	13	49
$r_j(s)$ & $r_j(o)$	13	4	0	2	2	21
$r_j(v)$ & $r_j(s)$ & $r_j(o)$	1	0	0	0	0	1
Total	41	41	41	41	41	205

correlational analysis (not reported here). The table also shows that for all three models the goodness of fit tends in general to decrease as the environmental uncertainty increases.

A final analysis identified the best prediction (or predictions when two or three coincide) for each subject and condition separately, and its results are summarized in Table 3.5. They support our previous conclusion regarding the predominance of the equality model formulated as equation (2).

Discussion

An implicit assumption underlying Hardin's parable is that the carrying capacity of the commons is known. This assumption also underlies most of the research of Messick and his associates, who have devised several experimental tasks to study structural solutions to resource dilemmas with a fixed and known threshold. We have argued—to continue with Hardin's parable—that the carrying capacity of the commons is in general not known exactly. Indeed, it is the uncertainty regarding the carrying capacity, in addition to the individual considerations of each herdsman, that may result in patterns of behavior leading to the destruction of the commons.

To study the effects of what was termed environmental uncertainty, we devised a single-trial resource dilemma in which only the distribution of the resource is common knowledge. Our experiment included five different uniform distributions with the same mean of 500 but different ranges. The uniform distribution is the simplest continuous probability distribution. Moreover, when the mean is divided by five—the group size in our study—the resulting value is an obvious focal point. Therefore, on the basis of symmetry considerations, we expected the expectations about others' requests, as well as the individual requests, to center around 100 for the fixed resource case. This expectation was fully realized. We had no hypotheses about focal points when the resource was variable. The model we proposed specifies how the subject arrives at his or her request by combining knowledge about the environment and expectations about the decisions of others; it makes no predictions about these expectations under conditions of environmental uncertainty. As a result of arguments made by Kahneman and Tversky (1979) about the discontinuity between certainty and uncertainty, we also anticipated possible differences between condition I and conditions II through V.

Indeed, the individual requests (Table 3.1), estimates of the (random) resource (Table 3.2), and estimates of the total request of the remaining four group members (Table 3.3) all increased on the average as the resource uncertainty was increased. The main difference was not between the certain (I) and four uncertain (II, III, IV, and V) conditions, but rather between the condition of extreme uncertainty (V) and conditions I through IV. However, the standard deviations of the requests and estimates increased monotonically as the range of the resource was widened. Finally, the mean estimates of the resource correlated positively and significantly with the mean expectations about the requests of others (0.61, 0.64, 0.58, and 0.62 for conditions II, III, IV, and V, respectively).

Several explanations for the various effects of the resource uncertainty come to mind. The increase in the mean estimate of the unknown resource may be explained by the fact that people tend to perceive the variability and central tendency of probability distributions to be positively correlated. As the mean and variance are often positively correlated in real-life applications, this perception may simply reflect generalization from experience. In the present task, the increase in the range of the random resource might have been associated with an upward shift in its estimated mean and, consequently, a higher probability of sampling relatively high values.

An alternative explanation of the same finding is that when people are asked to provide their best estimate of the unknown resource (note that we did not ask our subjects to estimate the mean or any other measure of central tendency), their estimate will be based on a weighted average of the two endpoints of the range in which the upper—and more desirable—endpoint is overweighted. Similar patterns of probability-outcome interaction were documented in the past (Morlock, 1967; Slovic, 1966; Einhorn & Hogarth, 1986). They have been labeled "optimism," "outcome desirability bias," or simply "wishful thinking" (Hogarth, 1987).

Expectations about the others' requests, as well as individual requests from the resource, correlated positively with the estimates of the resource size. Because the information about the resource was given to the subjects before they stated their requests and estimated the behavior of others, it is tempting to attribute the systematic increase in these quantities to misperception of the resource.

On the other hand, one can argue that the increase in the mean estimates of the random resource and the total contributions of others may reflect characteristics of our experimental design rather than a genuine effect of resource uncertainty. Like many other studies of social dilemmas, we have asked our subjects to specify their request and estimate what others would do. There are good reasons to believe that expectations and decisions are interrelated (Dawes, McTavish, & Shaklee, 1977). In the present study subjects might well determine their individual requests *before* making their estimates and then "tailor" their expectations regarding the resource or the total request of others to justify their own requests.

To test this artifactual explanation, we ran five additional groups ($n=25$) in a similar design. These subjects were also promised a 1 NIS payoff for every instance in which their estimates of the resource or the others' requests were within 25 points of the true values. The results of this group were very similar in most respects to the results reported above. In particular, the independent reward for accuracy in estimation did not eliminate, nor weaken, the relationship between requests and estimates. Thus, we reject the possibility that the observed pattern of results is purely artifactual.

Turning next to the comparison of the models, our results suggest that the subjects' behavior is best described as a request for an equal and fair share from the common (and misperceived) random resource. Several papers (e.g., Messick *et al.*, 1983; Samuelson *et al.*, 1986a; Rutte *et al.*, 1987) have shown that people perceive and respond differentially to environmental and strategic uncertainty. All of these studies have shown the former to be a stronger determinant of behavior, and our results follow the same pattern at the individual and group level. However, before rejecting the maximization of expected utility model in favor of simpler alternatives, we must recall that—because no utilities were assessed—our test was restricted to maximization of expected value, and did not take into account the subjects' misperception of the distribution of the source.

The equality model yields different predictions for the five levels of environmental uncertainty, since it incorporates the empirical estimates of the resource. Despite this fact, the fit of the model deteriorates as the variance of the source increases. This result, and the consistent growth in the variability of the requests, indicate that additional considerations affect the subjects' requests. One interesting possibility is that there are systematic differences in the ways individuals react, and expect others to react, to environmental uncertainty. Some, who believe that the others will behave as they do, will maintain a strict "equal share" norm. Others may demand more (or less) than an equal share if they are risk seekers (or avoiders), and expect their partners to become increasingly cautious (or risk taking) as the environmental uncertainty increases. Thus, we suggest that future studies in this domain collect measures of attitudes towards risk in order to allow precise tests of this explanation.

References

Dawes, R. M. (1980). Social dilemmas. *Annual Review of Psychology*, **31**, 169–193.

Dawes, R. M., McTavish, J., & Shaklee, H. (1977). Behavior, communication, and assumptions about other people's behavior in a commons dilemma situation. *Journal of Personality and Social Psychology*, **35**, 1–11.

De Vries, S., & Wilke, H. A. M. (1988). Resource management in an uncertain environment: Harvesting biases and effects of additional information. Paper presented at the Third International Conference on Social Dilemmas, Groningen, The Netherlands.

Einhorn, H. J., & Hogarth, R. M. (1986). Decision making under ambiguity. *Journal of Business*, **59**, S225–S250.

Hardin, G. R. (1968). The tragedy of the commons. *Science*, **162**, 1243–1248.

Hogarth, R. M. (1987). *Judgment and Choice: The Psychology of Decision*, 2nd edition. New York: Wiley.

Hovi, J. (1986). Binary games as models of public goods provision. *Scandinavian Political Studies*, **9**, 337–360.

Kahneman, D., & Tversky, A. (1979). Prospect theory: An analysis of decision under risk. *Econometrica*, **47**, 263–291.

Messick, D. M. (1984). Some effects of environmental uncertainty on optimal group behavior in social dilemmas. Unpublished manuscript, University of California at Santa Barbara.

Messick, D. M., & Brewer, M. B. (1983). Solving social dilemmas: A review. In L. Wheeler & P. Shaver (Eds), *Review of Personality and Social Psychology*, vol. 4, pp. 11–44. Beverly Hills: Sage.

Messick, D. M., Allison, S. T., & Samuelson, C. D. (1988). Framing and communication effects on group members' responses to environmental and social uncertainty. In S. Maital (Ed.), *Applied Behavioral Economics*, vol. 11. Brighton: Wheatsheaf.

Messick, D. M., Wilke, H. A. M., Brewer, M. B., Kramer, R. M., Zemke, P. E., & Lui, L. (1983). Individual adaptations and structural change as solutions to social dilemmas. *Journal of Personality and Social Psychology*, **44**, 294–309.

Morlock, H. (1967). The effect of outcome desirability on information required for decisions. *Behavioral Science*, **12**, 296–300.

Rutte, C. G., Wilke, H. A. M., & Messick, D. M. (1987). Scarcity or abundance caused by people or the environment as determinants of behavior in the resource dilemma. *Journal of Experimental Social Psychology*, **23**, 208–216.

Samuelson, C. D., & Messick, D. M. (1986a). Alternative structural solutions to resource dilemmas. *Organizational Behavior and Human Decision Processes*, **37**, 139–155.

Samuelson, C. D., & Messick, D. M. (1986b). Inequities in access to and use of shared resources in social dilemmas. *Journal of Personality and Social Psychology*, **51**.

Samuelson, C. D., Messick, D. M., Rutte, C. G., & Wilke, H. A. M. (1984). Individual and structural solutions to resource dilemmas in two cultures. *Journal of Personality and Social Psychology*, **47**, 94–104.

Selten, R. (1987). Equity and coalition bargaining in experimental three-person games. In A. E. Roth (Ed.), *Laboratory Experimentation in Economics: Six Points of View*, pp. 42–98. Cambridge: Cambridge University Press.

Slovic, P. (1966). Value as determiner of subjective probability. *IEEE Transactions on Human Factors in Electronics*, **HFE-7**, 22–28.

Smith, J. E. K. (1976). Data transformations in analysis of variance. *Journal of Verbal Learning and Verbal Behavior*, **15**, 339–346.

Suleiman, R., & Rapoport, A. (1989). Environmental and social uncertainty in single-trial resource dilemmas. *Acta Psychologica*, **68**, 99–112.

4

Efficacy as a Causal and Moderating Variable in Social Dilemmas[1]

NORBERT L. KERR
Michigan State University

Several theorists interested in social dilemmas (e.g., Buchanan, 1965; Kerr & Bruun, 1983; Marwell, 1982; Messick, 1976; Olson, 1965; Rapoport, 1985, 1987) have advanced the following argument: cooperation is discouraged in many social dilemmas, especially ones faced by very large groups, because cooperative (or, for that matter, defecting) behavior is perceived as having very little effect on the group's outcomes. Olson's (1965) comments are illustrative: "When a partnership has many members, the individual partner observes that his own effort or contribution will not greatly affect the performance of the enterprise, and expects that he will get his prearranged share of the earnings whether or not he contributes as much as he could have done" (p. 55). In many cases, especially when the group is very large, the impact of a personally-costly cooperative act on the collective welfare is often quite small. Conversely, the marginal harm to the group of the personally-rewarding defecting choice is also quite small. Of course, the tragedy of the commons (and many other social dilemmas) derives from the accumulated effect of many such "imperceptible" defecting acts.

Defining Efficacy in Social Dilemmas

Bandura (1986) defines perceived self-efficacy as "a judgment of one's capability to accomplish a certain level of performance" (p. 391). In experimental social dilemmas, there is typically little uncertainty about one's capability to make cooperative vs. defecting choices, but there is often considerable uncertainty about the likely consequences of one's actions (cf. Campbell *et al.*, 1970). A particularly salient consequence of cooperation in a social dilemma is achieving mutual cooperation (Pruitt

& Kimmel, 1977), since mutual cooperation leads to a better outcome than mutual defection in any social dilemma. Thus, a "level of performance" which one might hope to achieve through cooperation is the outcome associated with mutual cooperation—e.g., avoiding the collapse of the commons or obtaining a public good. In this paper we are interested in the perceived self-efficacy of cooperation for achieving such a public good—that is, the judgment that one's cooperative behavior will affect the chances of the group achieving a valued public good.

Paradigmatic Considerations

In our past and current work, we focus on a particular type of social dilemma—the step-level public good problem (Van de Kragt *et al.*, 1983).[2] Further, contributions to the public good in our paradigm are all-or-none. Such tasks simplify the operationalization of efficacy in social dilemmas. In many social dilemmas there are many levels of cooperative behavior possible and many potential degrees to which the public good might be provided. For example, in commons dilemmas, one may harvest at many different rates and the public good (e.g., preserving the commons) may be achieved to varying degrees (e.g., for different lengths of time). Theoretically, a group member might have a different sense of perceived self-efficacy for every possible pair of cooperative action-collective outcome combinations. However, in our step-level problems, there are only two behavioral choices and one either does or does not obtain a distinct public good. Thus, for such situations, the efficacy of cooperation for providing the public good has a single and well-defined meaning.

Efficacy as a Cause of Cooperation in Social Dilemmas

Much research by Bandura and others (e.g., see Bandura, 1986) has demonstrated that one is less likely to initiate or persist in a course of action if one feels a low sense of self-efficacy. Similarly, as noted above, many have speculated that an individual is less likely to cooperate in a social dilemma if he/she feels that the efficacy of his/her cooperative behavior for producing the public good is low. The proposition that the self-efficacy of cooperation is positively and causally related to the rate or probability of cooperation in social dilemmas is hereafter termed the *efficacy-cooperation* hypothesis.

There is a fair amount of evidence bearing on the efficacy-cooperation hypothesis. However, this evidence is rather indirect and inconclusive. The primary objective of the research reported in this chapter is to provide more direct and conclusive evidence on this hypothesis. Before describing our own research, it is worthwhile to briefly consider the most relevant prior research. It is of two types: (a) experimental research which manipulates some variable associated with the objective self-efficacy of cooperation and determines whether that variable affects cooperation rates, and (b) attempts to correlate cooperation with either direct or indirect subjective estimates of the efficacy of cooperation.

Experimental Evidence on the Efficacy-Cooperation Hypothesis

One obvious study of the first type is one which manipulates group size; for most social dilemmas, the impact of personal choice on group outcome declines with group size. There have been many social dilemma studies of group size, and the consensus of reviewers (cf. Messick & Brewer, 1983; Orbell & Dawes, 1981) is that cooperation tends to decline with group size, as the efficacy-cooperation hypothesis suggests. However, there are also many failures to observe group size effects on cooperation (e.g., Kerr, 1989; Liebrand, 1984; Rapoport *et al.*, 1989) as well as occasional complex interaction effects (e.g., Brewer & Kramer, 1986). And even if the group size effect were robust and reliable, it would still be difficult to attribute it unambiguously to self-efficacy. This is because manipulations of group size typically (and nearly inevitably, Orbell & Dawes, 1981) produce multiple confounds (e.g., group size also may affect one's share of group benefits, one's identifiability, one's degree of deindividuation, the level of group cohesiveness, the difficulty of coordination, and so on). To my knowledge, no one has been able to show, either via experimental or statistical (e.g., mediational analysis, Baron & Kenny, 1986) means, that a group size effect is unambiguously attributable to self-efficacy.

An indirect piece of evidence is Van de Kragt *et al.*'s (1983) finding that groups which were allowed to discuss step-level public goods problems *always* provided themselves with the public good, unlike groups not allowed to discuss such problems. Groups accomplished this by designating a *minimal contributing set* of group members equal to the provision point. Even when contribution decisions were made in complete privacy, every person who had been placed in such a set subsequently contributed toward the public good. Van der Kragt *et al.* attributed this result to subjects' recognition of the criticality of their behavior (i.e., to the efficacy of cooperation for providing the public good). Unless someone outside of the designated set also contributed (which rarely happened), the group could receive the public good if and only if each member of the set contributed. This seems quite plausible, but other explanations (e.g., promising, enhanced social identification, Orbell *et al.*, 1988) cannot be ruled out.

Another promising approach is to vary the impact of a cooperative act on group welfare more directly. This is the approach taken in a pair of studies by Rapoport and his colleagues (Rapoport, 1988; Rapoport *et al.*,

1989, Experiment 1). Functionally they posed the question, "Are wealthy individuals more likely to contribute toward the provision of public goods than poor individuals?" (Rapoport, 1988, p. 433). Because a wealthy person may have more money available to give, his/her contribution can be more efficacious (or, in Rapoport's terminology, more *critical*) for providing the public good than the contribution of a poor person. Subjects within a group were given different endowments which they could keep or contribute towards provision of a step-level public good. Endowment size did not significantly affect cooperation in the Rapoport (1988) study (although those with larger endowments tended nonsignificantly to contribute more often). In Rapoport *et al.* (1989),[3] those with larger endowments were significantly *less* likely to contribute, contrary to the efficacy-cooperation hypothesis. Unfortunately, as with the group size studies, manipulations of endowment size affect more than the efficacy of a cooperative choice. Despite their greater efficacy, those with larger endowments may have been less willing to contribute (a) because they stood to lose more if the public good was not provided, and (b) because it may have been considered inequitable to contribute more but to receive no more than other contributors.[4]

There are also two studies which have used similar endowment-size manipulations for public-good games permitting continuous contribution choices (Marwell & Ames, 1979; Wit, Wilke, & Oppewal, 1989). In both studies, those with larger endowments contributed more to the provision of the public good. However, these studies were not specifically designed to test the efficacy-cooperation hypothesis and have certain design flaws for that purpose. In some of Marwell and Ames's (1979) conditions the endowment size was confounded with the subject's share of the public good. Furthermore, concerns with equity (rather than efficacy) could also have produced these effects. Subjects could define a fair and equitable contribution either in terms of every member making an equal absolute contribution or an equal proportional contribution (cf. Gergen *et al.*, 1975). The latter principle would produce increasing absolute contributions with increasing endowment size, even if every group member contributed the same percentage of their endowment (e.g., 50 percent).[5]

Correlational Evidence on the Efficacy-Cooperation Hypothesis

Five studies employing the step-level public good paradigm have asked subjects to make direct estimates of the efficacy of making an all-or-none contribution to help provide a public good (Kerr, 1989, Experiments 1, 2, & 4; Rapoport *et al.*, 1989, Experiments 1 & 2). In every study, such efficacy judgments were positively (and significantly) correlated with subjects' decisions to contribute. Another approach has been to compute the efficacy of a cooperative choice in a step-level game using the subject's own estimates of the probability that other group members would contribute. In one such analysis (Rapoport, 1988), this indirect subjective efficacy estimate was significantly correlated with cooperative choices; in two others (Rapoport *et al.*, 1989, Experiments 1 & 2) it was not. Of course, the difficulty with such correlational findings is that causal inferences cannot be confidently drawn. It is possible, for example, that subjects minimize the perceived efficacy of cooperation to justify a non-cooperative choice.[6]

Summary

The pattern of findings in this literature is generally supportive of the efficacy-cooperation hypothesis. However, this support is equivocal. What is needed is experimental social dilemma research which incorporates powerful and unconfounded manipulations of self-efficacy. This was attempted by the pair of studies reported in this chapter. The key manipulation was a variation on the endowment-size manipulation used by Rapoport and his colleagues. In previous studies (e.g., Rapoport, 1988; Rapoport *et al.*, 1989) a cooperative choice always meant losing one's endowment and adding exactly that amount to the group's "account" (e.g., the total amount contributed toward providing the public good). In our studies, all group members were given the same endowment which they could either keep or contribute towards providing a step-level public good. However, a decision to contribute did not necessarily have equal impact on the group's account. For some subjects, the value to the group of a decision to contribute was greater than the endowment value; for some it was less. This procedure provided a clear and direct manipulation of the efficacy of cooperation without introducing confounds (e.g., in the cost of cooperation or in the "value of the public good-to-cost" ratio) and thereby provided a cleaner test of the efficacy-cooperation hypothesis.[7]

Efficacy as a Moderating Variable in Social Dilemmas

Besides its direct effect on cooperation, efficacy may also exert indirect, moderating effects; i.e., the effects of other variables on cooperation may change as the efficacy of a cooperative act varies (Baron & Kenny, 1986). This proposition is implied by a number of economic or rational-choice analyses (e.g., Olson, 1965; Rapoport, 1987) that suggest that because self-efficacy is very low in extremely large groups seeking public goods, few if any individuals will choose to contribute. This suggests that factors which normally serve as incentives to cooperative behavior may become irrelevant if cooperative behavior is ineffectual for obtaining the public good.

One reason this issue is important is that many significant social dilemmas occur in very large groups, where self-efficacy does tend to be low. However, most of the potential remedies for such social dilemmas have been investigated in small, laboratory groups, where personal self-efficacy is higher. Thus, exploring the moderating effect of self-efficacy may help clarify the ecological validity of social dilemma remedies identified under laboratory conditions.

Generally, remedies for social dilemmas consist of some objective or subjective transformation of the social dilemma's objective payoffs (Kelley & Thibaut, 1978). Excepting purely altruistic action, social dilemma solutions require that ". . . individual incentives must be changed so that the game is not a social dilemma" (Orbell & Dawes, 1981, p. 44). In the present context, it is useful to distinguish two non-exhaustive subclasses of transformations. Some transformations have the net effect of increasing the value the individual places on the public good. We might term these *public-good transformations* (PGTs). For example, public radio stations might increase voluntary contributions by convincing viewers that the programming they offer is particularly valuable. It has been suggested that cooperative social motives (e.g., Messick & McClintock, 1968; Kuhlman & Marshello, 1975)[8] or a strong in-group identity (Kramer & Brewer, 1986) may enhance cooperation by blurring the distinction between personal and collective welfare. If one values a public good not only because of its direct value to oneself, but also (to some degree) because it has value to others in the group, we might also classify solutions which rely on the manipulation of these variables as PGTs.

In transformations of the second type, which we might call *cooperation-contingent transformations* (CCTs), new incentives for cooperation (or disincentives for defection) are not contingent on obtaining the public good, *per se*, but rather are directly contingent on one's cooperative choice. Direct externally-supplied side payments (e.g., fines or penalties for defection, rewards for cooperation) are good examples of remedies of the second type. Such transformations may also reflect social or personal norms that prescribe cooperation, *per se*. Several studies (e.g., Van de Kragt *et al.*, 1986; Dawes *et al.*, 1977) have shown that pre-decision communication about the social dilemma among group members encourages cooperation. Recent research (Orbell *et al.*, 1988; Braver, in press) suggests that this effect is due, at least in part, to promising or commitment; group members who agree during group discussion to cooperate may feel bound to do so, even when cooperation lowers subjects' game payoffs (see Braver, in press). Kerr (in press) speculates that the personal costs (e.g., guilt, embarrassment) of violating social and personal norms proscribing breaking one's word may often be more salient than the objective payoffs inherent in the social dilemma.

We hypothesize that the perceived self-efficacy of cooperation has different moderating effects on variables that derive their effect (exclusively)[9] through these two types of transformations. In particular, we hypothesize that as the self-efficacy of cooperation declines, the effectiveness of a public-good remedy should decline as well. One simple way of seeing this is in instrumentality-value terms (e.g., Vroom, 1964). A remedy which enhances the value of a public good should generally increase the attractiveness of the behaviors (e.g., a cooperative choice in a social dilemma) which lead to that outcome. However, the strength of the relation between the value of the outcome and the attractiveness of the behavior also depends on how instrumental that behavior is for producing that outcome. At the limit, no matter how much the value placed on obtaining the public good was increased, you would not increase your level of cooperation if you were convinced that a cooperative act had no impact at all on attaining that public good.

However, the self-efficacy of cooperation should have no effect on a purely cooperation-contingent remedy. Even if efficacy were minimal, incentives strictly contingent on cooperation, *per se*, should still boost cooperation. For example, one might feel compelled to keep a promise to cooperate even if that cooperative act could not actually help the group. Another good example might be voting. Most voters will admit that the probability of their vote altering the outcome of an election is vanishingly small. Yet the act of voting itself may offer sufficient rewards to justify voting [e.g., the opportunity to "bask in the reflected glory" of the winning candidate (Cialdini *et al.*, 1976); the value-expressive payoff of supporting an ideologically acceptable candidate (Katz, 1960); the satisfaction of fulfilling the role of "good citizen"].[10]

In the two studies reported here, we test the first of these two hypotheses for one purported public-good transformation remedy—viz., enhancing one's group identity (Kramer & Brewer, 1986). There are at least two ways in which these studies might be useful. First, they may reveal an interesting limit on the external validity of a potential social dilemma remedy; viz., show that the lower the perceived self-efficacy of cooperation, the less benefit enhancing group identity will have on cooperation. They may also help illuminate the psychological basis for the remedial effect of enhancing group identity. Confirmation of the moderation interaction prediction would bolster the claim (e.g., Kramer & Brewer, 1986) that enhancing group identity increases one's concern for the group's welfare.

Group Identity and Self-efficacy

The design of our studies also permitted a first empirical test of an interesting conjecture proposed by Messick & Brewer (1983). They suggested that group identification may enhance cooperation, in part, by enhancing the perceived self-efficacy of a cooperative act. They note ". . . when individuals feel . . . that their actions are representative of some larger social entity, the perceived impact of those actions is magnified and the individual's sense of personal responsibility for collective outcomes enhanced" (p. 28). This argument is reminiscent of Quattrone and Tversky's (1984) "voter's illusion"—voting is more likely given the belief that one's vote is diagnostic of many others' votes. Essentially, Messick and Brewer suggest that strong group identification strengthens a similar belief about the diagnosticity of one's own cooperative response.

Summary

To summarize, the primary objective of the following studies was to provide a direct experimental test of the efficacy-cooperation hypothesis. The secondary objective was to test the prediction that manipulated self-efficacy would moderate the group identity-cooperation relationship. The third and final objective was to test Messick and Brewer's (1983) conjecture that strengthening group identity would bolster the perceived efficacy of cooperative behavior.

EXPERIMENT 1

The method of manipulating the self-efficacy of cooperation was as outlined above—endowments were equal but giving up the endowment had different impact on achieving the public good. In Experiment 1, group identity was manipulated using a variant of a procedure introduced by Kramer and Brewer (1984; Experiments 1 & 2)—group composition was varied to enhance or blur the differentiation of subgroups based on university enrollment.

Method

Subjects and Design

The subjects were 136 students recruited from introductory psychology classes. Their participation fulfilled a class requirement. The experimental design was a 2 (Group identification) × 2 (Sex) × 3 (Efficacy) factorial. The latter factor was manipulated within-subjects.

Procedure

Subjects were scheduled at one of four sequential, hour-long sessions. Approximately 45 students were run per session. Two of these sessions (the first and the third) received low group-identification (Low GI) instructions; the second and fourth received the High GI instructions. The audiotaped instructions indicated that the present experiment was being run simultaneously at three different universities: the subject's university (MSU) and two others (UM and NU). All subjects participated as part of a nine-person group. In the Low GI condition, the anonymous members of this group were distributed (three MSU, three UM, three NU). In the High GI condition, subjects were told that their own group contained nine MSU students and that (besides there being a number of additional homogenously-MSU groups) there were also homogenous groups being run at UM and NU. To strengthen this treatment, High GI subjects were told that one purpose of the study was to compare how the MSU groups' task performance would compare with the groups from the other schools; subjects in the Low GI condition were told simply that it was of interest to see how heterogeneous groups like theirs performed the task.

An "investment game" (Kerr, 1989) step-level public goods task was then described. All group members received a $10 endowment which they could keep or "invest." Invested money was lost, but if $45 or more was invested, then every group member received a $25 "jackpot" (the public good). Since subjects' cooperative choices involved an all-or-none contribution, the functional provision point was five investors out of nine group members. Investment choices were made anonymously by group members who never interacted directly.

The various possible outcomes of the game were described and subjects then took a brief written test of their understanding. The experimenters checked subjects' answers and when errors were detected, the rules of the game were reviewed with the subject and an alternate form of the test was administered. Experimenters noted whether and how many errors were made on this second form.

Subjects were then told that they would actually play a slightly different version of the game. The difference was that although a decision to invest always cost a person $10, it did not necessarily contribute $10 to the group's investment total. Rather, when a person invested, the total invested by the group was increased by an "investment value" which could differ from the endowment value. As in the earlier, simpler version of the game, the group had to collectively invest $45 or more to earn the $25/member public good. Each player would know his/her own investment value but would not know the corresponding investment values for other group members. He/she did know, however, that the sum of the investment values across the nine group members would always be $90, just as in the simpler version of the game.

The four dependent variables were then described. They were: (a) a dichotomous invest/keep choice; (b) an estimate of the total amount likely to be invested by the *other* eight members of one's group; (c) a subjective probability estimate of the likelihood that the group would provide the public good; and (d) an estimate of how important one's own decision to invest/keep was for the group's chances to obtain the public good. The latter was to be expressed as the difference in the group's probability of obtaining the public good when the subject did vs. did not invest. The last judgment operationalizes the self-efficacy of cooperation in this paradigm (cf. Kerr, 1989; Rapoport *et al.*, 1989); the next-to-last judgment operationalizes collective efficacy.

To give the game outcomes some real utility, it was explained that one randomly selected participant in the study would actually receive the amount of money earned through his/her own and the other group members' invest/keep choices. Because each person would play the game three times, the total amount the selected person would earn could vary from \$0 to \$105.

Subjects then played the game three times. Variation of the investment values across trials constituted the efficacy manipulation. The manipulated investment values were \$2, \$10, and \$18. Thus, on one trial the subject had the "expected" investment value (\$10 = \$90 total investment value in the group/nine group members); on another he/she had an investment value well below this expected value and on another one well above. Since the total investment values of group members was fixed (=\$90), this manipulation involved varying both the absolute and proportional investment value of one's own choice compared to the average other group member. All possible orders of considering these three games were used and with approximately equal frequency. Two response item orders were used [(a, c, d, b) and (d, b, a, c)] with approximately equal frequency. This was because the primary interest was in the cooperation and self-efficacy measures, and this procedure counterbalanced their order.

After considering the three games, subjects filled out a brief questionnaire. They were to indicate the number of MSU, UM, and NU students in their group. There were also four scales checking the social identity manipulation. On seven-point scales, subjects rated (a) how strongly they felt part of a group; (b) whether they would prefer to have been in a different group; (c) similarity with the people in their group; and (d) whether they would choose to work together again with their group. Two other items probed their concern for the collective welfare: (e) a rating of their concern that the group get the public good, and (f) whether they played the game for the group (vs. for themselves). An open-ended item checked subject suspicion.

Results

Six subjects (five males, one female) were dropped from analyses because they missed several items on the check of task understanding. Thus, the final sample analyzed included 131 subjects. (Due to class composition, females outnumbered males in approximately a 3:1 ratio.)

Checks of Experimental Manipulations

The primary analyses were 2 × 2 × 3 (GI × Sex × Efficacy) repeated-measures ANOVAs. First, it was clear that the efficacy manipulation was effective. There was a strong main effect for the efficacy treatment on subjective ratings of self-efficacy, $F(2,240) = 55.31$, $p < .001$ (mean subjective probability ratings were $2 investment value = .18, $10 = .41, and $18 = .51; all three means differed significantly from one another by Newman–Keuls tests, $p < .01$).

Nearly all (62/66 = 94 percent) of the Low GI subjects correctly reported that there were only three MSU students in their group. Only 10 percent (6/62) of the High GI subjects reported that there were any non-MSU students in their group. However, these differences in group composition had little effect on subjects' perceptions of and reactions to their groups, at least as revealed by the manipulation check items. The GI treatment produced no significant effects in univariate analyses of the four manipulation check items. Although this manipulation appears to have failed, the GI factor was retained in subsequent analyses to see whether it might still have had some impact on behavior.

Cooperation and Efficacy Analyses

The only significant effect obtained on the ANOVA on the dichotomous invest/keep choices was a main effect of the efficacy treatment, $F(2,240) = 58.08$, $p < .001$; as subjects' investment value and hence efficacy increased, so did their probability of cooperation. The means were $2 investment value = 31.5 percent cooperative responses, $10 = 81.5 percent, and $18 = 89.5 percent. Only the latter two means did not differ significantly ($p < .05$) by the Newman–Keuls procedure; ceiling effects were clearly a possibility. Unsurprisingly, in light of the manipulation check data, the GI treatment had no effect on cooperation ($F < 1$). Nor did the GI treatment affect subjects' ratings of concern that the group get the public good or the degree to which the game was played for the group's benefit.

Besides the powerful effect of the efficacy treatment, only one other effect emerged on the subjective self-efficacy ratings, a Sex × GI interaction effect, $F(1,120) = 4.08$, $p < .05$. Males reported feeling somewhat more self-efficacious when social identification was high (Hi GI = .37 vs. Lo GI = .29), but females displayed the opposite pattern (Hi GI = .33 vs. Lo GI = .42).

To further explore the role of perceived self-efficacy for mediating the observed effects of the manipulation of objective efficacy, an analysis of covariance was run using subjects' subjective self-efficacy ratings as a covariate. The strength of the efficacy main effect was attenuated

[$F(2,239) = 32.29$ vs. $F(2,240) = 58.08$ without the covariate] in the ANACOVA. This might be taken as evidence of partial but not complete mediation of the objective efficacy main effect on cooperation by subjective self-efficacy. However, even if the effect were totally mediated by subjective self-efficacy, this pattern would also obtain if the subjective efficacy ratings were unreliable (Baron & Kenny, 1986), a plausible interpretation given the extreme complexity of these judgments (viz., a difference in subjective probabilities for highly uncertain events).

Ancillary analyses

Analyses of the collective efficacy judgments resulted in two significant effects. The greater subjects' personal investment value/efficacy, the more likely they thought it was that the group would provide the public good [$F(2,240) = 98.73$, $p < .001$; \$2 investment value = .37; \$10 = .65; \$18 = .77]. The other effect was a sex main effect, $F(1,120) = 4.07$, $p < .05$; females thought it was more likely that their groups would provide the public good (.61) than males (.54).

The same two effects emerged on an analysis of subjects' estimates of others' likely contribution. First, the greater subjects' own investment value, the more they believed the *other* group members would invest, $F(2,240) = 30.57$, $p < .001$ (\$2 investment value mean = \$39; \$10 inv. value = \$54, \$18 inv. value = \$56). This was despite the fact that the amount that others could invest potentially declined with one's own investment value; thus, subjects thought that as their own personal efficacy rose, the likelihood of others investing rose. Finally, there was a significant ($p < .05$) Sex × GI interaction, $F(1,120) = 4.05$; males tended to expect higher levels of contribution in the High GI condition (\$47.35 vs \$40.75) while females tended weakly in the opposite direction (Hi GI = \$45.76 vs. Lo GI = \$48.82).

Discussion of Experiment 1

Experiment 1 provided strong support for the efficacy-cooperation hypothesis. However, it was not possible to test the moderation hypothesis because the group identification manipulation was not successful. Perhaps subjects saw introductory psychology students at the different universities as undistinctive, preventing strong subgroup differentiation in the Low SI condition. Experiment 2 was carried out to provide a cleaner and stronger manipulation of group identity and to replicate the test of the efficacy-cooperation hypothesis.

EXPERIMENT 2

This study was structurally similar to Experiment 1. The primary difference was the method of manipulating group identity. Subjects were told that the experiment was being run simultaneously at five different universities. Furthermore, all subjects were members of one of five national fraternities (or sororities). Subjects in the High GI condition were told that their five-person group was composed of five members of the same national fraternity/sorority, one from each university. These subjects were reminded repeatedly that all the people in their group were brothers/sisters in the same fraternity/sorority. In the Low GI condition, subjects were told that to maximize diversity in the groups, group members would differ from one another in both university and fraternity/sorority membership.

Method

Design

The experiment employed a 2 (Group identity) × 2 (Sex) × 8 (Efficacy) factorial design. The latter factor was manipulated within subjects.

Pretest Screening

Students in several large (300–500 student) sections of introductory psychology were surveyed as to their membership in various social, academic, and athletic organizations, including social fraternities or sororities. Subjects who were currently members of a MSU fraternity or sorority were contacted by phone and scheduled. A total of 73 subjects (22 males, 51 females) were recruited for the experiment.

Task and Procedure

The investment game differed slightly from the one used in Experiment 1. Endowments were $10, and the public good was worth $15. A pool of 100 "points" was to be randomly divided among the five members of each group with the single constraint that no single player's "share" could be larger than 50 points. Subjects knew the size of their own share of the 100-point pool but did not know the share sizes of the other four group members. The shares of all group members who chose to invest their endowment were totaled; if that total exceeded 50 points, the public good was provided. The efficacy manipulation was achieved by varying the subject's share across eight plays of the game. The eight share values used were 1, 8, 15, 22, 29, 36, 43, and 50 points. The order in which these were considered was randomized separately for each subject. In addition, the same four response scales used in Experiment 1 were randomly ordered for each play of the game.

Besides the differences already noted, the other non-trivial differences between Experiment 2 and Experiment 1 were as follows: (a) Experiment 2 was run at individual computer stations. (b) Subjects were unable to continue with the program until they could correctly answer a series of questions about the rules of the game. (c) In order to familiarize subjects with the structure of the game, all went through a series of ten hypothetical plays of the game. Their own point shares varied from 5 to 47 points. After making an investment choice, investment choices for the remaining group members were simulated by randomly selecting from the range of allowable point-total values. Subjects were told explicitly that these were random values selected only for purposes of illustration and were not representative of actual group choices. Subjects were shown what outcome would have resulted from their own actual choice as well as the opposite choice. (d) Subjects did not know in advance how many separate plays of the game they would engage in. (e) To make subjects' choices consequential, they were told that one group would be randomly selected, and then for each play of the game, one player in that group was to be randomly selected. That player would actually receive the amount of money earned through the choices he/she and the other group members made. (Of course, since groups were not actually formed, a Monte Carlo procedure was used to approximate this payoff contract.) (f) At the end of the study, subjects were asked to identify the number of persons in their group who were members of their own fraternity/sorority.

Results

Checks of Experimental Manipulations

A 2 × 2 × 8 (GI × Sex × Efficacy) repeated-measures ANOVA showed that subjects' subjective ratings of self-efficacy were strongly influenced by the efficacy manipulation, $F(7,483) = 93.08$, $p < .001$. As one can see in Table 4.1, these ratings increased steadily with assigned share size.

A large majority (86 percent) of the subjects in the High GI condition reported that all the subjects in their group were members of their own fraternity/sorority, whereas a comparable majority (viz., 80 percent) in the Low GI condition reported that they were the only person in their group drawn from their own fraternity/sorority. Not only were subjects aware of the manipulated group composition, it also appeared to affect their sense of group identification. Subjects in the High GI condition reported feeling more a part of the group ($p < .002$), preferred to remain in the same group ($p < .02$), felt more similar to others in the group

TABLE 4.1 *Effects of Manipulated Efficacy (Experiment 2)*

Subject's share size	Subjective efficacy	Proportion investing	Collective efficacy	Estimated total points by others
1	.11	.07	.45	49.4
8	.20	.12	.42	47.9
15	.32	.29	.45	45.6
22	.45	.59	.52	39.8
29	.50	.66	.61	37.9
36	.59	.78	.63	31.4
43	.74	.85	.76	26.7
50	.86	.92	.88	22.8

($p < .001$), and tended to want to work together again with the same group members more ($p < .09$) than subjects in the Low GI condition.

Cooperation and Efficacy

A 2 × 2 × 8 ANOVA on the dichotomous invest/keep choices showed that as in Experiment 1, as the efficacy of a cooperative choice for providing the public good increased, so did their rate of cooperation, $F(7{,}483) = 51.19, p < .001$. And, again, as in Experiment 1, the major such increase occurred when the subject's share size passed the point of expected share size across group members (here, a 20-point share = 100 total points/five group members); as one can see in Table 4.1, there was a sharp increase in cooperation as one went from a share of 15 to a share of 22 points. It is not surprising, given the data in Table 4.1, that subject cooperation and subjective self-efficacy were highly correlated (mean within-subject, across-play correlation = .628, $p < .001$). As in Experiment 1, inclusion of subjective efficacy judgments as a covariate in a repeated-measures ANACOVA of cooperative choices resulted in a sharp attenuation but not the elimination of the main effect for the efficacy treatment [$F(7{,}482) = 12.16$ with the covariate; $F(7{,}483) = 51.19$ without].

No other effects were significant in the ANOVA of investment choices. In particular, although subjects certainly identified more with their group in the High GI condition, they were not significantly more likely to invest in this condition, $F(1{,}69) < 1$. Similarly, subjects did not report in the post-experimental questionnaire that they were more concerned with group welfare ($F < 1$) or felt gladder when others won ($F < 1$) when the group was composed of their fraternity/sorority brothers/sisters than when it was not.

There was no support in these data for Messick and Brewer's (1983) conjecture that stronger social identification might produce a stronger sense of personal effectiveness or efficacy for cooperation, $F(1{,}69) = 1.48$, ns. Other than the check on the efficacy manipulation reported above, there were no significant effects on the subjective self-efficacy measure.

Ancillary Analyses

Two effects were significant in the analysis of the collective efficacy judgments. First, as subjects' own investment value-efficacy increased, so gradually did their mean sense of collective efficacy (see Table 4.1), $F(7,483) = 36.14$, $p < .001$. It might be assumed that this was entirely due to the fact that subjects were more likely to cooperate as investment value increased and these choices produced a larger proportion of the total necessary to obtain the public good. However, using investment choices as a covariate did not eliminate the effect ($p < .001$). Thus, greater personal efficacy seems to have been accompanied by a greater sense of collective efficacy as well.

The other significant effect was a main effect of group identity, $F(1,69) = 5.64$, $p < .02$. Surprisingly, subjects in the High GI groups actually reported that their groups were *less* likely to earn the public good (mean = .56) than those in the Low GI groups (mean = .62) (even though the High GI subjects did not feel personally less willing or able to bring that result to pass; recall GI had no effect on cooperation or self-efficacy).

Finally, as investment value/efficacy increased, the expected amount contributed by others decreased, $F(7,483) = 32.99$, $p < .001$ (see Table 4.1). However, this was simply a consequence of the fact that the potential contribution of others declined linearly with the size of the subject's own investment value. When we looked at the expected proportion (relative to the maximum possible value) of contributing by others, it was found to hover near 50 percent and not vary significantly ($p = .078$) with investment value.

General Discussion

The primary objective of these studies was met—in both studies, direct manipulations of the objective self-efficacy of cooperation were accompanied by strong effects on both subjective self-efficacy and cooperative behavior. These results confirm and bolster the prior equivocal experimental and correlational findings supporting the efficacy-cooperation hypothesis. When the perceived self-efficacy of cooperation is clearly low, cooperation is strongly attenuated. The present results also suggest that prior instances in which experimental treatments have produced significant effects on subjective self-efficacy but not parallel effects on cooperation (e.g., Kerr, 1989, for group size; Rapoport, 1988, for endowment size) may reflect either confounds which give rise to opposing processes or relatively weak (albeit significant) perceived self-efficacy effects (at least relative to the present effect sizes for self-efficacy).

In our prior discussion of the efficacy-cooperation hypothesis we have assumed an instrumentality-value model—the attractiveness of the cooperative choice should increase as the instrumentality of cooperation for obtaining a valued public good increases. However, other processes could also produce or contribute to the effects we have obtained.[11] For example, they would also follow from a norm which holds that it is the duty of those who are more capable of helping to do so [e.g., a variation of Berkowitz's (1972) norm of social responsibility]—those who can assist the group should; those who cannot, need not. A refinement of such a norm may be that public goods also be provided as efficiently as possible. Because collective welfare is reduced by overcontribution, groups may not only value obtaining the public good, but doing so at the minimum cost to its members. In the present paradigm, that would consist of providing the public good with the minimum number of invest choices, and would tend to relieve low efficacy members from responsibility to invest.

Our second objective was to test the moderating effects of self-efficacy for group identity, alleged to be an example of a public-good social dilemma remedy.[12] This objective was not realized because the group identity manipulation failed to have any affect on cooperation in either study; hence, the moderating effect of efficacy could not be examined. This was not particularly surprising in Experiment 1, where the manipulation apparently did not work, but was rather more surprising in Experiment 2, where the manipulation did seem to affect perceptions of group identity in appropriate ways. Certain features of our procedures and social identity manipulations may have weakened these manipulations.[13] For example, in both studies, the contingency for actual cash payoffs involved lotteries affecting only individual group members, not the entire group. Brewer and Kramer have shown (e.g., 1986, Experiment 3) that such individualized fate arrangements undermine social identity and cooperation. The incentives for the lottery winners were also sizeable (up to $105 in Experiment 1; up to $200 in Experiment 2); such amounts may have sharpened egoistic concerns at the expense of collective concerns. Finally, although the members of our high solidarity groups in Experiment 2 were from the same fraternity/sorority, they also always were enrolled at different universities. There is evidence (Vanbeselaere, 1987) that typical in-group biases are sharply attenuated in groups with such crossed social categorizations.[14]

Although it is not our present objective to explore the basis for and generality of the group identity effect, *per se*, our results underscore a conclusion that emerges from a detailed examination of prior group identity research (see Kramer & Brewer, 1986; Brewer & Kramer, 1986;

Wit & Wilke, 1988)—viz., that although the overall pattern suggests that superordinate group identity enhances cooperation, it does not invariably or uniformly do so. The present paradigm is distinctive in this literature in several ways—it uses an all-or-none, dichotomous cooperate/defect choice in a step-level public-goods task, whereas prior successful demonstrations of group identity effects have tended to use commons dilemma paradigms and/or continuous response and outcome formats.[15] In fact, Brewer & Kramer (1986) even found the opposite of the usual group identity effect with a large-group public-goods task. Clearly, more careful work is required to identify when and why a superordinate group identity enhances cooperation. With respect to our current objective, probably the most efficient way of testing the hypothesis of differential moderating effects of efficacy for group-welfare and personal-welfare remedies is to add efficacy manipulations to research paradigms which have reliably demonstrated remedies of each type.

Finally, no support was obtained for Messick and Brewer's (1983) interesting conjecture that group members would feel more self-efficacious when group identity was strong. However, before dismissing this conjecture, it should still be tested using group identity treatments which actually affect cooperation levels, unlike the present group identity treatments. This underscores the value of replicating the present design using alternative and proven group identity treatments. Such follow-up work is now in progress in our laboratory.

Conclusions

This research strengthens our confidence that the efficacy of cooperative behavior for obtaining a public good may directly affect cooperation. We have also posed but ultimately left unanswered several questions about the moderating role of self-efficacy in social dilemmas. With a weak sense of personal efficacy being a likely reaction to many real-world social dilemmas (involving very large groups of anonymous, noninteracting persons where defection is widespread, habitual, and even socially accepted), we think it is worthwhile to pursue these questions systematically in future research.

References

Bandura, A. (1986). *Social Foundations of Thought and Action: A Social Cognitive Theory*. Englewood Cliffs: Prentice-Hall.

Baron, R. M., & Kenny, D. A. (1986). The moderator-mediator variable distinction in social psychological research: Conceptual, strategic, and statistical considerations. *Journal of Personality and Social Psychology*, **51**, 1173–1182.

Berkowitz, L. (1972). Social norms, feelings, and other factors affecting helping and altruism. In L. Berkowitz (Ed.), *Advances in Experimental Social Psychology*, vol. 6. New York: Academic Press.

Braver, S. (in press). Social contracts and the provision of public goods. In D. Schroeder (Ed.), *Social Dilemmas: Social Psychological Perspectives*. New York: Pergamon.
Brewer, M. B., & Kramer, R. M. (1986). Choice behavior in social dilemmas: Effects of social identity, group size, and decision framing. *Journal of Personality and Social Psychology*, **50**, 543–549.
Buchanan, J. M. (1965). Ethical rules, expected values, and large numbers. *Ethics*, **76**, 1–13.
Campbell, J. P., Dunnette, M. D., Lawler, E. E., & Weick, K. E. (1970). *Managerial Behavior, Performance, and Effectiveness*. New York: McGraw-Hill.
Cialdini, R., Borden, R., Thorne, A., Walker, M. R., Freeman, S., & Sloan, L. R. (1976). Basking in reflected glory: Three (football) field studies. *Journal of Personality and Social Psychology*, **34**, 366–375.
Dawes, R. M., McTavish, J., & Shaklee, H. (1977). Behavior, communication, and assumptions about other people's behavior in a commons dilemma situation. *Journal of Personality and Social Psychology*, **35**, 1–11.
De Vries, S., & De Vos, H. (1989). Niet-egoistisch gedrag in sociale dilemma's: Groepsaltruisme of sociale rechtvaardigheid? (Non-egoistic behavior in social dilemmas: Group altruism or social justice?) Unpublished manuscript, University of Groningen, The Netherlands.
Fox, J., & Guyer, M. (1978). "Public" choice and cooperation in *N*-person prisoner's dilemma. *Journal of Conflict Resolution*, **22**, 469–481.
Gergen, K., Ellsworth, P., Maslach, C., & Seipel, M. (1975). Obligation, donor resources, and reaction to aid in three cultures. *Journal of Personality and Social Psychology*, **31**, 390–400.
Jorgenson, D. O., & Papciak, A. S. (1981). The effects of communication, resource feedback, and identifiability on behavior in a simulated commons. *Journal of Experimental Social Psychology*, **17**, 373–385.
Katz, D. (1960). The functional approach to the study of attitudes. *Public Opinion Quarterly*, **24**, 163–204.
Kelley, H. H., & Thibaut, J. W. (1978). *Interpersonal Relations: A Theory of Interdependence*. New York: Wiley.
Kerr, N. L. (1983). Motivation losses in task-performing groups: A social dilemma analysis. *Journal of Personality and Social Psychology*, **45**, 819–828.
Kerr, N. L. (1989). Illusions of efficacy: The effects of group size on perceived efficacy in social dilemmas. *Journal of Experimental Social Psychology*, **25**, 287–313.
Kerr, N. L. (in press). Norms in social dilemmas. To appear in D. Schroeder (Ed.), *Social Dilemmas: Social Psychological Perspectives*. New York: Pergamon.
Kerr, N. L., & Bruun, S. (1983). The dispensability of member effort and group motivation losses: Free rider effects. *Journal of Personality and Social Psychology*, **44**, 78–94.
Kramer, R. M., & Brewer, M. B. (1984). Effects of group identity on resource use in a simulated commons dilemma. *Journal of Personality and Social Psychology*, **46**, 1044–1057.
Kramer, R. M., & Brewer, M. B. (1986). Social group identity and the emergence of cooperation in resource conservation dilemmas. In H. Wilke, D. M. Messick, & C. G. Rutte (Eds), *Experimental Social Dilemmas*. Frankfurt am Main: Verlag Peter Lang.
Kuhlman, D. M., & Marshello, A. (1975). Individual differences in game motivation as moderators of preprogrammed strategic effects in prisoner's dilemma. *Journal of Personality and Social Psychology*, **32**, 922–931.
Liebrand, W. B. G. (1983). A classification of social dilemma games. *Simulation and Games*, **14**, 123–138.
Liebrand, W. B. G. (1984). The effect of social motives, communication and group size on behaviour in an *N*-person multi-stage mixed-motive game. *European Journal of Social Psychology*, **14**, 239–264.
Marwell, G. (1982). Altruism and the problem of collective action. In V. Derlega & J. Grzelak (Eds), *Cooperation and Helping Behavior: Theories and Research*. New York: Academic Press.
Marwell, G., & Ames, R. E. (1979a). Experiments on the provision of public goods, I: Resources, interest, group size, and the free-rider problem. *American Journal of Sociology*, **84**, 1335–1360.

Marwell, G., & Ames, R. E. (1979b). Experiments on the provision of public goods, II: Provision point, stakes, experience, and the free-rider problem. *American Journal of Sociology*, **85**, 926–937.
Messick, D. M. (1976). To join or not to join: An approach to the unionization decision. *Organizational Behavior and Human Performance*, **10**, 145–156.
Messick, D. M., & Brewer, M. B. (1983). Solving social dilemmas: A review. In L. Wheeler & P. Shaver (Eds), *Annual Review of Personality and Social Psychology*, vol. 3. Beverly Hills, CA: Sage.
Messick, D. M., & McClintock, C. G. (1968). Motivational basis of choice in experimental games. *Journal of Experimental Social Psychology*, **4**, 1–25.
Messick, D. M., Wilke, H. A. M., Brewer, M. B., Kramer, R. M., Zemke, P. E., & Lui, L. (1983). Individual adaptations and structural change as solutions to social dilemmas. *Journal of Personality and Social Psychology*, **44**, 294–309.
Olson, M. (1965). *The Logic of Collective Action: Public Goods and the Theory of Groups*. Cambridge, MA: Harvard University Press.
Orbell, J., & Dawes, R. M. (1981). Social dilemmas. In G. Stephenson & J. H. Davis (Eds), *Progress in Applied Social Psychology*, vol. 1. Chichester: Wiley.
Orbell, J., Dawes, R., & Van de Kragt, A. (1988). Explaining discussion induced cooperation. *Journal of Personality and Social Psychology*, **54**, 811–819.
Quattrone, G. A., & Tversky, A. (1984). Causal vs. diagnostic contingencies: On self-deception and on the voter's illusion. *Journal of Personality and Social Psychology*, **46**, 237–248.
Rapoport, A. (1985). Provision of public goods and the MCS experimental paradigm. *American Political Science Review*, **79**, 148–155.
Rapoport, A. (1987). Research paradigms and expected utility models for the provision of step-level public goods. *Psychological Review*, **94**, 74–83.
Rapoport, A. (1988). Provision of step-level public goods: Effects of inequality in resources. *Journal of Personality and Social Psychology*, **45**, 432–440.
Rapoport, A., & Bornstein, G. (1987). Intergroup competition for the provision of binary public goods. *Psychological Review*, **94**, 291–299.
Rapoport, A., Bornstein, G., & Erev, I. (1989). Intergroup competition for public goods: Effects of unequal resources and relative group size. *Journal of Personality and Social Psychology*, **56**, 748–756.
Schroeder, D. A., Jensen, T. D., Reed, A. J., Sullivan, D. D., & Schwab, M. (1983). The actions of others as determinants of behavior in social trap situations. *Journal of Experimental Social Psychology*, **19**, 522–539.
Vanbeselaere, N. (1987). The effects of dichotomous and crossed social categorizations upon intergroup discrimination. *European Journal of Social Psychology*, **17**, 143–156.
Van de Kragt, A., Orbell, J., & Dawes, R. M. (1983). The minimal contributing set as a solution to public goods problems. *American Political Science Review*, **77**, 112–122.
Van de Kragt, A. J. C., Dawes, R. M., Orbell, J. M., Braver, S. R., & Wilson, L. A. (1986). Doing well versus doing good as ways of resolving social dilemmas. In H. A. M. Wilke, D. M. Messick, & C. G. Rutte (Eds), *Experimental Social Dilemmas*. Frankfurt: Peter Lang.
Vroom, V. (1964). *Work and Motivation*. New York: Wiley.
Wit, A., & Wilke, H. A. M. (1988). Effecten van gemeenschappelijke versus individuele lotsbepaling op cooperratief keuzegedrag in drie soorten sociale dilemma's. (Effects of common fate vs. individual fate on cooperation in three types of social dilemmas.) In A. van Knippenberg *et al.* (Eds), *Fundamentele Social Psychologie*, vol. 2, pp. 51–70. Tilburg: Tilburg University Press.
Wit, A., Wilke, H. A. M., & Oppewal, H. (1989). Asymmetrische sociale dilemma's; Het effect van verschillen in middelen en profijt tussen groepleden op hun bijdrage aan een gezamenlijk belang. (Asymmetric social dilemmas: The effect of differential resources and profits on contributions to a public good.) In M. Poppe *et al.* (Eds), *Fundamentele Sociale Psychologie*, vol. 3, pp. 93–110. Tilburg: Tilburg University Press.

Notes

1. Support for the research reported in this chapter was provided by NSF Grant BNS-8818952. The author wishes to thank Barbara Campbell, Lisa Isaacs, Hector Lee,

Julio Sosa, and Tracey Thompson for serving as experimenters, to Sjerp de Vries for supplying unpublished findings, and to Sjerp de Vries, Arjaan Wit, and editors Wim Liebrand and David Messick for their comments on an earlier draft of the chapter.

2. Step-level public-good problems do not meet the original, strict definition of social dilemmas (e.g., Orbell & Dawes, 1981), which requires that defection completely dominates cooperation. That is because under one specific level of others' cooperation (viz. when the group is only one contributor short of obtaining the public good), cooperation produces a better outcome than defection in a step-level problem. But a step-level problem does qualify as a social dilemma under a looser but commonly-used definition (e.g., Liebrand, 1983) which only requires that defection often (although not necessarily always) produces higher outcomes than defection.
3. In this study, subjects did not play a simple step-level game, but rather played the intergroup public goods game (Rapaport & Bornstein, 1987) in which the public good is provided to whichever of two groups accumulates the larger contribution total. The greater uncertainty about the provision point that this paradigm creates does not alter its relevance to the efficacy-cooperation hypothesis.
4. Of course, such equity concerns may deter any cooperation. Contributors to a public good, regardless of endowment size, receive no more than non-contributors. Many people may refuse to cooperate rather than "play the sucker" (Kerr, 1983).
5. Interestingly, Wit *et al.*'s (1989) subjects seemed to conform to such a rule; the *proportional* share contributed did not vary across endowment sizes (mean = 57 percent). Marwell & Ames's (1979; unequal resources/equal interest conditions) subjects seemed to compromise between the equal-absolute and equal-proportional contribution rules, since proportional contribution declined with endowment size.
6. The uncertainty surrounding the causal link between efficacy and cooperation is reminiscent of early research attempting to link expectations of others' cooperation with own cooperation in social dilemmas. Early work (e.g., Dawes *et al.*, 1977) established a positive correlation between these variables, but it was only later experimental work (e.g., Messick *et al.*, 1983; Schroeder *et al.*, 1983) that established that this correlation was due to more than just post-choice justification or projection.
7. One recent unpublished study by de Vries and de Vos (1989) employed a somewhat similar manipulation. Subjects were given identical endowments which they could invest in either a personal or group account. The value of a contribution to the group account was varied across group members. Counter to the efficacy-cooperation hypothesis, group members whose group contributions were multiplied by four contributed less than those whose group contributions were simply doubled. The methodology of this study differs in several important ways from the present research (e.g., group contributions benefit only others, not the self; the public good is continuous, not step-level). Perhaps the most important difference is that in de Vries and de Vos's paradigm, a "high-impact" group member had to contribute less than a "low-impact" member to produce the same absolute contribution to the equally-shared public good (i.e., the group account). Again, equity rather than efficacy considerations may have been most salient.
8. Social motives or orientations are not typically viewed as social dilemma remedies. But research on social motives does suggest that one way to increase cooperation in social dilemmas is through group composition—i.e., by maximizing the number of altruists and cooperators and minimizing the number of individualists and competitors in the group.
9. It is likely that many variables known to affect cooperation in social dilemmas may produce both kinds of transformations. For example, we know that anonymity decreases cooperation (e.g., Fox & Guyer, 1978; Jorgenson & Papciak, 1981). Greater anonymity may both decrease the value placed on the public good (via disidentification with the group and a reduced concern with collective welfare) [a PGT] and reduce potent social sanctions for defecting (prescribed by social norms) [a CCT]. But it is also likely that some remedies reflect pure exemplars of each type of transformation.
10. Another way of thinking about such a situation is that one may see an action as totally inefficacious for producing a public good (e.g., electing a leader), yet see it as highly efficacious for producing other valued goals (e.g., fulfilling a civic duty).

11. Thanks to Sjerp de Vries for suggesting these possibilities.
12. An efficiency norm would complicate interpretation of the hypothesized moderating role of self-efficacy for PGT remedies. Manipulations which increase the value one places on the public good (e.g., enhanced social identity) might also be expected to increase the power of relevant social norms, including an efficiency norm. Both processes would have the same consequence—the greater the perceived self-efficacy, the greater the impact of the manipulation on cooperation. Hence, without additional experimental controls and measures, one would not be able to unambiguously interpret such a "fan" interaction as evidence that the manipulation was in fact enhancing the value placed on the public good.
13. Thanks to editors Wim Liebrand and Dave Messick for noting these possibilities.
14. Unfortunately, it was not feasible to avoid this crossed categorization in Experiment 2. Few if any members of subjects' local fraternity/sorority chapters were in the subjects' psychology class from which all local subjects were recruited. Thus, the experimental cover would have been implausible had we attempted to further enhance social identification by alleging that the other four group members were from the same local fraternity/sorority chapter.
15. For example, since strong in-group identity is often achieved through implicit or explicit comparison with an out-group, perhaps the all-or-none nature of the step-level game offers no competitive advantage to the in-group to cooperate any more than is necessary to provide the public good, whereas in continuous outcome games (e.g., commons dilemma games, continuous public good games) the desire for a favorable social comparison with outgroups may encourage incrementally higher levels of cooperation. (Thanks to Arjaan Wit for raising this possibility.)

5

Constrained Egoism and Resource Management Under Uncertainty

SJERP DE VRIES
University of Groningen
The Netherlands

HENK A. M. WILKE
University of Leiden
The Netherlands

Resource management (RM) situations are defined as situations in which members of a collective have free access to a common resource. Collective resource management often results in overuse of the resource: the sum of individual harvests exceeds the optimal harvest with respect to the collective payoff. Examples are overfishing of the world seas and "brown-outs" due to excessive use of air-conditioners during a heat-wave. These and other societal problems (e.g., environmental pollution) signify the importance of understanding harvesting behavior in RM situations.

In the following we will try to contribute to this understanding by focusing on two possible reward structures underlying resource management situations, and their effect on individual harvesting behavior. More specifically, we will study their effects when there is uncertainty regarding the optimal collective harvest, a circumstance quite common in real-life RM situations. It will be argued that harvesting behavior is motivated by constrained egoism. The constraint is due to one's tendency to follow the rule of fairness that other participants, occupying equal positions, are entitled to equal outcomes. Egoism is involved because uncertainty regarding what constitutes fair behavior tends to lead to egoistic biases.

Resource Management Situations: Social Dilemmas and Coordination Games

The first type of resource situation we will consider is the one having a social dilemma structure. A social dilemma structure implies that (a) each member of the collective has a dominant strategy (harvest as much as you can), and (b) these dominant strategies intersect in a deficient equilibrium (overuse of the collective resource). However, resource management dilemmas differ from most other social dilemmas (e.g., "Take Some" games; Hamburger, 1974), in that taking less is not always advantageous for the collective as a whole (cf. Schelling, 1973). In a resource management dilemma *it is also possible to underuse the resource*. The presence of a collective optimum implies that the effect of one's harvesting behavior on own and others' outcomes depends on (a) the size of the optimal collective harvest (OCH), and (b) the harvesting behavior of others. For example, if one wishes to maximize the collective payoff, one's harvest should equal the OCH minus the combined harvests of others.

Not all resource management situations have the reward structure described above. Besides the social dilemma type, a type of RM-situation may be distinguished in which individuals have no dominant strategy. We will label this second type of RM situation, without a dominant strategy, a *coordination game*. Whereas the overfishing example mentioned before constitutes a social dilemma, the "brown-out" example constitutes a coordination game. In the overfishing example harvesting as much as possible is a dominant strategy. At least in the short run, increasing one's harvest increases one's payoff, *even if the OCH has already been reached*. Although from that point on harvesting more reduces the fish population in the next season, this decrease in future gains is outweighed by the present increase. In the "brown-out" example, on the other hand, it is clear that if one knows how much electricity one can use before the collective power-supply will fail, exceeding this limit is not in one's best interest. Furthermore, it may be noted that in coordination games maximizing one's own payoff coincides with maximizing the collective payoff: given that the OCH and others' behavior are known, the same harvest maximizes own as well as the collective payoff.

In social dilemmas increasing one's harvest always has positive consequences for the own payoff, albeit less positive once the combined harvest of all group members exceeds the OCH. In coordination games the consequences are positive as long as the combined harvest does not exceed the OCH, and negative thereafter. As for the consequences of one's behavior for others, we may note that, as long as the OCH has not been reached, increasing one's harvest has no consequences. Once the OCH has been reached, however, increasing one's harvest has a negative effect on others' payoffs. This holds for social dilemmas as well as for coordination games.

The previous paragraph clearly indicates that in coordination games the consequences of increasing one's harvest are conditional upon the OCH and the behavior of others. This is also true, although to a lesser degree, for resource management social dilemmas. When, as in our games, the OCH and others' behavior cannot be influenced by individual players, players are likely to act as if they were the last player making a decision. They will consider the marginal consequences of their behavior given an estimated OCH and given an estimated joint harvest of others. An important question, then, is how they will evaluate the consequences of their behavior for self and others.

Fairness

That an increase in one's own payoff, by itself, is evaluated positively needs no discussion. However, empirical research suggests that the own payoff is not all that matters. People in social dilemma situations do not always maximize their own payoff (see Dawes, 1980; Messick & Brewer, 1983 for overviews). The question to be answered is: what distracts them from doing so? We propose that fairness considerations are crucial. People want to maximize their own payoff, within the restriction that this is done by fair means: they try to avoid exploiting others to their own benefit. Put differently, people try to act fairly, at the lowest possible costs to themselves. At this point it is important to distinguish between striving for a fair distribution of payoffs and fairness as a restriction on own gain maximizing. What we propose is that people will respect others' entitlements: they will refrain from hurting others. That is: at least as long as these others respect one's own entitlements. People are not supposed to pursue a fair distribution for its own sake. Fairness considerations are thought to function solely as a restriction on hurting others. Therefore, we have termed our hypothesis the *constrained egoism hypothesis*.

In order to apply the constrained egoism hypothesis, we need to specify what subjects are likely to consider fair behavior in the situation at hand. Although this may be difficult in some situations, in symmetric situations it seems rather evident: since all participants occupy equal positions, they are entitled to equal payoffs (see Rutte, Wilke, & Messick, 1987 for empirical support). Given this restriction of equal payoffs, an equal share of the OCH is the highest harvest possible without risking infringement on others' entitlements. However, what should one do if others do not adhere to the equal sharing rule? First consider the possibility that others harvest less than an equal share. In that case one may compensate for their underharvesting by harvesting more than an equal share oneself. This is not unfair because the underharvesters are not harmed by doing so. One might argue that if the underharvesters are harmed at all, they harmed themselves by harvesting less than they were entitled to. In case others harvest more than an equal share, things are more complex and we need to consider the type of RM situation.

If in a social dilemma situation others harvest more than an equal share and thereby try to increase their payoff, one is entitled to do the same oneself: one is allowed to harm others (if one wishes to do so) to the degree that these others have harmed oneself. So, although harvesting an equal share of the OCH is never unfair to others, in case others harvest more, matching their behavior offers a higher payoff without being unfair. In sum, in social dilemmas we expect most people to refrain from increasing their harvest beyond their fair share if this has negative consequences for others, to the degree that others have done the same.

In coordination games, when others try to increase their payoff by overharvesting, one is also entitled to overharvest oneself. However, in contrast with the social dilemma situation, such overharvesting now *lowers* the own payoff. Since a fair distribution is not a goal in itself, we do not expect that subjects will take this course of action. One's payoff is maximal if one gives in to the overharvesting of others and harvests as much as is left of the OCH after subtraction of others' harvests. In sum, in coordination games we expect most people to harvest as much as is left of the OCH by others. This may be more than a fair share, or less.

Social and Environmental Uncertainty

Since in both types of RM-situation the consequences of one's behavior for own and others' payoff depend on the OCH and on the harvests of others, subjects may be confronted with two sources of uncertainty: environmental uncertainty (what is the OCH?) and social uncertainty (how much will others harvest?). What will be the effects of these two kinds of uncertainty on individual harvesting behavior? In the following, predictions are derived from the constrained egoism hypothesis with respect to the effects of environmental and social uncertainty. We will consider social uncertainty first. Strictly speaking, when simultaneous decisions have to be made, one does not know how others are going to behave. They may harvest nothing at all, or as much as their harvesting-capacity allows. At this point we make an additional assumption. When there is no explicit reason for subjects to assume that others systematically differ from oneself, one thinks that fairness considerations (which are important for oneself) are important for others too. Given the mutually assumed importance of fairness and a self-evident rule for dividing the OCH, we suggest that one is willing to restrict oneself to an equal share of the OCH, and expects others are willing to do the same. Moreover, it may be noted that in RM social dilemmas harvesting more than an equal share oneself means obtaining an advance on the egoism of others. Given the assumed importance of own behavior being fair, one needs to justify to oneself why it is reasonable to expect that others will overharvest. In case no obvious justification is available, others are likely to be given the benefit of the doubt. So, social uncertainty is thought to be strongly reduced by the presence of a clear normative rule for dividing the OCH.

Furthermore, due to giving others the benefit of the doubt, the social uncertainty that remains is not likely to result in sizeable harvesting biases. With harvesting biases we mean: motivationally based tendencies to take more or less than an equal share of the OCH, as estimated by oneself.

Harvesting biases resulting from social uncertainty are especially unlikely when the situation has a coordination game structure. As long as others are thought to adhere to the equal sharing rule, deviating from the rule oneself will never increase one's payoff, or, for that matter, the collective payoff. Harvesting more than an equal share then results in overuse, lowering one's own payoff and that of others, while harvesting less than an equal share results in underuse, lowering only one's own payoff. Furthermore, since an equal share of the OCH forms a focal point for tacit coordination (Schelling, 1977), it is likely that others will adhere to this rule, even if they do not have fairness at heart. Therefore one might even say that in a RM coordination game fairness considerations are not needed to expect others' adherence to the equal sharing rule.

Environmental uncertainty, in contrast to social uncertainty, cannot be reduced by social conventions or norms. Therefore it may very well lead to observable harvesting biases. Our prediction for RM social dilemmas, based on the constrained egoism hypothesis, runs as follows. While harvesting less than an equal share of the OCH hurts oneself with absolute certainty, harvesting more than an equal share *may* hurt others. The deciding factor is how much these others harvest. If, on average, they harvest less than an equal share, this lessens the negative impact of one's own overharvesting. If they overharvest, one's own overharvesting hurts them, but is (at least partly) justified. So, own overharvesting only hurts others unjustifiably when these others overharvest less than oneself, harvest exactly an equal share, or harvest not enough less to compensate for own overharvesting. Furthermore, one is likely to consider it less aversive to hurt others (by harvesting more than an equal share), than to hurt oneself (by harvesting less than an equal share). Therefore, subjects are expected to display an upward harvesting bias in RM social dilemmas: they are predicted to harvest more than an equal share, according to their own best estimate of the OCH.

In RM coordination games hurting others means hurting oneself. Therefore, fairness considerations are likely to have a much lower saliency than in a social dilemma. Everyone is expected to adhere to the equal sharing rule out of self-interest. This implies that deviations from the rule will also be interpreted in terms of self-interest. So, in coordination games the only effects of over- and underestimating the OCH likely to be considered, are those on the *own payoff*. These effects depend on the exact reward-structure: contributing to overuse may have less severe, equally severe, or more severe consequences for the own payoff than contributing to underuse. Consequently, depending on the reward-structure, the bias may be upward, absent, or downward.

Study No. 1. Two Coordination Games Compared

In this first study we examine the hypothesis that in RM coordination games only the consequences of over- and underestimating the OCH for the own payoff are taken into account. The importance of investigating this hypothesis is in its assertion that others' payoffs are *not* taken into account, when one considers the consequences of deviating from an equal share.

Subjects are confronted with two reward-structures which differ in the effect of contributing to over- or underuse for their own payoff. The structures are more or less equal, however, with regard to the consequences of over- and underuse for the collective payoff: in both structures overusing the resource has far more aversive consequences for the collective payoff than underusing it. In a first structure both "mistakes" have equally aversive effects on the own payoff. So, given our hypothesis that consequences for the own payoff are mainly considered, no harvesting bias is expected (no bias expected = NOBI). The NOBI-condition is created by the following rule: if the four-person group as a whole harvests more than the optimal amount, each individual has to pay a fine. The size of this individual fine is twice the amount by which the group has overused the resource. For example: suppose the OCH is 80 units and the other three players have already harvested 60 units. The optimal harvest for the fourth player now is 20 units. A harvest of 15 units results in a payoff of only those 15 units. A harvest of 25 units results in a fine of twice the amount of overuse: 2 * 5 = 10 units per person. Therefore the fourth player's payoff is (25 − 10) = 15 units, as before. However, this time the payoff of each of the other players is lowered with 10 units. So, although at an individual level contributing to overuse is as bad as contributing to underuse, the collective payoff decreases seven times as fast by overuse as by underuse: collective fine (= 4 * 2 * "overuse") minus extra profit for one individual (= "overuse").

In the second structure contributing to overuse has far more serious consequences for the own payoff than contributing to underuse. Therefore, we expect to find a downward harvesting bias in this condition (downward bias expected = DOBI). Biases are defined as deviations from an equal share of the OCH, as estimated by subjects themselves. The DOBI-condition is created by the following rule: if the group as a whole harvests more than the optimal amount, all harvests will be confiscated. For example: suppose once again the OCH is 80 units and the other three players have already harvested 60 units. The optimal harvest for the fourth player remains 20 units. A harvest of 15 units still results in a payoff of

15 units. However, a harvest of 25 units now results in a zero payoff, not only for oneself but also for the other players. So, at an individual level contributing to overuse has become much worse than contributing to underuse. At the collective level overuse has much worse consequences for the collective payoff than underuse, as before.

Reducing Environmental Uncertainty: an Adviser

Since the biases are supposed to be caused by uncertainty regarding the optimal collective harvest (OCH), and their size is assumed to be positively related to the degree of environmental uncertainty, decreasing this uncertainty might reduce the biases. One way to reduce uncertainty is showing the participants the *optimal average individual harvest* (OCH divided by the number of participants) as estimated by an outsider, e.g., an adviser. So, after subjects had indicated their intended harvest, they were shown a recommended individual harvest and then asked for their definite harvest.

That receiving advice will reduce biases presupposes that a correct integration of the available information has taken place. Two independent estimates of an equal share of the OCH, when correctly combined, permit a more accurate final estimate. However, we are not dealing with a situation in which one tries to make the best estimate possible. Motivational biases are likely to influence the integration of own intention and recommendation into a definite harvest. Research by Birnbaum and Stegner (1979) suggests that during the process of integration people will (a) tend to ignore that their intention was already biased, and (b) tend to assign more weight to the estimate, own intention or recommendation, that is consistent with the bias in intention. That is: the estimate that, when compared with the other estimate, goes in the same direction as the bias. This latter form of biasing is referred to as configural weighing. Basing ourselves on the Birnbaum and Stegner study, we predict that when recommendations are systematically varied around own intentions, average definite harvests will be *more* biased than average intended harvests. People will comply more with recommendations that go in the direction of their original bias, than with recommendations that go in the opposite direction. This prediction, of course, can only be made if intended harvests are expected to be biased themselves, that is: in the DOBI-condition. In the NOBI-condition we predict that upward and downward recommendations will be complied with to the same degree.

Summarizing the above, we come to two predictions: (1) a main effect of reward structure on the way intended harvests deviate from an equal share of estimated OCHs (DOBI < 0; NOBI $= 0$), and (2) an interaction-effect between reward-structure and direction of advice (upward/downward) on compliance with advice (DOBI: upward $<$ downward; NOBI: upward $=$ downward).

Overview Procedure and Design Study No. 1

Subjects, forty-eight students of a secondary school in Groningen, were enlisted in groups of five. The role of adviser was said to be randomly assigned to one of the subjects, leaving four subjects to harvest. In reality there was no adviser and recommended harvests were fixed in advance, as will be explained later on. Subjects made harvesting decisions during two consecutive periods, each consisting of ten harvesting trials with independent poolsizes. For half of the subjects the reward structure of the first harvesting period was the NOBI-structure. For the other half of the subjects it was the DOBI-structure. The reward structures were switched for the second harvesting period. Subjects were not told beforehand that the reward structure would change during the session. The reward structure for a given harvesting period was explained thoroughly (see also our introduction).

On each trial subjects started by estimating the optimal collective harvest (range: 50–250). An OCH was indicated by the numbers of characters in a picture. This picture was shown on a video-monitor for a short time. After having estimated the OCH, subjects reported their intended harvest (range: 0–60) and then received a harvesting advice. Finally they decided on their definite harvest (range: 0–60). In five of the ten trials the advice was to take more, and in the other five trials the advice was to take less than intended. The discrepancy between intention and recommendation was varied between 2 and 7. When, due to an extreme intention, the planned discrepancy between the intended and recommended harvest would result in illogical advice, the advice was truncated at the logical limit. For example: since subjects were told that the lowest possible OCH was 50 units and they knew that the number of participants was four, the lowest recommendation an adviser could reasonably give was 12 units. In case no truncations were needed, the discrepancies between intentions and recommendations amounted to 23 units by direction of advice.

The between-subjects design consisted of an order-of-reward-structure factor (NOBI,DOBI/DOBI,NOBI). The within-subjects design consisted of a reward-structure factor (NOBI/DOBI) and a direction-of-advice factor (upward/downward). The main dependent variables per period were the average harvesting intention and the level of compliance, aggregated by direction of advice. Compliance was calculated as the shift between intention and definite harvest. A shift was counted as positive when it went in the direction of advice.

Results Study No. 1

Intended Harvests

In each of the twenty trials subjects estimated the optimal amount to harvest as a group, before indicating their intended individual harvest.

Analysis shows that the estimates of the OCH were not influenced by the reward structure of the situation. Since subjects thought four persons were harvesting, harvesting biases were calculated by subtracting a fourth of the estimated OCH from the intended harvest. An analysis on these deviations showed a main effect of reward structure: $F(1,43) = 7.63$; $p < .01$. Aggregated over all trials per period harvesting biases were $M = +4.1$ in the NOBI-condition and $M = -3.1$ in the DOBI-condition.

The bias in the DOBI-condition was as expected: downward. The upward bias in the NOBI-condition, however, puzzled us: how could one rationally expect to gain by upwardly deviating from an equal share of one's own estimate of the OCH? A first explanation that suggests itself, is that others were thought to harvest less than an equal share. However, when asked how much others were likely to have harvested in comparison to oneself [much more (1)—much less (7)], subjects in the NOBI-condition thought it unlikely that others had harvested less ($M = 3.74$). Another possible explanation will be suggested in the discussion of this study.

Compliance

After subjects had indicated their intended harvest for that trial, a recommended individual harvest was given by the adviser. Before analyzing the compliance data, we checked whether the planned discrepancies between intended and recommended harvests were realized to the same degree in all conditions. The check revealed that aggregated discrepancies were significantly smaller for downward recommendations ($M = 20$) than for upward recommendations ($M = 26$). Therefore we have corrected aggregated levels of compliance in a particular direction by dividing them by the total amount of discrepancy between intentions and recommendations the subject experienced in the direction at hand. Consequently, subjects that followed all recommendations in a particular direction received a compliance score of 100 percent for that direction of advice.

An analysis on the percentages of compliance revealed a significant interaction between the reward structure and the direction of advice: $F(1,44) = 25.07$; $p < .001$. Paired t-tests on levels of compliance per reward structure and direction of advice indicated that, as expected, in the DOBI-condition compliance with downward recommendations ($M =$ 65 percent) was higher than compliance with upward recommendations ($M =$ 53 percent; $p < .05$). In the NOBI-condition compliance with upward recommendations ($M =$ 62 percent) was higher than compliance with downward recommendations ($M =$ 51 percent; $p < .05$). This latter bias was not predicted, but is in accordance with the upward bias in intended harvests (and therefore may be explained in the same way). Compared between reward structures, compliance with upward recommendations was higher in the NOBI-condition, whereas compliance with downward recommendations was higher in the DOBI-condition (both $p < .05$).

Discussion Study No. 1

Due to unexpected low estimates of optimal amounts to harvest as a group, the systematic manipulation of the discrepancy between intended and recommended harvests was not successful. By using percentages of compliance, instead of absolute amounts, levels of compliance were corrected for differences in discrepancy between intentions and recommendations by direction of advice.

Our hypotheses were largely confirmed. When contributing to overuse of the resource had more aversive consequences for the own payoff as well as for the collective payoff (DOBI-condition), on average intended harvests were below an equal share of the OCH as estimated by oneself. When, only considering one's own payoff, contributing to overuse was no worse than contributing to underuse (NOBI-condition), intended harvests were above an equal share of the OCH. This although for the collective payoff overuse had much more aversive consequences than underuse. Moreover, in the DOBI-condition compliance with downward recommendations was higher than compliance with upward recommendations, while in the NOBI-condition the reverse was found.

We did not expect the upward bias for intended harvests and compliance in the NOBI-condition. A possible reason for these biases in the NOBI-condition is that subjects considered their own estimates of the OCH to be on the low side. And in fact these estimates were low, even to the degree that planned downward recommendations had to be adjusted in order to prevent them from becoming illogical. What remains to be explained then, is how subjects came to make such low estimates. A likely explanation is that subjects thought that the maximum possible OCH, which was said to be 250 units, would completely fill the picture which was shown to them. This heuristic leads subjects to giving much too low estimates, since a completely filled picture would not have contained 250, but almost 550 characters. Furthermore the indicated range for the OCH (50–250) is likely to suggest a base rate expectancy for the OCH of 150, the midpoint. Combining such a base rate expectancy with own estimates will lead to upward adjustments. Given that estimated OCHs in the DOBI-condition did not differ significantly from those in the NOBI-condition, the above process may also have operated in the DOBI-condition. This implies that -3.1 is a conservative estimate of the motivational harvesting bias in the DOBI-condition.

What are the implications of our findings? That we found a downward bias in the DOBI-condition is not surprising: for both the individual and the group as a whole harvesting more than one's equal share was likely to have very strong negative consequences. The absence of a similar downward tendency in the NOBI-condition, however, is more informative. Considering the consequences at a group level the reward structure rendered overuse of the resource much more unattractive than underuse: overuse decreased the group payoff seven times as fast as underuse. The fact that in spite of this we found no downward tendency in the NOBI-condition confirms our hypothesis that harvesting biases are based on the consequences of one's behavior with respect to *one's own outcomes*, and not on the consequences with respect to the group outcomes. Once fairness is satisfied, others' outcomes seem of little interest. Our confidence in the robustness of our results is strengthened by the fact that the bias in intentions is replicated by a bias in compliance. This configural weighing of recommendations (Birnbaum & Stegner, 1979) decreases the effectiveness of an adviser as a means to counteract biases.

Study No. 2. Social Dilemma and Coordination Game Compared

In the first study adherence to the equal sharing rule could also be explained by a need for tacit coordination, instead of by the mutually assumed importance of fairness considerations. In this second study we want to test the importance of fairness more directly. According to the constrained egoism hypothesis people in social dilemma resource management situations will also strive to harvest an equal share of the OCH. However, in social dilemmas uncertainty is expected to always lead to upwardly biased harvesting: harvesting more than one's share is less bad than harvesting less than one's share. We already argued in our introduction that in a RM social dilemma social uncertainty will be strongly reduced by the presence of an unambiguous distribution rule for the OCH, in this case: equal shares for all. Furthermore, even if one doubts that others will adhere to this rule, one has to be able to justify to oneself why others are likely to behave less fairly than oneself, before acting upon it. Therefore we predict that only environmental uncertainty will generate upward biases.

To test our prediction we compared harvesting behavior in a RM social dilemma with that in a RM coordination game. To make both situations as comparable as possible, the consequences of over- and underuse for the collective payoff were held constant. In contrast to the first study, overuse and underuse now had the same aversive effect on the collective payoff. Furthermore, the consequences of contributing to underuse of the resource for one's own payoff were the same in both situations. So the only thing that distinguished the two situations was the effect of contributing to overuse on the own payoff. While in the social dilemma condition contributing to overuse naturally heightened the own payoff, in the coordination game condition contributing to overuse lowered the own payoff to the same degree as contributing to underuse. Consequently, in the coordination game (COGA) condition (as in the NOBI-condition of the previous study) no harvesting bias was expected, while in the social dilemma (SODI) condition an upward bias was expected.

The COGA reward structure was created in the following way. Harvesting cost money. If harvests could be sold, the gain was twice the investment; therefore profit (gain minus investment) equalled investment in size. However, in case of overharvesting not all harvests could be sold. Everyone was allowed to sell an equal share of the amount that could be sold (the OCH). If someone had harvested less than an equal share, the additional amount was equally divided between those who harvested more than an equal share. The remainder of one's harvests had to be considered investments with no return. The SODI-condition differed in what happened in case of overharvesting: everyone was stuck with an equal share of the dead stock. This implied that even if the OCH was already reached, in a five-person group one could still sell 4/5 of any additional harvests made, resulting in a profit of (2 * 4/5 gain minus 5/5 investment) = 3/5 on investment.[1]

In this second study subjects also received a recommended average individual harvest from an adviser. Once again we expect compliance to be biased in the same direction as intended harvests. In the coordination game condition we predict no difference in compliance with upward versus downward recommendations, and in the social dilemma condition we predict more compliance with upward recommendations than with downward recommendations.

As a further test of our theorizing, we manipulated the size of the OCH. Given a certain maximum harvesting capacity, as the size of the OCH increases, taking an equal share of the OCH differs less from taking all one can. For example, if the OCH equals the product of group size and individual harvesting capacity, taking an equal share *is* taking all one can. If we assume that it is unlikely that someone will harvest less than an equal share, the degree of theoretically possible social uncertainty decreases with an increasing OCH. We argued before that this possible uncertainty is reduced by the mutually assumed importance of fairness and the presence of an unambiguous rule to divide the OCH. If our reasoning is correct, only environmental uncertainty, which is the same for high and low OCHs, will lead to biases. Therefore the size of the OCH will have no effect on the size of the bias. However, if our reasoning is incorrect, we may expect larger biases if the OCH is small than if the OCH is high, due to a larger degree of social uncertainty in case of low OCHs.

As already mentioned before, we mainly expect *egoistic biases due to environmental uncertainty*. Since environmental uncertainty will not be very large, we expect intentions to be quite close to an equal share of the OCH, especially when taking the range of possible intentions into consideration. Since we expect intentions to be clearly lower than the midpoint of the range between an equal share and the maximum harvest allowed, one might suggest that we expect people to be very cooperatively oriented, that is: willing to forego own gain in order to maximize collective gain. However, in strong contrast to this interpretation, we expect that compliance with recommendations will show a clear egoistic bias. Therefore we think that, if our predictions are confirmed, we have some evidence that in social dilemmas people are not as much concerned with the collective payoff as with respecting normative constraints on own gain maximization.

Overview Procedure and Design Study No. 2

Subjects, fifty-one students of two professional schools in Groningen, were enlisted in groups of five. They were asked to perform two tasks: an estimation task and a harvesting task. Each group started by estimating the percentage of white squares in a picture that was shown on their video-monitor for a short period. Without subjects knowing this, the twenty pictures shown to them were to be used again later on, to indicate OCHs in the harvesting task. Because this first task was a mere estimation task, answers can be regarded as unbiased estimates of the OCH. Next, subjects were informed about the reward structure of the harvesting task that would follow. Half of the subjects was randomly assigned to the coordination game (COGA) condition, the other half to the social dilemma (SODI) condition. After the reward structure was explained (see also our introduction to this study), the adviser was introduced: a participant in an earlier study that was merely asked to estimate the percentage of white squares in the pictures that for the present subjects would indicate the size of the OCH (range: 0–100). Recommended average individual harvests were the adviser's estimates, divided by five.

The harvesting task consisted of twenty trials. Each trial started by showing subjects a picture to indicate the OCH. On eight trials the OCH was high (60), on eight other trials the OCH was low (40). On the four remaining trials, the OCH was either 30, 50 (twice) or 70. In contrast to the first study, subjects were not asked to estimate the OCH. Instead they could indicate their intended harvest right away (range: 0–20). On the high OCH trials, downward advice was given, while on the low OCH trials upward advice was given. On the four remaining trials no advice was given. The confounding of size of OCH and direction of advice was deliberate, in order to have a better chance to realize planned discrepancies between intentions and recommendations. Since our interest concerns the effect of reward structure on the difference between compliance with upward and downward recommendations, rather than on absolute levels of compliance, the confounding has no serious consequences. The discrepancies ranged from 2 to 4, adding up to 24 per direction of advice. A more complete description of the procedure may be found elsewhere (De Vries & Wilke, submitted).

The design for intended harvests has one between subjects factor (reward structure: COGA/SODI) and one within subjects factor (size of OCH: high/low). In the design for compliance the size-of-OCH factor becomes the direction-of-advice factor (upward/downward). Compliance is defined the same way as in study no. 1. Predictions are that (1) intended harvests in the COGA-condition will equal a fifth of the OCH as estimated by the subjects themselves in the pre-task, whereas in the SODI-condition intended harvest will be above an equal share; (2) in the COGA-condition compliance with upward recommendations will equal that with downward recommendations, whereas in the SODI-condition compliance with upward recommendations will be higher than that with downward recommendations.

Results Study No. 2

Intended Harvests

An analysis on the deviations of intentions from an equal share of the OCH, as estimated by oneself before one knew the reward structure of the situation, shows a main effect of reward structure: $F(1,49) = 8.17$; $p < .01$. On average intended harvests in the SODI-condition were $M = 0.6$ above an equal share of the OCH, while in the COGA-condition intended harvests were $M = -0.5$ below an equal share. Whereas we expected an upward deviation in the SODI-condition, we did not predict the downward tendency in the COGA-condition. The size of the OCH had no effect on the bias, neither on itself ($p = .90$), nor in interaction with the reward structure ($p = .37$). In the SODI-condition the mean was $M = 0.4$ for the low OCH and $M = 0.7$ for the high OCH. So the theoretically possible higher degree of social uncertainty for low OCH trials, as compared to high OCH trials, did not result in an enlarged bias.

Compliance

The check whether the planned discrepancies between intentions and recommendations were realized to the same degree for both directions of advice revealed that this time we succeeded almost completely. Therefore analyzing absolute levels of compliance and analyzing procentual levels of compliance amounts to the same. For the sake of consistency with the first study, we have chosen to report percentages instead of absolute amounts. The analysis of variance revealed an interaction between the reward structure and the direction of advice: $F(1,49) = 14.82$; $p < .001$. As predicted, in the SODI-condition compliance with upward recommendations ($M = 24$ percent) was higher than compliance with downward recommendations ($M = 18$ percent; $p < .05$). In the COGA-condition, instead of equal levels of compliance we found that compliance with downward recommendations ($M = 27$ percent) was higher than compliance with upward recommendations ($M = 18$ percent; $p < .05$). Although this effect was unexpected, it is consistent with the bias found in intentions. Comparison between reward structures showed a significant difference in compliance with downward recommendations only ($p < .05$). We may note that because of the configural weighing of recommendations the mean definite harvest per period was more biased than the mean intended harvest per period. For example, in the SODI-condition intended harvests had a bias of 0.6, whereas definite harvests had a bias of 0.7.

When asked how much they thought that others had harvested, on a scale running from "much more than I did" (1) to "much less than I did" (7), subjects' mean answer was $M = 3.90$. There was no effect of reward structure ($p = .73$). So, as in study no. 1, others were expected to have harvested at least as much as oneself.

Discussion Study No. 2

Results were largely in agreement with predictions. In the SODI-condition intended harvests deviated upwardly from an equal share of the OCH. Furthermore, compliance with upward recommendations was higher than compliance with downward recommendations. For the COGA-condition the results were unexpected, although internally consistent. Intended harvests deviated downwardly from an equal share of the OCH and compliance with downward recommendations was higher than that with upward recommendations. The first question we will address is how these downward biases in the COGA-condition may be explained.

In the COGA-condition contributing to overuse had the same negative effect on the own payoff as contributing to underuse. However, during the debriefing a subject remarked that he thought it less annoying to forego a profit than to incur a loss of the same size after having made his harvest. This remark suggests that although objective consequences were the same, subjects were more concerned with avoiding a possible loss than with the risk of foregoing a gain. Such a framing effect is consistent with Kahneman and Tversky's Prospect Theory (1979). Another explanation is that having to "pay back" part of one's earnings due to overuse was experienced as a punishment, with the connotation of transgressing a norm. This may have added to the disutility of contributing to overuse. Both explanations seem plausible to us, and do not exclude each other. We may point out that the processes implied by these explanations are equally likely to have operated in the SODI-condition.

Despite the small size of the biases relative to the range of behavioral alternatives, we think they are important in at least two respects. First, it should be remembered that a bias of for example 0.6 on an individual level implies a bias of $(5 * 0.6) = 3$ on the aggregate level of the five-person group. Second, the amount of environmental uncertainty was not especially large in the present study. Let us assume a symmetric 100 percent confidence interval of twenty units around an estimated OCH of 50 units: $P(40 < \text{OCH} < 60) = 1$. For computational ease we will further assume a linear decline of the probability within the interval as one moves further away from the estimate given. This hypothetical confidence interval implies that in the social dilemma condition the preferred risk-ratio of harvesting less than an equal share versus harvesting more than an equal share is three to one.[2] Consequently, if subjects had been told that the OCH could range from 0 to 100, and that the probability distribution was uniform, we might have expected a collective harvest of $(100 * 3/4) = 75$, whereas the unbiased collective harvest obviously is only 50 units. An unpublished earlier study (De Vries, Van Knippenberg, & Wilke, 1987) offers some empirical support for the effect of the degree of environmental uncertainty. Subjects, in groups of five, were confronted with a social dilemma structure similar to the one employed in the present SODI-condition. When they were told that the OCH could range from 0 to 270 units, the average collective harvest was 197 units, instead of an unbiased 135. When they were told that the OCH was exactly 135 units, the average collective harvest was 155. So, the large degree of environmental uncertainty increased overharvesting by 42 units, or 8.4 units per person on average. The results of Rapoport, Budescu, Suleiman, and Weg (1988) point in a similar direction. Although they employed a different type of resource management game, they also found that with increasing levels of environmental uncertainty the upward deviation of harvests from an equal share of the OCH also increases.

General Discussion

In this paper we introduced the constrained egoism hypothesis. This hypothesis states that people want to maximize their payoffs, but restrict themselves to fair means in doing so. A first implication of this hypothesis was that if fairness has a low saliency, e.g., because one cannot exploit others to one's own advantage, people will neglect the effects of their behavior on others and only look at the consequences of their behavior for their own payoff. Study no. 1 supports this prediction to a large degree. When harvesting more than an equal share was likely to have more aversive consequences for the own payoff than harvesting less than an equal share, we found downward biases in both intended harvests and compliance. When, however, the consequences of contributing to over- and underuse for one's payoff were equally aversive, no downward bias was found. Instead biases were directed upward. This although in this second condition, as in the first condition, overuse had much more detrimental consequences for the collective payoff than underuse.

Neglect of the consequences of one's behavior for others suggests that in social dilemmas dominant strategies will be followed. However, social dilemmas differ from coordination games in that own gain maximization exploits others that do not act similarly. The constrained egoism hypothesis now suggests that fairness constraints will be applied. One is willing to refrain from contributing to overuse to the degree that others (are expected to) do the same. An additional assumption was made: given no specific information regarding others, one is likely to think that fairness considerations are important to others too, or at least to give these others the benefit of the doubt. Therefore we supposed that harvesting behavior in a social dilemma would not differ as much from that in a coordination game as the results of the first study seemed to suggest. Study no. 2 was designed to test this prediction.

In our second study we found upward biases for intended harvests when the situation had a social dilemma structure. Biases were downward when the situation had a coordination game structure that was intended not to give rise to biases. Biases were not affected by the size of the OCH, suggesting that social uncertainty was not the cause of the biases. Therefore deviations of intended harvests from an equal share of the OCH may indeed be interpreted as egoistic biases due to environmental uncertainty. The bias-interpretation of deviations was corroborated by a similar bias in compliance with recommendations. Taken together the studies provide strong support for the idea that in social dilemma situations non-egoistic behavior is better explained as due to the wish to respect other people's entitlements than as due to a strong concern for the collective payoff.[3]

The constrained egoism hypothesis suggests that the critical question for behavior in social dilemma situations is: how much can I harvest without infringing upon other people's entitlements? The answer to this question depends on the size of the optimal collective harvest, the fair way to distribute this optimal harvest, and whether others will respect one's own entitlements. In our introduction we already argued that in symmetric games, as employed in the present studies, it is rather obvious what constitutes a fair distribution of the OCH: equal shares for all. However, what if positions are asymmetrical and people may think differently about what constitutes a fair distribution? Research on allocations of a fixed amount of money among people differing in one or more relevant aspects, suggests that allocators display an egoistic bias in deciding what is a fair allocation (Messick & Sentis, 1983; Krebs, 1982). Given that most real-life resource dilemma are asymmetrical in nature, it seems worthwhile to investigate whether, when the situation has a social dilemma structure, ambiguity regarding the fair way to distribute a common resource indeed leads to a higher degree of overuse next.

References

Birnbaum, M., & Stegner, S. (1979). Source credibility in social judgement: bias, expertise and the judge's point of view. *Journal of Personality and Social Psychology*, **37**, 48–74.

Dawes, R. (1980). Social dilemmas. *Annual Review of Psychology*, **31**, 169–193.

Hamburger, H. (1974). Take some—a format and family of games. *Behavioral Science*, **19**, 28–34.

Kahneman, D., & Tversky, A. (1979). Prospect theory: an analysis of decision under risk. *Econometrica*, **47**, 263–291.

Krebs, D. (1982). Prosocial behavior, equity and justice. In J. Greenberg & R. Cohen (Eds), *Equity and Justice in Social Behavior*. New York: Academic Press.

Messick, D., & Brewer, M. (1983). Solving social dilemmas. In L. Wheeler & P. Shaver (Eds), *Review of Personality and Social Psychology*, vol. 4, pp. 11–44.

Messick, D., & Sentis, K. (1983). Fairness, preference and fairness biases. In D. Messick & K. Cook (Eds), *Equity Theory*, pp. 61–94. New York: Praeger.

Rapoport, A., Budescu, D., Suleiman, R., & Weg, E. (1988). Social dilemmas with uniformly distributed resource. Paper presented at the Third International Conference on Social Dilemmas, Groningen, The Netherlands.

Rutte, C. G., Wilke, H. A. M., & Messick, D. (1987). Scarcity or abundance caused by people or the environment as determinants of behavior in the resource dilemma. *Journal of Experimental Social Psychology*, **23**, 208–216.

Schelling, T. C. (1973). Hockey helmets, concealed weapons, and daylight saving. A study of binary choices with externalities. *Journal of Conflict Resolution*, **17**, 381–428.

Schelling, T. C. (1977). *The Strategy of Conflict*. London: Oxford University Press (reprint).

Vries, S. de, & Wilke, H. A. M. Resource management in an uncertain environment: harvesting biases and configural weighing of recommendations. Submitted to the *Journal of Personality and Social Psychology*.

Vries, S. de, Van Knippenberg, D., & Wilke, H. A. M. (1987). Onderzoeksverslag project Sociale Dilemma's II: het effect van beloningsstructuren in resource management situaties. (Research report of Social Dilemma project II: the effect of reward-structures in resource management situations). Unpublished manuscript.

Notes

1. To illustrate the consequences of both reward structures, an example is given below for a situation in which the combined harvest of the group is 53, while the OCH is only 40 units.

Player	Harvest	Payoff COGA	Payoff SODI
A	8	8	2.8
B	15	1	9.8
C	10	6	4.8
D	12	4	6.8
E	8	8	2.8
Total	53	27	27

2. The computation goes as follows. Preferred risk ratio = $P(\text{OCH} < 53)/P(\text{OCH} > 53)$.

   Some probabilities:

   $P(\text{OCH} = 40) = P(\text{OCH} = 60) = 0$
   $P(\text{OCH} = 45) = P(\text{OCH} = 55) = .05$
   $P(\text{OCH} = 50) = .1$
   $P(\text{OCH} < 50) = P(\text{OCH} > 50) = .45$
   $P(\text{OCH} < 53) = .45 + .1 + .09 + .08 = .72$
   $P(\text{OCH} > 53) = .01 + .02 + .03 + .04 + .05 + .06 = .21$
   Preferred risk ratio: $.72/.21 = 3.4$

3. One might argue that this strong support is partially due to the use of an adviser. The adviser, by recommending optimal average individual harvests, making the equal sharing norm highly salient. There is ample evidence, however, that in symmetric games the equal sharing norm is already highly salient by itself. Another argument to invalidate our results might be that payoffs were hypothetical in nature. Therefore there were no real costs linked to obeying the equal sharing norm. As for this argument, it is important to note that there were no real costs associated with showing concern for the collective payoff either. So, although we grant that employing hypothetical payoffs is likely to have heightened the degree of non-egoistic behavior, we still feel justified to conclude that it were normative constraints that led to this non-egoistic behavior, and not concern for the collective payoff.

6

The Provision of Public Goods by Experts: The Groningen Study*

DAVID M. MESSICK
University of California, Santa Barbara
USA

CHRISTEL G. RUTTE
Erasmus University Rotterdam
The Netherlands

It is a rare opportunity when one can perform an experiment in which the subjects are among the world's foremost experts on the subject matter of the experiment. Such an opportunity was provided during the Third International Conference on Social Dilemmas, held on 25–29 July 1988 in Groningen, The Netherlands. The scholars in attendance, mostly social psychologists and sociologists, were among the most distinguished in the field of social dilemma research. Collectively, they have been associated with a large majority of the experiments that have been conducted and subjects that have been used in this line of research. It is unlikely, however, that many of these scholars have ever been subjects in an experiment that was designed by someone else. The current exercise was undertaken to provide such an experience.

An historical context for the present study was created during the First International Conference on Social Dilemmas also held in Groningen four years previously. During that meeting, the first author created a public goods game in which each of the fifteen members of the audience for the concluding paper would be given 10 Dutch guilders if twelve or more of these participants placed 5 guilders in an envelope that had been provided for them. Thus, for a group investment of 60 guilders, the group was able to gain 150 guilders, a clear profit of 90 guilders. The level of prosocial

* The data reported in this paper were collected at the Third International Conference on Social Dilemmas held in Groningen, The Netherlands, 25–29 July 1988. The paper was written while the first author was a participant in the Research Group on Game Theory and the Behavioral Sciences and a guest of the Center for Interdisciplinary Research of the University of Bielefeld, Germany, during August 1988.

behavior was as high as it could have been since all fifteen of the participants gave 5 guilders.

The current exercise was designed with this previous outcome in mind. In particular, we decided that we would make it somewhat more difficult to apply simple decision rules or heuristics. This decision was based on the outcome of an experiment by Allison and Messick (1988) in which it was found that rather trivial factors that hinder the use of a choice principle like equal division result in people trying to take more than an equal share of a common resource. A research paper describing this study had been presented to the conference participants earlier in the same day that the present study was conducted. First we described the game and then the steps we took to make it more challenging than the previous one.

The game was simple. Every person in the lecture hall where the first author was giving concluding remarks was given an envelope. The audience was told that if they wished they could put money in the envelope and that the envelopes would be collected presently. If the total amount of money collected was Dfl. 250 (about US$ 125) or more, everyone in the audience would be given Dfl. 10. A stack of fifty bills of Dfl. 10 was displayed so that the audience would know that the promise could be fulfilled without trouble. Each person was also asked to make a prediction about the total amount that would be collected in the experiment by writing the predicted amount on the inside of their envelopes. The only procedural constraint was that the group could not discuss the task and make a collective decision. There was, nevertheless, considerable discussion among the participants.

Among the questions that were answered were the following. What if one did not want to participate? The answer was that nonparticipation was allowed—it simply counted as a contribution of zero. The experimenters declined to make change for the participants but permitted the participants to make change among themselves. The only foreign currencies that would be accepted were United States dollars and West German marks, and these would be counted on a one to one basis. This constitutes a 50 percent loss for the dollar and a loss of roughly 10 percent for the mark. Promissory notes were not acceptable. The experimenter also declined to state the number of people in the room, but did not prevent anyone from counting. The room contained forty-three participants and two experimenters.

There are at least two perspectives from which to analyze the game. An expected value maximization approach would focus on the probability that one's contribution would be critical since that is the only condition in which contributing is instrumental in increasing one's expected income. A game theoretic analysis would identify two symmetric equilibria. The first is when no one contributes anything. When all contribute nothing, no one has any reason to make a contribution. A second equilibrium exists when all contribute an equal part of the provision amount. Under this circumstance, each player is critical and has no incentive to reduce the contribution size. While the latter equilibrium dominates the first with regard to payoff size, the first is considerably less risky. From this perspective, the game presents a coordination problem in which the players are better off all doing the same thing, either giving nothing or giving an equal share, but in which there is a conflict between risk and payoff.

Several factors augured well for the ability of the group to raise the funds necessary to provide the public good. First the subjects were experts who comprehend the factors that lead groups to perform inefficiently. Second, the group was cohesive, composed of colleagues who were good friends and, often, collaborators. Finally, there was a sense of shared fate directed against the first author for having created the game and having made the audience, involuntarily, subjects in it. These factors should work to reduce the risk of contributing or to enhance the value of successfully providing the good.

The features that were designed to make success less than certain included these. There was no predetermined amount that each participant could give or not. The outcome was binary, but contributions were continuous. The equal contribution amount could be estimated, but only by counting the people in the room and dividing that number into 250. The required amount was rather an ugly number, Dfl. 5.82, when one divided by 43, a number about which there was considerable uncertainty. The group size was larger by a factor of three than it had been four years before. The refusal to make change or to accept promissory notes made it more difficult for people to give their most preferred amount, and the ratio of the amount won for the amount to be provided made this game less rich than the previous one. In the last game, the group could get 150 for 60, whereas in the present game the group could attain 430 for 250. Finally, the larger size of the current group also entailed greater heterogeneity, with greater uncertainty about what others would do. These factors enhanced the risk of contributing by making the all contribute option less stable and by reducing the value of the bonus to be provided.

For about 20 minutes after the game was introduced, the first author harangued the audience with his thoughts about the conference. During this time, the second author collected the envelopes, counted the money, and tallied the responses. These are given in Table 6.1. The total amount contributed was Dfl. 245.59, less than 5 guilders under the amount needed to provide the good. Thus the bonus was not provided and contributions were lost. The mean amount provided was 5.71, a quantity that is quite close to the 5.82 required to provide the bonus. In this type of task, being close but below the provision point is more frustrating than failing by a large margin. It is easy to imagine simple scenarios in which minor changes

TABLE 6.1 *Raw Data from Public Goods Experiment Conducted in Groningen, 29 July 1988*

S no.	Est.	Contrib.	S no.	Est.	Contrib.
1	270	6.25	23	270	6.00
2	200	6.00	24	300	10.00
3	275	6.75	25	200	0
4	under	0	26	270	5.00
5	275	10	27	300	8.49
6	240	1.00	28	280	7.40
7	above	8.00	29	270	8.00
8	260	6.20	30	225	5.00
9	300	10	31	***	10
10	***	1.00	32	***	10
11	100	0	33	300	6.00
12	300	5.00	34	265	6.00
13	260	7.00	35	300	6.00
14	270	6.00	36	320	10
15	255	7.00	37	420	10
16	400	10	38	270	6.50
17	under 150	0	39	200	0
18	180	4.00	40	275	7.00
19	160	0	41	225.40	0
20	275	6.00*	42	400	6.00*
21	300	6.00	43	280	6.00
22	200	6.00			

Subject numbers are arbitrary, estimates and contributions were in Dutch guilders. (Three US dollars and about 6 Deutschmarks were included in the contributions.)
* These two individuals made a joint donation and so indicated in their envelope.
*** indicates that estimated total contribution was not given. The minimum *per capita* donation needed to provide the good was 5.82 (=250/43).

would have altered the outcome ("if only one more person had coughed up 6 guilders we would have made it") and such circumstances create intense regret (Kahneman & Tversky, 1986).

Of the 40 people who made predictions about the magnitude of the aggregate contribution, 28 or 70 percent predicted a successful outcome. Thus, nearly three-quarters of the experts were incorrect in their predictions. The mean prediction (of those 37 colleagues who gave numerical predictions) was 267.31.

There are two ways in which we can assess the relationship between predicted outcome and contribution. First we can compute the correlation between these quantities for the 37 participants who made numerical predictions. This correlation is .70. A second way to examine this relationship is to categorize the participants into those who believed they were critical ($n = 1$, S no. 15 in Table 6.1), those who made no prediction ($n = 3$), those who predicted failure to secure the bonus ($n = 12$), and those who predicted success but who did not think their donation would be critical ($n = 27$). The mean contributions for these groups is presented

TABLE 6.2 *Mean Contributions as a Function of Predicted Outcome*

Prediction	Mean contribution
Critical (S no. 15) (n = 1)	7.00
No prediction (n = 3)	7.00
Predict failure (n = 12)	1.83
Predict success (n = 27)	7.24

in Table 6.2. Inspection of these means reveals that the average donation of all but one of the groups was close to 7 guilders. This exceptional group was the group that predicted failure, and the mean donation for that group was less than 2 guilders (M = 1.83). It is interesting to note that while subjects in both the bottom two groups in Table 6.2 believed (according to their predictions) that their contributions would not be critical, the optimistic group contributed nearly four times as much on the average as the pessimistic one. Twenty-five of the 27 people in the optimistic group contributed at least 6 guilders, while 10 of the 12 in the pessimistic group contributed less than 6 guilders.

What conclusions may we draw from the outcome of this exercise? First, the group of experts who participated failed to provide the collective bonus, and most failed to predict that failure. To be sure, the aggregate contribution was very close to the provision point and it is easy to imagine how the provision point might have been surpassed, in which case the group outcome and the modal prediction would have been successful. Second, the participants seem to have been motivated more by fear of losing their contribution than by the greedy desire to ride free on the contributions of others. Those who believed that the provision point would be reached and that their contributions would be superfluous, nevertheless contributed over 7 guilders on average, rather than taking a free ride on the contributions of others. Those who believed that the bonus would fail to be provided, however, contributed very little. Third, rather trivial features of the situation like not being able to get exact change, not having precise knowledge of the number of players, or not having an equal share that is divisible, may be sufficient to disrupt the efficient equilibrium.

Finally, what inferences can be drawn about the decision processes of our expert subjects? First, for only one of the contributors is the relationship between the prediction and the contribution consistent with an expected value maximization hypothesis. So even though many participants were undoubtedly vague about the total amount that would be provided, and even though the choices of those people who declined to contribute are consistent with expected value maximization, the hypothesis does not seem useful in explaining the behavior of most of the contributors.

What seems more likely is that the participants were thinking in terms of choice heuristics that would lead to an equilibrium outcome. For purposes of discussion, let us propose the following choice model. First, a participant asks himself/herself whether he/she believes it is possible for the group to succeed or not. If the answer is "no," the participant contributes nothing. If the answer is "yes," the participant will contribute and must decide on the magnitude of his/her contribution. The first step is to calculate the "fair share" which is the total provision required, 250 guilders in the present study, divided by the total number of participants. Next, the participant decides on the size of a "cushion" to be added to the fair share to compensate for the fact that some participants will not contribute. The total contribution of course must not exceed the magnitude of the bonus to be awarded to the decision maker if the group is successful. The size of the cushion may depend on other factors, such as the importance of having the group succeed, but it should also increase, up to a point, as the estimated number of non-contributors increases. At some point, however, there will be too many non-contributors to be compensated for by the contributors, so at that point the decision maker decides to become a non-contributor himself/herself.

This model, which we will formalize presently, is attractive for two reasons. First it is generally consistent with the observed data. It predicts that there will be bimodal distributions with some people giving nothing and some giving a lot. It postulates that people who are pessimists will give less than others; in fact it assumes that they give nothing at all. It proposes that those who expect success will make contributions, and therefore leads to the prediction of a positive relationship between expectations and contributions. Finally, it presumes that those who anticipate success will give at least the fair share and that they may "cushion" their contributions to allow for the fact that some will not contribute. Data from only five subjects in Table 6.1 violate the assumptions of this model. They are the five subjects who predicted failure and made contributions anyhow, and the two subjects who predicted success and contributed only 5 guilders, somewhat less than the fair share.

The second nice feature of this idea is that it can be developed formally and used to specify conditions for the existence of the asymmetric equilibria that the behavioral model implies. Let us define the following symbols. Let a = the proportion of non-contributors; n = the number of participants; P = the provision amount required; $F = P/n$, the fair share of the provision amount; B = the bonus to the decision maker for successful provision of the good; $c(j)$ = the jth participant's cushion; and $d(j)$ = the jth player's donation $= F + c(j)$.

From the assumptions made above, we know that $c(j) < (B-F)$.

The total contribution will be

$$\sum^{n} d(j) = \sum^{n(1-a)} d(j),$$

since only $n(1-a)$ of the participants contributed. When this total is equal to P, the outcome is in equilibrium since neither the contributors nor the non-contributors have an incentive to change their choices. This condition can be rewritten in the following way by substitution.

$$n(1 - a)F + \sum^{n(1-a)} c(j) = P$$

or, equivalently, since $F = P/n$,

$$\sum^{n(1-a)} c(j) = aP.$$

If the term on the right-hand side of this equation exceeds the maximum possible sum of the contributors' cushions, then no asymmetric equilibrium can exist. Since the maximum cushion for any player is $(B - F)$, the maximum of the sum on the left side can be rewritten as $n(1 - a)$ $(B - F)$. Substituting in the expression above and solving for a, we can write the following as a necessary condition for the existence of an asymmetric equilibrium.

$$\frac{n(B - F)}{P + n(B - F)} > a$$

In terms of the study discussed in this paper, with $(B - F) = 4$, $n = 43$, and $P = 250$, we compute that if the rate of non-contribution had been greater than about 41 percent, no solution would have been possible. However, the rate of non-contribution was considerably below 41 percent and, as we have described, the group came remarkably close to providing the good and to achieving such an equilibrium.

References

Allison, S. T., & Messick, D. M. (1988). Decision making in the use of shared resources: Rational choices or decision heuristics. Unpublished manuscript.

Kahneman, D., & Tversky, A. (1984). Choices, values, and frames. *American Psychologist*, **39**, 341–350.

Part III

Structure and Interpretations

A. Transformation of Outcomes

7

Judgments of Cooperation and Defection in Social Dilemmas: The Moderating Role of Judge's Social Orientation

D. MICHAEL KUHLMAN
The University of Delaware

CLIFFORD BROWN
Wittenburg University

PAUL TETA
The University of Delaware

General Introduction

Assume that a person chooses cooperatively in a social dilemma. What social goal motivated this choice? A desire to maximize the collective welfare of all participants? A selfless concern for the welfare of the others? Similarly, we can ask what social goal motivates the decision to defect. A desire to do better than others? A strictly individualistic concern with maximizing one's own welfare? A desire to inflict social harm, even at a cost to one's own welfare?

That cooperation and defection in social dilemmas can be driven by any of several different goals creates an interesting theoretical issue for social scientists attempting to understand the causes of each behavior. It also creates an important attributional problem for the layperson who confronts cooperation and defection in others on a daily basis.

The present chapter deals with two issues, one of which is the attributional problem just described. Its second focus concerns the connotative meaning that laypersons assign to cooperation and defection in dilemmas. Consistent with the work of Liebrand, Jansen, Rijken and

Suhre (1986) we concentrate on the ubiquitous dimensions of Good-Bad and Potency-Weakness. How does the layperson locate cooperation and defection in this two-dimensional space? Do the subject's social motivational analyses of cooperation and defection help us to understand the verbal meanings assigned to each act?

To address the above questions we asked our subjects to make two types of social judgment for each of two target persons who differ in their approach (cooperative vs noncooperative) to a social dilemma. For one judgment, the subject is asked to decide what type of social goal the target was attempting to achicve. For the second type of judgment, the subject is asked to provide verbal descriptions of what each target is like. Is the cooperative (noncooperative) target wise or foolish, good or bad, strong or weak, and so on?

The fundamental assumption of the present paper is that both types of social judgment will be influenced by the subject's own social orientation, or characteristic approach to situations of social interdependence. In the following paragraphs social orientation will be described and the details of its expected influence on social judgment presented.

Social Orientation

In 1968 Messick and McClintock published a classic paper demonstrating that choice behavior in socially interdependent situations can be driven by any of a number of underlying social motivations or orientations, each defined in terms of the decision maker's preferences for the distribution of rewards to self and interdependent others (McClintock, 1978).

Although an infinite number of social orientations are theoretically possible (Griesinger & Livingston, 1973; MacCrimmon & Messick, 1976; Liebrand & Van Run, 1985), most empirical work has focused on five. *Altruism* (Al) is a preference for outcomes which maximize the gains of the other, with no concern for gains to self. *Cooperation* is a preference for outcomes which maximize Joint Gain (J), or the sum of outcomes to self and other(s). *Individualism* is a preference to maximize Own Gain (O), or the outcome to self. *Competition* is a preference for outcomes which maximize Relative Gain (R), or the algebraic difference of outcomes to self minus outcomes to others. *Aggression* (Ag) seeks to minimize gains to the other, again with no concern for gains to the self.

In almost all social orientation research, the subject's orientation is assessed by means of some variation of the decomposed game technique first developed by Messick and McClintock. Because of their central role in the present research, decomposed games and a related concept of dominance structure will be presented next.

Decomposed Games and Dominance Structure

Table 7.1 gives an example of each of the four different decomposed games used here. A decomposed game involves a choice between *n* alternatives, (here, $n = 3$) each possessing two numerical outcomes: (a) Self is the outcome to self, and (b) Other is the outcome to another with whom self has been randomly paired. For example, a choice of column B in Game I of Table 7.1 would produce 50 units for self and 20 units for the other, whereas column A would produce 40 units for each person.

TABLE 7.1 *Examples of the Four Decomposed Game Structures Used in the Present Study*

	Game I			Game II			Game III			Game IV		
Structure:	AlJ.O.RAg			AlJ.OR.Ag			AlJO.R.Ag			Al.JORAg.U		
	A	B	C	A	B	C	A	B	C	A	B	C
Self	40	50	40	40	50	20	80	70	50	20	60	40
Other	40	20	0	30	10	0	70	50	40	20	0	10

Decomposed games differ in terms of how their choices dominate with respect to each type of social orientation. Following Messick and McClintock's notation, the dominance structure of a three-choice game is given by three groups of letters separated by periods. The letters Al, J, O, R and Ag correspond to the five social orientations defined above. If one of the three groups is the single letter U, this means that one choice in the game maximizes none of the five motives. Each group of letters shows the motive(s) maximized by a single choice in the game. For example, in the AlJ.O.RAg game Altruism and Joint Gain are maximized by one choice, Own Gain by another, and Relative Gain and Aggression by the third.

Although the specific form of the decomposed game task has varied, numerous studies dealing with individual differences in social orientation (e.g., Kuhlman & Marshello, 1975; Kuhlman & Wimberley, 1976; Liebrand & Van Run, 1985) have shown that most people display either Cooperation, Individualism or Competition as their characteristic social orientation. Henceforth we will refer to Cooperators, Individualists and Competitors as Js, Os and Rs, reflecting their concern with Joint, Own and Relative gain respectively.

The present chapter seeks to understand how the subject's social orientation influences judgments of cooperation and noncooperation in social dilemmas. Our expectations are based on two previous lines of social orientation research dealing with cognitive differences between Js, Os and Rs. One focuses on the beliefs held by Js, Os and Rs as to the levels of social orientations in the general population (Kuhlman &

Wimberley, 1976). The other deals with the use of evaluative versus potency dimensions to describe prosocial and nonprosocial orientations (Liebrand, Jansen, Rijken, & Suhre, 1986).

Cognitive Domain One: Interpretation of Cooperation and Defection in Terms of Underlying Social Orientations

In the present study subjects observed a Prisoner's Dilemma interaction between two targets, one of whom was consistently noncooperative and the other showed a preference for cooperation. In terms of the social orientations underlying each target's actions, numerous possibilities exist. That is, in a social dilemma cooperation can result either from a desire to benefit the other at a cost to self (Altruism) or a desire to maximize collective welfare which includes benefit to the self (Joint Gain). Defection can result from Individualistic, Relative Gain, or Aggressive motivation.

How do subjects interpret each target's behavior in terms of underlying social orientation? Is cooperative choice seen as Altruistic, or Cooperative? Is Individualism, Competition, or Aggression used to explain defection in the PDG? How does the judge's own social orientation play a role in the interpretation of these acts? Past research on beliefs of Js, Os and Rs concerning levels of social orientation in the general population suggests possible answers (Kuhlman & Wimberley, 1976).

Kuhlman and Wimberley asked subjects to estimate the proportion of 100 fellow students that would choose each alternative in the four classes of decomposed games shown in Table 7.1. Across these four game classes the subject's orientation covaried with population expectations as follows. The Js expected high levels of Joint Gain, followed by Own and then Relative Gain. The R judges expected high levels of Relative Gain, followed by Own and then Joint Gain. The expectation profile of Os was a single peaked function with a mode at Own Gain. Expected levels of Altruism and Aggression were low for all groups, indicating that these motives are assumed to be quite rare by practically all subjects. Henceforth, we refer to these results as the Structured Assumed Similarity Bias (SASB).

The SASB has important implications for the way in which Js, Os and Rs might interpret choice behavior in Prisoner's Dilemma. Cooperation maximizes both Joint Gain and Altruism. Since all three types of subject have low expectations of Altruism, we could expect that it would play only a small role in the interpretation of Cooperation. Therefore, it seems likely that Js, Os and Rs would tend to make similar, Joint Gain interpretations of the Cooperative Target.

Of the three motives that could lead to Defection, Individualism and Relative Gain are seen as common in the general population, making the Defector motivationally ambiguous. We assume that subjects will resolve this ambiguity in terms of which motive they consider most likely in the general population. By this argument, Rs should interpret Defection more than Os and Js in terms of Relative Gain, whereas both Os and Js should judge it as an attempt to maximize Own Gain.

The second focus of the present work was on the connotative meanings subjects assign to cooperation and defection, specifically in terms of their goodness and power. Again, prior work (Liebrand, Jansen, Rijken, & Suhre, 1986) leads us to expect that the subject's social orientation will influence the manner in which each of these dimensions are used.

Cognitive Domain Two: Might and Morality as Bases for Construing Cooperation and Defection in Social Dilemmas

Liebrand *et al.* led their subjects to believe that they were playing a series of decomposed games with each of four different "partners." The partners differed in terms of which social orientation (Altruism, Joint Gain, Individualism, Relative Gain) they displayed on every trial. One partner was 100 percent Altruistic, another 100 percent Cooperative, and so on. Thus, each partner's social orientation was directly and unambiguously displayed to the subject.

Following the decomposed game interaction, each player was rated on a series of semantic differential items. Factor analysis of the items revealed the expected factors of Evaluation (Morality) and Potency (Might). Liebrand *et al.* found that the subject's social orientation moderates the extent to which subjects discriminate prosocial orientations (Altruism, Cooperation) from nonprosocial (Individualism, Competition) ones in terms of Morality and Might. Compared to Os, Js make heavier use of morality concepts in distinguishing Altruism and Cooperation from Individualism and Competition. Compared to Js, Os make heavier use of power constructs. This is referred to as the Might Over Morality effect.

In the present study, subjects were asked to rate cooperative and noncooperative targets in a Prisoner's Dilemma Game. On the surface, this procedural variation might seem to threaten the applicability of the Liebrand *et al.* findings to the present study. However, we think there is good reason to expect that the judgments of our Js and Os will be very much like those of Liebrand *et al.* Specifically, in Prisoner's Dilemma cooperation and defection perfectly partition the set of prosocial (Altruism, Cooperation) from the nonprosocial (Individualism, Competition) orientations. Although Liebrand *et al.* did not include Rs in their study, we anticipate that Rs and Os will agree in their use of might and morality constructs.

In addition to demonstrating the importance of social orientation to social judgments of behavior in social dilemmas, we also hope to add this study to a growing body of evidence demonstrating that social orientation can be regarded as a temporally stable personality variable that covaries with a variety of behaviors in interdependent contexts (Kuhlman, Camac, & Cunha, 1986; Bem & Lord, 1979; McClintock & Allison, 1989). This issue was addressed by assessing the social orientation of our subjects from three to six weeks prior to the social judgment tasks.

Method

General Overview

Initially, decomposed games were used to assess the social orientation of a group of 140 undergraduates. A subset of these students was selected to participate in a subsequent experiment which took place three to six weeks later. In this later experiment students performed three tasks. First, they estimated population choice proportions in the four classes of decomposed games described above. This allowed for a demonstration of the temporal stability of social orientation.

Before performing tasks two and three all subjects observed a Prisoner's Dilemma interaction between two confederates in which one made the NonCooperative choice on every trial and the other chose Cooperatively 60 percent of the time. We will refer to these two students as the Defector and Cooperator, respectively.

After observing this interaction, subjects were asked to rate each target in two different ways. First, decomposed games were used to allow each subject to give their interpretation of the type of social goal (e.g., Joint Gain, Own Gain) each target was pursuing. Second, each target was rated on a set of semantic differential items. Five of the items were included as manipulation checks and the others served as measures of the Might and Morality attributed to each target.

Initial Session: The Assessment of Social Orientation

Subjects

One hundred and forty subjects (58 males and 82 females) participated in this phase of the study as partial fulfillment of an introductory psychology research requirement.

Procedure

Groups of same-sex subjects were randomly seated in a classroom at least one chair apart and faced a common projection screen. Tape recorded instructions explained that each subject had been randomly and anonymously paired with another for a decision making task, and that each subject's outcomes in that task would depend on what the two of them chose together. A sample decomposed game (AlJ.O.RAg) was projected and used to explain how the subjects' combined choices would determine the total units each received.

Following the instructions, a written quiz was administered to determine subjects' comprehension of the decomposed game task, after which subjects were asked to indicate their choices for twenty game slides each presented for 20 seconds. They were told to imagine that the units involved with the games had value, and that ". . . both you and the other student should want to accumulate them." Before the first trial, the subjects were told to ". . . make the decision that you consider the best on each trial." When the task was completed, subjects were thanked for their participation and asked not to talk about the experiment with other students until it was discussed in class later in the term.

Classification of Subjects

An examination of the comprehension quiz revealed that 3 of the 58 males and 4 of the 82 females had missed 3 or more of the 18 responses required. These subjects were eliminated from further consideration.

Of the twenty decomposed games presented in Phase I, 11 were of the AlJ.O.RAg type. In order to be classified as a J, O or R a subject had to make a plurality of choices in these 11 games consistent with Own, Relative, or Joint Gain, respectively. Ties between two motives prevented classification. A second requirement for the classification of a J is based on the fact that in the AlJ.O.RAg game the cooperative choice can maximize either Joint Gain or Altruism. Thus to be classified as a J, the subject's choices in the Al.JORAg.U game were examined. Only those who consistently chose the JORAg alternative were classified as Js. This produced a total of 92 subjects (41 males and 51 females) who were eligible for the experiment held 3 to 6 weeks later, including 40 Js, 22 Os and 30 Rs. Consistent with previous research, a chi-square computed on the 3 (motive) × 2 (sex) contingency table was not significant ($\chi^2 = 4.44$).

The Subsequent Experiment

SUBJECTS

Three to six weeks after the assessment of social orientation, 67 subjects (34 males and 33 females) participated in a second study as partial fulfillment of an introductory psychology course requirement. One of these subjects (a male R) was excluded from the reported analyses due to suspicion about the authenticity of a confederate's behavior. The remaining subjects included 25 Js, 18 Os and 23 Rs and were run in groups of size 4 to 6 which were sexually homogeneous with regard to subjects, experimenters and confederates.

Procedure

Students who were not initially classifiable as Js, Os, or Rs served as confederates, one acting as the Cooperative target, the other as the Defector. Different confederates were used in each experimental session and arrived 15 minutes before the actual subjects. After being informed as to their special role in the experiment, the confederates left through a back door, and arrived again with the naive subjects. By means of a rigged lottery held in front of all subjects, the confederates were selected to serve "special roles" in the experiment.

The two confederates were led to a room where their upcoming PDG interaction would be observed by the other subjects through a one-way mirror. The mirror allowed a clear view of the PDG payoff matrix, but the confederates were seated so they could not be seen by the subjects.

Tape recorded instructions began by explaining that a few weeks ago everyone had participated in a "Decision Study" which was interested in how they made decisions. They were told that the present study was interested in how well they understood how other people make decisions. The first task required subjects to look at four of the twenty slides they had seen a few weeks ago and to indicate how many of 100 classmates of their own sex they thought would choose A, B, and C. These are the games shown in Table 7.1.

Following the estimation task, subjects were asked to observe the two students in the other room participate in a decision task, and told that following their observation they would be asked to complete various questionnaires regarding the two students.

The students then listened to tape recorded instructions which explained the Prisoner's Dilemma payoff matrix, and indicated that it would be the basis for the decision task of the two targets. The instructions indicated that the task was concerned with how pairs of people make decisions when each person's outcome was partly determined by his/her own decision and partly determined by the other person's decision. Subjects heard that once both targets had made a choice, one of the four lights in the matrix would come on depending on the choices both made.

Since the payoff matrix was in clear view of all subjects, they were able to see the choices made by each target on each of the ten trials of the PDG interaction, although they could not see the targets. Prior to the first trial, subjects heard the targets being told to regard the payoff units in the matrix as valuable, and that each was to make the choice they considered best on each trial.

Across all 10 trials the Defector consistently chose NonCooperation.

The Cooperator chose cooperation on trials 1, 2, 4, 7, 9, and 10, demonstrating persistent cooperative intent, but for the sake of realism and consistency with previous research (Kelley & Stahelski, 1970; Kuhlman & Marshello, 1975; Kuhlman & Wimberley, 1976) did not permit excessive exploitation.

Following the tenth trial the experimenter covered the PDG matrix with a white projection screen, and the instructions continued. Though they were (ostensibly) addressed to Targets 1 and 2, the observers (as intended) heard them also. The targets were told:

> In the next part of this experiment, you two students will see the same twenty slides you saw earlier. What I want you to do is make the choice for each slide which is most consistent with the way you made your choices in the Decision Task you just completed. That is, Student 1, you chose either X or Y on each trial. Student 2, you either chose A or B on each trial. Only you know why you made these ten choices. What I want each of you to do now is look at the twenty slides and for each of them choose A, B, or C. Make the choice that is most consistent with your behavior in the Decision Task you just completed.

Next, the instructions requested the observers to use the decomposed games to make similar judgments of the targets, showing which choice was most consistent with the way each behaved in the PDG task. It was made clear to the observers that the same choice could be used to describe each Target on a given slide, or that different choices could be used. The twenty slides previously shown during Phase I were then displayed, each for 20 seconds.

Following this, subjects were asked to rate each Target on ten bipolar adjective rating scales; the 6-point scales used were: cruel-kind, smart-stupid, weak-strong, bad-good, wise-foolish, selfish-generous, successful-unsuccessful, yielding-persistent, intentional-unintentional, and cooperative-competitive. The instructions emphasized that the answers to these questions would be kept strictly confidential and that the ratings should be based solely on behavior exhibited during the 10-trial decision task.

A final open-ended questionnaire was administered which was designed to give subjects a chance to verbalize any suspicions they might have had. Subjects were completely debriefed, asked not to talk about the experiment with other students, and allowed to leave.

Results

Population Expectations of Js, Os and Rs in the Four Decomposed Games

If social orientation is temporally stable, the expectations of Js, Os and Rs in each class of decomposed game should vary in a fashion consistent with the SASB. Also, since the SASB is an important basis for predictions regarding the social orientation interpretation of the PDG targets, we present these findings first.

Population Expectations in AlJ.O.RAg

As shown in Fig. 7.1 expectations of each social orientation group mirrored those originally reported by Kuhlman and Wimberley. Across the Joint, Own and Relative choices in this game the Js show decreasing expectations, Rs increasing, and Os' expectations are peaked in the middle. Expectations were analyzed via ANOVA in which Orientation and Choice served as factorially crossed independent variables, with Choice treated as a repeated measures factor. A reliable interaction between Orientation and Choice obtained. (Rao's $F = 5.0369^1$, $df = 4{,}124$, $p = 0.001$). The $2-df$ effect for Orientation was decomposed in terms of $1-df$ contrasts, one comparing Js and Rs and the other Js and Os. In each case, the effect was significant. (For Js versus Rs, $F = 8.9593$, $df = 2{,}62$, $p < 0.001$. For Js versus Os, $F = 5.06785$, $df = 2{,}62$, $p = 0.009$.) As shown in the following paragraphs, subjects' expectations in the other game classes were also consistent with the SASB.

Population Expectations in AlJ.OR.Ag

This game is most similar to Prisoner's Dilemma,[2] so that expectations should show Kelley and Stahelski's (1972) Trinagular pattern, in which

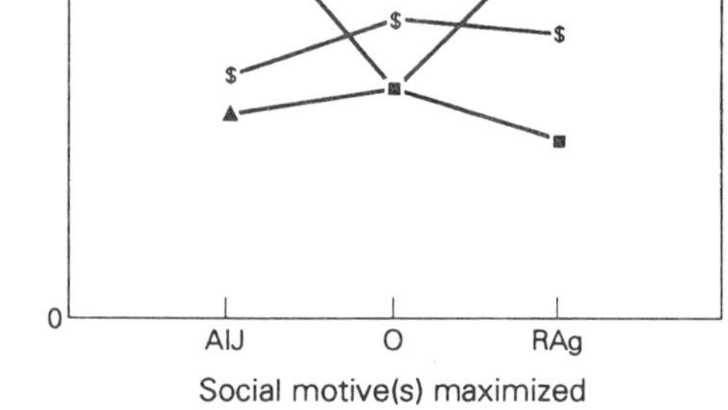

FIG. 7.1 Population expectations of Js, Os and Rs in the AlJ.O.RAg game.

Js show relatively little bias and Os and Rs show strong bias for the expectations of OR. As Fig. 7.2 indicates, across the J and OR choices, Os and Rs show biased expectations for the OR choice, whereas this bias is reversed and smaller among the Js. An ANOVA using the same design as above showed a significant interaction between Orientation and Choice (Rao's $F = 4.76859$, $df = 4{,}120$, $p = 0.001$). Contrasts for the decomposition of the Orientation effect involved Js versus Rs, and Js versus Os. In both cases, the interaction was significant. (For Js versus Rs, $F = 8.24172$, $df = 2{,}60$, $p = 0.001$. For Js versus Os, $F = 5.96310$, $df = 2{,}60$, $p = 0.004$.)

Although the expectations for this PDG structure support the Triangular pattern, with Js showing less biased expectations than Os and Rs, it is important to note that Kuhlman and Wimberley argued that Triangularity is more a result of the motivational structure of PDG than of a general tendency for Js to be non-biased. That is, in PDG the competitive choice maximizes both Individualism and Relative gain. Hence Os and Rs would both show fairly high competitive expectations since this choice maximizes two motives which both groups consider to be fairly probable. The relatively smaller bias among Js is a consequence of one choice maximizing Joint Gain (considered probable by Js) and the other Own (also considered somewhat probable by Js).

Kuhlman and Wimberley tested their Triangularity interpretation by examining expectations in the AlJO.R.Ag game where Individualism is paired with Joint gain, leaving Relative gain as the only motive leading

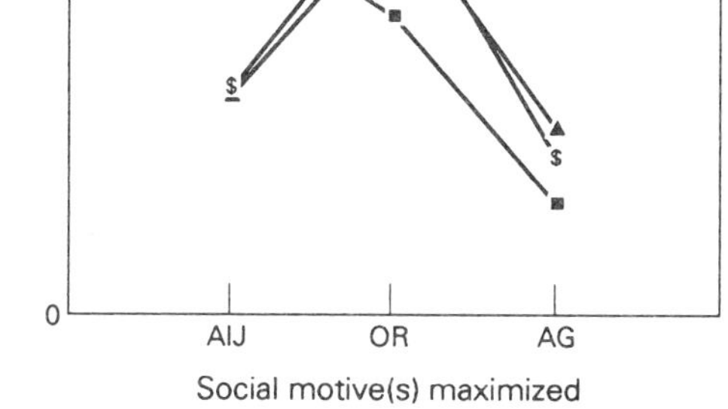

FIG. 7.2 Population expectations of Js, Os and Rs in the AlJ.OR.Ag game.

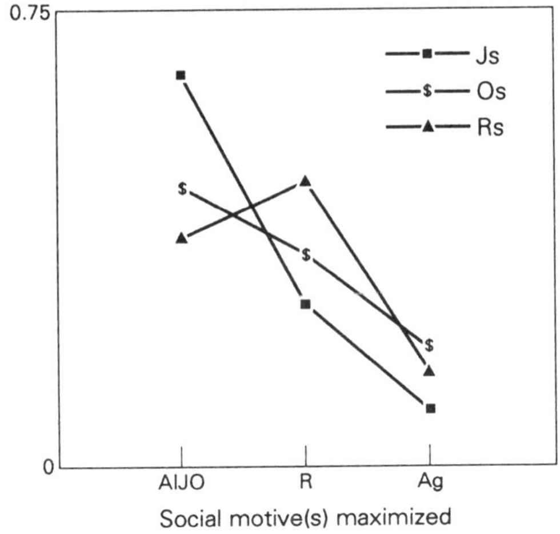

FIG. 7.3 Population expectations of Js, Os and Rs in the AlJO.R.Ag game.

to the competitive choice. As expected, they found that Rs "became" less biased and Js and Os showed higher bias. A similar reversal occurred in the present experiment.

Population Expectations in AlJO.R.Ag

As can be seen in Fig. 7.3 Js and Os show biased expectations of cooperative choice, whereas among Rs the expectation is reversed and less biased. The ANOVA yielded a significant Orientation by Choice interaction. (Rao's $F = 4.86368$, $df = 4{,}124$, $p = 0.001$). The 1−*df* contrasts for the analysis of this game were Js and Os versus Rs, and Js versus Rs. In both cases, the interaction was significant. (For Js and Os versus Rs, $F = 4.92258$, $df = 2{,}62$, $p = 0.010$. For Js versus Rs, $F = 8.50274$, $df = 2{,}62$, $p = 0.001$.)

Population Expectations in Al.JORAg.U

In this final game class, a single choice maximizes all three motives considered most probable by Js, Os and Rs (Joint Gain, Individualism, and Relative Gain). Here then, the expectations of this "triple motive" alternative should be high, and relative to the other game classes, effects for judge's Orientation should be reduced. As can be seen in Fig. 7.4, the expectation of all three Orientation groups peaks over the JOR choice. An ANOVA showed no global interaction between Orientation and Choice (Rao's $F = 1.73984$, $df = 4{,}124$, $p = 0.145$), nor did either of the 1−*df*

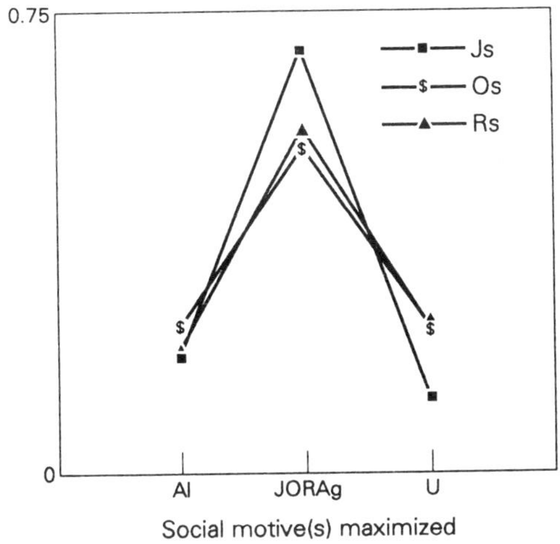

FIG. 7.4 Population expectations of Js, Os and Rs in the Al.JORAg.U game.

Orientation contrasts achieve significance. (For Js versus Rs, $F = 2.58410$, $df = 2{,}62$, $p = 0.084$, and for Js versus Os, $F = 2.2356$, $df = 2{,}62$, $p = 0.103$.)

In summary, these results show that the SASB guided the population expectations of the present subjects. In this regard at least, Orientation appears to be exerting temporally stable effects. In the next section we examine the social motivational interpretations of our subjects, to see if they support the SASB based predictions developed earlier.

Social Orientation Interpretation of the Cooperative Target

Based on the SASB, we assumed that all three types of judge would interpret the cooperator in terms of Joint Gain. This did not happen. Table 7.2 shows the decomposed game interpretations of the Cooperative Target made by each of the Orientation groups. For example, the table shows that in the AlJ.O.RAg game J judges made a strong ProSocial interpretation (0.804) whereas the Os and Rs were less extreme (0.515 and 0.675 respectively). The three rightmost columns of the table show p-values resulting from ANOVAs which tested three null-hypotheses: (a) No main effect for Orientation, (b) Js and Os do not differ, and (c) Js combined with Os do not differ from Rs.

As the table indicates, ProSocial interpretations in AlJ.O.RAg were affected by judge's Orientation ($p = 0.034$), and the $1-df$ contrasts suggest this was primarily due to a difference between Js and NonJs. The table further shows the only other judgment affected by Orientation was of

TABLE 7.2 *Interpretation of the Cooperator in Each Game Class as a Function of the Judge's Social Orientation*

		Expectations of			p-values		
Class	Choice	Js	Os	Rs	Overall	J vs O	JO vs R
I	AlJ	0.804	0.515	0.6752	0.034	0.01	0.863
I	O	0.1452	0.2972	0.2174	0.282	0.114	0.962
I	RAg	0.0504	0.1856	0.1065	0.104	0.034	0.828
II	AlJ	0.7736	0.4822	0.6383	0.042	0.012	0.914
II	OR	0.1596	0.3139	0.13	0.126	0.1	0.174
II	Ag	0.0664	0.2039	0.2313	0.116	0.128	0.204
III	AlJO	0.6404	0.4628	0.6961	0.129	0.127	0.139
III	R	0.2532	0.2394	0.0861	0.055	0.862	0.018
III	Ag	0.1056	0.2956	0.217	0.071	0.025	0.814
IV	Al	0.5068	0.4083	0.58	0.397	0.427	0.241
IV	JORAg	0.3332	0.3144	0.217	0.549	0.875	0.29
IV	U	0.1592	0.2767	0.203	0.349	0.149	0.826

Note: The column labeled "Overall', shows p-values for the overall Orientation effect ($df = 2,63$). The two columns to the right show p-values for *a-priori* contrasts of Js with Os and then with Js and Os compared with Rs. The df for each of these columns = 1,63.

ProSocial behavior in the AlJ.OR.Ag game. Again, Js make a stronger ProSocial interpretation than Os and Rs, who do not differ.

In both cases, the ProSocial choice could either be seen in terms of Joint Gain or Altruism. Results for the Al.JOR.Ag game show that judges of all three types had fairly high and equal expectations of the purely altruistic choice ($p = 0.397$), suggesting that the Orientation effect in the other games was a result of Js seeing more Joint Gain intention on the part of the Cooperator than either Os or Rs. Although all groups agree that the Cooperator was rather altruistic, the J judges also saw a component of self-interest (i.e., Joint Gain involves maximizing the sum of gains to Self and Other) in this target. Contrary to our SASB predictions then, Altruism was seen as a potent motive by all groups. And, the only group that saw any Joint Gain motivation was the Js.

Social Orientation Interpretation of the NonCooperative Target

For this target, SASB based predictions were that Js and Os would make Individualistic interpretations, and that Rs would see Relative Gain as the driving force. Table 7.3 gives decomposed game interpretations of the Defector made by judges in each group. There were five instances where a reliable Orientation effect emerged, four of which provide strong support for our predictions.

As expected, the Defector's behavior was seen as a matter of Individualism by J and O judges. In the AlJ.O.RAg game, both Js and Os made strong Own Gain interpretations (.656 and .565, respectively), whereas Rs saw considerably less Individualism (.225). The p-values show that the overall effect for Orientation involves a difference between Rs and NonRs. Similar results for Own Gain interpretation occurred in the AlJO.R.Ag game which is the only other structure which separates Own and Relative gain.

Also as expected, the Defector was interpreted as a Relative Gainer by the R judges. In the two game classes which separate Relative from Own gain (AlJ.O.RAg and AlJO.R.Ag), Rs make strong Relative Gain interpretations compared to Js and Os who did not differ on this dimension. There were two game classes in which Aggression was separate from Relative Gain (AlJO.R.Ag and AlJ.OR.Ag), and in both cases all judges made hardly any interpretive use of this motive. Thus, the Rs appear to be interpreting the Defector as motivated by Relative Gain.

The final case where an effect for Orientation emerged involved the use of Altruism in the Al.JORAg.U game. Although all groups saw extremely low levels of this motive, Os saw reliably more than Js and Rs. We are presently unable to confirm this effect.

Semantic Differential Ratings

Of the ten semantic differential items five were intended as manipulation checks. Specifically, we expected that the Defector would be judged more

TABLE 7.3 *Interpretation of the Defector in Each Game Class as a Function of the Judge's Social Orientation*

		Expectations of			p-values		
Class	Choice	Js	Os	Rs	Overall	Js vs Os	JOs vs Rs
I	AlJ	0.080	0.0961	0.0157	0.373	0.793	0.164
I	O	0.656	0.565	0.2252	0.001	0.445	0.001
I	RAg	0.264	0.3389	0.7591	0.001	0.521	0.001
II	AlJ	0.08	0.0922	0.0143	0.396	0.845	0.176
II	OR	0.92	0.815	0.913	0.344	0.18	0.486
II	Ag	0.001	0.0928	0.0722	0.116	0.057	0.523
III	AlJO	0.7068	0.6661	0.2161	0.001	0.713	0.001
III	R	0.2932	0.2783	0.74	0.001	0.895	0.001
III	Ag	0.001	0.0556	0.043	0.225	0.113	0.6
IV	Al	0.0132	0.0733	0.001	0.018	0.024	0.051
IV	JORAg	0.9468	0.8522	0.8843	0.294	0.134	0.773
IV	U	0.0396	0.0744	0.1157	0.361	0.54	0.222

TABLE 7.4 *Mean Ratings of the Cooperator and Defector Averaged Over the Judge's Social Orientation*

	Defector	Cooperator	*F*-value	*p*-value
Selfish	4.11	1.49	132.76	0.000
Successful	4.11	1.71	69.05	0.000
Persistent	5.45	2.47	155.06	0.000
Intentional	4.53	2.23	88.88	0.000
Competitive	5.46	2.43	122.15	0.000
Cruel	3.88	1.25	166.75	0.000
Bad	2.49	1.98	1.96	0.166
Smart	3.87	2.46	24.69	0.000
Strong	4.73	3.15	32.58	0.000
Wise	3.55	2.49	13.91	0.000

Note: Ratings were made on a 6-point scale, with no neutral point. Degrees of freedom for all reported *F*s = 1,63.

Selfish, Successful, Persistent, Intentional, and Competitive than the Cooperator. As can be seen in Table 7.4, this was the case for each of these items. Furthermore, on these five the judge's Orientation did not moderate the main effects for target. (The *p*-values for the Orientation by Target interaction were 0.748, 0.077, 0.392, 0.157 and 0.142 for Selfish, Successful, Persistent, Intentional, and Competitive respectively.)

The absence of interactions with Orientation suggests that Js, Os and Rs do not make qualitatively different judgments of Cooperation and Defection on all dimensions. We **did** anticipate interactions on dimensions associated with Might and Morality, which results follow.

Ratings on Dimensions of Might and Morality

Main Effects for Target

For each target, *a-priori* Morality and Might scores were computed by averaging the ratings on Good-Bad with Kind-Cruel, and the ratings on Strong-Weak, Smart-Stupid, and Wise-Foolish respectively. Each derived measure served as the dependent variable in an ANOVA with Orientation and Target as the independent variables. Both ANOVAs yielded a significant main effect for Target (For Morality $F = 47.56$, $df = 1,63$, $p < 0.001$. For Might, $F = 32.14$, $df = 1,63$, $p < 0.001$.) Overall, the Cooperative Target was judged as more Moral and less Mighty than the Defector. (Means for Morality=4.385 and 2.816. Means for Might=2.698 and 4.045.)

The Might Over Morality Effect

In addition, both ANOVAS yielded a significant interaction between Orientation and Target. (For Morality, $F = 3.52$, $df = 1,63$, $p = 0.036$.

For Might, $F = 8.80$, $df = 2,63$, $p < 0.001$.) The 2-*df* effect for Orientation was decomposed via *a-priori* 1−*df* contrasts in which Js were compared with Os and Rs, and Os were compared with Rs. For both measures, the only significant contrast involved Js versus Os and Rs. (For Morality, F(J vs OR) = 5.22, $df = 1,63$, $p = 0.026$; F(O vs R) = 2.30, $df = 1,63$, $p = 0.136$. For Might, F(J vs OR) = 16.57, $df = 1,63$, $p < 0.001$; F(O vs R) = 0.49, $df = 1,63$, $p = 0.486$.)

As can be seen in Figs. 7.5 and 7.6, the mean ratings of Js, Os and Rs demonstrate the Might Over Morality effect. On the Might dimension (Fig. 7.5) results are straightforward: Js do not differentiate the targets at all, whereas both Os and Rs assign much higher Might to the defector than the Cooperator. Examination of the means for the individual items comprising this scale (Strong-Weak, Wise-Foolish, Smart-Stupid) show results virtually identical to those for the composite.

On Morality (Fig. 7.6) the effects are less straightforward, and a bit surprising. The Js do indeed differentiate the two targets more than NonJs (aggregated Rs and Os), but surprisingly the Rs and Os are themselves quite different. The Rs appeared to be making Morality distinctions almost as large and of the same type as the Js. Although we had not planned to do so, Fig. 7.6 led us to a statistical comparison of the slopes of Js and Rs. The result ($F = 1.41$, $df = 1,63$, $p = 0.240$)[3] indicates that the Orientation effect on Morality is primarily a difference between Os and NonOs.

Means for the individual items comprising the Morality scale (Good-Bad, Kind-Cruel) are given in Table 7.5. As the table shows, the J versus

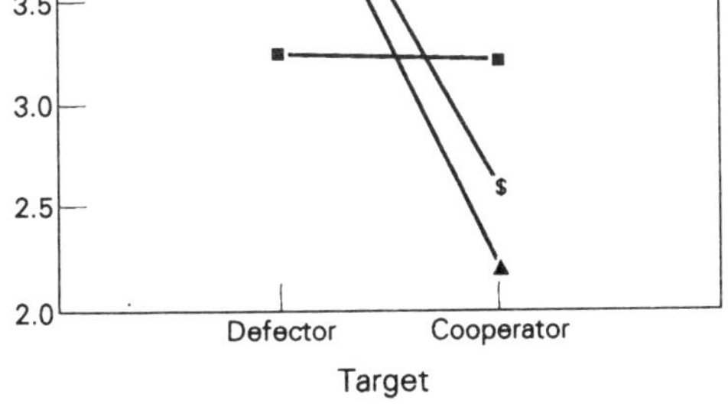

FIG. 7.5 Might ratings of the Cooperator and Defector made by Js, Os and Rs.

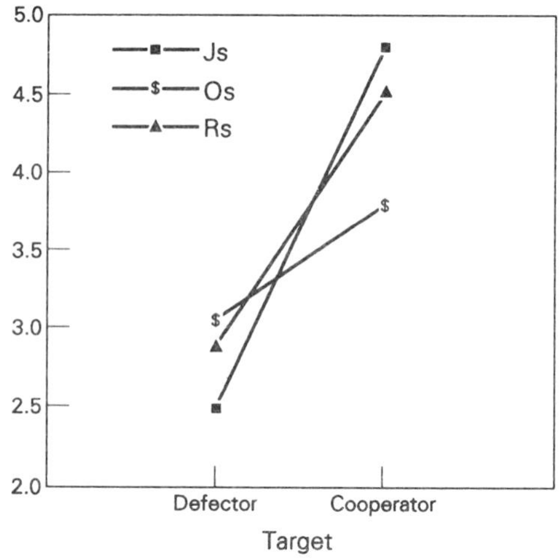

FIG. 7.6 Morality ratings of the Cooperator and Defector made by Js, Os and Rs.

TABLE 7.5 *Mean Ratings of the Defector and Cooperator on Good-Bad and Kind-Cruel*

	Rating on Bad		Rating on Cruel	
Judge	Defector	Cooperator	Defector	Cooperator
J	3.96	0.84	3.04	1.60
O	3.67	2.00	2.22	2.34
R	4.00	0.91	2.22	2.00

O difference is consistent with the Might versus Morality effect for both pairs. Among Rs, however, this is only the case with Good-Bad. Overall, these results demonstrate a temporally stable tendency, especially strong on the dimension of Might, for Js, Os and Rs to differentiate Cooperative from NonCooperative acts in Prisoner's Dilemma.

Discussion

Social Motive Interpretations of Cooperation and Defection

Although social orientation was assessed at least three weeks prior to the social judgment study reported here, our subjects' estimates of decomposed choice behavior in the general population were very consistent with the SASB originally reported by Kuhlman and Wimberley. Further, each social orientation group had a unique pattern of social motivational interpretations of the PDG targets, although these differences were not totally consistent with the predictions based on the SASB.

Interpretation of Cooperation

All social orientation groups attributed the same high levels of Altruism to the cooperator, and Js attributed significantly higher levels of Joint Gain to this target than either Os or Rs. Any social orientation effect predicted by the SASB position, however, would be just the opposite. That is, Os and Rs should be less likely to use Altruism and more likely to use Joint Gain, since the latter is closer to their own positions on the social orientation continuum.

It appears that something similar to a contrast effect (Sherif & Hovland, 1961) occurred here, in which the cooperative target was sufficiently different from the O and R anchors that it was placed in an extremely pro-social (Altruistic) as opposed to moderately pro-social (Joint Gain) category. In addition to seeing Altruism in the cooperator, the Js saw significantly higher levels of Joint Gain than the Os and Rs. As a result of this target's proximity to the Js, they showed assimilation, judging the cooperator as motivationally similar to its own position.

The apparent tendency of Js to assimilate and of Os and Rs to contrast the cooperative target have important implications for their tendency to behave cooperatively in real-world dilemma settings. In their review of twenty years of PDG research, Pruitt and Kimmel (1977) point out that trust, or the expectation that others will cooperate, is a necessary condition to cooperative behavior. Laboratory studies can manipulate trust by providing the subject with clear feedback as to the partners' choices. In the real world, however, trust is a matter of generalized and largely unverifiable beliefs as to what ". . . most of the other people are doing. . . ."

Behavior which is totally self-indifferent and other-enhancing (Altruism) is very rare, the stuff of military heroes and religious saints rather than a chronic property of human nature. Hence, Os and Rs may have a difficult time believing that most others would cooperate in real-world dilemmas, and so have very good reason for not doing so themselves. More than Os and Rs, however, the Js see prosocial behavior as driven by a desire to benefit self. This allows for a stronger conviction that others can be counted on to act prosocially and a greater readiness to do so themselves.

Interpretations of Defection

Again, Sherif and Hovland's work provides a framework for the interpretation of decomposed game judgments. For this target, an assimilation bias appears to have occurred for all three types of judge.

Both Os and Rs are familiar with targets who consistently defect in PDG, and in both cases this target was assimilated to the motivational position of the particular group. Since it is logically impossible to see defection in terms of Joint Gain or Altruism, the Js were forced to choose between three non-prosocial interpretations (Own, Relative, Aggression) differing in proximity to their own position. The Js show an assimilative, Own-gain interpretation of the defector, implying that this target is not wholly alien to them.

That Js have considerable experience both with cooperation and defection in others is a central point in the description of cooperativeness provided by Kelley and Stahelski (1972). Hence, the Js' motivational judgment of the defector was not a contrasting displacement to an extreme category, but rather was as close to their own motivational position as they could logically make.

Judgments of Might and Morality

Although the procedures of the present study differed in a number of ways from those of Liebrand *et al.*, Js and Os differed in their use of might and morality constructs in a fashion wholly consistent with the original effect. The judgments of the Rs, however, only partially support our expectations that they would use these dimensions like Os.

The Rs agreed with the Os that cooperation and defection differ strongly in terms of might, but they also agreed with the Js that these behaviors differ just as much on morality. Thus, each type of judge had unique might and morality profiles. We think that the social motivational interpretations of the three groups may help to increase our understanding of these differences in verbal judgment.

Judgments of Might

In this experiment, the two PDG targets were instructed to regard the points in the PDG payoff matrix as valuable to themselves, so that presumably each target should have been attempting to obtain some. The fact that in PDG defection dominates cooperation in terms of own gain makes it a reasonable, effective, mighty way to achieve such a goal. If cooperation is seen only in terms of benefitting the other with no concern for self, as appears to have occurred with Os and Rs, then their judgments of it as ineffective, weak, irrational, is understandable.

However, at the very heart of the dilemma is the fact that the cooperative behavior, if mutual, can also maximize one's own welfare. If self interest is seen as a partial motivation for cooperation, then it too can be judged as sensible, effective, mighty. Unlike Os and Rs, J judges interpreted the cooperative target as (at least partially) driven by Joint Gain, which includes a component of self-interest. Hence the Js could see the behavior of this target as more mighty than the purely altruistic cooperation seen by Os and Rs. Unlike Os and Rs then, Js see both types of behavior as ways to benefit self, which might account for their tendency to make balanced judgments of each act's effectiveness.

Judgments of Morality

The Js see both cooperation and defection as behaviors that are driven by self-interest. Cooperation, however, provides benefit to the other as well. Thus, Js may reason that the major difference between cooperation and defection involves a choice between benefitting the other, and being indifferent to his or her needs. While such (latter) aloofness might be morally acceptable if it involves cost to the self, it may be judged rather immoral if, as in PDG, it is relatively free.

The Os see little difference in the morality of cooperation and defection. Their social motivational interpretations of each act suggest that they view cooperation and defection as pro-other, self-indifferent, and as pro-self, other-indifferent respectively. Given that morality is not seen exclusively in terms of benefits to others, but also includes a belief that the self is worthy of reward, the judged morality of each target could achieve the sort of balance observed in this group.

Like Js, the R judges saw a large difference in the morality of cooperation and defection. Their social motive interpretations suggest that these acts are seen in terms of a desire to benefit or to surpass and dominate the other, to help or to hurt. Such a view could lead to the different morality judgments observed in this group.

In the present study then, differences in the might and morality judgments of Js, Os and Rs can be understood in terms of the social motivations each group sees as responsible for the targets' actions. The general utility of such an approach can only be demonstrated in future research which takes a strongly parametric approach to the might versus morality effect itself. That is, under what conditions does the effect obtain, and when does it not? Are changes in might morality judgments accompanied by changes in social motivational interpretations, and do these latter changes help to rationalize the might and morality results?

References

Bem, D. J., & Lord, C. G. (1979). Template matching: A proposal for probing the ecological validity of experimental settings in social psychology. *Journal of Personality and Social Psychology*, **37**, 833–846.

Griesinger, D. W., & Livingston, J. W., Jr. (1973). Toward a model of interpersonal motivation in experimental games. *Behavioral Science*, **18**, 173–188.

Kelley, H. H., & Stahelski, A. J. (1970). Social interaction bases of cooperators' and

competitors' beliefs about others. *Journal of Personality and Social Psychology*, **16**, 66–91.
Kuhlman, D. M., & Marshello, A. (1975). Individual differences in game motivation as moderators of preprogrammed strategy effects in prisoner's dilemma. *Journal of Personality and Social Psychology*, **32**, 922–931.
Kuhlman, D. M., & Wimberley, D. C. (1976). Expectation of choice behavior held by cooperators, competitors, and individualists across four classes of experimental game. *Journal of Personality and Social Psychology*, **34**, 69–81.
Kuhlman, D. M., Camac, C., & Cunha, D. A. (1986). Individual differences in social orientation. In H. Wilke, D. Messick, and C. Rutte (Eds), *Experimental Social Dilemmas*. New York: Verlag Peter Lang.
Liebrand, W. B. G., & Van Run, G. J. (1985), The effects of social motives on behavior in social dilemmas in two cultures. *Journal of Experimental Social Psychology*, **21**, 86–102.
Liebrand, W. B. G., Jansen, R. W. T. L., Rijken, V. M., & Suhre, C. J. M. (1986). Might over morality: Social values and the perception of other players in experimental games. *Journal of Experimental Social Psychology*, **22**, 203–215.
MacCrimmon, K. R., & Messick, D. M. (1976). A framework for social values. *Behavioral Science*, **21**, 86–100.
McClintock, C. G. (1978). Social values: Their definition, measurement, and development. *Journal of Research and Development in Education*, **12**, 121–137.
McClintock, C. G., & Allison, S. (1989). Social value orientation and helping behavior. *Journal of Applied Social Psychology*, **19**, 353–362.
Messick, D. M., & McClintock, C. G. (1968). Motivational bases of choice in experimental games. *Journal of Experimental Social Psychology*, **4**, 1–25.
Pruitt, D. G., & Kimmel, M. J. (1977). Twenty years of experimental gaming: Critique, synthesis and suggestions for the future. *Annual Review of Psychology*, **28**, 363–392.
Sherif, M. & Hovland, C. I. (1961). *Social Judgement: Assimilation and Contrast Effects in Communication and Attitude Change*. New Haven: Yale University.

Notes

1. All repeated measures effects reported here were tested via the Multivariate Analysis of Variance model.
2. Formally our decomposed PDG differs from classic Prisoner's Dilemma by providing an Aggression choice separate from that which maximizes both Own and Relative Gain.
3. This test is a $1-df$ contrast of Rs and Js. The p-value is not "corrected" for being based on a *post-hoc* test. Under the circumstances, this creates no problem regarding the decision to retain the Hn, since any *post-hoc* test would be more conservative.

8

Rationality and Morality in Social Dilemmas: The Influence of Social Value Orientations*

PAUL A. M. VAN LANGE
Free University, Amsterdam, The Netherlands

In social dilemmas, people are faced with a conflict between the pursuit of their own individual outcomes and the pursuit of collective outcomes. Such a decision problem underlying these dilemmas arises from two conflicting definitions of rationality, one individualistic the other collectivistic (Kahan, 1974). Individual rationality prescribes noncooperation because this leads to higher individual outcomes than cooperation, irrespective of others' choices. Collective rationality, however, prescribes cooperation because individual outcomes for each participant will be higher if all cooperate than if all do not. Given these two conflicting definitions, the social dilemma structure reflects a decision problem with *no objective rational* solution.

In addition, the decision problem underlying social dilemmas may also be seen or experienced as a moral issue. In most social dilemmas the noncooperative choice implies individual gain at some costs to others, while the cooperative choice implies gain to others at some costs to oneself. The extent to which one should (noncooperation) or should not (cooperation) pursue own gain at the expense of the well-being of others, is likely to be seen in terms of fairness, or *morality* (cf. Dawes, 1980; Deutsch, 1982; McClintock & Van Avermaet, 1982; Liebrand, Jansen, Rijken, & Suhre, 1986). Indeed, people do tend to evaluate choices in social dilemmas in moral terms.

* The present chapter was completed while the author was an NWO-Fellow (Netherlands Organization for Scientific Research) at the Department of Psychology at the University of Delaware, USA. The author would like to thank Michael Platow for his very helpful comments on an earlier version of this chapter. Correspondence concerning this chapter should be addressed to Paul van Lange, Department of Social Psychology, Free University Amsterdam, De Boelelaan 1081, 1081 HV Amsterdam, The Netherlands.

The way in which social dilemmas are interpreted in terms of rationality and morality, however, may vary from person to person. One major assumption underlying the present chapter is that pre-existing individual differences in *social value orientations* influence such interpretations.

Below we first discuss social value orientations, including their theoretical relevance for social dilemma situations. Following this, we discuss how interpretations of social dilemmas in terms of rationality and morality may be influenced by individuals' social value orientations. Finally, we describe two experiments designed to study interpretations of either rationality or morality.

Individual Differences in Social Value Orientations

More than twenty years ago, Messick and McClintock (1968) were among the first to demonstrate that people differ in how they typically evaluate outcomes for themselves and others. Using a "decomposed game" approach, they identified three distinct social value orientations, which they referred to as *cooperation* (i.e., the preference to maximize joint outcomes), *individualism* (i.e., the preference to maximize own outcomes with no regard for others' outcomes) and *competition* (i.e., the preference to maximize relative advantage in favor of self). More recent research has shown that these individual differences tend to be temporally stable (Kuhlman, Camac, & Cunha, 1986; McClintock & Allison, 1989), are predictive of overt behavior, such as helping behavior (McClintock & Allison, 1989), and are related in a number of meaningful ways to other personality characteristics (Kagan & Knight, 1981) as well as personality descriptions made by roommates and friends (Bem & Lord, 1979).

The consistent finding across social dilemma studies is that cooperators (also referred to as "pro-socials") show more self-restraint, or more cooperative choice behavior (Kramer, McClintock, & Messick, 1986; Kuhlman & Marshello, 1975; Liebrand & Van Run, 1985; McClintock & Liebrand, 1988) and also expect more cooperation from others than individualists or competitors do (Grzelak, 1982; Kelley & Stahelski, 1970a, b; Kuhlman & Wimberley, 1976).

The influence of individuals' social value orientation on both their own choice behavior and their expectations of others' choice behavior in social dilemmas can be understood in terms of Kelley and Thibaut's (1978) *transformation analysis* (cf. McClintock & Liebrand, 1988). This analysis assumes that the presented or objective outcome interdependence structure of a task, "*the given matrix*," undergoes a series of psychological transformations to become a "*subjective matrix*" from which individuals make their choices.

Kelley and Thibaut (1978) assume that these transformations are in part dictated by the relative weights that one assigns to own, other's, and the difference between own and other's outcomes. Cooperators or pro-socials are assumed to transform a given matrix into a subjective matrix by assigning positive values to both own and other's outcomes. Individualists are assumed to transform a given matrix by placing the heaviest or exclusive weight on outcomes for self. Finally, competitors are assumed to transform a given matrix by computing the differences between own and other's outcomes, valuing the set of outcomes providing the greatest relative advantage to self.

The importance of these transformations dictated by one's social value orientation is at least twofold. First, the transformation analysis helps to describe and explain why pro-socials are more likely than individualists and competitors to make cooperative decisions in a variety of social dilemma tasks.

Second, the transformation analysis helps to explain why some external forces to cooperate or not cooperate can differentially influence people with different social value orientations. A demonstration of such a moderating influence of social value orientations is provided by Kuhlman and Marshello (1975) and McClintock and Liebrand (1988). These studies show that, relative to the 100 percent cooperative strategy, the effectiveness of the well-known Tit for Tat (TFT) strategy (Axelrod, 1984) is dependent upon social value orientation. Specifically, compared to a 100 percent cooperative other, TFT produces only a significant increase in cooperation by people holding individualistic value orientations. Pro-socials and competitors do not respond significantly different to these two strategies. The transformation analysis provides an explanation why external punishments for noncooperation are less essential to pro-socials (who are *a priori* inclined to maximize joint gain) than they are to individualists. Further, punishments for noncooperation are also less important to competitors for whom relative benefits do not increase by cooperative responses to TFT than they are to individualists for whom individual benefits do increase by cooperative responses to TFT.

Finally, research on the influence of social value orientations on choice behavior in social dilemmas (Kuhlman & Marshello, 1975; McClintock & Liebrand, 1988) as well as Kelley and Thibaut's (1978) transformation analysis provide support for the proposition that not all people pursue exclusively own gain. Hence, departures from "rational self-interest" or *homo economicus* assumptions (cf. Roth, 1988) are not necessarily irrational or foolish, but may be perfectly consistent with a cooperative or a competitive transformation of a "given" social dilemma. Thus, understanding such transformation processes, as well as the way in which people with different social value orientations define or construe social dilemma situations, provide a stronger basis for understanding both social decision making in general, and ways in which cooperative solutions to social dilemmas can be promoted in particular.

Two Experiments on Rationality and Morality

Given Kelley and Thibaut's transformation analysis, it is likely that people with different social value orientations will have different interpretations or evaluations of cooperative and noncooperative choices in social dilemmas. Prior research conducted to examine such differential interpretations have done so by asking subjects to make judgments of cooperation and noncooperation. Among the possible interpretations, the dimensions of rationality or intelligence and morality have been shown to be important (McClintock & Liebrand, 1988; Van Lange, Liebrand, & Kuhlman, 1990). The line of research described in this chapter, however, extends this previous work by utilizing a substantially different paradigm. Specifically, this paradigm employs a two-person social dilemma in which subjects are led to believe that the other is either high or low on intelligence (Experiment 1), or high or low on morality (Experiment 2). As will be discussed, the dimensions of intelligence and morality are of theoretical and empirical relevance not only for interpretations of social dilemmas, but they reflect two ubiquitous dimensions of person perception as well. Specifically, intellectual (i.e., intelligent vs. unintelligent) and social desirability (good vs. bad) have been shown to be two distinct dimensions along which people tend to organize impressions of their social worlds (cf. Rosenberg & Sedlak, 1972; Schneider, 1973).

The major purpose of the present line of research is threefold: (1) to demonstrate that expected cooperation from another will be influenced by perceptions of other's intelligence and morality, (2) to examine the moderating influence of social value orientations, and (3) to examine the mediating role of expected cooperation for one's own cooperative choice behavior. The present line of research utilizes a single trial social dilemma so as to avoid strategic and temporal considerations influences on perceptions of rationality and morality.

Consistent with previous research (e.g., McClintock & Liebrand, 1988), both experiments described here consisted of two major tasks. Initially, subjects responded to a series of decomposed games (Messick & McClintock, 1968) in order to assess each subject's dominant social value orientation. In the second task a two-person social dilemma was explained. The dilemma provides five options varying in the degree to which they optimize joint welfare. After subjects received personality information about the interdependent other, they were asked to indicate the choice they expected the other to make, and the choice they wished to make themselves. The experiments we discuss in the present chapter, Experiments 1 and 2, have been described in more detail by Van Lange and Liebrand (1991a) and Van Lange and Liebrand (1991b), respectively.

Experiment 1. Rationality in Social Dilemmas

As mentioned before, there is no objective rational solution to a social dilemma. This is not to imply, however, that people do not have their own subjective rational solutions to social dilemmas. Indeed, there is evidence that "naive" participants, as well as formal game theorists, are inclined to perceive solutions to social dilemmas in terms of rationality (Van Lange, Liebrand, & Kuhlman, 1990). Specifically, cooperative individuals associate cooperation with high intelligence and noncooperation with low intelligence, whereas noncooperative individuals make just the opposite association.

The specific transformations people make of the given matrix has strong implications for whether a cooperative is perceived as more, or less, intelligent than a noncooperative choice in social dilemmas. If individuals with pro-social value orientations base their perceptions of intelligent behavior on a subjective matrix in which outcomes for self and the other are positively combined, then they should be inclined to take the collective perspective on rational behavior, viewing cooperation as more rational, and hence more intelligent, than noncooperation. Conversely, if individualists and competitors base their perceptions of intelligent behavior on a subjective matrix in which own outcomes or relative outcomes are valued, then they should be inclined to take a strong individualistic or egocentric perspective of rational behavior, viewing noncooperation as more intelligent than cooperation. Thus, individuals' social goal or value orientation should influence the perceived relationship between rationality and cooperation in social dilemmas, with pro-socials perceiving a positive relationship and individualists and competitors a negative relationship. This is referred to as the *Goal Prescribes Rationality Principle* (cf. Van Lange *et al.*, 1990; Van Lange & Liebrand, 1991a).

Effects of Social Value Orientation and Other's Intelligence on Expected Cooperation

When no information about others is available, pro-socials, individualists and competitors expect others to have similar social value orientations as themselves (Kuhlman & Wimberley, 1976). That is, people with different social value orientations are inclined to assume that others will make the same transformations of the given matrix as they do themselves (Maki, Thorngate, & McClintock, 1979). Pro-socials should expect others to take a collective perspective on rationality and individualists and competitors an egocentric perspective in a social dilemma task. These expectations are further influenced by direct evidence that the other person is indeed rational or intelligent.

When the other is perceived as relatively unintelligent, however, people will have reason to doubt the other's rational approach to social dilemmas. On the basis of the Goal Prescribes Rationality Principle, we assumed that pro-social subjects believe that an unintelligent other is less likely to take a collective perspective of rationality than an intelligent other. Hence, it was predicted that pro-socials would expect less cooperation from an unintelligent other than from an intelligent other. Individualistic and competitive subjects, however, were assumed to believe that an unintelligent other is less likely to take an individualistic or egocentric perspective of rationality than an intelligent other. Hence, it was predicted that individualists and competitors would expect more cooperation from an unintelligent other than from an intelligent other.

As can be seen from Fig. 8.1a, support is found for the Goal Prescribes Rationality Principle. Pro-socials did indeed expect more cooperation from another seen as intelligent than from another seen as unintelligent, whereas individualists and competitors tended to expect relatively more cooperation from another seen as unintelligent.

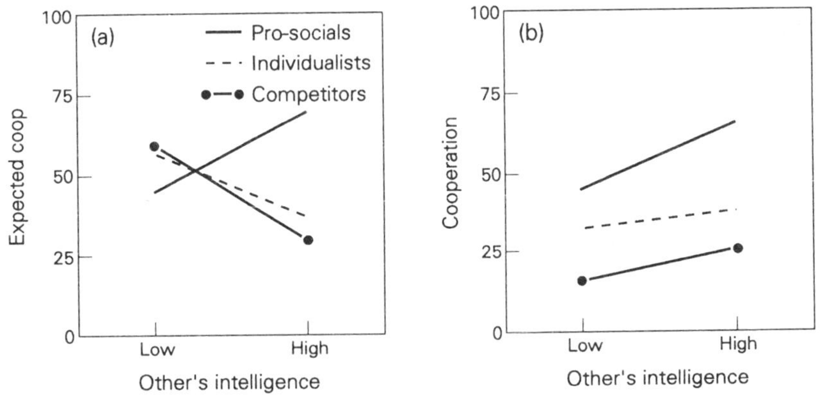

FIG. 8.1 Expected cooperation from the other (a), and own cooperative choice behavior (b) as a function of social value orientation and other's intelligence.

Effects of Social Value Orientation and Other's Intelligence on Own Cooperative Choice Behavior

Transformations depend not only upon individual's social value orientations, but on the specific transformation they expect the other(s) to make as well (cf. Kelley & Thibaut, 1978). In iterated or sequential social dilemmas for two persons, pro-social subjects have been shown to be cooperative unless they have sufficient evidence, based upon previous trials, that the other is making individualistic or competitive transformations (Kelley & Stahelski, 1970a; Kuhlman & Marshello, 1975; McClintock & Liebrand, 1988). This movement of pro-socials toward noncooperative behavior as a result of other's repeated noncooperation has been referred to as *behavioral assimilation* (Kelley & Stahelski, 1970a).

Interestingly, the above studies indicate also that behavioral assimilation is an asymmetric process. That is, competitors and individualists tend not to assimilate to cooperative behavior when they have strong evidence (based upon previous trials) that the other is making cooperative transformations. Thus, individualists and competitors show *no* behavioral assimilation to other's repeated cooperation.

The asymmetric nature of behavioral assimilation has strong implications for the extent to which expected cooperation influences cooperative choice behavior in a single-trial two-person social dilemma. Given pro-socials' concern for collective outcomes coupled with their reluctance to being exploited, we assumed a strong correspondence between expected cooperation and own willingness to cooperate. That is, pro-socials will cooperate to the extent that the other is expected to do the same. In contrast to this, individualists' and competitors' concern for own and relative outcomes, coupled with their readiness to exploit cooperation, we assumed a relatively weak correspondence between expected cooperation from the other and own cooperative behavior. That is, individualists and competitors tend not to cooperate, regardless of their expectations of other's choice behavior.

The above analysis led us to hypothesize, first, that pro-socials will cooperate more toward others from whom they expect high levels of cooperation (another perceived as intelligent) than toward others from whom they expect lower levels of cooperation (another perceived as unintelligent). Second, we hypothesized that individualistic and competitive subjects will not tend to cooperate, regardless of their expectations of other's high (another perceived as intelligent) or low (another perceived as unintelligent) levels of cooperation.

As can be seen from the results in Fig. 8.1b, pro-socials did cooperate more toward another seen as intelligent than toward another seen as unintelligent. Further, individualists and competitors tended to cooperate more toward another seen as intelligent than toward another seen as unintelligent. An increase in the level of cooperation expected from an unintelligent other, relative to an intelligent other, does not seem to enhance cooperative choice behavior in individualists and competitors at all.

Experiment 2. Morality in Social Dilemmas

In many societies, behaviors reflecting cooperative intentions or a concern for the well-being of others have a strong moral meaning. With regard to social dilemma situations, Dawes (1980) was among the first to stress the importance of morality in enhancing cooperative decisions. For example, people may evaluate the "rights" and "wrongs" of a decision, and, in doing so, decide on a course of action which they consider as right, even at some personal costs. Indeed, cooperative decisions tend to increase in frequency when an experimenter emphasizes the rights of cooperation and wrongs of noncooperation (described in Dawes, 1980).

Even in the absence of such "moralizing," people tend to evaluate the "rights" and "wrongs" of decisions in social dilemmas. That is, subjects' judgments or causal attributions of cooperative and noncooperative choices in social dilemmas reveal that cooperation is viewed as considerably more moral (e.g., fairer, more honest) than noncooperation (e.g., Kelley *et al.*, 1970; Liebrand *et al.*, 1986; McClintock & Liebrand, 1988; Van Lange *et al.*, 1990).

There is evidence, however, that the extent to which cooperation is seen as more moral than noncooperation is moderated by social value orientations. Consistent with their prediction based upon the *Might over Morality Hypothesis*,[1] Liebrand *et al.* (1986) observed that people with pro-social orientations discriminated cooperation and noncooperation in social dilemmas more in terms of morality than people with individualistic or competitive orientations did. Thus, pro-socials perceive a stronger positive relationship between morality and cooperation than do individualists and competitors.

Effects of Social Value Orientation and Other's Morality on Expected Cooperation

If pro-socials perceive a stronger relationship between morality and cooperation than do individualists and competitors, then cooperative expectations based upon different levels of perceived morality may be moderated by individuals' social value orientations. Specifically, on the basis of the Might over Morality Hypothesis, we predicted that the differential magnitude of expected cooperation from another perceived as highly moral than from another seen as low on morality would be greater for pro-socials than for individualists and competitors.

As can be seen from Fig. 8.2a, we found a strong main effect for perceptions of other's morality. Contrary to our Might over Morality prediction, however, this effect was *not* moderated by individual differences in social value orientations. Surprisingly, but consistent with other research (cf. Van Lange & Liebrand, 1991b), subjects of all social values expected (considerably) more cooperation from another seen as highly moral than from another seen as low on morality.

The present findings indicate that people with different social value orientations do not differ in how they interpret morality information (i.e.,

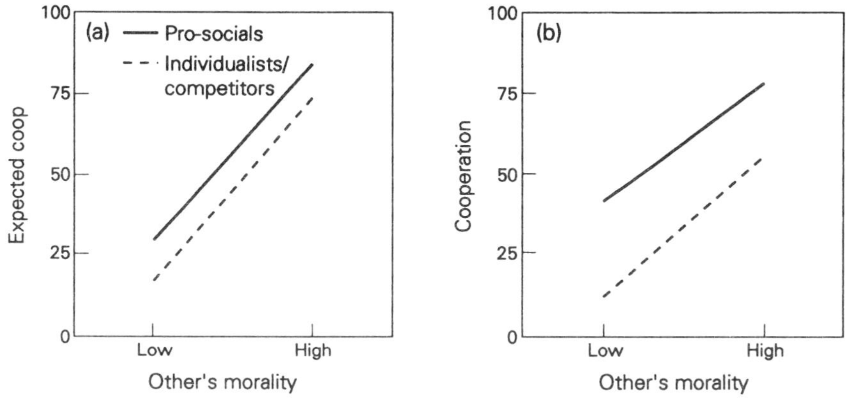

FIG. 8.2 Expected cooperation from the other (a), and own cooperative choice behavior (b) as a function of social value orientation and other's morality. [*Note*: Because relatively few subjects could be classified as individualistic or competitive in this experiment, we collapsed across these two social value orientations.]

they all see a positive relationship between morality and cooperation), and more interestingly, they do not seem to differ in the absolute importance, or perhaps informativeness, they assign to morality. Apparently, morality has an important meaning in social dilemmas, regardless of individuals' social value orientation.

Effects of Social Value Orientation and Other's Morality on Own Cooperative Choice Behavior

Given the asymmetric nature of behavioral assimilation, i.e., that pro-socials assimilate to noncooperation, and individualists and competitors do not assimilate to cooperation, we expected again that expected cooperation from the other would influence cooperative choice behavior by pro-socials to a larger extent than that of individualists and competitors. As for expected cooperation from other, it was observed that pro-socials' choice behavior as well as that of individualists and competitors were strongly influenced by different levels of perceived morality. As can be seen from Fig. 8.2b, another perceived as high on morality elicited considerably more cooperation than another seen as low on morality. Further, expected cooperation was strongly correlated with own cooperation for pro-socials as well as individualists and competitors, suggesting a relatively strong mediating role of expected cooperation.

The present finding that individualists and competitors behaved considerably more cooperatively to another from whom they expect high (a highly moral other) than another from whom they expect low (another low on morality) levels of cooperation, gives rise to a number of interesting questions. For example, why do individualists and competitors not cooperate when they can be reasonably confident (based upon previous trials) that a 100 percent cooperative other is going to make a cooperative choice in the next trial (cf. Kuhlman & Marshello, 1975; McClintock & Liebrand, 1988)?

One plausible explanation is that individualists and competitors should also be relatively confident that the other person has true and intentional cooperative intentions. When the other cooperates 100 percent of the time, even if they themselves do not cooperate, they indeed might attribute weakness and ignorance rather than an intrinsic concern for the well-being of others to the other (cf. Liebrand *et al.*, 1986). These judgments or attributions of cooperative others to weakness and ignorance may help to rationalize their own exploitation.

Finally, the present findings are important because they indicate that individualists and competitors can be stimulated to cooperate, without changing the payoff structure in ways that enable them to pursue their *a priori* goals of own and relative gain, respectively. Hence, it seems indeed likely that the transformations individualists and competitors tend to make depend not only upon own values, but upon perceived characteristics of the other as well (cf. Kelley & Thibaut, 1978).

Conclusions

The major purpose of the research described in this chapter was threefold: (1) to demonstrate that expected cooperation from another will be influenced by perceptions of other's intelligence and morality, (2) to examine the moderating influence of social value orientations, and (3) to examine the mediating role of expected cooperation for one's own cooperative choice behavior.

Expected Cooperation as a Function of Perceived Intelligence and Morality

First of all, the present research indicates that the dimensions of both intelligence and morality are important for how much cooperation interdependent actors anticipate from one another. Generally, expected cooperation from interdependent others was significantly influenced by different levels of perceived intelligence and perceived morality for all three groups of social value orientations. This indicates the general importance of rationality and morality as different ways in which social dilemmas can be understood.

The effect of perceived intelligence on expected cooperation was generally consistent with the predictions based upon the Goal Prescribes

Rationality Principle (Van Lange *et al.*, 1990; Van Lange & Liebrand, 1991a). The finding that pro-socials perceive a positive and individualists and competitors a negative relationship between intelligence and cooperation is consistent with the view that people with different social value orientations use different transformed matrices to reach their ultimate decisions (cf. Kelley & Thibaut, 1978). The general conclusion is that a significant number of people do not associate the pursuit of own benefits in social dilemmas with intelligence, and indeed, departures from self-interest are not necessarily (seen as) irrational, as recognized earlier by Kuhlman and Marshello (1975) and McClintock and Liebrand (1988).

The effect of perceived morality on expected cooperation revealed strong similarities between people with different social value orientations. In Experiment 2 we observed that people expected considerably more cooperation from another seen as highly moral than from another seen as low on morality, and this effect was *not* moderated by social value orientation when only morality information about the other was given. As mentioned earlier, this prediction has been supported in studies where subjects are asked to judge cooperative and noncooperative behavior (Liebrand *et al.*, 1986). The judgmental paradigm used by Liebrand *et al.* may also elicit other interpretations than morality (e.g., intelligence, or potency), and hence subjects may differ in the weight they assign to morality interpretations *relative* to other possible interpretations. In Experiment 2, subjects were provided only with morality information. Therefore, it seems likely that they did not weigh the importance of morality information relative to other kinds of information to the extent they did in the Liebrand *et al.* study. A recent study of Van Lange and Kuhlman (1991) has addressed this issue by providing subjects with both morality and intelligence information about the interdependent other. Consistent with the above reasoning, it was found that pro-social subjects used morality information more heavily than individualists and competitors. Thus, the findings of this study in combination with the findings of Experiment 2 suggest that subjects with different social value orientations do not differ so much in the absolute importance they assign to morality, but more so in the importance they assign to morality relative to intelligence.

Finally, an interesting implication of the intelligence and morality findings together is that people with different social value orientations might differ in their implicit personality theories (e.g., Schneider, 1973), or perceived interrelationships between personality attributes. Pro-socials are inclined to infer cooperation from the two different positive personality attributes of intelligence and morality, whereas individualists and competitors tend to infer cooperation from morality and *un*intelligence. Within the framework of cooperation and competition, these findings indicate that pro-socials tend to perceive intelligence and morality as positively related, whereas individualists and competitors tend to see these attributes as negatively related. This would lead to the interesting idea that pro-socials might view people seen as simultaneously intelligent *and* moral as more common in their social worlds than individualists and competitors who might view unintelligent and moral or intelligent and nonmoral people as relatively more common.

The Relationship between Expected Cooperation and Own Cooperative Choice Behavior

Previous work on iterated social dilemmas has indicated that pro-socials come to behave similarly to noncooperative others, whereas individualists and competitors do not show behavioral assimilation to cooperative others (Kelley & Stahelski, 1970a; Kuhlman & Marshello, 1975; McClintock & Liebrand, 1988). On the basis of this work, it was generally assumed that expected cooperation would influence own cooperative behavior more among the people with pro-social orientations than among those with individualistic or competitive orientations.

The present studies utilizing a single-trial social dilemma show that things are more complicated. For pro-socials we found, indeed, that different levels of both perceived intelligence and perceived morality produced a similar effect on expected cooperation and own cooperation. For individualists and competitors, we found that the effects for perceived morality only produced similar effects on expected cooperation and own cooperation: They expected more cooperation from, and cooperated more with, moral others than others seen as low on morality. With regard to the effect for perceived intelligence, however, we found that individualists and competitors expected relatively more cooperation from unintelligent others, but tended to cooperate more with others seen as intelligent.

The pattern of findings indicate that individualists and competitors are more likely to cooperate when they have cooperative expectations that are based upon perceived morality than when such expectations are based upon a perceived lack of intelligence. This suggests that the extent to which expected cooperation influences own cooperative behavior in individualists and competitors is mediated by the reasons why they think the other is likely to cooperate.

Given the finding that individualists and competitors do cooperate with moral others, why then do they not cooperate with others seen as low on intelligence, from whom they also expect cooperation? One possible explanation is that low intelligence is a negative personality attribute that allows one to easily blame the other for irrational behavior, thereby rationalizing their own exploitation. As mentioned before, such perceptions may explain why individualists and competitors do not cooperate with others who cooperate all the time (cf. Liebrand *et al.*, 1986). A complementary explanation would be that individualists and competitors were not very confident about the cooperation they expected on the basis of low intelligence, and preferred to give themselves rather than the other the benefit of the doubt.

Finally, the present chapter describes evidence for the influence of both individual differences in social value orientation and characteristics of others on one's own choice behavior. One of the major conclusions in this regard is that perceptions of certain characteristics of the other strongly influence cooperative choice behavior of people with different social value orientations. The effects of perceived characteristics in terms of morality were so strong that pro-socials were willing to display behaviors inconsistent with their values (i.e., when the other is seen as nonmoral). Similarly, individualists and competitors can be motivated to display behaviors that are quite inconsistent with their values (i.e., when the other is seen as moral). The latter finding is of both theoretical and practical interest in that it suggests that individualists and competitors do not necessarily tend to choose for egocentrically rational options; that is, they do not seem to be unconditionally noncooperative in their interpersonal orientation. This suggests that there are important possibilities to stimulate cooperative behavior in individualists and competitors.

References

Axelrod, R. (1984). *The Evolution of Cooperation.* New York: Basic Books.

Bem, D. J., & Lord, C. G. (1979). Template matching: A proposal for probing the ecological validity of experimental settings in social psychology. *Journal of Personality and Social Psychology*, **37**, 833–846.

Dawes, R. M. (1980). Social dilemmas. *Annual Review of Psychology*, **31**, 169–193.

Deutsch, M. (1982). Interdependence and psychological orientation. In V. Derlage & J. Grzelak (Eds), *Cooperation and Helping Behavior: Theories and Research.* New York: Academic Press.

Grzelak, J. L. (1982). Preferences and cognitive processes in interdependence situations: A theoretical analysis of cooperation. In V. Derlage & J. Grzelak (Eds), *Cooperation and Helping Behavior: Theories and Research.* New York: Academic Press.

Kagan, S., & Knight, G. P. (1981). Social motives among Anglo American and Mexican American children: Experimental and projective measures. *Journal of Research in Personality*, **15**, 93–106.

Kahan, J. P. (1974). Rationality, the prisoner's dilemma, and population. *Journal of Social Issues*, **4**, 189–210.

Kelley, H. H., & Stahelski, A. J. (1970a). Social interaction basis of cooperators' and competitors' beliefs about others. *Journal of Personality and Social Psychology*, **16**, 66–91.

Kelley, H. H., & Stahelski, A. J. (1970b). Errors in perception of intentions in a mixed-motive game. *Journal of Experimental Social Psychology*, **6**, 379–400.

Kelley, H. H., & Thibaut, J. W. (1978). *Interpersonal Relations.* New York: Wiley.

Kelley, H. H., Shure, G. H., Deutsch, M., Faucheux, C., Lanzetta, J. T., Moscovici, S., Nuttin, J. M., Rabbie, J. M., & Thibaut, J. W. (1970). A comparative experimental study of negotiation behavior. *Journal of Personality and Social Psychology*, **16**, 411–438.

Kramer, R. M., McClintock, C. G., & Messick, D. M. (1986). Social values and cooperative response to a simulated resource conservation crisis. *Journal of Personality*, **54**, 576–592.

Kuhlman, D. M., & Marshello, A. (1975). Individual differences in game motivation as moderators of preprogrammed strategic effects in prisoner's dilemma. *Journal of Personality and Social Psychology*, **32**, 922–931.

Kuhlman, D. M., & Wimberley, D. C. (1976). Expectation of choice behavior held by cooperators, competitors, and individualists across four classes of experimental game. *Journal of Personality and Social Psychology*, **34**, 69–81.

Kuhlman, D. M., Camac, C., & Cunha, D. A. (1986). Individual differences in social orientation. In H. Wilke, D. Messick, and C. Rutte (Eds), *Experimental Social Dilemmas*. New York: Verlag Peter Lang.

Liebrand, W. B. G., & Van Run, G. J. (1985). The effect of social motives across two cultures on behavior in social dilemmas. *Journal of Experimental Social Psychology*, **21**, 86–102.

Liebrand, W. B. G., Jansen, R. W. T. L., Rijken, V. M., & Suhre, C. J. M. (1986). Might over Morality: Social values and the perception of other players in experimental games. *Journal of Experimental Social Psychology*, **22**, 203–215.

Maki, J. E., Thorngate, W. B., & McClintock, C. G. (1979). Predictions and perceptions of social motives. *Journal of Personality and Social Psychology*, **37**, 203–220.

McClintock, C. G. (1978). Social values: Their definition, measurement, and development. *Journal of Research and Development in Education*, **12**, 121–137.

McClintock, C. G., & Allison, S. (1989). Social value orientation and helping behavior. *Journal of Applied Social Psychology*, **19**, 353–362.

McClintock, C. G., & Liebrand, W. B. G. (1988). The role of interdependence structure, individual value orientation and other's strategy in social decision making: A transformational analysis. *Journal of Personality and Social Psychology*, **55**, 296–409.

McClintock, C. G., & Van Avermaet, E. (1982). Social values and rules of fairness: A theoretical perspective. In V. Derlage & J. Grzelak (Eds), *Cooperation and Helping Behavior: Theories and Research*. New York: Academic Press.

Messick, D. M., & McClintock, C. G. (1968). Motivational basis of choice in experimental games. *Journal of Experimental Social Psychology*, **4**, 1–25.

Rosenberg, S., & Sedlak, A. (1972). Structural representations of implicit personality theory. In L. Berkowitz (Ed.), *Advances in Experimental Social Psychology*. New York: Academic Press.

Roth, A. E. (1988). Laboratory experimentation in economics: A methodological overview. *The Economic Journal*, **98**, 974–1031.

Schneider, D. J. (1973). Implicit personality theory: A review. *Psychological Bulletin*, **79**, 294–309.

Van Lange, P. A. M., & Kuhlman, D. M. (1991). Social value orientation and the effects of perceptions of other's intelligence and other's morality in a social dilemma. Unpublished paper. Free University Amsterdam.

Van Lange, P. A. M., & Liebrand, W. B. G. (1991a). Social value orientation and the effects of other's intelligence in a social dilemma: A test of the Goal Prescribes Rationality Principle. *European Journal of Social Psychology*, **21**, 273–292.

Van Lange, P. A. M., & Liebrand, W. B. G. (1991b). The influence of other's morality and own social value orientation on cooperation in two countries. *International Journal of Psychology*, **26**, 429–449.

Van Lange, P. A. M., Liebrand, W. B. G., & Kuhlman, D. M. (1990). Causal attribution of choice behavior in three *N*-person prisoner's dilemma. *Journal of Experimental Social Psychology*, **26**, 34–48.

Note

1. The Might over Morality Hypothesis is not only concerned with differential interpretations of cooperation and noncooperation along the morality, or the good vs. bad dimension, but also along the potency, or the strong vs. weak dimension (cf. Liebrand *et al.*, 1986; McClintock & Liebrand, 1988).

9

Information Preferences in a Two-person Social Dilemma

CURT CAMAC
Roanoke College

Choice behavior within social dilemmas is a well researched topic in social psychology. Studies have examined the effects of payoff parameters (Guyer & Rapoport, 1972; Komorita, Sweeney, & Kravitz, 1980) and the effects of individual difference variables such as social values or social orientations (Messick & McClintock, 1968; Kuhlman & Marshello, 1975; Liebrand, 1984; Liebrand & Van Ruen, 1985) on social dilemma outcomes. However, with the exception of research concerning the relationship between cooperative expectations and choice behavior (Kelley & Stahelski, 1970; Dawes, McTavish, & Shaklee, 1977; Kuhlman & Wimberley, 1976; Messé & Sivacek, 1979), relatively few studies have examined the cognitive processes which underlie individual decision-making in social dilemmas. (Although, as may be noted from several of the chapters in this text and from recent studies such as McClintock & Liebrand (1988), study of these cognitive processes is increasing.)

The primary focus of this chapter is on one cognitive process, information search, which has received little attention in the social dilemma context, but which has been shown to have predictable effects in the area of social perception (Fiske & Taylor, 1984). The basic principle is that our perception and memory for persons, situations, and events are influenced by cognitive structures or schemata which are organized representations of our beliefs, knowledge, motivations, and behavioral tendencies (Markus & Zajonc, 1985). Given that individuals also bring motivations, beliefs, and behavioral tendencies to social dilemma situations, it follows that these should influence the course of decision making in a systematic way. For example, a cooperative individual may attend to outcomes (in a prisoner's dilemma game or PDG) which result from joint cooperation *before* considering those based on exploitation. In this way the cooperative person's goals could be seen to influence his or her information search.

Grzelak (1981) reports data which supports the notion that information search is related to the goal that one wishes to maximize. In his study, subjects who were sensitive to their partner's outcomes sought more information about the other's payoffs and other's characteristics than did individualistically oriented subjects. While Grzelak's results bolster the plausibility of the basic idea addressed here, the current study focuses on somewhat different sources of information. In the current study subjects are shown 2 × 2 matrices where several payoff parameters have been manipulated. Before making a choice in the dilemma, outcome information must be sought since the payoffs contained in the matrix have been hidden. This allows for the study of "on-line" processing, which may disclose an underlying cognitive procedure which impacts on decision making (Fiske & Taylor, 1984). It also creates a context that allows for the possibility that subjects will seek information concerning parameters that are consistent with their motivations or intentions. Discovering these underlying processes is important since preferences for one type of information over another may help us to better understand the bases for individual's choice behavior within social dilemmas. In addition, if search patterns are related to personal motivations, expectations, or predispositions, then evidence of biased decision making, such as the well known confirmation bias (Chapman & Chapman, 1982), is provided as well.

In order to describe the types of information which were manipulated in the current study, and in order to see how these may relate to individual differences in information search, the following sections describe recent research which has examined the effects of payoff manipulations and research which examines the impact of social orientations on social dilemmas.

Interest in Payoff Parameters

Research concerning choice behavior in two- and *N*-person dilemma games has focused on individual responses to payoff parameters. Several parameters have been examined, including Rapoport's (1967) index of cooperation or *K*, and Harris's (1972) parameters, *r3* and *r4*, which have become known as fear and greed, respectively. Basically, fear is the difference in payoffs as one moves from cooperation to defection if one assumes that the other will defect, while greed is the same difference under the assumption that the other cooperates. The cooperative index captures the motivation or incentive for cooperative behavior presented by the situation. It relates to the differences in payoffs offered by joint defection as compared to joint cooperation, and can also be stated as a function of fear and greed. Specifically, $K = 1 - (r3 + r4)$.

Investigators have manipulated these parameters in order to estimate the relative importance of each in determining individual choice behavior;

however, these experiments have produced discrepant results. For example, in one of the earliest studies looking at the effects of fear and greed on choice behavior in two-person games, Wyer (1969), found relatively weak effects. Further study (Wyer, 1971) showed the parameters to be better predictors if one took into account a subject's expectations regarding cooperation. Not surprisingly, greed was a better predictor of choice behavior when subjects expected the other to choose cooperatively than when they expected the other to defect. Similarly, fear was a better predictor when expected cooperation was low.

Komorita and his colleagues have extended the examination of these parameters beyond two-person dilemmas. For instance, Komorita, Sweeney, & Kravitz (1980) examined an *N*-person extension of the *K* index, and also *N*-person extensions of Harris's parameters. They found that greed was a more heavily weighted parameter than fear, and that the cooperative index was only a moderately good parameter for estimating choice behavior. In contrast, Yamagishi & Sato (1986), who also examined choice in the context of an *N*-person dilemma, observed that fear was a more salient motivator, while Liebrand, Wilke, Vogel, & Wolters (1986) manipulated these parameters in an *N*-person context and found that fear and greed were equally important determinants of choice behavior.

Individual Differences in Information Preferences

Individual differences, in the form of social orientations, were also examined by Liebrand *et al.* (1986), who observed that the parametric influences were the same for cooperators and noncooperators. However, Camac & Kuhlman (1987) examined the three parameters described above in both a two-person and six-person dilemma. While observing that fear and greed were equally important determinants of choice behavior, they also found that responsiveness to changes in game parameters depended on social orientation. Specifically, cooperators (and to a lesser extent individualists) became increasingly likely to defect as the cooperative incentive decreased while, in contrast, competitors were unaffected by changes in *K*.

Although these studies have not provided unequivocal evidence that people respond to one parameter more than another, a particularly interesting possibility is that people are differentially predisposed to look for fear, greed or *K* information. A preference for one type of information would be an indication of a cognitive bias which operates in the context of social dilemmas.

For instance, imagine that during a serious drought (such as the one which gripped much of the United States in 1988) you must decide how much water to use—a lot or a little. Before making your decision what would you rather know? Would you like to know how much better off you could be if your neighbors conserve water and you do not (greed)? Or, would you rather know how much worse off you will be if you conserve water but your neighbors do not (fear)? Or perhaps, you would rather know how much better off you (and your neighbors) will be if you all cooperate rather than all defecting (cooperative incentive). While this example is not exhaustive, since it is possible that people might prefer some source of information other than those considered above, it helps illustrate that having a preference could lead persons to act in certain ways. The person who focuses on the fact that his or her neighbours are not using water may feel that less harm will be done by using more water his or herself. On the other hand, the person who focuses on mutual losses or gains would be likely to conclude that both should conserve water.

The research of Grzelak (1981) suggests that it is likely that you might prefer to look for information which bolsters your existing intentions. Given the ubiquitous nature of the effects of social orientations within social dilemmas (Liebrand, 1986), it also seems reasonable to consider the possibility that these preferences or biases will be different for different types of actors. In fact, research on social orientations which does not focus on responsiveness to game parameters does suggest some direction for making predictions regarding the nature of a search bias.

The work of Kuhlman & Marshello (1975) and Cunha (in Kuhlman, Camac & Cunha, 1986) suggests that cooperators tend to see dilemmas in terms of mutual cooperation versus mutual defection rather than in terms of "off diagonal" outcomes which allow for exploitation. They will cooperate with another who reciprocates cooperation; however, they will turn to defection when faced with a noncooperative partner. This research also suggests that they are not greedy, since they do not exploit a partner who offers noncontingent cooperation. A reasonable prediction for this group would thus be that they will be least interested in greed information (although they might respond to it when it is given) and most interested in information relevant to mutual cooperation or mutual defection.

This same work suggests that noncooperators are much more willing to consider off diagonal outcomes. For example, Kuhlman and Marshello (1975) showed that noncooperators exploited the noncontingent cooperation of their partners, while Cunha (in Kuhlman, Camac, & Cunha, 1986) found that noncooperators were low in interpersonal trust (i.e., fearful). These data suggest that noncooperators should focus on off diagonal outcomes, and the aforementioned studies suggest that they may be greedy, that is, willing to exploit others. Therefore, the prediction for this group is that they will prefer the off diagonal cells, that is fear or greed information.

A Method for Examining Information Preferences

These hypotheses were tested in an experiment where a series of prisoner's dilemma games in which fear, greed, and *K* systematically varied were presented via a video display terminal (VDT). The participants (85 introductory psychology students) were greeted by the experimenter who oriented them toward the VDT, and from that point on all instructions and tasks were presented on the VDT. The study proceeded in two parts.

In part 1, participants were instructed in the determination of outcomes in decomposed games. After attending to these instructions they responded to twelve, three-alternative decomposed games. Half of the games were triple dominance games; that is, each alternative maximized a single type of social gain. Of the remaining games, three were J—OR games (one alternative maximized joint gain while another maximized both own and relative gain), and three were JO—R games (one alternative maximized relative gain while the other maximized own and relative gain). Subjects' responses were compared to choice patterns generated by joint, own, and relative gain strategies. This comparison was used to classify subjects as being either cooperative (max-joint), or noncooperative (max-own or max-rel). Responses (choice and time in 100ths/second) were collected by a Zenith Z-200 computer. (See Kuhlman & Wimberley, 1976, or Kuhlman, Camac, & Cunha, 1986 for a more detailed presentation of the decomposed game procedure.)

In part 2, participants were instructed in the determination of outcomes in a matrix game task (prisoner's dilemma). These instructions stressed that choices were jointly determined (although they would not receive feedback as to the choices of the other), and that they should think of the payoffs as having real value; they and the other should desire to accumulate as many points as possible.

Next, it was explained that we were interested not only in their final choices, but also in the way that they reached their decisions. Thus, we explained that we were going to cover the outcome matrix and that in order to reach their decisions they would have to "uncover" the matrix.

This uncovering task proceeded in one of two ways: In the full information condition participants were told that they would be able to uncover all four cells before making their row choice. However, they were asked to uncover the cells in order of decreasing importance. In the partial information condition participants were informed that they would have the opportunity to uncover only two cells before making their row choice, and again they should uncover the cells in order of decreasing importance. This partial condition was included as an additional means of ensuring that subjects considered the importance of the information they were seeking when they uncovered the cells.

After these instructions, the participants completed a practice trial in order to see how the uncovering and choice process would proceed. They were then informed that we wished to familiarize them with the 18 outcome matrices, which were shown on the VDT. They were allowed to view each matrix for as long as they wished; proceeding to the next by pressing "c" on the keyboard.

The outcome matrices were of three types: In the first type, fear was held constant while greed varied over six levels, ranging from .1 to .7. In the second type, greed was held constant while fear varied over six levels in the same range as above. In the last type, both fear and greed varied in approximately equal increments ranging from .14 to .85. Within each type of outcome matrix, Rapoport's *K* index varied from a low of .1 to a high of .7. All games were symmetric with the sucker's payoff set at 0. All other values (the reward for mutual cooperation, the punishment for mutual defection and the temptation for defection) varied; however, values were allowed to repeat. Still faced with the covered matrix, subjects could not "construct" the full outcome matrix without uncovering at least three cells. With the exception of three games, all matrices conformed to a PDG structure. The three games which did not conform violated the requirement that prevents an alternating strategy. However, the violation of this requirement should be unimportant in this case since each game was responded to only once, and since no feedback regarding own outcomes or other's choices were given. Table 9.1 contains two sample PDG from the current study.

TABLE 9.1 *Sample PDG used in the Current Study*

	Game 1			Game 2	
	C	D		C	D
C	40,40	0,50	C	20,20	0,25
D	50,0	5,5	D	25,0	15,15

Note: The row player's payoffs are to the left of the comma.

After familiarizing themselves with the set of matrices, subjects responded to the covered matrices which were presented in a single random order. They were informed that the ordering of the stimuli would be random and most likely different from the order in which they just viewed the complete matrices. On each trial subjects provided two uncoverings (or four in the full information condition) and a row choice which was recorded by the computer.

In order to address the main questions of interest, participants' first two uncoverings were coded in terms of several *a priori* patterns. Since the games in the current study were symmetric, information relevant to greed could be obtained in two ways. By uncovering the upper-left (cell 1) and lower-left (cell 3) cells, information concerning greed from the row player's or subject's perspective would be obtained. However, the same information from the column player's perspective could be obtained by uncovering cell 1 and the upper-right cell (cell 2). Thus, greed information was available in basically two ways albeit from different perspectives. A similar situation holds for fear information. From the row player or subject's perspective it would be obtained by uncovering cell 2 and the lower-right cell (cell 4). However, the same information from the column player's perspective could be obtained by uncovering cells 3 and 4.

Thus, for each of the 18 games, if the subject responded with cells 1 and 3 in any order or cells 1 and 2 in any order then "greed information" (GI) was increased by the corresponding number of matches. If the subject responded with cells 2 and 4 in any order or 3 and 4 in any order then "fear information" (FI) was incremented for each match. Finally, if the subject responded with cells 1 and 4 in any order then the variable "main-diagonal information" (MD) was incremented for each match.

The use of this coding scheme creates the opportunity to respond with GI or FI twice as often as with MD. In fact, data generated using random responding (see below) disclosed means for GI and FI which were twice as high as MD. Thus, in the statistical analyses which follow, GI and FI for each subject were divided by 2. This is especially important when considering the null hypothesis for preferring one type of information over the other. Without this division a difference between GI and FI as compared to MD would be expected, even if subjects were responding randomly.[1]

Is Information Search Systematic?

To determine whether or not subjects' responses were systematic rather than random two pieces of evidence were examined. If the participants were reasoning when making their selections, then all or at least most of their uncoverings should fit the three *a priori* patterns. Since the games were symmetric, it would not be sensible to uncover cells 2 and 3 since the exact same information is contained in each cell. Also, it would not be sensible to uncover the same cell more than once since no additional information would be obtained before making a choice decision. In actuality, 83 percent of the average responses fit the three *a priori* patterns.

Additional evidence was provided by using a computer program to generate random data. Using an $SPSS_x$ input routine, 18 pairs of random uncoverings were generated for 1000 cases. The coding procedure described above was then applied to these data and the average GI, FI, and MD were calculated. Given the symmetric nature of the games and coding scheme employed, we should expect the average amounts of GI and FI to be greater than MD if the data are random. (Essentially, twice as many response patterns would lead to GI or FI while only one pattern is coded as MD.) The computer generated data provided averages (before the division described above) of 5.97, 6.04, and 3.01 for GI, FI, and MD, respectively.[2] The overall averages from the actual data were 6.8 for GI, 2.6 for FI, and 5.46 for MD. There is some evidence then to conclude that information search is a systematic rather than random process.

Analysis of Information Preferences

As can be seen in Table 9.2, there were moderate correlations among the three coded variables. Thus, the three dependent measures were analyzed in a multivariate analysis of variance (MANOVA) which employed a 2 (subject's sex) × 2 (social value orientation) × 2 (information condition) between subject design. In order to determine if there were any effects for the type of information sought, an additional analysis which applied two orthogonal contrasts to the dependent variables was conducted. The first comparison combined GI and FI and contrasted these with MD. The second contrasted GI and FI.

TABLE 9.2 *Correlations Between GI, FI, and MD*

	GI	FI	MD
GI	1.0	−.35	−.57
FI		1.0	−.21
MD			1.0

With respect to general information preferences, the analysis including the orthogonal contrasts on the dependent measures indicated that indeed subjects did show preferences beyond the chance level, $F(2,72) = 36.99$, $p < .0001$. Figure 9.1 presents the means associated with this main effect. Univariate analyses indicated that the first contrast (comparing GI and FI to MD) was statistically reliable [$F(1,73) = 7.81$, $p = .007$], while the second contrast (comparing GI to FI) was highly significant [$F(1,73) = 42.4$, $p < .0001$]. It would appear that overall, greed information was sought out to a greater degree than fear information, and that MD was sought most overall. The analysis using contrasts on the dependent variables produced only one other global effect which was for Social Value Orientation, $F(2,72) = 9.51$, $p < .0001$. The univariate contrasts showed that there were significant differences between the responses of cooperative and noncooperative subjects when considering the first contrast [$F(1,73) = 9.86$, $p = .002$] and the second [$F(1,73) = 16.29$, $p = .0001$]. As can be seen in Fig. 9.2, these effects are largely due to differences between cooperative and noncooperative subjects when focusing on GI and MD.

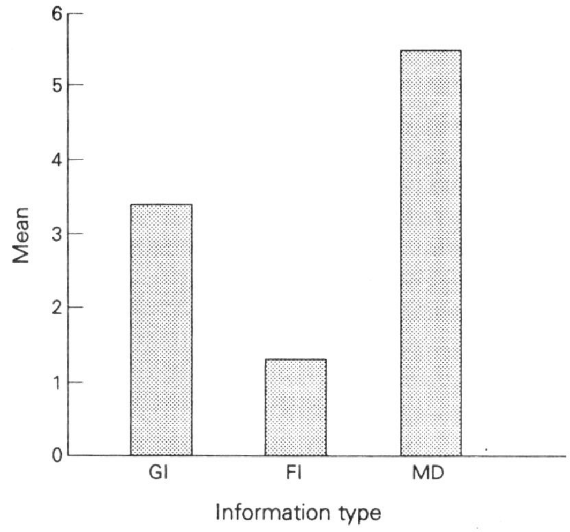

FIG 9.1 Mean preference as a function of information type.

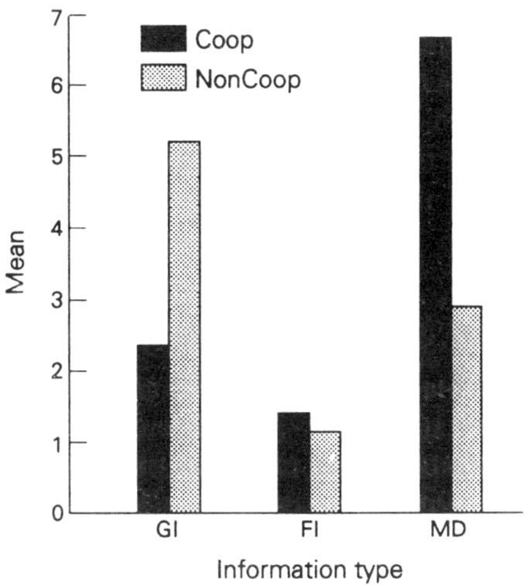

FIG. 9.2 Mean preference as a function of social orientation and information.

Information Preferences and Social Orientations

The MANOVA analyses which did not employ contrasts on the dependent variables also provide clear evidence that general information preferences were moderated by social orientations. There was an overall multivariate effect for social orientation on the set of information categories, $F(3,71) = 8.31$, $p < .0001$. Univariate analyses indicated that there was a significant difference between cooperators and noncooperators in the extent to which they sought information concerning MD [$F(1,73) = 7.32$, $p = .008$] and GI [$F(1,73) = 24.01$, $p < .0001$]. As is shown in Fig. 9.2, cooperators showed more interest in MD information than did noncooperators, while noncooperators showed significantly more interest in greed information than cooperators. In addition, the analysis disclosed a two-way interaction involving orientation and information condition, $F(3,71) = 3.37$, $p = .023$. The univariate analyses indicated that the effect concerned GI information only [$F(1,73) = 3.9$, $p = .05$], and examination of the means associated with the interaction showed that preference differences between cooperators and noncooperators were greater in the full information condition than in the partial condition. One possible reason for this result is that all participants, regardless of their orientation, tended to show greater interest in fear information under partial conditions. There were no other main or interaction effects in this analysis.

At this point it seems that the data provide support for the notions that information preferences do exist, and that these preferences are related to social orientations.

Proportion of Cooperation

In order to see if previous results (Camac & Kuhlman, 1987) involving an interaction between payoff parameters and social orientation could be replicated in these somewhat different circumstances, an analysis of choice behavior was conducted with subject's sex, social orientation, and the parameters K (with 6 levels) and game type (fear changes, greed constant; greed changes, fear constant; both change) as factors.

The planned analyses also disclosed significant effects on the level of cooperation. Consistent with many past studies, there was a main effect for social orientation, $F(1,72) = 21.64$, $p < .0001$. Overall, cooperators had a significantly higher proportion of cooperative choice than did noncooperators. The average choice proportions were .51 and .19, respectively. There was also a significant main effect for the cooperative index (K), $F(5,68) = 2.6$, $p = .03$. Figure 9.3 illustrates that this effect was largely linear and positive. The figure also suggests the presence of an orientation by K interaction which would be consistent with the previous results of Camac & Kuhlman (1987). Although the statistical analysis indicated that this interaction effect did not attain significance, simple effects analyses which tested the effect of K within each orientation group did provide evidence of an interaction. There was a significant effect for K within the cooperative group ($p = .033$) but no significant effect within the noncooperative group ($p = .396$). As in the Camac & Kuhlman study, there was no indication of a game type effect. The only other significant global effect was an unpredicted three-way interaction

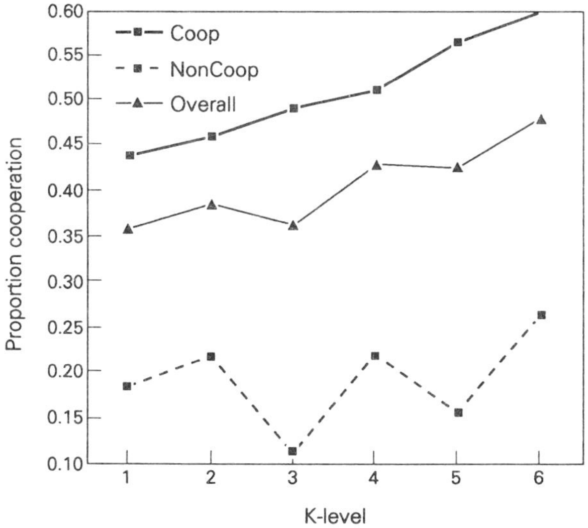

FIG. 9.3 Proportion of cooperation as a function of *K* and social orientation.

involving sex, information condition, and game type [$F(2,71) = 5.19$, $p = .008$].

Implications and Conclusions

Regarding Information Search and Social Orientation

The main prediction of the current study, that information seeking would be related to one's social orientation, received strong support. Cooperative subjects, who in previous studies have been shown to have cooperative expectations and intentions (Kelley & Stahelski, 1970; Kuhlman & Wimberley, 1976), here demonstrated a strong preference for MD information. This information, which contrasts the outcomes for mutual cooperation with mutual defection, should bias the decision maker towards a cooperative choice. Indeed, consistent with past studies, participants identified as cooperators through a decomposed game procedure evidenced the highest degree of cooperative choice in the dilemma game. Competitive subjects, on the other hand, have been shown to expect defection from others and to hold intentions to defect (Kelley & Stahelski, 1970; Kuhlman & Wimberley, 1976; Kuhlman *et al.*, 1986). Consistent with these intentions and beliefs, noncooperative subjects in the current study showed a stronger preference for information which contrasted payoffs which allow for exploitation. Most notably, this interest was in greed information, which would indicate an appetitive motivation for defection.

As has occurred in many studies now, noncooperators in the current study were also very uncooperative in terms of their dilemma game choices.

These results, along with those of Grzelak (1981), support the notion that cooperative and noncooperative persons apply somewhat different schemata to social dilemma situations, and that these structures influence information search. The current results also suggest that the effect of these search patterns may result in a type of confirmation bias. By focusing on MD information, for example, cooperators examine information which supports their cooperative motivation.

At a more general level, these results add to an increasing list of studies (Liebrand, Jansen, Rijken, & Sure, 1986; McClintock & Liebrand, 1988; Van Lange, Liebrand, & Kuhlman, 1990) which demonstrate differences in social information processing between cooperative and noncooperative people. A consistent finding across all of these studies is that relationships exist among one's orientation, processing of social information, and decision making in social dilemmas. For example, people who are identified as cooperative are more likely to expect cooperation from others, more likely to interpret the behavior of others along a morality dimension and more likely to act cooperatively in social dilemmas. The results of the current study suggest that we may add to this list: more likely to seek information which supports cooperative behavior. In contrast, persons who are identified as noncooperative are more likely to expect competition from others, more likely to interpret behavior using a potency dimension, and more likely to defect in social dilemmas. To this list we may add: more likely to search for information that supports defection.

Regarding Payoff Parameters and Behavior

The results of the analysis of choice proportions are consistent with the previous findings of Liebrand *et al.* (1986) and Camac & Kuhlman (1987). Fear and greed appear to be equal determinants of choice behavior. In addition, analysis of the simple effects involved in the orientation by cooperative index interaction produced results which were consistent with Camac & Kuhlman's previous study. The proportion of cooperation observed within the cooperative group was influenced by incentive level, while the proportion of cooperation within the noncooperative group was not significantly affected by changes in incentive level. This result is at least partially consistent with the information search data. Given the limitations of the current task, those subjects most likely to obtain MD information (cooperators) would be predicted to be most responsive to K level. Those most likely to obtain only greed (noncooperators) or fear information would be predicted to be less responsive to the K index. Evidence for a more direct link between information preferences and choice would be stronger if a game type effect had been present.

The overall preference for greed information as opposed to fear information would appear to support the payoff studies of Komorita *et al.* (1980) who found that choice behavior was more responsive to changes in greed than in fear. However, as mentioned above, the choice behavior obtained here is inconsistent with that study. Additional caution is warranted since one aspect of the particular payoff structures used in the current study may have contributed to this effect. Specifically, the sucker's payoff was constant at 0 throughout the experiment. This could have strengthened interest in GI while decreasing interest in FI.

While the current results may appear to do little to untangle the inconsistencies found in studies of the effects of payoffs, they suggest one avenue for future investigation. For differences in information search to be schematically based, it is not necessary that cooperators hold different schemas than noncooperators. It is possible that both groups hold many similar cognitive structures which could be applied in social dilemma tasks. The observed differences could instead be related to differences in schema activation. For instance, a more recently used schema is more likely to be activated than a less recently used one (Higgins & King, 1981). Schema activation is also related to the frequency with which schemata have been applied over time (Wyer & Scrull, 1980). In addition to recency and frequency, schema activation may also be influenced by other factors such as the nature of one's goals, motivation and affect (Fiske & Taylor, 1984). Thus, the difference in information search between cooperators and competitors may be attributed to a difference in schema activation, perhaps because of the recency or frequency with which certain schemas have been activated in the past.

Implications for Future Study

The current chapter presents a paradigm for studying information search and some initial results which bear on this process. The current study provides evidence that information search is an orderly process which can be quantified and studied systematically. In addition, one variable (social value orientation) which was suggested to influence information search appears to do so. However, there could be at least two reasons for the social value effect.

One possibility is that cooperative or pro-social persons have different schemas concerning social dilemma situations than noncooperative or self-interested persons. Such a conclusion would certainly be consistent with prior studies of expectations (e.g. Kelley & Stahelski, 1970) and with the recent research concerning other cognitive processes mentioned above (e.g., Liebrand *et al.*, 1986). If such is the case, then factors such as instruction set or game class would be expected to have little effect on the search patterns of people with various social values. That is, cooperative persons should always seek information which supports cooperation while noncooperative or self-interested people should seek information which supports individual rationality.

A second possibility is that cooperative and noncooperative persons have similar schemas concerning social dilemma situations; however, the schemas normally activated within cooperative persons differ from those normally activated within noncooperative people. If this latter possibility is true, then it would follow that a manipulation of goals or motives should result in the activation of different schemata. These in turn might influence cognitive processes such as information search, and ultimately choice behavior. Hence, if one were to change one's chronic social orientation through role-playing or through instruction set, for example, then one might see chronic noncooperators demonstrating a search pattern more exemplary of cooperators and vice versa. Examination of this "reversal hypothesis" provides one direction for future research which may illuminate some of the questions raised by the current work. In addition, if a link between information search and choice behavior in social dilemmas can be firmly established, then the manipulation of the schema activation process could provide an avenue for resolving the conflict between individual and collective rationality inherent in the social dilemma.

References

Camac, C., & Kuhlman, D. M. (1987). Individual differences in social orientation as moderators of payoff effects in social dilemmas. Unpublished manuscript, Roanoke College.

Chapman, L. J., & Chapman, J. P. (1982). Test results are what you think they are. In D. Kahneman, P. Slovic, & A. Tversky (Eds), *Judgment Under Uncertainty: Heuristics and Biases*. New York: Cambridge University Press.

Dawes, R. M., McTavish, J., & Shaklee, H. (1977). Behavior, communication, and assumptions about other people's behavior in a commons dilemma situation. *Journal of Personality and Social Psychology*, **35**, 1–11.

Fiske, S. T., & Taylor, S. E. (1984). *Social Cognition*. New York: Random House.

Grzelak, J. L. (1981). Social interdependence: do we know what we want to know? *Polish Psychological Bulletin*, **12**, 125–135.

Guyer, M., & Rapoport, A. (1972). 2 × 2 games played once. *Journal of Conflict Resolution*, **16**, 409–431.

Harris, R. J. (1972). An interval scale classification system for 2 × 2 interval-symmetric games. *Behavioral Science*, **17**, 371–383.

Higgins, E. T., & King, G. A. (1981). Accessibility of social constructs: Information-processing consequences of individual and contextual variability. In N. Cantor & J. F. Khilstrom (Eds), *Personality, Cognition, and Social Interaction*. Hillsdale, N.J.: Erlbaum.

Kelley, H. H., & Thibaut, J. W. (1978). *Interpersonal Relations: A Theory of Interdependence*. New York: Wiley.

Komorita, S. S., Sweeney, J., & Kravitz, D. A. (1980). Cooperative choice in the *N*-person dilemma. *Journal of Personality and Social Psychology*. **38**, 504–516.

Kuhlman, D. M., & Marshello, A. F. J. (1975). Individual differences in game motivation as moderators of preprogrammed strategy effects in Prisoner's Dilemma. *Journal of Personality and Social Psychology*, **32**, 922–931.
Kuhlman, D. M., & Wimberley, D. L. (1976). Expectations of choice behavior held by cooperators, competitors, and individualists across four classes of experimental game. *Journal of Personality and Social Psychology*, **34**, 69–81.
Kuhlman, D. M., Camac, C. R., & Cunha, D. A. (1986). Individual differences in social orientations. In H. Wilke, D. Messick, & C. Rutte (Eds), *Experimental Social Dilemmas*. New York: Peter Lang.
Liebrand, W. B. G. (1984). The effects of social motives, communication and group size on behavior in an *N*-person multi-stage mixed-motive game. *European Journal of Social Psychology*, **14**, 239–264.
Liebrand, W. B. G. (1986). The ubiquity of social values. In H. Wilke, D. Messick, & C. Rutte (Eds), *Experimental Social Dilemmas*. New York: Peter Lang.
Liebrand, W. B. G., & Van Ruen, G. J. (1985). The effects of social motives on behavior in social dilemmas in two cultures. *Journal of Experimental Social Psychology*, **21**, 86–102.
Liebrand, W. B. G., Jansen, R. W. T. L., Rijken, V. M., & Sure, C. J. M. (1986). Might over Morality: Social values and the perception of other players in experimental games. *Journal of Experimental Social Psychology*, **22**, 203–215.
Liebrand, W. B. G., Wilke, H. A. M., Vogel, R., & Wolters, F. J. M. (1986). Value orientation and conformity in three types of social dilemma games. *Journal of Conflict Resolution*, **30**, 77–97.
Markus, H. & Zajonc, R. B. (1985). The cognitive perspective in social psychology. In G. Lindzey & E. Aronson (Eds), *Handbook of Social Psychology*. New York: Random House.
McClintock, C. G., & Liebrand, W. B. G. (1988). Role of interdependence structure, individual value orientation, and another's strategy in social decision making: a transformational analysis. *Journal of Personality and Social Psychology*, **55**, 396–409.
Messé, L. A., & Sivacek, J. M. (1979). Predictions of others' responses in a mixed motive game: Self-justification or false consensus? *Journal of Personality and Social Psychology*, **37**, 602–607.
Messick, D. M., & McClintock, C. G. (1968). Motivational basis of choice in experimental games. *Journal of Experimental Social Psychology*, **4**, 1–25.
Rapoport, A. (1967). A note on the "index of cooperation" for prisoner's dilemma. *Journal of Conflict Resolution*, **11**, 101–103.
Van Lange, P. A. M., Liebrand, W. B. G., & Kuhlman, D. M. (1990). Causal attribution of choice behavior in three *N*-person prisoner's dilemmas. *Journal of Experimental Social Psychology*, **26**, 34–48.
Wyer, R. S., (1969). Prediction of behavior in two-person games. *Journal of Personality and Social Psychology*, **13**, 222–238.
Wyer, R. S., (1971). Effects of outcome matrix and partner's behavior in two-person games. *Journal of Experimental Social Psychology*, **7**, 190–210.
Wyer, R. S., & Srull, T. K. (1980). The processing of social stimulus information: A conceptual integration. In R. Hastie, T. M. Ostrom, E. B. Ebbesen, R. S. Wyer, D. Hamilton, & D. E. Carlston (Eds), *Person Memory: The Cognitive Basis of Social Perception*. Hillsdale, N.J.: Erlbaum.
Yamagishi, T., & Sato, K. (1986). Motivational bases of the public goods problem. *Journal of Personality and Social Psychology*, **50**, 67–73.

Notes

1. Analyses conducted before dividing GI and FI by 2 lead to the same conclusions regarding the reliability of global effects as those which are reported in the text.
2. If this procedure is applied to the data after GI and FI are divided by 2, then the respective means were 2.99 and 3.02.
3. The author would like to acknowledge the assistance of Sherry Bailey, Trina Bogle, Doug Burson, and Joshua McNair, in conducting this study. In addition, he would like to thank the editors and several anonymous reviewers for their helpful comments on an earlier draft of this chapter.

B. Asymmetric Conflicts

10

The Effects of Leverage and Payoffs on Cooperative Behavior in Asymmetric Dilemmas*

J. KEITH MURNIGHAN and THOMAS R. KING
Department of Business Administration
University of Illinois

The establishment of cooperation is a common goal in interpersonal interaction. All too often, however, cooperative behaviors do not emerge. The difficulty frequently centers on each individual's reluctance to unilaterally contribute his or her own resources while others may not be contributing. When outcomes are symmetric, people with cooperative intentions risk inequitable distributions: they may receive less than their fair share if they cooperate, and they know that noncooperators simultaneously protect themselves and may gain better outcomes. When outcomes are asymmetric (and known to both parties), mutual cooperators may find themselves receiving different outcomes even when their contributions and their risks are perceived to be equal. Thus, the problem of cooperation becomes even more difficult when the parties know that, even when they cooperate, their outcomes will differ.

Asymmetric dilemmas (ADs), i.e., games where similar choices by the parties yield different, known outcomes, model conflict with greater generality and complexity than the symmetric dilemmas studied in most

* We thank Sjerp de Vries for several extremely helpful comments on an earlier version of this paper. Both his general and his specific suggestions would ordinarily necessitate a series of footnotes throughout the paper. Instead, we hope this single acknowledgement will be sufficient thanks for his tremendous assistance. His comments have significantly improved the paper. Needless to say, any remaining errors are ours. We also thank Michael Bowen, Deborah Lundberg, and James Wishloff for their assistance in data collection and analysis. Work on this project was supported, in part, by a grant from the National Science Foundation of the United States.

previous research. This paper presents two experiments on iterated ADs that investigated the effects of two variables, leverage and the value of the parties' mutually cooperative outcomes, which our previous research and theory (Murnighan, King, & Schoumaker, 1990) have indicated are important determinants of AD strategies and cooperative behavior. We discuss both variables in greater depth below.

As a first step in the study of ADs, our research focuses on asymmetric variations of the standard 2 × 2 iterated prisoner's dilemma (PD) game, where the payoffs to the Traitor (b_1 for player 1; b_2 for player 2) are greater than the payoffs for mutual cooperation (a_1 and a_2) which are greater than the payoffs for mutual noncooperation (c_1 and c_2) which arc greater than the payoffs to the Sucker (d_1 and d_2). We studied games that asymmetrically varied a_1 and a_2 (the mutually cooperative payoffs) and b_1 and b_2 (the mutually noncooperative payoffs) while keeping the payoffs to the Traitor (b_1 and b_2) and to the Sucker (d_1 and d_2) symmetric and constant. The main diagonal outcomes are the most frequently observed outcomes in previous research on iterated PD games and, therefore, should respond most notably to manipulations of asymmetry. Also, we focused on games where the players are aware of each other's outcomes (cf. Roth & Murnighan, 1982) and can communicate about their different expectations about their interaction. Both of these structural conditions were included to increase the richness of our research participants' responses.

Background

Previous models and research on cooperative play in iterated dilemmas have almost exclusively investigated symmetric games. One exception (McClintock, Gallo, & Harrison, 1965) focused primarily on the likelihood of retaliatory behavior following cooperation or noncooperation in asymmetric games. As far as we know, however, no studies other than our own have addressed the basic phenomena of the effects of known asymmetric outcomes in iterated dilemmas.

In our first study (reported in Murnighan, King, & Schoumaker, 1990), we investigated two symmetric and two asymmetric games. Our research was based on earlier work (Roth & Murnighan, 1978) that had identified the conditions when a cooperative equilibrium could exist in iterated two-person PD games. When a cooperative equilibrium exists, both players can benefit from repeated mutually cooperative choices, even given the risk of one or the other defecting. We replicated research on two symmetric games, including one with a cooperative equilibrium and one without, and extended the domain of our research to two ADs. Both established the conditions for a cooperative equilibrium for only one of the two parties (Individual 1) but not the other (Individual 2; see Table 10.1 for an example). Since a cooperative equilibrium requires cooperation from both

TABLE 10.1 *An Asymmetric Dilemma*

		Player 2	
		Cooperative choice	Noncooperative choice
Player 1	Cooperative choice	(36,24)	(0,40)
	Noncooperative choice	(40, 0)	(4,18)

Note: The first number in each pair is the payoff for Player 1; the second number in each pair is the payoff for Player 2.

parties, our *a priori* prediction was that cooperation would be unlikely in these asymmetric games. Although one party would find mutual cooperation very rewarding, the other would have little interest or benefit from mutual cooperation and could unilaterally shift his behavior to induce the ever-present noncooperative equilibrium.

The symmetric game results supported our prediction that a cooperative equilibrium would generate more cooperative behavior. The AD results, however, were unexpected: some pairs implemented a scheme of alternation, whereby one or both parties allowed the other to choose noncooperatively without retaliating. We observed two forms of alternation: (1) simple alternation, where the parties made a continuing series of alternating cooperative-noncooperative and noncooperative-cooperative choices, resulting in the highest and lowest payoffs (the off-diagonal outcomes) for each, every other trial; and (2) complex alternation, where one party allowed the other to make regular, intermittent noncooperative choices, while still maintaining consistent cooperative choices.

Our subsequent research, including these two studies, has been designed to identify when these alternation strategies might occur. In particular, our work assumes that, by themselves, asymmetric outcomes make cooperative behavior more unlikely and that either form of alternation provides a satisficing if not optimizing solution that is far superior to the deficient solution of mutual noncooperation.

Simple alternation provides both parties with less than Pareto optimal outcomes (i.e., both could do better), but removes much of the motivation to defect so often observed in symmetric dilemmas. It also provides equal outcomes if play ends after an even number of trials. Complex alternation does yield Pareto optimal outcomes (one party could not do better without the other doing worse) that, depending on the payoffs, are usually less than the joint maximum obtainable from mutually cooperative choices.

Complex alternation represents a creative, integrative (Pruitt, 1981) solution to a complicated dilemma. On the one hand, players with little leverage (those who are interested in mutual cooperation but cannot enforce it) are allowed to obtain some high payoffs from mutual cooperation. At the same time, they must swallow their pride and let the players with leverage have several very high payoffs while they occasionally receive nothing. Once this strategy is discovered and implemented (no small feat), defection provides only small immediate benefits and the motivation to defect is considerably reduced, especially compared to the motivation to defect from mutual cooperation in symmetric games.

Thus far, our research is limited to iterated games where the Sucker payoffs (d_1 and d_2) are fixed and normalized to zero and the Traitor payoffs (b_1 and b_2) are fixed at 40. Within these constraints, we have allowed the mutually cooperative and noncooperative payoffs to vary. The relationships among these outcomes provides the basis for identifying two variables which our early studies (Murnighan, King, & Schoumaker, 1990) indicate are important determinants of alternating strategies. The first, leverage, depends on the idea that both parties in a dilemma have potential regret: if everyone chooses noncooperatively, all lose relative to mutual cooperation. We define the difference between the mutually cooperative and noncooperative outcomes as potential regret, $R_i = (a_i - c_i)$. When one party has much less potential regret than the other, e.g., Individual 2 in Table 10.1, that party has leverage, $L = (R_i - R_j)$.

The concepts of leverage and regret assume that knowledgeable players will use their mutually cooperative and noncooperative outcomes as baselines for evaluating their ultimate payoffs. In symmetric PD games, the negotiation typically concerns whether the players will establish a pattern of mutual cooperation (which would break down with a defection by either side) or mutual noncooperation. Thus, regret identifies the potential costs a party may incur from mutual noncooperation. Either party can enforce this outcome by repeatedly choosing noncooperatively. This enforcement inflicts regret on the other party.

Since the party with leverage has less to lose from mutual noncooperation and less to gain from mutual cooperation, they may be more tempted to choose noncooperatively. Their one-time gain from the Traitor's payoff may more than compensate them for the regret they might suffer from subsequent c payoffs if the other player retaliates. Players without leverage, however, will have less temptation and less benefit from defection. Instead, they hope to continue mutual cooperation for as long as possible.

The model predicts that, as leverage increases, so will the power of the leverage player. In essence, the player with leverage has fate control (Thibaut & Kelley, 1959) over the other player. The non-leverage player does not have such power. An increase in leverage (power, control) should motivate some leverage players to use their power to increase their payoffs. The only feasible outcome that can accomplish this is the Traitor's payoff, b. Unilaterally invoking this outcome, however, invites retaliation. Thus, in an iterated game, leverage players are predicted to use both simple and complex alternation strategies to increase their payoffs as their leverage increases.

Our earlier research also suggested that the players' mutually cooperative outcomes were critical to the emergence of alternation. Negotiators apparently discover simple alternation before they discover complex alternation. When a party's mutually cooperative outcome (a) is less than they would receive from simple alternation [i.e., $(b + d)/2 > a$ for an even number of plays], simple alternation is attractive. But if the non-leverage player's mutually cooperative payoff is greater than $(b + d)/2$, simple alternation is not Pareto optimal. Thus, both players can do better with either mutual cooperation or complex alternation. Since complex alternation is difficult to discover, it becomes more likely when the leverage player's payoffs are less than $(b + d)/2$.

Study 1 was designed to systematically vary leverage and the players' mutually cooperative payoffs (see Table 10.2). When leverage is low, the model predicts that neither simple nor complex alternation should occur. As leverage increases, the opportunity for the leverage player to suggest and implement a scheme of complex alternation increases. This opportunity, however, may not be discovered when the leverage player's mutually cooperative payoff is high and Pareto optimal outcomes come from mutual cooperation. When their mutually cooperative outcome is low, however, players with leverage should be motivated to find ways to

TABLE 10.2 *The Experimental Design*

	Leverage*					
Mutually Cooperative Payoffs	High (L = 28,28,14)*		Moderate (L = 14,14,5)*		Low (L = 0,0,0)	
High/High	36,24	0,40	36,24	0,40	36,24	0,40
$a_1 = 36$ $a_2 = 24$	40,0	4,20	40,0	18,20	40,0	32,20
High/Low	36,18	0,40	36,18	0,40	36,18	0,40
$a_1 = 36$ $a_2 = 18$	40,0	4,14	40,0	18,14	40,0	32,14
Low/Low	18,16	0,40	18,16	0,40	18,16	0,40
$a_1 = 18$ $a_2 = 16$	40,0	4,12	40,0	9,12	40,0	14,12

* The first number in each pair in the 2 × 2 matrices is the payoff for Player 1; the second number in each pair is the payoff for Player 2, who has Leverage in each of the nine games. The leverage values, L, are listed for the three payoff conditions: High/High, High/Low, Low/Low. Values drop for the Low/Low payoff condition due to constraints on the values of a_1 and a_2.

increase their payoffs. Simple alternation is the most obvious, especially if $a < (b + d)/2$. Complex alternation, however, can provide considerably greater benefits for both players. Thus, a combination of a low mutually cooperative payoff for the leverage player, high leverage, and a high mutually cooperative payoff for the non-leverage player should lead to the highest frequencies of complex alternation: the non-leverage player obtains some mutually cooperative payoffs and the leverage player does better than the mutually cooperative payoff or the payoff from simple alternation.

When the mutually cooperative payoffs are low for both parties, simple alternation is an equilibrium strategy that provides them with increased benefits. The effects of leverage under this low payoff condition should be negligible. Complex alternation requires that the mutually cooperative payoff of the non-leverage player be high; otherwise there is little to be gained from complex alternation. When mutually cooperative payoffs are both low, complex alternation should not surface, even with leverage.

Study 1

The Games

The two variables, leverage and the mutually cooperative outcomes of the players, were varied in a 3 × 3 design (see Table 10.2). Our research and analysis has always set $b = 40$ and $d = 0$, arbitrary choices that limit the values of R and L. Increasing the value of b or decreasing the value of d would expand the range of possibilities for R and L and might change the theoretical analysis, especially if some outcomes are negative (Kahneman & Tversky, 1979). In a game where all the payoffs take integer values, where $b > a > d$ (as defined by the prisoner's dilemma), and where $a_1 > a_2$ and c_1 does not equal c_2, the maximum leverage in any game is 37 (i.e., when $a_1 = 39$; $a_2 = x$; $c_1 = 1$; and $c_2 = x - 1$, where x is between 2 and 38). The minimum is zero. The three leverage conditions in this experiment (High, Moderate, and Low) took values of 28, 14, and 0.

For the mutually cooperative outcomes, a relatively high value indicated that a player's outcome exceeded $(b + d)/2$; a low value indicated that his or her outcome did not exceed $(b + d)/2$. Lower values in the low/low condition were possible but would have made the simple alternation solution even more obvious.

Both within and across conditions, values in the outcome matrices were fixed as much as possible. The off-diagonal outcomes (40 and 0) were fixed in all conditions. The mutually cooperative outcomes were fixed within the levels of the leverage condition. The nine games that were included in the study span a considerable range of values for leverage and the mutually cooperative outcomes.

Method

Subjects

Thirty students in an MBA course at the University of Illinois participated in the study as part of their course project. They chose this experiment from a variety of possible projects. Their performance in the games and their analysis of their strategies, submitted after the experiment was completed, contributed to part of their course grade.[1]

Design and Procedure

Each person bargained anonymously with different bargainers for each of four games. Individuals knew the game they would be playing in advance, but were randomly chosen as Individual 1 or Individual 2 (e.g., Table 10.1). Negotiations were scheduled approximately one week apart. Each of the nine games was played first, second, third, and fourth by either one or two bargaining pairs. Fifteen different game orderings were used, with two individuals seeing each of these orderings.

An extensive introduction to the games and the procedures was provided in the class preceding the groups' first sessions. The task was introduced as the Strawberry Bidding Game. Participants acted as representatives of one of two firms bidding for a limited supply of fresh strawberries in any particular season. The discussion explained that each firm could bid either low or high in each week of the season. If both firms bid low, their profits would be relatively large, and each would receive some of the supply. If both firms bid high, their profits would drop, but each would again receive some of the crop. If one firm bid high and the other bid low, the high bidder would receive the entire week's supply and would be able to reap large profits while the other party received zero profits. The outcomes for different games and different firms varied due to different market conditions. The outcome for one party bidding low and the other bidding high, however, remained the same for any game and any firm; controlling the supply gave a firm the same benefit (40) regardless of market conditions.

Subjects were told that a random number generator determined how many weeks (trials) each session (season) would continue (modeling the onset of the wet season, when strawberry production would end) with a fixed termination probability of .13. In actuality, the experimenter never terminated the session until the parties had completed at least eight trials. Sessions could be terminated by the experimenter, depending on time constraints, if they ran over fifteen trials. When time was available, and after eight trials had been completed, the termination trial was randomly determined with a probability of .13.

Each firm submitted their bid simultaneously and secretly. The results from each trial's bids were announced prior to the next bid. For the first two trials, bids were made without communication. After outcome feedback was provided for the second bidding trial, firms were allowed to communicate with one another via written messages. The only restriction on messages was that the players could not identify themselves. Once both parties submitted their bids, the outcome (agreement) for that trial was determined and announced to the two players.

The participants were encouraged to prepare well for each session. Everyone was required to submit "Strategic Considerations," which described theirs and the other party's expected strategies.

Analysis

The analysis focused on the first eight trials, completed by all pairs. Bids were partitioned into two sets: the first two trials, where messages were not possible, and the next six, where messages were possible. Time to reach agreement was recorded for all trials. Message frequencies were tabulated for the last six trials.

The most important dependent variable was each pair's strategy. Three independent, trained judges used the players' Strategic Considerations, messages, and bids (excluding the first two trials) to categorize the strategies as cooperation, noncooperation, defection, simple alternation, or complex alternation. Cooperation included mutually cooperative choices throughout the session. Noncooperation included consistent, mutually noncooperative choices. Defection began with cooperative choices; one firm eventually chose noncooperatively, usually in combination with a cooperative message. This typically led to mutual noncooperation thereafter. Simple alternation consisted of a series of cooperative-noncooperative, noncooperative-cooperative choices. Complex alternation consisted of a series of cooperative choices by one party with occasional noncooperative choices by the other. In addition to these pure categories, some pairs moved from one strategy to another within a single game. Finally, we also identified the party who chose noncooperatively first within the defection, simple, and complex alternation strategies.

Results

An overall analysis of variance on the players' bids, with leverage (three levels), mutually cooperative payoffs (three levels), players (firm 1 and firm 2), and trials (eight levels, a repeated factor) as independent variables led to significant effects for payoffs [$F(2,102) = 12.76$, $p < .001$], trials [$F(7,714) = 68.32$, $p < .001$], and the payoffs by trials interaction [$F(14,714) = 1.73$, $p < .05$]. (See Table 10.3 for means.) Analysis of the

TABLE 10.3 *Mean Proportion of Cooperative Choices for the Payoffs by Trials Interaction, the Mean Time to Reach Agreement, and the Frequency of Messages (Study 1)*

Mutually Cooperative Payoffs	Trials 1	2	3	4	5	6	7	8	Mean	Mean (trials 3–8)
High/High	.07	.05	.90	.92	.82	.82	.81	.77	.64	.84
High/Low	.12	.07	.76	.74	.74	.76	.67	.67	.57	.72
Low/Low	.08	.02	.50	.50	.50	.55	.55	.50	.40	.52
Mean	.09	.05	.72	.72	.69	.71	.68	.64	.54	.69
Time	61	66	332	79	82	53	47	56	97	108
Messages	—	—	22	4.4	.4	.3	.2	.3	—	4

Note: Cooperative bids were coded as ones; noncooperative bids were coded as zeros. Higher means indicate more cooperative choices. Time is expressed in seconds.

communication trials only yielded a significant effect for payoffs: $F(2,102) = 13.32, p < .001$. As values increased, over all trials or only the message trials, cooperative bids also increased.

Similar analyses for the time to reach agreement and message frequencies yielded significant effects only for trials: $F(7,777) = 21.95, p < .001$ and $F(5,555) = 21.41, p < .001$, respectively (see Table 10.3). The trials where messages first became possible took longer and produced the most messages.

Strategies

Three judges sorted each pair's bids into one of the five strategy categories, or "Other." Unanimous agreement was reached in 88.4 percent of the cases. Those cases where one judge disagreed (there were no cases of everyone disagreeing) were resolved by discussion (usually with the acquiescence of the disagreeing judge). Due to the relatively small sample size, contingency tables were constructed for the leverage and payoff manipulations, but not for their interaction (see Table 10.4).

The frequencies were insufficient for analysis using χ^2 (Siegel, 1956) even when categories were consolidated. Some regularities, however, are suggestive. Mutual noncooperation was rare. Unlike previous two-person dilemma research (e.g., Murnighan & Roth, 1983), only six pairs (10 percent) were consistently noncooperative. Defection was slightly more frequent (7.5 pairs; 12.5 percent), more often when mutually cooperative outcomes were both high.

Mutual cooperation was most prevalent in the low leverage and the high/high payoff conditions and least prevalent in the high leverage and the low/low payoff conditions. This is in contrast to the frequencies of complex alternation: when leverage was high or when the mutually cooperative payoffs were high/low, complex alternation was most frequent. These results matched our predictions.

Simple alternation was apparently unaffected by leverage. Instead, the mutually cooperative payoffs seemed to determine their frequency completely. Of the twenty bargaining pairs in the low/low payoff conditions, sixteen used simple alternation. These were the only cases of pure simple alternation. (Other pairs used a mix of simple alternation and other strategies.)

TABLE 10.4 *The Strategy Frequencies of Bargaining Pairs in the Leverage and Mutually Cooperative Payoff Conditions (Study 1)*

	Leverage			Mutually Cooperative Outcomes		
Strategies	HI	MOD	LO	High/High	High/Low	Low/Low
Cooperation	2.5	5.5	9.5	10.5	6	1
Noncooperation	1	1	3	1	3	1
Defection	3	3.5	1	4	2.5	1
Simple alternation	6.5	6	4.5	.5	.5	16
Complex alternation	8	4	1	3	9	1

The final dependent variable identified the player who chose noncooperatively first. With low leverage, first noncooperations split 4–3 between players 1 and 2. With moderate or high leverage, 38 noncooperations were spread fairly evenly across the three strategies. In simple alternation, the players also split almost equally (5 for player 1, 7 for player 2). In the remaining pairs, the player with leverage always chose noncooperatively first: 7 of 7 defectors; 12 of 12 in complex alternation.

Discussion

Rapoport and Chammah (1956) suggested that the mutually cooperative payoffs in an iterated prisoner's dilemma game should never be less than the outcomes attainable from simple alternation.[2] We know of no data other than the current study that actually tested their assumption that simple alternation would result. Clearly, their hypothesis was correct. Various levels of leverage had virtually no effect here. Also, the presence of a simple alternation equilibrium, satisfied only in the low/low payoff condition (Murnighan, King, & Schoumaker, 1990), led to the only cases of pure simple alternation in this study.

The frequencies of cooperation and complex alternation showed markedly different patterns, as suggested by our theory. Although some instances of complex alternation occurred when both parties' mutually cooperative outcomes were high, cooperation was much more frequent. When leverage was high or when the mutually cooperative outcomes were high/low, complex alternation was most prevalent. When these two conditions were combined, six of seven bargaining pairs used complex alternation. These results support our predictions, but, due to the small sample, cannot be considered conclusive.

Study 2

Two issues were foremost in the design of the second study: (1) our assumption that complex alternation was desirable but difficult to discover in asymmetric dilemmas; and (2) the fact that only small sets of data have documented its frequency. The first issue was addressed by including a manipulation that provided some participants with information on potential strategies. Prior to play, they were shown a set of strategies that included cooperation, noncooperation, defection, simple alternation, and several forms of complex alternation. If complex alternation is desirable but difficult to discover, players with this strategy information should use complex alternation more often.

The second issue was addressed by collecting considerably more data on a smaller set of games. Study 2 is a partial replication of Study 1, including the four games in the high and moderate leverage and the high/high and high/low payoff conditions.

Different complex alternation schemes allow the leverage player a varying number of noncooperative choices. A study that observed more complex alternation would allow analysis of the frequency of different types of complex alternation and their relation to leverage and mutually cooperative payoffs. As discussed earlier, being the first to choose noncooperatively is one indication of the use of leverage. A stronger indication is the frequency of noncooperative choices. Thus, Study 2 may provide the opportunity to test the proposition (Murnighan, King, & Schoumaker, 1990) that increased leverage leads to a greater frequency of noncooperative choices within different complex alternation schemes.

Study 2 also provided sufficient data to compare the success of individual bargainers and their efficiency in maximizing joint benefits in the four games.

Method

The first study's procedures were repeated in Study 2. The participants were 120 students enrolled in the following two semesters in the same course as those of Study 1. Eighty MBA students (two classes) participated in the first semester; forty (one class) in the second. Each bargainer met an anonymous opponent for each of the four games. The games were ordered so that each would be played 1st, 2nd, 3rd or 4th an equal number of times. A secondary concern was mixing the orderings so that the same two games followed each other the same number of times. With a slight departure,[3] this was successfully accomplished. Since most cell sizes were unequal but were not a function of the independent variables, all analyses of variance used the unweighted means approach.

As in Study 1, participants were provided with background information and instructions in the class prior to the beginning of play. Included in these instructions was the strategy manipulation. The members of one first semester class and the only second semester class were given a list titled "Eight possible choice pairings for any of the four games." The list included: (1) consistent mutually cooperative choices; (2) consistent noncooperative choices; (3) non-message trial noncooperation followed by consistent cooperation; (4) defection after four trials of cooperation; (5) simple alternation; and (6) three forms of complex alternation. One form of complex alternation allowed only one of the players noncooperative choices; the other two allowed both players noncooperative choices, but one player took more. This information was included in the written instructions and the class discussion prior to play.

The analyses were expanded to include several additional variables. The first compared the number of defections from mutual cooperation versus either form of alternation. Defections were identified by a noncooperative choice which broke from the previous pattern of bids and was typically followed by mutual noncooperation thereafter. Defections from both studies were pooled. In addition, success measures for each player were calculated as their mean outcome on the first six trials after messages were available (trials 3–8). These scores were compared to the original payoff matrix values. In addition, they provided the basis for an efficiency score for the pairs, i.e., the percentage of the maximum joint benefit attained.

Results

Two analyses were conducted to determine whether the samples in the two studies differed. The first compared the behavior of players in the no strategy conditions in Study 2 with the behavior of players in the same four games in Study 1. A study (two levels) of leverage (2) × payoffs (2) × trials (8) analysis of variance led to only one effect that included study, the study by payoffs interaction, $F(1,206) = 5.90$, $p < .02$. *Post hoc* tests indicated that people made significantly more cooperative bids in Study 2.

The second analysis compared the behavior of the students from different semesters, conducted only for participants who received strategy information. No effects were found for semester in an analysis of variance with leverage, payoffs, players, and trials as independent variables.

Overall Analyses

The bids were analyzed in a 2 (leverage) × 2 (mutually cooperative payoffs) × 2 (strategy information) × 2 (players) × 8 (trials; a repeated factor) analysis of variance. All of the main effects were significant; each was included in a significant interaction. The strategies by payoffs interaction [$F(1,464) = 5.32$, $p < .03$] indicated that not providing strategy information in the high/high payoff condition led to higher levels of cooperative bidding (mean = .72) than the other three conditions (means = .62, .62, and .63). The means from the leverage by trials [$F(7,3248) = 3.29$, $p < .01$] and leverage by players by trials [$F(7,3248) = 2.06$, $p < .05$] interactions are shown in Table 10.5. Leverage players were less cooperative than the other players, especially when leverage was moderate on the later trials. The comparable analysis of the message trials yielded the same effects except for the three-way interaction.

The analysis of time to reach agreement and message frequency led to significant effects for trials [$F(7,3304) = 77.95$ and $F(5,2360) = 27.38$, respectively; $p < .001$; see Table 10.5] and a difficult to interpret strategies by payoffs by trials interaction for time [$F(7,3304) = 2.83$, $p < .01$]. Time was long and messages were frequent as soon as messages became available. Unlike Study 1, messages were also frequent in the later trials. This may have been due to the increase in complex alternation strategies and the need for communication to insure their implementation. The interaction remained in the message trials analysis.

Strategies

Three judges again categorized strategies, with 95.3 percent unanimous agreement. As before, a brief discussion led to a consensus for categorizing each pair.

Almost no pairs used the pure form of simple alternation (see Table 10.6). None used this strategy in these four games in Study 1. Several used a form of complicated simple alternation, defined as a series of cooperative and noncooperative choices by both players that, in the end, equalizes their noncooperative choices. This strategy is something like a mix of complex and simple alternation, with more similarities to simple alternation. It was most frequent when leverage was moderate and the payoffs were high/low.

TABLE 10.5 *Mean Proportion of Cooperative Choices for the Leverage by Players by Trials Interaction, the Mean Time to Reach Agreement, and the Frequency of Messages (Study 2)*

		Trials								
Leverage	Player	1	2	3	4	5	6	7	8	Mean
	1	.12	.11	.91	.93	.90	.87	.84	.85	.69
High	2	.12	.05	.78	.85	.76	.71	.82	.72	.60
	Mean	.12	.08	.84	.88	.83	.79	.83	.78	.64
	1	.28	.17	.93	.90	.88	.87	.88	.77	.71
Moderate	2	.08	.07	.81	.82	.72	.74	.68	.59	.56
	Mean	.18	.12	.87	.86	.80	.80	.78	.68	.64
Time (seconds)		33	52	385	83	84	93	73	87	111
Message Frequency		—	—	1.9	.3	.3	3.8	2.9	3.3	2.1

Note: Cooperative bids were coded as ones; noncooperative bids were coded as zeros. Higher means indicate a higher proportion of cooperative choices. Time is expressed in seconds.

The lack of pure simple alternation strategies may be due to the non-leverage player's large mutually cooperative outcome ($a_1 = 36$) in all four games in this study. Had this value been lower, simple alternation might have been more attractive. Instead, this high payoff provided the players with an opportunity to benefit from complex alternation; the frequency of this strategy was high.

These data were analyzed in a series of χ^2 analyses. Following a significant overall χ^2, one factor was removed from each successive χ^2. Significant analyses with a variable included and not significant with it excluded indicated that this variable contributed substantially to the previous, significant effect.

The first analysis excluded the infrequent strategies (noncooperation, complicated simple alternation, and the two mixed strategies); it included cooperation, defection, and complex alternation in separate categories crossed by leverage and payoffs. The test was significant: $\chi^2(14) = 28.13$, $p < .02$. The defection strategy, which was most frequent under the high/high payoffs (as in Study 1), was eliminated from the next test. Cooperation and complex alternation frequencies were still significant between conditions, $\chi^2(7) = 23.56$, $p < .01$. Collapsing across either the leverage, the payoff, or the strategy conditions did not remove the significant χ^2: in each case $\chi^2 > 20.2$, $p < .01$. Removing combinations of leverage and strategies or leverage and payoffs had little effect; the analyses remained significant at the .01 level (both $\chi^2 > 10.06$). Removing the strategies-payoffs combination, however, removed the significance of the χ^2 (= 1.87, ns), suggesting that they interacted to affect the observed strategies.

The data in Table 10.6 lead to the suggestion that when payoffs are high/low and strategies are provided, complex alternation is frequent; when payoffs are high/high and strategies are not provided, complex alternation is less frequent. Strategy information, high leverage, or high/low payoffs increased complex alternation; cooperative strategies were most frequent when strategy information was not provided. The frequency of complex alternation in the strategy-provided conditions follows the pattern we predicted: High leverage, high/low payoffs ($n = 26$) > Moderate leverage, high/low payoffs ($n = 18$) = High leverage, high/high payoffs ($n = 18$) > Moderate leverage, high/high payoffs ($n = 13$).

TABLE 10.6 *The Strategy Frequencies of Bargaining Pairs in the Leverage, Payoffs, and Strategies Conditions (Study 2)*

Leverage	High		High		Moderate		Moderate		
Mutually Cooperative Payoffs	High/High		High/Low		High/High		High/Low		
Strategies provided	Yes	No	Yes	No	Yes	No	Yes	No	Totals
Observed Strategies:									
Cooperation	10	9	7	6	16	10	7	5	70
Noncooperation	0	1	1	3	3	1	2	1	12
Defection	7	3	4	3	7	6	3	2	35
Complex alternation	18	3	26	6	13	2	18	8	94
Complicated Simple Alt.	2	2	0	2	0	0	8	3	17
Defection + Cooperation	1	1	0	0	0	0	0	0	2
Complex Alt. + Defection	2	1	1	0	1	1	1	1	8
Simple Alt. + Defection	0	0	1	0	0	0	1	0	2
Totals	40	20	40	20	40	20	40	20	240

Other Variables

While strategies of continuous mutual cooperation outnumbered defections two to one across the two studies (105 non-defections/ 50 defections), complex alternation outnumbered its defections at a rate of about twelve to one (94 non-defections/ 8 defections).

As in Study 1, the leverage player was the first noncooperator much more often (117 times versus 16) than the non-leverage player in the defection and complex alternation strategies. The results were consistent across game-strategy combinations; no other systematic tendencies were apparent.

The proportion of non-reciprocated noncooperative choices by the leverage player in complex alternation, called the complexity proportion (CP), was analyzed in a leverage (2) × payoffs (2) analysis of variance. For instance, when the leverage player alternated between cooperative and noncooperative choices on every other trial and the non-leverage player chose cooperatively throughout, CP equals .5.

CPs were calculated for each complex alternation scheme in both studies. No significant differences resulted; the complexity proportion was unaffected by these games.

TABLE 10.7 *Mean Outcomes for the Players in Each Condition (and the Percentage of Maximum Joint Gain Achieved) Across the First Six Communication Trials (Study 2 and comparable Study 1 data)*

	Leverage	
	High	Moderate
High/High Payoffs	36,24 0,40 40, 0 4,20	36,24 0,40 40, 0 18,20
Mean Outcomes (trials 3–8), Player 1–Player 2:		
All Pairs		
No Strategies	30.1 – 24.9	32.0 – 25.1
(% max. joint gain)	(91.7%)	(95.2%)
Strategies	26.5 – 26.2	28.9 – 25.3
(% max. joint gain)	(87.8%)	(90.3%)
Only Complex Alternation Pairs		
No Strategies	26.0 – 28.4	27.0 – 28.0
(% max. joint gain)	(90.7%)	(91.7%)
Strategies	25.8 – 27.3	27.3 – 27.2
(% max. joint gain)	(88.5%)	(90.8%)
High/Low Payoffs	36,18 0,40 40, 0 4,14	36,18 0,40 40, 0 18,14
Mean Outcomes (trials 3–8), Player 1–Player 2:		
All Pairs		
No Strategies	26.2 – 20.3	29.1 – 20.6
(% max. joint gain)	86.1%)	(92.0%)
Strategies	25.0 – 22.0	27.2 – 20.9
(% max. joint gain)	(87.0%)	(89.1%)
Only Complex Alternation Pairs		
No Strategies	26.7 – 22.9	26.9 – 22.6
(% max. joint gain)	(91.9%)	(91.7%)
Strategies	24.8 – 23.9	26.3 – 23.4
(% max. joint gain)	(90.2%)	(92.0%)

The players' success at increasing their outcomes and their efficiency at attaining or approaching the joint maximum outcome are shown in Table 10.7 for the strategy, payoff, and leverage conditions for the first six trials after communication was possible. The data for pairs using the complex alternation strategy are also included.

Over all pairs, non-leverage players averaged higher outcomes than the leverage players, in every condition. However, they never averaged as much as their mutually cooperative outcome. Leverage players' average outcome, on the other hand, uniformly exceeded their mutually cooperative outcome. Providing strategies or reducing the leverage players' mutually cooperative payoff (i.e., the high/low payoff condition) reduced the non-leverage players' outcomes. Compared to their mutually cooperative outcome, leverage players' payoffs increased most when leverage was high and the payoffs were high/low. When payoffs were high/high and the players used complex alternation, the leverage players' outcomes increased to be higher than those of the non-leverage player; they increased with complex alternation in the high/low condition, but were still less than the outcomes of the non-leverage players.

Efficiency in attaining the maximum joint gain is highest when both payoffs are high and leverage is moderate, i.e., the conditions where leverage should have its least effect. Efficiency is higher when leverage is moderate or when strategies are not provided. Complex alternation, however, does not reduce efficiency overall and leads to increased efficiency in the high leverage-high/low payoff condition.

Discussion

The data from these two studies provide the first test of our model of asymmetric dilemmas (Murnighan, King, & Schoumaker, 1990); they are generally very supportive. The findings are also pertinent to questions concerning the frequency of mutual cooperation and complex alternation in ADs of this type. Cooperation was rare when messages were not allowed; it increased significantly when mutually cooperative payoffs increased or when strategies were not provided. Complex alternation was frequent in both studies when leverage was high or when cooperative payoffs were high/low; it increased in Study 2 when strategy information was provided. The high frequency of complex alternation when strategies were provided, leverage was high, and cooperative payoffs were high/low provided strong support for the model. In addition, the overwhelming number of first noncooperative choices by the leverage player in defection and complex alternation strategies attests to its importance.

The model also predicts, however, that conditions promoting frequent use of complex alternation should generate high complexity proportions. This prediction was not supported. Although only a first test, these data suggest that the discovery and implementation of a complex alternation scheme may be where negotiators stop. Our model suggests that negotiators will bargain over different complex alternation schemes and that greater leverage and low mutually cooperative payoffs for leverage players should give them an advantage in these negotiations. At least in this study, the differences among these schemes were not systematically different, even when the leverage players' strength varied. Future research might explore the reasons for this finding. The current findings suggest that implementation of complex alternation may be a discrete phenomenon, supporting a simple game theoretic prediction.

Providing bargainers with information about possible strategies was clearly important. When strategy information was not provided, more mutual cooperation and less alternation resulted but efficiency was higher (possibly due to the task being simpler). We can't help but wonder whether the continued accumulation of different payoffs might not lead players with lower mutually cooperative outcomes (the leverage players in this study) to defect at some time in a protracted interaction. Indeed, the non-leverage players' reactions to such a defection would be critical: If they reacted in a tit-for-tat or a punitive way, play would probably degenerate into mutual noncooperation and they would receive repeated low payoffs. If they accepted the defection and tried to resurrect mutual cooperation, they would signal to the leverage player that they would tolerate an occasional defection. In this way, a form of complex alternation might develop. Several of our non-leverage subjects realized that repeated mutually cooperative choices kept them on the brink; they reported that they were amazed when the leverage player cooperated through the entire session. They kept waiting for the axe to fall; it never did. The introduction of strategic information, however, allowed leverage players to realize that simple cooperative choices were not the only way to achieve a mutually satisfactory solution to the dilemma. Some choices that would normally be defined as noncooperative were clearly possible in a scheme that provided mutual benefits.

These results clearly indicate that discovering complex alternation schemes is difficult. The data also show that complex alternation schemes were more frequent after bargainers' first negotiations. Experience plus information increased the number of pairs using complex alternation. Once discovered and implemented, complex alternation was stable: defections were rare compared to mutual cooperation.

Conclusions

The study investigated a particular form of asymmetric dilemma with a limited range of payoffs. Both issues provide a basis for alternative explanations and additional research.

For instance, the payoff variable did not include mutually cooperative outcomes for the leverage player that were equal to or higher than the non-leverage player's. Thus, attempts by the leverage players to increase their outcomes may not have resulted from the use of power; instead, they may have resulted from a simple desire to equalize outcomes. Although this equity-based explanation is best tested directly, the current study's results can address this issue. The players' mean outcomes were about equal when they used complex alternation in the high/high payoff conditions (Table 10.7); leverage players' outcomes were considerably lower than the non-leverage players' in the high/low conditions. Equal outcomes were not achieved here, even though complex alternation predominated.

Another important limitation of the current study is that all the payoffs were positive. As we noted earlier, prospect theory (Kahneman & Tversky, 1979) suggests that people react differently to gains and losses. Shifting the outcomes in these games into negative values, then, should accentuate the effects of leverage and payoffs: players with leverage who can obtain positive payoffs only from Traitor (*b*) payoffs should be even more motivated to discover strategies (i.e., complex alternation) that will avoid losses. Further research would be very valuable here.

Finally, adding more asymmetries to the payoffs would expand the complexity of the game and might generate additional dynamics similar to our discovery of alternation schemes.

In summary, most empirical research on social interactions is characterized by conditions of symmetry and equality. This study departed from that trend and found encouraging new results, including a new model of asymmetric dilemmas and the potential for other asymmetry-induced interpersonal dynamics and the modeling of more complex interactions and dilemmas.

References

Kahneman, D., & Tversky, A. (1979). Prospect theory: An analysis of decisions under risk. *Econometrica*, **47**, 263–291.

McClintock, C. G., Gallo, P., & Harrison, A. A. (1965). Some effects of variations in other strategy upon game behavior. *Journal of Personality and Social Psychology*, **1**, 319–325.

Murnighan, J. K., & Roth, A. E. (1983). Expecting continued play in prisoner's dilemma games: A test of several models. *Journal of Conflict Resolution*, **27**, 279–300.

Murnighan, J. K., King, T. R., & Schoumaker, F. (1990). The dynamics of cooperation in asymmetric dilemmas. In E. J. Lawler, B. Markovsky, C. Ridgeway and H. A. Walker (Eds), *Advances in Group Processes*, vol. 7, pp. 179–202. Greenwich, Conn.: JAI Press.

Oskamp, S. (1971). Effects of programmed strategies on cooperation in the prisoner's dilemma and other mixed-motive games. *Journal of Conflict Resolution*, **15**, 274–283.

Pruitt, D. G. (1981). *Negotiation Behavior*. New York: Academic Press.

Rapoport, A. & Chammah, A. M. (1965). *Prisoner's Dilemma*. Ann Arbor: Univ. of Michigan Press.

Roth, A. E., & Murnighan, J. K. (1978). Equilibrium behavior and repeated play in prisoner's dilemma games. *Journal of Mathematical Psychology*, **17**, 189–198.
Roth, A. E., & Murnighan, J. K. (1982). The role of information in bargaining: An experimental study. *Econometrica*, **50**, 1123–1142.
Siegel, S. (1956). *Nonparametric Statistics*. New York: McGraw-Hill.
Thibaut, J. W., & Kelley, H. H. (1959). *The Social Psychology of Groups*. New York: Wiley.

Notes

1. The use of an instructor's students in his or her research raises the ethical issue of potential coercion to participate. The safeguards we took to avoid this can be obtained from the first author.
2. This recommendation became a requirement in subsequent research (cf. Oskamp, 1971).
3. Five pairs bargained in each game-order-strategy or semester combination except for the high leverage, high/high payoff, no strategy combination. Three pairs played this game first and seven played it second.

11

Fairness in Asymmetric Social Dilemmas*

ARJAAN WIT, HENK WILKE and HARMEN OPPEWAL
University of Leiden, The Netherlands

A social dilemma poses a conflict of choice between one's private interest and the welfare of a group to which one belongs. When behaviors that are gratifying for the individual imply harm for the group at large, individuals may be tempted to serve their private interests at the expense of the group interests. However, the more group members choosing so as to pursue their private interests, the more a group falls short in efficiently pursuing its common interests. To give an example, consider a group of local residents in a urban neighborhood who want to erect a playground where children can play safely. Since all local residents can enjoy the collective benefits from efficient goal achievement, irrespective of their own contribution, it may seem profitable to each of them to refrain from contributing and to free ride on other residents' efforts. However, if all residents refrain from contributing, the playground will not be realized and they will all be worse off than if all would have contributed to realize this so-called public good (Olson, 1965).

Asymmetric Social Dilemmas

Previous experiments on social dilemmas (see Dawes, 1980; Messick & Brewer, 1983; Wilke, Messick, & Rutte, 1986) have primarily focused on situations in which the group members occupy interchangeable positions within their group: each of the group members had equal amounts of resources at his or her disposal and each of them would make equal profit from realizing the common interest. In real life, however, symmetric group compositions are more an exception than the rule (see also Hardin, 1982; Marwell & Oliver, 1984; Oliver, Marwell, & Teixeira,

* Address correspondence to Henk Wilke, Department of Social and Organizational Psychology, University of Leiden, P.B. 9500, 2300 RB Leiden, The Netherlands.

1985; Oliver & Marwell, 1988). Within most groups, members differ substantially with respect to the resources available to contribute. In our playground example, some local residents may have more resources (such as money, skill and leisure time) available than others. Furthermore, group members may differ in the amount of profit they make from the realization of the common interest; for residents having children, a playground is more important than to those without children. The present chapter then focuses on contributions to the common interest as a function of a group member's resources and profit.

In this chapter we consider social dilemmas from the perspective of a fair exchange between group members. The outcome interdependency in social dilemmas confronts group members with the question how many private costs each of them is willing to make in order to provide collective benefits from which each group member receives his or her share. As such, behavior in social dilemmas may be interpreted as a means of distributing costs and benefits between the group members (Pepitone, 1971). By noncooperative choice behavior (i.e., refraining from contributing to the common interest) one saves oneself the costs, but at the same time one decreases the benefits to all group members. In contrast, by cooperative choice behavior (i.e., contributing to the common interest) one raises one's own costs, but one also raises the benefits to all group members. Earlier research in two-person and *N*-person asymmetric interdependence situations shows that group members strive for a fair exchange. Some of this research will be described below. Thereafter we will report an experimental study, which tries to increase our understanding of fairness in asymmetric social dilemmas.

Asymmetries in Two- and *N*-person Interdependence Situations

In a study on cooperation in asymmetric dyads, Pepitone (1971) showed that subjects who found themselves in a favored monetary position relative to the other player at the onset of a multi-trial Prisoner's Dilemma Game tended to cooperate more than their behind partners. It appeared that the rich player was tolerant of the non-cooperative behavior of the poor player (see also Marwell, Ratcliff, & Schmitt, 1969).

Rijman and Poppe (1977) created a dyadic exchange situation in which the two persons occupied equal starting positions but differed with respect to their ability to gain profits from the exchange. It appeared that subjects who found themselves in a high profit position relative to the other player chose more cooperatively than their disfavored partners. The high profit subjects appeared to be tolerant of the non-cooperative behavior of the low profit persons (see also McClintock, Messick, Kuhlman, & Campos, 1973; Wilke, Liebrand, Lotgerink, & Buurma, 1986).

It should be noted, however, that these studies investigated two-person exchange situations which were either asymmetric as for starting positions or profit positions. Furthermore, the subjects were involved in continued play during several trials in which feedback was provided about each other's choice behavior. This made it possible for both persons, i.e., the one in the favorable position as well as the one in the unfavorable position, to coordinate their responses to attain what they considered to be a fair exchange (see also Messick & Thorngate, 1967; Kerr, 1983; Kerr & Bruun, 1983). Social dilemmas, however, most of the time involve more than two persons, who do not only occupy differential starting positions (e.g., resource positions) but at the same time differ as for their profit positions. Furthermore, in *N*-person situations choice behavior is less identifiable for the fellow group members than in two-person situations, so that it is more difficult to coordinate responses to attain a fair exchange of costs and benefits. Empirical studies on asymmetric *N*-person social dilemmas have been scarce, however. Three studies are of particular relevance.

Rapoport (1988) examined cooperative behavior in five-person asymmetric groups. The subjects were provided with an endowment which they could either keep for themselves or contribute to a step-level public good: if six or more resource units would be contributed, the collective benefits would be provided. The group members differed as for their resources: two rich group members had three resource units each, an intermediate one had two units, while the two poor ones had only one unit each. The group was symmetric as for profit, i.e., each group member would receive an equal share of the collective benefits. The results show a marginally significant tendency for group members to contribute more often, the higher their resources. These results were interpreted by Rapoport in terms of two motives operating in opposite directions. On the one hand, group members with high resources may feel designated to contribute because their contributions would have most effect on the realization of the public good. On the other hand, group members with high resources risk great losses if the group would fail to realize the public good. It may be assumed that these two motives more or less cancelled each other, although the data suggested that subjects weighted their feelings of personal designation somewhat more heavily.

A more recent study by Rapoport, Bornstein, and Erev (1989), however, showed that group members with high resources are less likely to contribute to the public good than group members with smaller amounts of resources. These findings were interpreted by Rapoport *et al.* (1989) as evidence supporting the idea that group members with high resources risk greater losses than group members with low resources. The results of the above two studies raises the question what will happen if subjects are given the opportunity to contribute to the common interest in any amount they wish, instead of making binary decisions whether or not to contribute their entire endowment.

The study of Marwell and Ames (1979) may provide an answer to this question. Their subjects were provided with resources which they could keep for themselves or contribute to realize a step-level public good, in any amount they wished: if 400 or more units were contributed, the public good returned approximately four times as much per unit as when the units were kept for oneself. Within the four-person asymmetric groups, one member occupied a favorable position: this group member had 405 resource units at his or her disposal, whereas the three fellow group members had only 165 resource units available each; furthermore, the first mentioned group member would receive 45 percent of the returns from the public good, whereas the three fellow group members would only receive 18 percent each. As predicted, subjects occupying a favorable position showed more cooperative behavior than subjects occupying unfavorable positions. In fact, most of the subjects in the favorable position contributed all, or nearly all, of their resources to the public good. In contrast to Olson's (1965) notion that "the small tend to exploit the great," it appeared that subjects in the unfavorable positions did not free ride on the efforts of those in the favorable positions: they contributed about two-thirds of their resources (see also Marwell & Ames, 1980). Additional data showed that there was an impressive degree of consensus that contributing a substantial amount of one's resources was the fair thing to do.

However, the Marwell and Ames (1979) study raises two important questions. A first question is to what extent the large contribution by the group member in the favorable position was due to this person's high resources or profit, since resources and profit were perfectly correlated within the asymmetric groups. In their 1979 study, Marwell and Ames wanted group members high in profit to have the resources to act in terms of their interest, and were not interested in the behavior of group members whose resources and profit positions did not match. In order to disentangle their separate effects, an experimental design is needed in which a subject's resources vary independently of a subject's profit.

A second question is whether the large contribution by the group member in the favorable position should be considered as group-interested behavior or as self-interested behavior. In Marwell and Ames's (1979) four-person groups, the person in the favorable position had enough resources to provide the step-level public good unilaterally, and would receive about half of the collective benefits. Given other group members' contributions, this person's benefit from contributing exceeded his or her costs. It may be suggested that the group member in the favorable position contributed so many resources to the public good because his or her contribution would receive the particularly high return available at the provision point. In further research by Marwell & Ames (1980, 1981), employing eighty-person groups, it appeared that the step-level character of the public good game employed cannot in itself explain the high level of contribution by the group members in the favorable position, but it also appeared that when a group member in a favorable resources and profit position has not enough resources to provide the step-level public good unilaterally and receives much less than 45 percent from the public good, his or her contribution drops dramatically (Marwell & Ames, 1979).

Given the two research questions raised above, we conducted an experiment in which a subject's resources were manipulated independently of a subject's profit. Furthermore, the experiment employed a four-person linear public good game in which not-contributing is the dominating strategy for any group member, irrespective of his or her resources or profit position.

Assuming that group members strive for a fair exchange of costs and benefits, we predicted that subjects' contributions to the common interest would depend on their amount of resources and profit. In groups which are symmetric as for resources and profit, fairness may be easily defined (Adams, 1965; Adams & Freedman, 1976; Walster, Walster, & Berscheid, 1978; Messick & Cook, 1983): equal contributions by all group members will be considered fair, since these imply equal costs and benefits to all group members. The main problem facing symmetric groups, then, is to take care that each group member contributes equally.

In asymmetric social dilemmas, however, finding fair arrangements of costs and benefits is not a matter of equality versus inequality, but one of equality with respect to what (Hardin, 1982; Messick & Sentis, 1983). What will be considered fair will depend on how the relative costs and relative benefits are weighted by the group members. As for asymmetry in *resources*, two alternative lines of reasoning may be followed. On the one hand, if subjects attach much weight to an interpersonal comparison of relative costs, they may consider it fair if the rich group members contribute more than the poor ones, since a contribution of one resource unit may be perceived as a lower cost to the rich than to the poor. This line of reasoning and earlier research findings obtained in two-person situations (Pepitone, 1971; Marwell, Ratcliff, & Schmitt, 1969) and in N-person situations (Rapoport, 1988) lead to the prediction that group members with high resources will contribute more to the common interest than group members with low resources. On the other hand, if subjects attach much weight to an interpersonal comparison of relative benefits, they may consider it fair if the rich group members contribute less than the poor ones, since a contribution of one resource unit may be perceived to yield a lower marginal benefit to the rich than to the poor; the rich may be perceived to have a lower interest in the public good than the poor. Following the latter line of reasoning, it may be predicted that the rich will contribute less than the poor. Given these two lines of reasoning, the question arises how strong these two opposing motives will be.

As for asymmetry in *profit*, it may be predicted that group members with high profit from the public good will contribute more than group members with low profit. This prediction follows from considering the relative benefits associated with contributing. A contribution of one resource unit yields higher benefits to high profit group members than to low profit group members: the first ones have higher interest in the public good than the latter ones. Earlier research in symmetric social dilemmas (Kelley & Grzelak, 1972; Bonacich, Shure, Kahan, & Meeker, 1976; Komorita, Sweeney, & Kravitz, 1980) has demonstrated that the higher the benefit of contributing, the weaker the temptation to defect. In these studies, however, the experimenters varied the benefits of all members of a group, rather than the relative benefits of some of its members. The question then arises whether subjects in asymmetric social dilemmas consider it fair if high profit group members contribute more than low profit ones.

The Experiment

In fictitious four-person laboratory groups the effects of differential resources and differential profits on subjects' contributions to a linear public good were examined in a 3 (Resources: *High, Equal, Low*) × 3 (Profit: *High, Equal, Low*) between-subjects factorial design. The subjects (133 secondary school students) received a specified amount of resource units which one could keep for oneself or contribute to the group interest. Subjects were requested to divide all their resource units between these two options in any way they wished. Each of these options converted units into coins. The more certain way was to keep the units for oneself: one would receive a fixed amount of one coin for every unit kept for oneself. These so-called "private coins" would accrue only to the individual. Fellow group members' decisions did not affect the payoff from this option, nor did they benefit from a unit a subject kept for him or herself. In contrast, the returns of contributing depended on the total amount contributed by all of the four group members: every resource unit contributed to the group interest would be converted into two so-called "group coins" to be divided by all the four group members according to a preset formula. No member could be excluded from receiving his or her share from these collective benefits. The final payoffs of a subject consisted of the sum of his or her private coins and his or her share from the group coins. These final payoffs would be converted into money: the more coins one accumulated, the more money one would receive. The subjects were to be paid individually in their own rooms at the end of the experimental session and no information about their decisions would be disclosed.

As for the RESOURCE conditions, subjects in the *High Resources*

TABLE 11.1 *Experimental Design Resources and Profit of Subject (A, underlined) and of Fellow Group Members (B, C, D)*

		Profit											
		High				*Equal*				*Low*			
		A	B	C	D	*A*	B	C	D	*A*	B	C	D
Resources													
High	Prof.	33%	33%	17%	17%	25%	25%	25%	25%	17%	17%	33%	33%
	Res.	20	10	20	10	20	20	10	10	20	10	20	10
Equal	Prof.	33%	33%	17%	17%	25%	25%	25%	25%	17%	17%	33%	33%
	Res.	15	15	15	15	15	15	15	15	15	15	15	15
Low	Prof.	33%	33%	17%	17%	25%	25%	25%	25%	17%	17%	33%	33%
	Res.	10	20	10	20	10	10	20	20	10	20	10	20

condition had 20 resource units available, while the fellow group members had 20, 10 and 10 units available each; subjects in the *Equal Resources* condition had 15 resource units available, just as the fellow group members; subjects in the *Low Resources* condition had 10 resource units available, while the fellow group members had available 10, 20, and 20 units each.

As for the PROFIT conditions, subjects in the *High Profit* condition would receive 33 percent of the group coins, while the fellow group members would receive 33, 17 and 17 percent each; subjects in the *Equal Profit* condition would receive 25 percent of the group coins, just as the fellow group members; subjects in the *Low Profit* condition would receive 17 percent of the group coins, while the fellow group members would receive 17, 33 and 33 percent each. The complete 3 × 3 design is depicted in Table 11.1.

Each individual would be better off by keeping the resource units for himself than by contributing, but the group as a whole would be worse off the lower the total contribution to the common interest. Each individual would be best off if he or she would keep the resource units for him or herself while everyone else would contribute to the group interest. An individual would be worst off if he or she would contribute while everyone else would keep the resources for him or herself.

Results

The present study addresses two research questions: (1) Do group members with high resources contribute more to the common interest than group members with low resources (given that a contribution of one resource unit may be perceived as a lower cost by the rich than by the poor), or do group members with high resources contribute less to the common interest than group members with low resources (given that a contribution of one resource unit may be perceived to yield a lower marginal benefit to the rich than to the poor)? (2) Do group members with high profit from the public good contribute more than group members with low profit (given that a contribution of one resource unit yields a higher benefit to high profit group members than to low profit group members)?

Perceived Costs and Benefits

In order to investigate the perceived costs and benefits associated with contributing to the public good (group coins), two questions were posed. When asked "How large are the losses you risk if you would contribute 10 resource units?", it appeared that the higher a subject's amount of resources, the lower the perceived losses one would risk by contributing. This may be taken as evidence for the presumption that contributing incurs the rich group members with lower subjective costs than the poor group members.

When asked "How much interest do you have in the realization of group coins?" it appeared that the higher a group member's profits, the higher his or her perceived benefits from the realization of group coins. Furthermore, it appeared that the higher a subject's resources, the lower his or her interest in group coins; this may be taken as evidence that contributing yields the rich group members lower subjective benefit than the poor group members.

Contribution (in Absolute Amounts)

Analysis of subjects' actual contributions revealed a Resources main effect [$F(2,124) = 34.7$, $p < .001$]: subjects with High Resources ($M = 12.0$; see Table 11.2) contributed more than subjects with Equal Resources ($M = 8.1$; $t = 5.1$, $p < .05$), who in their turn contributed more than subjects with Low Resources ($M = 5.8$; $t = 3.1$, $p < .05$).

The Profit main effect [$F(2,124) = 7.2$, $p < .001$] indicates that subjects with High Profit ($M = 9.9$) contributed somewhat more than subjects with Equal Profit ($M = 9.0$; $t = 1.1$, $p < .29$), who in their turn contributed more than subjects with Low Profit ($M = 7.0$; $t = 2.7$, $p < .05$).

TABLE 11.2 *Main Results: Contribution by the Subject*

Resources	Profit: *High*	*Equal*	*Low*	
High	$_{x}13.4^{a}$	$_{x}12.6^{a}$	$_{x}9.8^{a}$	$_{x}(12.0)$
Equal	$_{y}9.7^{a}$	$_{y}8.1^{ab}$	$_{y}6.6^{b}$	$_{y}(8.1)$
Low	$_{z}6.4^{a}$	$_{y}6.4^{a}$	$_{y}4.8^{a}$	$_{z}(5.8)$
	$(9.9)^{a}$	$(9.0)^{a}$	$(7.0)^{b}$	((8.6))

Note: a,b,c: Means which have no superscript in common differ significantly from one another in a row ($p < .05$);
x,y,z: Means which have no subscript in common differ significantly from one another in a column ($p < .05$).

Fairness

When asked "What do you consider a fair contribution for yourself?" it appeared that subjects' actual contributions (across conditions: $M = 8.6$) were generally lower than what they considered a fair contribution for themselves (across conditions: $M = 9.4$; $t = 2.3$, $df = 132$, $p < .02$). The correlation between subjects' actual contribution and a fair contribution was rather high (across conditions: Pearson $r = .74$).

The Resources main effect [$F(2,124) = 19.2, p < .001$] indicates that subjects with High Resources ($M = 12.3$) considered it fair to contribute more than subjects with Equal Resources ($M = 9.4$; $t = 3.1, p < .05$), who in their turn considered it fair to contribute more than subjects with Low Resources ($M = 6.8$; $t = 2.9, p < .05$).

The marginal effect of Profit [$F(2,124) = 2.4, p < .09$] indicates that subjects with High Profit ($M = 10.3$) considered it fair to contribute somewhat more than subjects with Equal Profit ($M = 9.8$; $t = .6$, n.s.), who in their turn considered it fair to contribute somewhat more than subjects with Low Profit ($M = 8.3$; $t = 1.5$, n.s.). The only significant difference ($t = 2.1, p < .05$) is between the High and Low Profit conditions.

Mutual Expectations

The subjects were asked to estimate the contributions to be made by each of the three fellow group members B, C, and D. The results are depicted in Table 11.3.

A 3 × 3 ANOVA on the estimated group's total contribution to the common interest (i.e., the actual contribution by the subject added to the estimated contributions of the three fellow group members) reveals no significant effects: on an average, subjects expected a total contribution of 33.8 resources, irrespective of the subject's own Resources of Profit.

Furthermore, it can be seen in Table 11.3 that higher contributions were expected from fellow group members with higher Resources and/or Profit.

Discussion

The overall pattern of results shows that a subject's resource and profit position are two independent factors affecting subject's contributing behavior. It appeared that subjects with High Resources contributed more resource units to the common interest than subjects with Low Resources. Apparently, group members with High Resources weighted their relatively low costs of contributing more heavily than the fact that they had not so much interest in the public good. A closer look at subjects' contributions reveals that subjects contributed about equal proportions of their private resources to the common interest, independent of the Resource condition. Subjects with High Resources on an average contributed 60 percent of their private resources to the common interest, subjects with Equal Resources contributed 54 percent, while subjects with Low Resources contributed 58 percent of their resources to the common interest. In an analysis of variance of these proportions the Resources

TABLE 11.3 *Contribution by the Subject A (underlined), and the Contributions the Subject Expected from B, C and D*

	A	B	C	D	*A*	B	C	D	*A*	B	C	D
Prof.	*33%*	33%	17%	17%	*25%*	25%	25%	25%	*17%*	17%	33%	33%
Res.	*20*	10	20	10	*20*	20	10	10	*20*	10	20	10
	13.4	6.1	8.5	4.4	12.6	12.4	5.8	5.7	9.8	5.4	10.9	5.9
Prof.	*33%*	33%	17%	17%	*25%*	25%	25%	25%	*17%*	17%	33%	33%
Res.	*15*	15	15	15	*15*	15	15	15	*15*	15	15	15
	9.7	9.6	7.3	7.5	8.1	9.3	8.7	8.9	6.6	6.8	8.9	10.7
Prof.	*33%*	33%	17%	17%	*25%*	25%	25%	25%	*17%*	17%	33%	33%
Res.	*10*	20	10	20	*10*	10	20	20	*10*	20	10	20
	6.4	11.0	4.9	9.9	6.4	5.8	11.1	11.9	4.8	9.3	7.1	12.6

main effect disappears [$F(2,124) = .64$, n.s.], suggesting that, on an average, subjects in the three different resource positions incurred about equal costs.

Furthermore, it appeared that High Profit subjects contributed more resource units to the common interest than Low Profit subjects. High Profit subjects, who would benefit more from the group coins than Low Profit subjects, contributed 65 percent of their private resources to the common interest, Equal Profit subjects contributed 60 percent, while Low Profit subjects contributed only 47 percent of their private resources to the common interest [$F(2,124) = 6.6, p < 002$, no significant Resources × Profit interaction]. Thus, group members who would bencfit more from the public good contributed more of their private resources than group members who would benefit less from the public good.

These results and the ancillary data on fairness suggest a normative consensus among the group members that contributing in accordance with one's resources and/or profit position was the fair thing to do. In order to further examine the motives underlying subjects' decisions, we posed the question "To what extent do you consider yourself designated to contribute?" It appeared that the higher a subject's resources, the more the subject felt designated to contribute to the common interest. Furthermore, the higher a subject's profit, the more the subjects felt designated to contribute. These data and subjects' expectations about the contributions by the fellow group members provide further evidence that there existed a normative consensus that group members should contribute in accordance with their resources and profit positions. In order to examine if the effects of Resources and Profit on subjects' contributions would be mediated by subjects' feelings of personal designation to contribute, we included the self-designation variable as a covariate in the model. It appeared that the correlation between self-designation and contribution was positive and about equally strong in all experimental conditions. Self-designation as a covariate accounted for 63 percent of the explained variance in subjects' contributions. Inclusion of this variable in the model drastically reduced the Resources main effect and eliminated the Profit main effect. Thus, subjects' feelings of designation to contribute strongly mediated subjects' actual contributions.

It should be noted, however, that the observed pattern of proportional contributions may apply only to situations in which the different positions have no relation to group members' personal merits. In the present study some group members were arbitrarily put in a favorable resource and/or profit position, which enabled them to attain higher final outcomes than other group members. Earlier research in two-person asymmetric exchange situations (Marwell *et al.*, 1969; Pepitone, 1971; McClintock *et al.*, 1973; Rijsman & Poppe, 1977; Wilke *et al.*, 1986) has demonstrated that if the exchange arbitrarily favors some persons over the others, the persons in the favorable position as well as those in the unfavorable position coordinated their actions to reduce the discrepancy in their final outcomes, whereas this tendency to equalize the final outcomes was less apparent when group members' achieved their differential positions on the basis of personal merit. Let us consider the effect of the observed contributions on subjects' final outcomes in the present study. The experimental design allows us to estimate each group member's final outcomes if our subjects would really have affected each others' outcomes. Consider, for instance, a four-person group (as depicted in the upper-left cell of Fig. 11.1), consisting of a High Resources/High Profit member, a Low Resources/High Profit member, a High Resources/Low Profit member, and a Low Resources/Low Profit member. When we take the observed means in each of the four corner cells of the design as predictors of the contributions to be made by each of these four types of group members, the final outcomes would have ranged from 29.5 coins for the group member in the most favorable position (i.e., High Resources/High Profit) to 16.7 coins for the one in the least favorable position (i.e., Low Resources/Low Profit). The discrepancies between these group members' final outcomes would have been much larger if the subjects would have contributed equally rather than proportionally. For example, if each of the group members would have contributed 8.6 units (i.e., the mean contribution), then the final outcomes would have ranged from 34.3 coins for the High Resources/High Profit group member to 12.9 coins for the Low Resources/Low Profit group member.

It may be hypothesized that in an experimental set-up in which the Resource and Profit positions would be assigned on the basis of merit rather than chance, particularly group members in a favorable position will be less concerned about equalization of potential differences in final outcomes and will show a stronger preference for equal contributions (see also Pepitone, 1971; Messé, Vallacher, & Phillips, 1975; Komorita & Chertkoff, 1973). This may result in a decrease in contributions from the group members in the favorable positions. If the group members in the unfavorable positions do not at the same time increase their contributions, this will ultimately result in an even lower level of group efficiency than in the present study, in which only 58 percent of the potential collective benefits (group coins) were realized. This constitutes only one of the many questions we need to address in future research.

However, besides being concerned with the way in which individuals' positions within the group influence their preferences for certain distribution rules, perhaps we also need to focus on mutually agreed upon solutions reached in face-to-face bargaining. Until now, bargaining in social dilemmas has merely been studied in symmetric dilemma games. Van de Kragt, Orbell, and Dawes (1983) showed that subjects who are allowed to communicate about their contributions toward a step-level public good, organize themselves by explicitly designating a subset of all group members as contributors, just large enough to reach the provision point. It appeared that the members of such a coalition, the so-called "minimal contributing set," adhered to their assigned role. Van de Kragt *et al.* (1983) suggest that it is the apparent criticalness of their contributions that ensured mutual cooperation from all members of this set. The results of the present study show that even in a linear public good situation in which not-contributing is the dominating strategy for all group members, subjects tacitly coordinated their actions to attain a self-generated—although suboptimal—efficiency level and fulfilled the obligations of normative but less patently critical roles.

This leads us to a challenging research question, i.e., whether the gap between research on coalition formation (for a recent overview, see Wilke, 1985) and social dilemma research can be narrowed. In coalition experiments it is generally more attractive for an individual to join the coalition than to stay out of it; joining the coalition yields the individual more private outcomes than not-joining. In a linear-public good situation, by contrast, it is always more attractive to stay out of the providing coalition than to join it, since free riding always yields higher private outcomes than contributing. The process to be studied in future research is essentially a bargaining game between a cooperative and a noncooperative coalition over the allegiance of individual players (Schofield, 1975). This bargaining process in asymmetric dilemmas is interesting insofar as it is always rational for an individual to leave the cooperative coalition, even though he or she may be attracted back to the cooperative coalition by normative considerations which place a heavier burden on privileged and/or highly interested group members than on the other ones.

References

Adams, J. S. (1965). Inequity in social exchange. In L. Berkowitz (Ed.), *Advances in Experimental Social Psychology*. New York: Academic Press.

Adams, J. S., & Freedman, S. (1976). Equity theory revisited: Comments and bibliography. In L. Berkowitz (Ed.), *Advances in Experimental Social Psychology*. New York: Academic Press.

Bonacich, P., Shure, G. H., Kahan, J. P., & Meeker, R. J. (1976). Cooperation and group size in the *N*-person Prisoner's Dilemma. *Journal of Conflict Resolution*, **20**, 687–705.

Dawes, R. M. (1980). Social dilemmas. In M. R. Rosenzweig and L. W. Porter (Eds), *Annual Review of Psychology*, **31**, 169–193.

Hardin, R. (1982). *Collective Action*. Baltimore: Johns Hopkins University Press.

Kelley, H. H., & Grzelak, J. (1972). Conflict between individual and common interest in an *N*-person relationship. *Journal of Personality and Social Psychology*, **21**, 190–197.

Kerr, N. L. (1983). Motivation losses in small groups: a social dilemma analysis. *Journal of Personality and Social Psychology*, **45**, 819–828.

Kerr, N. L., & Bruun, S. E. (1983). The dispensability of member effort and group motivation losses: free rider effects. *Journal of Personality and Social Psychology*, **44**, 78–94.

Komorita, S. W., & Chertkoff, J. M. (1973). A bargaining theory of coalition formation. *Psychological Review*, **80**, 149–162.

Komorita, S. S., Sweeney, J., & Kravitz, D. A. (1980). Cooperative choice in the *N*-person dilemma situation. *Journal of Personality and Social Psychology*, **38**, 504–516.
Marwell, G., & Ames, R. E. (1979). Experiments on the provision of public goods. I: Resources, interest, group size, and the free-rider problem. *American Journal of Sociology*, **84**, 1225–1360.
Marwell, G., & Ames, R. E. (1980). Experiments on the provision of public goods. II: Provision point, stakes, experience, and the free rider problem. *American Journal of Sociology*, **85**, 926–937.
Marwell, G., & Ames, R. E. (1981). Economists free ride, does anyone else? Experiments on the provision of public goods, IV. *Journal of Public Economics*, **15**, 295–310.
Marwell, G., & Oliver, P. (1984). Collective action theory and social movements research. *Research in Social Movements*, 7, 1–28.
Marwell, G., Ratcliff, K., & Schmitt, D. R. (1969). Minimizing differences in a maximizing differences game. *Journal of Personality and Social Psychology*, **12**, 158–163.
McClintock, C. G., Messick, D. M., Kuhlman, D. M., & Campos, F. T. (1973). Motivational bases of choice in three-choice decomposed games. *Journal of Experimental Social Psychology*, **9**, 572–590.
Messé, L. A., Vallacher, R. R., & Phillips, J. L. (1975). Equity and the formation of revolutionary and conservative coalitions in triads. *Journal of Personality and Social Psychology*, **31**, 1141–1146.
Messick, D. M., & Brewer, M. B. (1983). Solving social dilemmas: A review. In L. Wheeler and P. Shaver (Eds), *Review of Personality and Social Psychology*, **4**, 11–44.
Messick, D. M., & Cook, K. S. (1983). *Equity Theory*. New York: Praeger.
Messick, D. M., & Sentis, K. (1983). Fairness, preference, and fairness biases. In D. M. Messick and K. S. Cook (Eds), *Equity Theory*. New York: Praeger.
Messick, D. M., & Thorngate, W. B. (1967). Relative gain maximization in experimental games. *Journal of Experimental Social Psychology*, **3**, 85–101.
Oliver, P., & Marwell, G. (1988). The paradox of group size in collective action. A theory of the critical mass, II. *American Sociological Review*, **53**, 1–8.
Oliver, P., Marwell, G., & Teixeira, R. (1985). A theory of the critical mass. I. Interdependence, group heterogeneity, and the production of collective goods. *American Journal of Sociology*, **91**, 522–556.
Olson, M. (1965). *The Logic of Collective Action: Public Goods and the Theory of Groups*. Cambridge, MA: Harvard University Press.
Pepitone, A. (1971). The role of justice in interdependent decision making. *Journal of Experimental Social Psychology*, **7**, 144–156.
Rapoport, A. (1988). Provision of step-level goods: Effects of inequality in resources. *Journal of Personality and Social Psychology*, **54**, 432–440.
Rapoport, A., Bornstein, G., & Ervev, I. (1989). Intergroup competition for public goods: Effects of unequal resources and relative group size. *Journal of Personality and Social Psychology*, **56**, 748–756.
Rijsman, J., & Poppe, M. (1977). Power differences between players and level of matrix as determinants of competition in a MDG. *European Journal of Social Psychology*, 7, 347–367.
Schofield, N. (1975). A game theoretic analysis of Olson's game of collective action. *Journal of Conflict Resolution*, **19**, 441–461.
Van de Kragt, A. J. C., Orbell, J. M., & Dawes, R. M. (1983). The minimal contributing set as a solution to public goods problems. *American Political Science Review*, **77**, 112–122.
Walster, E., Walster, G. W., & Berscheid, E. (1978). *Equity Theory: Theory and Research*. London: Allyn & Bacon.
Wilke, H. A. M. (1985). *Coalition Formation*. Amsterdam: North Holland Publishers.
Wilke, H. A. M., Messick, D. M., & Rutte, C. G. (Eds) (1986). *Experimental Social Dilemmas*. Frankfurt am Main: Verlag Peter Lang.
Wilke, H. A. M., Liebrand, W. G., Lotgerink, B., & Buurma, B. (1986). Equity and individual preferences in a MDG. *European Journal of Social Psychology*, **16**, 131–148.

12

Discretionary Databases as Social Dilemmas

TERRY CONNOLLY, BRIAN K. THORN and ALAN HEMINGER
University of Arizona

The intent of this paper is to extend the analysis of social dilemmas (Dawes, 1980; Messick & Brewer, 1983) to include certain classes of multiperson information sharing and decision making processes. The processes of interest are those in which each of several motivationally myopic individuals initially holds information that has decision relevance to at least some of the others, and has access to some medium of publication (a "database") which would make the information available to the interested users. If a cost (such as money, effort, delay, potential embarrassment, or loss of strategic advantage) is associated with such publication, the incentive structure may take on the character of a "public goods" or "commons" problem: The individually dominant strategy, regardless of the choices of others, is to withhold one's information; the aggregate of such choices is the individually less-preferred, socially deficient equilibrium in which no information is contributed.

A number of situations may be represented in this way. A group decision making task, for example, might involve several individuals, each holding information that would be helpful to others, but each restrained from contributing it to the common pool by personal or tactical factors. A large corporation must commonly include individuals whose expertise would be of value to others, but who are deterred from attempting to share their information by the effort and difficulty of preparing reports for the corporate database. Perhaps, in the absence of exogenous pressures to publish, researchers in a scientific speciality would be discouraged from submitting their papers by the tedium of writing, though still hoping their more conscientious colleagues would maintain a flourishing literature. (We shall consider below the more familiar case in which publication *per se* is positively, rather than negatively, valued.)

It should be noted that our implementation of public goods ideas in the context of organizational communication processes is related to, but somewhat different from, that of Bonacich and Schneider in this volume. In their procedure individuals may communicate information to specific other players, balancing a share in a group prize against an individual prize for solving the problem first. In our procedure an individual may choose to contribute, at some cost, to the shared database. If he does so, the information contributed becomes available to all other players, who thereby earn more from their individual-level decisions. The two procedures thus model somewhat distinct real-world processes, a contrast that may be worth exploring in future studies.

A shared database is in many ways a paradigmatic public good, the defining characteristics of which are jointness of supply and impossibility of exclusion (Olson, 1965; Rapoport, 1987). A database clearly satisfies the first criterion, since information is neither consumed nor diluted by being used. The marginal cost of additional users is close to zero, neglecting such practical constraints as the physical wear on library copies of journals and the computing facilities required to access a database (see Barry & Hardin, 1982, p. 181). Similarly, though other rules may be imposed, one typically thinks of a database as accessible to all relevant users. However, a database is somewhat unlike a classic public goods (a lighthouse, a public radio station) in that the benefit to the user is probabilistic rather than deterministic. The payoff from regular access to a given source of information is an expected value over instances, not a fixed sum for each instance. In the typical public goods experiment the good, if provided, benefits the participants with certainty (though see Rubenstein, Watzke, Doktor, & Dana, 1975, for an exception). In contrast, a manufacturer may be no better off on any given day by knowing that demand for his/her product in some remote region is "normal"—though he/she may be greatly benefited the following day to learn that demand will be exceptionally high or low. In this sense the situation is closer to decision making under risk than under certainty. Payoffs of this expected value form appear to be the general case for informational public goods of the type considered here, as well as by Bonacich and Schneider.

We define a "discretionary database" as a pool of data, held in common by some set of participants, to which each may, if he chooses, contribute information. We shall assume that each contributor incurs a cost, c, for each contribution. In the simplest case we shall assume that an item of information has a lifetime of one period, after which it disappears from the database. Access to each item for a period generates an expected benefit, b, to each user. (Note that "costs" and "benefits" are intended broadly, not simply monetary gains and losses, as discussed above.)

Under these assumptions each participant faces the familiar "public goods" incentive structure. For any number of others contributing, he or she is better off by an amount c by not contributing. However, if all respond to this incentive by withholding, each receives a payoff which may be substantially less than that generated were everyone to contribute. The superiority of the all-contribute payoff depends, clearly, on the contribution costs, c, the slope of the payoff curve, and the number, N, of other players. Though the superiority may be very large indeed—a single phone call warning a city of a bomb attack, for example—the prediction remains that informational, like other public goods, will tend to be undersupplied by self-interested rational actors.

We report here an initial series of experiments exploring this general prediction for small laboratory groups under a variety of conditions. We first describe the laboratory procedures, and then report specific hypotheses and results.

Method

Student subjects participated in a simple business game, receiving course credit and game winnings as inducements. Each subject took the role of production manager in charge of agricultural output of one specific country, which produced a single product for worldwide distribution. Each manager's key task was to plan production level for his or her product period by period for twenty-four periods. Worldwide demand (the aggregate of demands in each country) varied from period to period, and production above or below this level resulted in penalties. The task structure was essentially parallel to that used in Connolly and Thorn (1986). The game was implemented on a network of up to eight microcomputers located in different rooms and connected to a central file-sharer.

The rationale for the information-sharing feature of the game was that each manager, being located in a different country, was in a position to assess the local economy and thus the likely demand for different products. Subjects were presented with this information at the start of each period and could, if they wished, contribute it to a database available to the other players, incurring a charge, c, if they did so. (To equalize earnings across experimental conditions, each subject received an initial monetary "stake", s, each period; contribution charges and penalty charges, if any, were deducted from this stake.) They were then shown the contents of the database for that period: a numerical demand for each nation that had contributed market estimates, and a Not Available (NA) code otherwise. They then set a production level for their own product for the subsequent period. When all players had done this they were shown actual demand for the period, penalties and charges were computed and displayed, and the game moved to the next period.

The subjects were recruited from undergraduate business classes with offers of pay and lab participation credit. On arrival at the lab they were seated around a table in a central room and briefed on the experimental procedures, purpose and equipment. They were then shown to separate rooms for the experiment proper. No direct discussion between subjects, either by voice or computer, was allowed. After twenty-four periods of play the subjects completed a brief post-experimental questionnaire, and were paid and released. Pay was based on performance, and typically ranged from \$3 and \$6 for a one-hour experiment.

Experiment 1 Effects of Changing Contribution Cost

Single-trial public goods experiments typically find contributions in the 30–50 percent range, with contribution rates tending to decline with repeated trials (Isaac, McCue, & Plott, 1985). A strict reading of the theory would lead to the prediction that, for any positive value of contribution cost, c, contribution rate will be zero, while any negative value of c will induce 100 percent contribution. More realistically, we hypothesize that a decrease in contribution cost, c, will produce higher contribution rates. Operationally, such a reduction might be achieved by a system-wide subsidy such as that operating in academic publishing. (It is worth noting that such a subsidy applies equally to all classes of information, useful, irrelevant, and positively harmful. It is easy to imagine payoff curves that are flat, or declining, with increasing numbers of contributors. In each case a subsidy sufficient to offset the contribution cost, c, results in a dominant individual strategy of contributing, regardless of the benefit (or cost) accruing to others. With declining payoff curves and publication subsidies, the publisher perishes, along with the readers and the publication system itself.)

To establish a base rate for contributions at different levels of contribution cost, we ran four four-person groups in each of three conditions: High cost (initial stake, s = \$.35/trial, contribution cost, c = \$.11); Medium cost (s = \$.30; c = \$.06); and Low cost (s = \$.25; c = \$.01).

Findings

Contribution rate declined sharply with increasing contribution cost: 68 percent overall when c = \$.01, 32 percent when c = \$.06, and 33 percent when c = \$.11 ($F = 11.71$; $p < .0001$). There was a marginally significant rise in contributions from the first twelve to the second twelve trials ($F = 3.22$; $p < .08$). Our subjects thus appear to treat contribution cost as binary, at least in this range. When cost is essentially zero, about two-thirds contribute; when cost is non-zero, only about one-third do so.

Experiment 2 Effects of Asymmetries

In Experiment 1 all players faced identical contribution and penalty charges, and controlled information of equal expected value to other players. In real settings it is likely that some participants will have access to better information than others, that some will stand to gain more from information of a given quality than do others, and that some face larger contribution costs than others. We shall refer to these asymmetries respectively as "sender," "user" and "contribution cost" asymmetries. Where such asymmetries are generally predicted to increase contribution for unitary public goods (see Oliver, Marwell, & Teixeira, 1985, pp. 528–530), it is not clear that they will do so in the present setting.

Let us suppose that part of the incentive to contribute information is the hope of eliciting reciprocity from others. A player controlling "good" information in a sender-asymmetric situation will want to induce cooperation from other "good" players, but will gain little from the contributions of "bad" players. The existence of these latter participants will thus reduce the first player's overall incentive to cooperate. Similarly, in a user-asymmetric situation, high-benefit users might be expected to contribute heavily in hopes of eliciting reciprocity, but the low-benefit users gain little from this largesse, and have little incentive to reciprocate. Finally, contribution-cost asymmetry should induce low-cost players to contribute, even if they benefit recipients little; but there seems little reason to expect reciprocity. On this analysis, then, asymmetries of all three sorts are predicted to reduce contribution rates below those obtained in the equivalent symmetrical cases.

We ran two asymmetrical conditions. In the source-asymmetric condition two members controlled information that was nine times as valuable (in expected penalty avoidance) as that available to the other two, with all four facing identical contribution and penalty functions. In the user-asymmetric condition, two members faced penalty functions nine times as steep as those for the other two, with all four controlling equally valuable information at equal contribution cost. Four groups were run in each asymmetry condition under low (c = \$.01) and medium (c = \$.06) contribution charges.

Findings

Mean contribution rates in the source-asymmetric condition were 55 percent (c = \$.01) and 29 percent (c = \$.06). In the user-asymmetric condition they were 49 percent (c = \$.01) and 22 percent (c = \$.06). Both rates are lower than the corresponding rates in Experiment 1 (68 percent for c = \$.01, 32 percent for c = \$.06). Two-way ANOVA showed significant main effects for both contribution charge ($F = 45.09$; $p < .0001$) and symmetry condition ($F = 3.62$; $p < .03$), giving support to the hypothesized reduction of contribution rates by asymmetries, as well as replicating the contribution cost effect found in Experiment 1.

Experiment 3 Effects of Group Size

Though group size has been widely studied in the public goods context, empirical findings are confusing. Several studies (e.g., Sweeney, 1973; Marwell & Ames, 1979; Komorita & Lapworth, 1982) have found lower contribution rates in larger groups. Others (e.g., Liebrand, 1984; Rapoport, Bornstein, & Erev, 1989; Isaac & Walker, 1988; Kerr, 1989) have found no effect; and still others (e.g., Brewer & Kramer, 1986) have found complex interactions of group size and other experimental variables. The social dilemma is a psychologically complex situation, and the opportunitics for complex (and possibly erroneous) reasoning are many. For example, many people believe that they are more likely to affect outcomes in small groups than in large ones (Kerr, 1989). Do they then contribute more in small groups (since they are likely to be the decisive actor) or less (assuming others sharing their beliefs will cooperate more)? Even without these complexities, it seems entirely likely that different psychological mechanisms will determine information sharing in groups of a half-dozen or so actors from those that operate in groups of the order of hundreds or thousands.

In the somewhat exploratory spirit of this series of experiments, we compared contribution rates of four-person and eight-person groups in the symmetrical, moderate contribution cost (c = $.06) condition, using both the standard procedure and two alternative bidding arrangements (described below), a "posted-price" and a "posted-bid" procedure. Four groups of each size were run in each of the three bidding conditions.

Findings

Four-person groups averaged contribution rates of 32, 50 and 64 percent across the three bidding conditions, eight-person groups averaged 34, 46 and 59 percent. A two-way analysis of variance showed a significant main effect for bidding condition ($F = 14.39$; $p < .0001$), but no significant effect for group size ($F < 1.0$). Though this is, clearly, a very preliminary exploration of the group size issue, it does appear that the thrust of the results is insensitive to group size, at least over the modest variation achieved here.

Experiment 4 Effects of Privatization

A wide variety of structural modifications has been proposed to overcome the public goods undersupply problem (e.g., Yamagishi, 1986; Messick & Brewer, 1983). One interesting possibility in the current context is "privatization" (Cross & Guyer, 1980): granting each participant a proprietary interest in the information he or she controls, and providing a mechanism for potential users to bid to induce contribution, so that contribution costs could be offset by revenues from users. Such a market-like arrangement would, ideally, ensure that all and only that information would be contributed whose contribution cost was exceeded by the aggregate benefit it generated for its users.

We explored two bidding arrangements of this kind. In the posted-price arrangement, each player established an asking price each period for his or her information, and users specified the amount they would be prepared to contribute to have the item available on the database. If the total exceeded the posted price, the item was placed on the database, and the contributing player received the net of total bids and contribution charge. In the posted-bid arrangement, players first made offers of what they would be prepared to contribute for the acquisition of each item. Each potential sender then reviewed the total offers made for his or her information and decided whether or not to contribute at that price. If the sender did contribute, all transactions cleared as before. Each procedure was run in symmetrical and both asymmetrical conditions under moderate contribution cost ($c = \$.06$), with four groups in each of the six conditions.

Findings

Experiment 2 found contribution rates of 32, 29 and 22 percent for the symmetric, source-asymmetric and user-asymmetric conditions respectively. The corresponding rates for posted-price conditions were 50, 40 and 41 percent; and for posted-bid, 64, 58 and 46 percent. A 3×3 ANOVA shows significant main effects for both bidding arrangement ($F = 21.11$; $p < .0001$) and symmetry condition ($F = 3.87$; $p < .03$). These bidding arrangements thus show a clear improvement in contribution rates over the simple structure, though contribution rates remain considerably short of 100 percent in all cases.

Experiment 5 Effects of Group-level Incentives

A second possible modification of the public goods structure is to incorporate the participants in a single overriding incentive structure. In an organizational context, for example, a company-wide profit-sharing scheme might return to each participant some fraction of the aggregate profit. Each participant would then have a two-part incentive, one part based on his or her own performance, the other on the aggregate performance of colleagues.

We devised a group bonus scheme in which each subject received, in addition to his or her individual profits, a share of a group bonus pool. The size of the pool was determined by multiplying the total individual profits by a factor g. The intent was to direct the subjects' attention towards their peers' performance as well as their own. Increasing g would be expected to induce larger contribution rates. We ran ten four-person symmetrical groups with moderate contribution costs ($c = \$.06$) in each of three group-bonus conditions: $g = 0$ (no bonus), $g = .2$, and $g = .5$, and with cost parameters adjusted so as to make expected earnings approximately equal across the three conditions.

Findings

Contribution rates for the three group-bonus conditions were 35, 43 and 50 percent. One-way analysis of variance showed a significant effect for g ($F = 4.65$; $p < .02$). This effect is in some ways unexpected, since the real monetary payoffs across the three conditions were quite close to equal. It seems likely that the increase in contributions engendered by the group incentive scheme is due at least in part to a rhetorical, symbolic or reframing effect of the (relatively small) group bonus, an effect similar to the ingroup identity effect noted by Messick and Brewer (1983, pp. 22–29) and others.

Discussion

The experiments summarized here provide, we believe, some substance to the claim that public goods theory provides a useful model for information-sharing processes of the kind we have referred to as "discretionary databases." Our evidence is, of course, constrained by the familiar limitations of brief experiments involving student subjects working unfamiliar tasks for modest rewards. Our results do, however, converge at many points with findings from conventional public goods experiments, while differing enough in detail to suggest that databases may be sufficiently unconventional public goods to merit separate treatment.

The primary finding is the familiar one of undersupply. Even when the disincentive for contribution is tiny (1 cent), almost a third of subjects refuse to contribute; and contributions fall sharply as cost increases. Asymmetries between players in either the quality of their information or the penalty for error reduce contribution further. Though the issue of group size is clearly open, the results do not seem idiosyncratic for groups of size four: We found no effect on contribution rate of increasing group size from four to eight. Finally, we found that structural modifications, either by allowing bidding for information or by introducing a group-wide incentive for cooperation, increased contribution considerably, even when (as in the bonus conditions) the group goal carried only modest financial backing.

We are encouraged that the approach outlined here offers some potential for improved understanding of multiperson communication and decision processes in general, and of such processes on computer-based networks in particular. The approach certainly leads to testable hypotheses for field studies. For example, it suggests that working databases will be common to the extent that the information they contain is generated cheaply, or as a byproduct of other activities (e.g., retail sales data, cash flow transactions, driver's licence applications), less common when the information must be specifically generated (e.g., market surveys, technology assessments, scientific experiments). Subsidies for contribution will generate high rates of contribution, but offer no guarantees of quality: Given large enough subsidy, actors with good, indifferent, irrelevant, or downright misleading information will all be equally encouraged to contribute. Where loss of strategic advantage is the primary cost factor (as in Bonacich & Schneider, this volume), lying may become an attractive tactic. Databases crossing organizational boundaries will, in general, be less common than will those internal to a single organization, since a host of mundane matters (vocabulary changes, timing issues, coding and data-handling protocols, and so on) add to obvious incentive and in-group factors to make contribution across boundaries costly. The analysis of databases in public goods terms thus rapidly generates potentially testable hypotheses for studies of organizational communication systems (see, for example, Connolly & Porter, 1989; Connolly, Jessup, & Valacich, 1990).

It seems likely that the development of computer technologies will bring network and database decision processes into increasing prominence. The social dilemmas model appears to offer some potential for understanding such processes and for guiding their development. It also suggests the extraordinary difficulties facing the designers of such systems. A central feature of discretionary databases as we conceive them is that potential contributors do not in general have any good estimate of how valuable their contribution might be to other users. Even if I am prepared, altruistically or by subsidy, to incur the cost of contributing my information, I simply do not know which parts of it are of value to other players, which merely adds further to their information clutter. This is the information that is potentially conveyed by the bidding schemes we explored in Experiment 4, where the market-like features convey both signal and incentive. Such schemes offer the potential for self-designing databases, if the costs and clumsiness of the arrangements can be overcome. We foresee generous scope for collaborations of theory-driven and problem-oriented work in this area.

References

Brewer, M. B., & Kramer, R. M. (1986). Choice behavior in social dilemmas: Effects of social identity, group size, and decision framing. *Journal of Personality and Social Psychology*, **50**, 543–549.

Connolly, T., & Porter, A. L. (1989). Discretionary databases in forecasting. *Journal of Forecasting*, **9**, 1–12.
Connolly, T., & Thorn, B. K. (1986). Predecisional information acquisition: Effects of task variables on suboptimal search strategies. *Organizational Behavior and Human Decision Processes*, **39**, 397–416.
Connolly, T., Jessup, L. M., & Valacich, J. S. (1990). Effects of anonymity and evaluative tone on idea generation in computer-mediated groups. *Management Science*, **36**, 1–15.
Cross, J. G., & Guyer, M. J. (1980). *Social Traps*. Ann Arbor: University of Michigan Press.
Dawes, R. M. (1980). Social dilemmas. *Annual Review of Psychology*, **31**, 169–193.
Isaac, R. M., & Walker, J. M. (1988). Group size effects in public goods provision: The voluntary contributions mechanism. *Quarterly Journal of Economics*, **103**, 179–199.
Isaac, R. M., McCue, K. F., & Plott, C. R. (1985). Public goods provision in an experimental environment. *Journal of Public Economics*, **26**, 51–74.
Kerr, N. L. (1989). Illusions of efficacy: The effects of group size on perceived efficacy in social dilemmas. *Journal of Experimental Social Psychology*, **25**, 287–313.
Komorita, S. S., & Lapworth, C. W. (1982). Alternative choices in social dilemmas. *Journal of Conflict Resolution*, **26**, 692–708.
Liebrand, W. G. (1984). The effect of social motives, communication, and group size on behavior in an *N*-person multi-stage mixed-motive game. *European Journal of Social Psychology*, **14**, 239–264.
Marwell, G., & Ames, R. (1979). Experiments on the provision of public goods. I. Resources, interest, group size, and the free-rider problem. *American Journal of Sociology*, **84**, 1335–1360.
Messick, D. M., & Brewer, M. B. (1983). Solving social dilemmas: A review. In L. Wheeler and P. Shaver (Eds), *Review of Personality and Social Psychology*, vol. 4, pp. 11–44. Beverly Hills, CA: Sage.
Oliver, P., Marwell, G., & Teixeira, R. (1985). A theory of the critical mass. I. Interdependence, group heterogeneity, and the production of collective action. *American Journal of Sociology*, **91**, 522–556.
Olson, M. (1965). *The Logic of Collective Action*. Cambridge, MA: Harvard University Press.
Rapoport, A. (1987). Research paradigms and expected utility models for the provision of step-level public goods. *Psychological Review*, **94**, 74–83.
Rapoport, A., Bornstein, G., & Erev, I. (1989). Intergroup competition for public goods: Effects of unequal resources and relative group size. *Journal of Personality and Social Psychology*, **56**, 748–756.
Rubenstein, F. D., Watzke, G., Doktor, R. H., & Dana, J. (1975). The effects of two incentive schemes upon conservation of a shared resource by five-person groups. *Organizational Behavior and Human Performance*, **13**, 330–338.
Sweeney, J. W. (1973). An experimental investigation of the free-rider problem. *Social Science Research*, **2**, 277–292.
Yamagishi, T. (1986). The structural goal/expectation theory of cooperation in social dilemmas. *Advances in Group Processes*, **3**, 51–87.

C. Framing and Categorization Processes

13

Motivational Arousal vs. Decision Framing in Social Dilemmas

S. S. KOMORITA and PETER CARNEVALE
Department of Psychology
University of Illinois at Urbana-Champaign

An important and pervasive feature of social interaction is the conflict between maximizing personal interests and maximizing collective interests. In many situations, if everyone behaves so as to maximize personal gain, everyone is worse off than if everyone behaves so as to maximize collective gain. A general definition that seems to capture the essential features of such situations is one proposed by Dawes (1980), which he called a social dilemma: A situation in which two or more persons receive a higher payoff for a competitive choice than for a cooperative choice—no matter what the other members choose—but all members are better off if all cooperate than if all compete.

Although a variety of experimental paradigms have been used to study social dilemmas, the present study was based on the *N*-person prisoner's dilemma (NPD), an extension of the two-person prisoner's dilemma to the case of larger groups. To illustrate this paradigm, consider the three-person NPD shown in Table 13.1.

TABLE 13.1 *Three-person Prisoner's Dilemma Game (NPD matrix game)*

	No. others choosing C		
	0	1	2
D	0	12	24
C	−6	6	18

Note: Entries represent payoffs of a given player, contingent upon the choices made by the other two players. As in the two-person case, the D-choice yields a higher payoff than the C-choice, no matter how many of the others choose C, but all are better off if all choose C (payoff of 18) than if all choose D (payoff of 0).

As in the two-person case, each person has one of two choices: a cooperative choice (C), and a competitive choice (D). The D-choice yields a higher payoff than the C-choice, no matter how many of the others choose C. Yet, if everyone chooses D, everyone receives a smaller payoff (6) than if everyone chooses C (12). Thus, it is individually rational for everyone to choose D, but collectively rational for everyone to choose C, and the axioms of individual and collective rationality are in conflict.

Cooperation and Variants of the Prisoner's Dilemma

Several variants of the prisoner's dilemma paradigm have been proposed. One commonly used variant is the matrix game shown in Table 13.1, hereafter called the matrix game. Another variant is the non-matrix game proposed by Hamburger (1973), called the "take-some" and "give-some" games. In the *Give-some game*, subjects are told that they will receive $X if they choose D, and $Y if they choose C. However, subjects are also told that each person will *receive $Z for each person who chooses C*. Of course, the values of X, Y, and Z are selected so as to satisfy the constraints of a social dilemma. The *Take-some game* is similar to the give-some game, but subjects are told that each person will be *penalized $Z for each person who chooses D*. Again, values of X, Y, and Z are selected so as to satisfy the constraints of the social dilemma. Thus, the two types of games simply differ in the values of X, Y, and Z. In the take-some game, the Z-parameter is negative, whereas in the give-some game, Z is positive in value. However, in both types of games, it is individually rational for each person to choose D, but collectively rational for all to choose C. According to Dawes (1980), the give-some game is a prototype of the problem of providing a public good, whereas the take-some game is a prototype of problems involving a negative externality (e.g., the decision to pollute or to over harvest from a common resource pool).

It can be shown that an infinite number of "give-some" and "take-some" games can be constructed with payoffs that are identical to a given matrix game. The main constraint is that the game must be "separable" (Hamburger, 1973) or uniform (Kahan, 1973). Dawes (1980) shows that an *N*-person prisoner's dilemma game is separable if the slopes of the payoff functions for the C- and D-choices are positive and equal.

One of the implications of the give-some games is that different types of games can be constructed with equivalent payoff structures. Several methods have been used to operationalize equivalent types of games. One method, proposed by Brewer and Kramer (1986), is based on asking subjects to maximize gain (take-some) or minimize loss (give-some). This method provides a convenient paradigm with which to test the effects of decision framing (Kahneman & Tversky, 1979, 1984). Kahneman and Tversky postulate that people are risk averse when asked to maximize gain, but are risk tolerant when asked to minimize loss. If so, people should be more cooperative in a take-some game than in an equivalent give-some game. Brewer and Kramer (1986) report data in support of this prediction, although Rutte, Wilke, and Messick (1987) found no difference between the two types of games.

Another method of operationalizing equivalent take/give-some games is based on the idea of decomposing a game into two component sources of reward: one source is based on a payoff resulting from one's own choice, and the second source is based on a payoff resulting from the other person's choice. To illustrate the principle of decomposing a game, consider some of the two-person games used by Pruitt (1967), shown in Table 13.2.

TABLE 13.2 *Games Used by Pruitt (1967, 1970)*

(a) 2 × 2 Prisoner's Dilemma Game		
	C	D
C	12, 12	0, 18
D	18, 0	6, 6
(b) Decomposed Game 1 (DPD-1)		
	Self	Other
C	6	6
D	12	−6
(c) Decomposed Game 2 (DPD-2)		
	Self	Other
C	−6	18
D	0	6

Note: In Decomposed Games (b) and (c), "Self" and "Other" refer to payoffs received by persons making the choice (self) and payoff awarded to the other person when the choice is made (other), e.g., in game (b), if a person chooses C, he/she receives 6 points and gives the other person 6 points.

The 2 × 2 PDG (Table 13.2a) is the "parent" game from which the two decomposed games were constructed. In the two decomposed games (DPDs), outcomes were based on two sources: an allocation to self (self) and an allocation to the other person (other), and on each trial their outcomes were based on the sum of the two sources. Note that for any combination of C- and D-choices, the sum of the payoffs for the two choices is identical to the 2 × 2 parent game.

Pruitt (1967, 1970) found a much higher level of cooperation in DPD-2 (Table 13.2c) than in DPD-1 (Table 13.2b). According to Pruitt, different DPDs arouse different motives in the players: DPD-2 evokes a high level of cooperation because it provides an opportunity to help the other at some cost to self, and thus elicits trust and the motive of mutual assistance. In contrast, DPD-1 evokes a low level of cooperation because the D-choice, once it is chosen by one or both players, punishes the other, and thus heightens the competitive motivation of the players.

Note that in DPD-2, if a person chooses C, the other person is rewarded 18 points; hence, this game can be interpreted as a special case of a give-some game. Similarly, DPD-1 can be interpreted as a special case of a take-some game because if a person chooses D, the other person is punished 6 points. Thus, this method of operationalizing take-some and give-some games emphasizes the negative externality (costs) involving the D-choice in the take-some game, and the positive reward involving the C-choice in the give-some game. Moreover, it can be shown that the constraints of a separable game are identical to the constraints of a decomposed game (Hamburger, 1973), namely, the slopes of the payoff functions for the C- and D-choices must be equal.

The results of Pruitt's studies (1967, 1970) suggest that a give-some game evokes a higher level of cooperation than a comparable take-some game. Based on the results found by Pruitt (1967, 1970), Komorita and Barth (1985) conducted a study involving a three-person NPD, and contrasted a standard matrix game (as in Table 13.1) with two payoff equivalent variants of this game. In the "give-some"variant, there was a positive external incentive (bonus) for each person who made a cooperative choice, and in the "take-some" variant, there was a negative external incentive (penalty) for each person who made the competitive choice. In accordance with the results found by Pruitt, the game with the positive incentive evoked a higher level of cooperation than the game with the negative incentive. In a replication experiment, they found that the size of the external incentive (bonus or penalty) directly affected the size of the difference.

Using the gain/loss paradigm (described earlier), Brewer and Kramer (1986) also found different levels of cooperation in two types of payoff equivalent social dilemmas. One type was a "give-some" variant in which subjects could contribute (give) to a common resource pool, and the other type was a "take-some" variant in which subjects could extract (take) from a common pool. Paradoxically, however, they obtained a higher level of cooperation in the "take-some" game than in the "give-some" game. To complicate matters, Schwartz-Shea and Simmons (1986), and Rutte, Wilke, and Messick (1987) found no significant difference between the "take/give" games.

There are many possible explanations of these discrepant findings. In addition to type of game, these studies differ in format, procedure, and payoff structures. Nonetheless, there is one critical way in which these studies can be distinguished, namely the number of trials that were administered. In the studies by Rutte *et al.* and by Schwartz-Shea and

Simmons, subjects were asked to make a single decision, and in both studies no significant difference between the two types of game was obtained. In the studies by Brewer and Kramer, Pruitt, and by Komorita and Barth, in contrast, multiple trials were administered, and in all of these studies, a significant difference was obtained. Thus, these data suggest that the two types of games are not likely to evoke different levels of cooperation in a one-trial game. This hypothesis was proposed by both Komorita (1987) and by Rutte *et al.* (1987). According to Rutte *et al.*, in a one-trial game subjects know from the start that they will make one and only one decision. In a multitrial game, in contrast, subjects may have a longer "decision perspective" (or planning horizon) in which they can compare and evaluate short-term vs. long-term gains and losses. Komorita's (1987) hypothesis is based on the fact that Pruitt (1967) found no significant differences between various decomposed games on trial 1, but found significant differences on subsequent blocks of trials. As we shall see, this difference between one-trial and multitrial experiments has important implications for the plausibility of various explanations.

Despite the plausibility of the above hypotheses, there remains the discrepancy in the direction of the difference obtained by Brewer and Kramer, on the one hand, and those obtained by Pruitt, Komorita and Barth, on the other. One plausible explanation for this discrepancy is that different methods were used to operationalize take/give-some games. For example, Brewer and Kramer did not use decomposed games and their study was based on a replenishable resource paradigm.

In an attempt to explain these discrepancy findings, Komorita (1987) conducted a study contrasting the three-person matrix NPD shown in Table 13.1 with two decomposed variants of the game. Table 13.3 shows the two DPDs. It can be shown that for any combination of C- and D-choices, the payoffs are the same in the three games. On the first trial, the take-some DPD evoked the highest level of cooperation (p = .71), the give-some DPD the lowest level (p = .57), and the matrix NPD was intermediate (p = .62). The direction of these effects support the results found by Brewer and Kramer (1986), but the differences were not significant at the .05 level. However, there was a significant main effect of games and an interaction between games and three blocks of 8 trials. Cooperation increased in the give-some game, whereas it decreased markedly in the take-some game. Moreover, cooperation was much greater in the give-some game than in the take-some game on the last block of trials. Thus, these results provide strong support for Pruitt's (1967) hypothesis that the give-some game elicits trust and the motive of mutual assistance. More importantly, the fact that the difference between the two DPDs was based on changes over trials—rather than on the initial trial—suggests that the effects are based on changes in the attitudes, intentions, and attributions of the individuals toward other members of the group.

TABLE 13.3 *Three-person Take-some and Give-some Decomposed Games (DPDs)*

	Self	Other
(a) DPD-1 (take-some)		
	Self	Other
C	6	6
D	12	−6
(b) DPD-2 (give-some)		
	Self	Other
C	−6	12
D	0	0

Note: For any combination of C- and D-choices, the payoffs in both of these games are identical to the payoffs in the matrix game of Table 13.1. In DPD-1 (take-some), the D-choice penalizes the others, and in DPD-2 (give-some), the C-choice rewards the others.

The results of these studies suggest that the responses of the other members of the group have important effects on an individual's propensity to cooperate, and in particular, the effects of others' behavior may interact with the nature of the decomposition. According to Komorita (1987), in the give-some decomposition, a cooperative choice communicates one's intention to cooperate, if the others are willing to reciprocate. Note in Table 13.2c that the C-choice involves a deliberate loss; hence, why would a person choose C, other than to communicate an intent to cooperate? In the take-some decomposition, in contrast, the C-choice does not involve a loss and does not necessarily communicate cooperative intent. Moreover, Table 13.2b (take-some game) shows that the D-choice punishes the other, and once one person chooses D, it is likely to escalate into a sequence of D-choices. Thus, the D-choice communicates competitive, self-serving intent. This hypothesis is consistent with the results of a study by Pincus and Bixenstine (1977), who found a difference in cooperative behavior between the standard matrix game and one of its decompositions. They report that the effect of decomposing the PDG is "due to the revealing of information that is not readily grasped from the standard matrix presentation format" (p. 519).

To the extent that these hypotheses are valid, it is reasonable to assume that preprogrammed feedback strategies, such as tit-for-tat, may also have differential effects on decomposed games. It is plausible that a tit-for-tat strategy may enhance the difference in cooperative behavior between the give-some and take-some games because it is completely reciprocal: It immediately retaliates (defects) if the subject defects, but immediately returns to cooperation (forgives) if the subject repents (returns to cooperation). Such a reciprocal strategy provides much more information about one's intentions in a decomposed game than in a standard matrix game. For example, in the give-some game in Table 13.2c, if subject switches from the D- to the C-choice on successive trials, a tit-for-tat strategy will immediately forgive and reciprocate the switch to the C-choice. But this switch to cooperation will involve a deliberate sacrifice, a loss of 6 points, and should communicate one's intent to reciprocate cooperation with cooperation. Thus, it is plausible that a reciprocal strategy may enhance the difference between the take- and give-some games. In an attempt to test this hypothesis, the study by Komorita (1987) was replicated with the use of two preprogrammed strategies that simulated the choices of two of the subjects.

Replication Study

In the previous study (Komorita, 1987), hereafter called Experiment 1, subjects sat around a large table and were separated by large wooden partitions. They simultaneously read and listened to a tape of the instructions, and were asked to make their choices by showing a card marked "A" or "B" (denoting the two choices) through a slot at the bottom of the wooden partition that separated them from the experimenter. After the three subjects had made their choices, an overhead projector was used to provide feedback on the number of persons who chose B (C-choice), and the total number of points awarded to those who chose A and B on that trial.

In the replication study, hereafter called Experiment 2, subjects were scheduled in groups of 4 to 8 persons in each session. Subjects were led to one of three experimental rooms, each containing two to four personal computers (IBM-PCs). Subjects were seated in front of a PC and all instructions and feedback were presented via the computer. Subjects were informed that they would be playing a three-person game, but none would be playing with anyone in the same room. To minimize suspicion of the deception, after the subject had made his choice on a given trial, there was a random time interval between his choice and presentation of outcome feedback on each trial.

The same three games that were used in Experiment 1 were used: the matrix game of Table 13.1, denoted the NPD, and the give-some and take-some decompositions shown in Table 13.3. As in Experiment 1, subjects were undergraduate students and were informed that they would be awarded prizes (school supplies) worth up to $3.00 at the end of the experiment, depending on their cumulative point total. In all conditions, a single naive subject played against two preprogrammed strategies, hereafter denoted P_1 and P_2. Both P_1 and P_2 chose C on the first trial. Thereafter, P_1 played tit-for-tat on subject's choice, and P_2 played tit-for-tat on P_1. In effect, this meant that P_2 was programmed to play tit-for-tat on subject's choice with a one-trial delay.

Based on the results of studies showing that the tit-for-tat strategy is the most effective in inducing cooperation (Oskamp, 1971), it was hypothesized that the mean proportion of cooperative choices (P_c) would be greater under the simulated conditions of Experiment 2 than in Experiment 1, where the subjects actually played with each other. It also was hypothesized that the difference between the two decomposed games (give-some vs. take-some) would be greater in Experiment 2 than in Experiment 1.

Results

Table 13.4 shows mean P_c over 3 blocks of trials for both Experiments 1 and 2. For the data of Experiment 2, a 3 × 3 (games by trial blocks) ANOVA showed two significant effects: the main effect of games, $F(2,99) = 7.57$, $p < .001$, and the main effect of trial blocks, $F(2,198) = 6.69$, $p < .002$.

TABLE 13.4 *Mean Proportion of Cooperative Choices in Experiments 1 and 2*[a]

		Trial Blocks[b]			
Experiment	Game	1	2	3	Mean
1	Give	.49	.49	.60	.53
	Take	.51	.21	.25	.32
	NPD[c]	.45	.33	.33	.37
2	Give	.49	.51	.54	.51
	Take	.64	.68	.71	.68
	NPD	.32	.39	.47	.39

[a] Data for Experiment 1 are based on the study by Komorita (1987), whereas data for Experiment 2 are based on replication study.
[b] Each trial block in Experiment 1 consisted of 8 trials, whereas each trial block in Experiment 2 consisted of 12 trials.
[c] NPD refers to the matrix game of Table 13.1.

It can be seen that the take-some game evoked the highest level of cooperation and the matrix game (NPD) evoked the lowest level. Table 13.4 also shows that cooperation increased over trial blocks in all three conditions. These results are clearly inconsistent with our hypotheses and inconsistent with the results of Experiment 1. Table 13.4 shows that in Experiment 1, the take-some game evoked the lowest level of cooperation, and there was a significant interaction between games and trial blocks: cooperation decreased markedly in the take-some game but increased slightly in the give-some game. Despite these discrepancies, there are some consistencies between the two experiments. If we compare the overall means in the two experiments, the last row of Table 13.4 shows that the data for the give-some and matrix games are quite comparable. It is in the take-some game that we find the greatest discrepancy: overall means of .32 versus .68.

Integrating Experiments 1 and 2

The results of Experiment 2 provide considerable support for the Brewer-Kramer hypothesis: They predict that the take-some game should evoke a higher level of cooperation than the give-some game. The intriguing question is why the take-some game evoked more cooperation in Experiment 2 than in Experiment 1. There are several plausible explanations for this discrepancy. One obvious factor is the difference in experimental procedure. In Experiment 1, the three subjects were seated around a common table with a partition separating them, whereas subjects in Experiment 2 sat alone in front of a personal computer. This factor would include subjects' "preplay contact" with each other as they were led to the experimental room from the reception room, and were seated at the common table. This preplay contact may have affected the "social climate" of the group, and may have aroused some "ingroup bias" (cf. Brewer, 1979). It is plausible, for example, that the ingroup bias may have enhanced the expectation of cooperation among the group members. In the give-some game, where cooperative behaviors rewarded the others, such ingroup feelings would be congruent with the receipt of rewards. In a take-some game, in contrast, a defection by a member punished each of the others, and such punishments would be incongruent with such ingroup feelings. This hypothesis is consistent with the results of Experiment 1, with preplay contact: Table 13.4 shows that cooperation decreased in the take-some game, and increased in the give-some game.

Another obvious explanation is the fact that three subjects actually interacted with each other in Experiment 1, whereas in Experiment 2, a single naive subject played against two simulated strategies. One important implication of this difference is that our programmed strategies were highly responsive to the behavior of the subject: P_1 immediately reciprocated the choice of the subject, while P_2 reciprocated the choice of the subject two trials later. One example of the importance of this responsiveness is that in the take-some game of Experiment 1, cooperation decreased markedly over the three trial blocks (.51, .21, .25). In Experiment 2, in contrast, cooperation did not decrease over trial blocks, and actually increased slightly.

Another important implication of this difference is that in all conditions of Experiment 2, both P_1 and P_2 chose C on the first trial and never defected unless the subject first defected. This has been called a "nice" strategy by Axelrod (1984). This meant that there were many cases in which all three "members" chose C on the first trial, hereafter denoted a (CCC) pattern or state. For subjects who chose C in the take-some game of Experiment 2 and "experienced" the (CCC) state on trial 1, mean P_c over the 36 trials was .89! For subjects who chose D and experienced the (DDC) state on trial 1, mean P_c was .40. This is an enormous difference, but this result is consistent with previous results on the effects of first choice (Terhune, 1968). In Experiment 1, in contrast, there were two triads with the (CCC) pattern on trial 1, and their mean P_c was only .26, and for the four triads with the (DCC) pattern, mean P_c was .36.

The main reason for these differences is that in Experiment 2 the transition probability of remaining in the (CCC) state was .95, whereas it was only .13 in Experiment 1. These results suggest that once one person defects from the (CCC) state, others are likely to reciprocate, and escalate the conflict. With our tit-for-tat strategy, P_1 and P_2 never initiated defection, and never escalated the conflict (always "forgave" and reciprocated cooperation if the subject returned to the C-choice). Thus, these data provide additional support for our hypothesis that the responsiveness of others may be one important factor that affects the likelihood that a person will cooperate.

To provide a partial test of some of these hypotheses, a third experiment was conducted to examine the effects of the give-some and take-some decomposed games. Two basic factors were manipulated using preprogrammed strategies: the "responsiveness" of the programmed strategies, and the "social climate" among the subjects, as manipulated by their preplay contact.

Experiment 3

In Experiment 3, subjects were scheduled in groups of 6 persons, and were led to one of six experimental rooms, each containing a personal computer (IBM-PCs). As in Experiment 2, subjects were seated in front of a PC and all instructions and feedback were presented via the computer; they were informed that they would be playing a three-person game. In the *no-preplay contact* conditions, subjects were told that they would not know the identity of the two people with whom they would interact. In the *preplay contact* conditions, before being seated in front of a PC, three subjects sat together for approximately five minutes and were told that they would interact with one another in the three-person game.

As in Experiment 2, a single naive subject played against two preprogrammed strategies, denoted P_1 and P_2. Unlike Experiment 2, P_1 chose C and P_2 chose D on the first three trials. Thereafter, in the *responsive* conditions, P_1 played tit-for-tat on subject's choice, and P_2 played tit-for-tat on P_1. This meant that P_2 was programmed to play tit-for-tat on subject's choice with a one-trial delay, as in Experiment 2. In the *low responsiveness* conditions, P_1 played tit-for-tat on subject's choice with a one-trial delay, and P_2 played tit-for-tat on P_1. This meant that P_2 was programmed to play tit-for-tat on subject's choice with a two-trial delay.

The same two decomposed games used in Experiment 2 were used (shown in Table 13.3). As in Experiments 1 and 2, subjects were undergraduate students and were informed that they would be awarded prizes (school supplies) worth up to $3.00 at the end of the experiment, depending on their cumulative point total. Based on our interpretation of the results of Experiments 1 and 2, it was hypothesized that the mean proportion of cooperative choices (P_c) would be greater when programmed strategies were responsive, and that the effects of responsiveness would be greater for take-some than give-some games. It also was hypothesized that there would be an interaction between games and preplay contact. We expected that preplay contact would inhibit cooperation in the take-some game, and that the absence of preplay contact would enhance cooperation in the take-some game.

Results

For the data of Experiment 3, a 2 × 2 × 2 × 3 (games by responsiveness by preplay contact by trial blocks) ANOVA showed four marginally significant effects: (a) the main effect of trial blocks, $F\ (2, 140) = 3.06$,

TABLE 13.5 *Mean Proportion of Cooperative Choices as a Function of Game Over Trial Blocks (Experiment 3)*

	Trial Blocks			
Game	1	2	3	Mean
Give	.53	.61	.66	.60
Take	.47	.47	.48	.47
Mean	.50	.54	.57	

TABLE 13.6 *Mean Proportion of Cooperative Choices as a Function of Responsiveness Over Trial Blocks (Experiment 3)*

	Trial Blocks			
Responsiveness	1	2	3	Mean
High	.51	.61	.63	.58
Low	.49	.47	.50	.49
Mean	.50	.54	.57	

$p < .06$; (b) the interaction of trial blocks and games, $F(2, 140) = 2.55$, $p < .09$; (c) the interaction of trial blocks and responsiveness, $F(2, 140) = 2.87$, $p < .07$; and (d) a three-way interaction between trial blocks, games, and preplay contact, $F(2, 140) = 2.93$, $p < .06$. Table 13.5 shows mean P_c over 3 blocks of trials for give-some and take-some games. Table 13.6 shows mean P_c over 3 blocks of trials for high and low responsiveness of the two programmed players.

The two *dfs* for the interaction between game and trial blocks were partitioned into two orthogonal contrasts (each tested for linear changes in cooperation over trial blocks). Table 13.5 shows that cooperation increased over trial blocks in the give-some game, $F(1,36) = 7.94$, $p < .008$, but remained constant in the take-some game, $F(1,39) = .01$, $p = .91$. The interaction between trial blocks and responsiveness was also partitioned into two orthogonal contrasts. Table 13.6 shows that cooperation increased over trials when programmed opponents were responsive, $F(1,38) = 8.50$, $p < .006$, but remained constant under low responsiveness, $F(1, 37) = .07$, $p = .79$. These results are consistent with our hypothesis that cooperative choices should be greater when programmed strategies are responsive than unresponsive, but are inconsistent with our hypothesis that the effects of responsiveness should be greater for take-some than for give-some games.

Table 13.7 shows mean P_c over three blocks of trials for give-some and take-some games for the two preplay contact conditions. The two *dfs* for the three-way interaction were partitioned into two orthogonal contrasts. These contrasts indicated a statistically significant linear interaction of game and trial blocks under preplay contact, $F(1, 35) = 5.70$, $p < .03$, but no significant effect in the no contact conditions.

Table 13.7 shows that with preplay contact, cooperation increased over trial blocks in the give-some game, but decreased in the take-some game.

TABLE 13.7 *Mean Proportion of Cooperative Choices as a Function of Game, Preplay Contact, and Trial Blocks (Experiment 3)*

	Trial Blocks		
	1	2	3
	Preplay Contact		
Give	.57	.70	.75
Take	.48	.43	.40
	No Preplay Contact		
Give	.49	.53	.58
Take	.47	.52	.56

Preplay contact simulates the conditions of Experiment 1 (the study by Komorita, 1987), whereas no preplay contact simulates the conditions of Experiment 2.

This interaction is consistent with the results of Experiment 1 (see Table 13.4).

Integrating Experiments 1, 2, and 3

In Experiment 1, greater cooperation was evoked from the give-some game than the take-some game, especially on later trials, a finding consistent with Pruitt's (1967, 1970) motives hypothesis. However, Experiment 2 produced the paradoxical finding that the take-some game evoked greater cooperation than the give-some game, a finding consistent with Kramer and Brewer's (1986) framing hypothesis. In Experiment 3, as in Experiment 1, cooperation increased in the give-some game and decreased in the take-some game (to levels virtually identical to that reported by Pruitt, 1967), but only when subjects had preplay contact; in the absence of preplay contact, the two DPDs evoked the same moderate level of cooperation. The latter effect suggests that preplay contact was an important component of the Experiment 1 procedure, and may have been negligible in Experiment 2.

If preplay contact was absent in Experiment 2, the high level of cooperation evoked by the take-some game in that study is especially intriguing. Equally intriguing is the low level of cooperation evoked by the take-some game when subjects had preplay contact in Experiment 3. To the extent that the two methods of manipulating give- and take-some games represent converging operations, the combined results seem to contradict Brewer and Kramer's (1986) social identity hypothesis that common identity leads to cooperative restraint in replenishing-resource-use dilemmas. If preplay contact induces common identity, the take-some game of Experiment 2 should have produced low levels of cooperation, and the take-some game of Experiment 3 should have produced high levels of cooperation.

These inconsistencies may be reconciled if one considers the expectations and motives elicited by preplay contact and the apparent intentions of the others in the group. The amount of initial contact between subjects may have produced an expectation of cooperation. In the preplay contact conditions of Experiment 3, when the others did not reciprocate their cooperation in the take-some game (in Experiment 3 the simulated players chose C and D on the first three trials), subjects may have reacted against this cooperative expectation by defecting. Defection escalates into more defection once it starts. In Experiment 2, which presumably had no preplay contact and thus no cooperative expectation, when the others offered cooperation in the take-some game (the programmed players both chose C on the first trial), subjects may have reacted favorably and reciprocated. Recall that for subjects who chose C in the take-some game of Experiment 2 and "experienced" the (CCC) state on trial 1, mean P_c

over the 36 trials was .89, whereas it was only .40 for those who experienced (DCC).

This explanation is consistent with Pruitt's (1967, 1970) hypothesis that different DPDs arouse different motives, and further suggests that preplay contact moderates expectations, attributions, and intentions that people have toward others in social dilemmas. Further evidence undoubtedly could come from direct measures of attitudes, intentions, and attributions (such as reported in Pruitt, 1970), as well as measures of risk perception and utility of gains and losses. We suggest that future tests of motivational arousal and decision framing hypotheses in social dilemmas include measures of this sort.

Taken together, the results are consistent with research that suggests the pattern of early experience (outcomes) has large effects on subsequent levels of cooperation. The results suggest that early experience interacts with context (give- vs. take-some games), and with the responses of others. However, the nature of early experience is a function not only of the choices of others but the subject's motivational orientation. Thus, it is plausible that the difference between the give- and take-some games will depend on the competitive motives of the subject(s). In other words, if subjects can be induced to choose C in a give-some game—and are rewarded for the C-choice (or not punished)—then the give-some game may evoke more cooperation than the take-some game. However, if subjects can be induced to choose C in a take-some game—and are rewarded for the C-choice—then the take-some game may evoke more cooperation than the give-some game.

In conclusion, if we consider the overall results of research on give- vs. take-some games, it is clear that the two types of games do not evoke comparable levels of cooperative behavior. What is not clear, at this state of research, is the generality of the effects. The differential effects of the two games have been shown to interact with several important variables, including a difference in the direction of the effect. Thus, what is needed is some theoretical ideas that will integrate and organize these results, and specify the boundary conditions of the effects.

References

Axelrod, R. (1984). *The Evolution of Cooperation*. New York: Basic Books.

Brewer, M. B. (1979). In-group bias in the minimal intergroup situation: A cognitive motivational analysis. *Psychological Bulletin*, **86**, 307–324.

Brewer, M. B., & Kramer, R. M. (1986). Choice behavior in social dilemmas: Effects of social identity, group size, and decision framing. *Journal of Personality and Social Psychology*, **50**, 543–549.

Dawes, R. M. (1980). Social dilemmas. *Annual Review of Psychology*, **31**, 169–193.

Hamburger, H. (1973). *N*-person prisoner's dilemmas. *Journal of Mathematical Sociology*, **3**, 27–48.

Kahan, J. P. (1973). Noninteraction in an anonymous three-person prisoner's dilemma game. *Behavioral Science*, **18**, 124–127.

Kahneman, D., & Tversky, A. (1979). Prospect theory: An analysis of decisions under risk. *Econometrica*, **47**, 263–291.
Kahneman, D., & Tversky, A. (1984). Choices, values, and frames. *American Psychologist*, **39**, 341–350.
Komorita, S. S. (1987). Cooperative choice in decomposed social dilemmas. *Personality and Social Psychology Bulletin*, **13**, 53–63.
Komorita, S. S., & Barth, J. M. (1985). Components of reward in social dilemmas. *Journal of Personality and Social Psychology*, **48**, 364–373.
Kramer, R. M., & Brewer, M. (1984). Effects of group identity on resource use in a simulated commons dilemma. *Journal of Personality and Social Psychology*, **46**, 1044–1057.
Oskamp, S. (1971). Effects of programmed strategies on cooperation in the prisoner's dilemma and other mixed motive games. *Journal of Conflict Resolution*, **15**, 225–259.
Pincus, J., & Bixenstine, V. E. (1977). Cooperation in the decomposed prisoner's dilemma game. *Journal of Conflict Resolution*, **21**, 519–530.
Pruitt, D. G. (1967). Reward structure and cooperation: The decomposed prisoner's dilemma game. *Journal of Personality and Social Psychology*, **7**, 21–27.
Pruitt, D. G. (1970). Motivational processes in the decomposed prisoner's dilemma game. *Journal of Personality and Social Psychology*, **14**, 227–238.
Rutte, C. G., Wilke, H. A. M., & Messick, D. M. (1987). The effects of framing social dilemmas as give-some or take-some games. *British Journal of Social Psychology*, **26**, 103–108.
Schwartz-Shea, P., & Simmons, R. T. (1986). The rhetoric of cooperation. Unpublished manuscript. Utah State University, Logan.
Terhune, K. W. (1968). Motives, situation, and interpersonal conflict within prisoner's dilemma. *Journal of Personality and Social Psychology Monograph Supplement*, **8**, 1–24.

14

Communication Networks and Collective Action*

PHILLIP BONACICH
University of California, Los Angeles, California,

SHERRY SCHNEIDER
Department of Management and Policy, University of Arizona, Tucson, Arizona

There is a strategic aspect to communication in organizations that can create conflicts between the interests of the organization and the interests of its subunits. Immediately after the tragic downing of Korean Airlines flight 007 in 1983 by the Soviets, many different government agencies competed to produce the most complete story for government officials as quickly as possible. As it turned out, the most accurate description was inferred by an Air Force intelligence unit that did not send its information to the Defense Intelligence Agency, the intelligence agency that had the most influence, because its director hoped to gain complete credit for his own unit (Hersh, 1986). As one officer put it, "The armed forces collaborate on everything except the hot stuff. They just don't do it if it's hot." This communications failure was one factor (among many) that led the United States to react as if the Soviets had purposefully shot down a civilian airplane when there was good evidence available that they had mistaken the civilian plane for a military reconnaissance plane that had been in the same area. Interestingly, Hersh says that there was free communication early on in the crisis between the lower levels of all the intelligence agencies and that keeping secrets existed only at the top levels.

Similar communication problems arose in the Challenger disaster in 1986 (Presidential Commission on Space Shuttle Challenger Accident,

* Direct all correspondence to Phillip Bonacich, Department of Sociology, University of California, Los Angeles, CA 90024.

The research for this paper was supported by National Science Foundation Grant No. SES 87 11781. We also wish to thank Marilynn Brewer of the Institute for Social Science Research at UCLA for making available the Center for Computer Based Behavioral Studies, and to Matt Futterman at CCBS for his programming expertise.

1986; McConnell, 1987). NASA was divided into three subdivisions. The Marshall Space Laboratory was given responsibility for the Orbiter's main engines, the external tank, and the solid rocket boosters. Marshall was the subunit that dealt with Morton-Thiokol, the manufacturer of the defective booster rockets. The Johnson Space Center in Houston, Texas was given responsibility for the Orbiter, and the Kennedy Space Center in Florida had the job of assembling the components, checking them out, and conducting launches.

NASA as a whole was facing intense political pressure to complete a large number of launches that year and much pressure was being put on its subdivisions and contractors to avoid delays. These pressures exacerbated pre-existing competitive feelings between the centers. The result was that even though Marshall representatives knew about Morton-Thiokol's O-ring booster problems, the difficulties were not divulged to the other centers.

The Presidential Commission on the Challenger disaster suggested that organizational problems within NASA were partly to blame; the project managers felt more loyalty to their centers than to the Shuttle Program as a whole. Their primary organizational suggestion was that the Shuttle Program Manager should have increased authority at the expense of the individual centers. Interestingly, it was lower-level non-managerial engineers at Morton-Thiokol who were the first to describe the long history of the O-ring problem to the Rogers Commission and who were also most communicative about the problem before the launch. Managers at the middle levels were chiefly responsible for the failures in the communication system.

A final example of strategic aspects of the decision whether or not to communicate concerns competition for priority in science. In *The Double Helix* (Watson, 1980), James Watson, one of the co-discoverers of the structure of DNA, recounts the social relationships existing among the competing sets of scientists working toward a solution to the same well-defined problem. There were three sets of scientists: Maurice Wilkins and his co-workers at the University of London; Crick and Watson at Cambridge; and Linus Pauling at the California Institute of Technology. Clearly, Watson was ambivalent about communicating with the other two groups. He and Crick wanted access to Wilkins's X-rays of DNA but did not take advantage of many opportunities to communicate their latest hypotheses to Wilkins. When Watson and Crick thought that Pauling was ahead of them they were anxious to find out what he was doing, but, near the end of the contest, Watson asked a colleague at the California Institute of Technology to whom he wrote about his solution not to communicate these results to Pauling: "I was still slightly afraid something would go wrong and did not want Pauling to think about hydrogen-bonded base pairs until we had a few more days to digest our position" (Watson, 1980, p. 217).

This type of situation is a "social dilemma" or "prisoner's dilemma" in the sense commonly used by social psychologists (Axelrod, 1984; Dawes, 1980; Messick & Brewer, 1983). A social dilemma is a conflict between individual and collective rationality; if every individual takes the action that is best for himself, all are worse off. The classic example is Hardin's "tragedy of the commons" (1968); a pastoral community's common grazing area may be overgrazed to the detriment of all if each community member benefits by grazing more animals on the common and no single individual's choices have a great effect. Choices about whether or not to communicate with others can have a similar pattern of consequences. Hoarding one's knowledge may be more rational than communicating it, but when all follow this individually rational strategy the group may not achieve its goal and all are worse off. Let us call this a "communications dilemma."

As the recent explosion in popularity of sophisticated information technologies shows, information is an important shared resource. Two chapters in this book (this one and Connolly, Thorn, & Heminger's Chapter 12) focus on information as a shared resource that may pose social dilemmas as serious as the natural resource problems more typically studied by researchers in this field.

Solutions to social dilemmas such as the communications dilemma may be either structural or psychological (Messick & Brewer, 1983). Structural solutions require external control to constrain individual choices in the collective interest.[1] Psychological solutions rely on individual preferences and social motives, maximizing those factors that influence individuals to include collective interests voluntarily in their personal decision making.

A strictly psychological approach taken by many social psychologists is that cooperativeness is a stable personality trait (Kuhlman & Marshello, 1975; Liebrand & Van Run, 1985; Liebrand *et al.*, 1986). In these studies, subjects are classified as cooperative, competitive, individualistic or altruistic on the basis of their consistent preferences concerning the relationship between their own rewards and the rewards of others. In this paper, on the other hand, cooperative behavior is seen as a product of group structure. In the first two experiments reported here, group structure is manipulated externally by constraining the communication channels available to members of the group, creating highly centralized or decentralized communication networks, and positions within those networks. In the third experiment, group structure is manipulated *psychologically* by two different methods—stressing a subgroup orientation based on position in the communication network, or by stressing a collective orientation, an "all for one, one for all" approach.

Communication Network Structure

The structural approach based on constraints on who may talk to whom in a communication network is particularly appropriate when studying communication in organizational settings. It is well known that organizations have approved communication routes. One must "go through channels." Even in informal structures, clearly defined social networks evolve. In this paper, cooperative or non-cooperative behavior is seen as a product of the structure of the communication network, and one's position in that network.

The traditional structural approach to group problem solving was developed by Leavitt (1951) and Bavelas (1950). Typically, five individuals were asked to identify a common symbol by communicating their information to one another through open mail slots. The experimenters manipulated the communication structure by controlling which slots were available to the participants. When all slots were open, the result was the "all-channel" network, in which all group members could communicate with one another. In the "wheel," all communication had to pass through a centrally located group member in order to be distributed to the rest of the group.

The likelihood of someone in a particular network guessing the common symbol depends on their position in it. Centrality of position is determined by how long it would take for all information to accumulate at that position (Bonacich, 1987). In the "wheel" network, there was little ambiguity about which position was most central. Information accumulated fastest in the lone position in the center of the network. In the "all-channel" network, however, all positions were of equal centrality.

Not only do positions differ in centrality within networks, networks differ in their degree of centralization. The centralization of a network refers to the degree to which centrality is monopolized by any one position in the network. Freeman (1979) mathematically defined the centralization of network as the sum of the differences in distance from the central point to all other points in the network divided by the maximum sum of the distances possible in a network of that size. Centralization is 0 if all positions are equally central, such as in the all-channel network, and 1 if the network is maximally centralized, such as the wheel network.

Intuitively, if a group were to organize a rational scheme for getting all available information to one person, the most central member should be the one to solve the group's problem first (Flament, 1963). However, competition to solve the problem can weaken the position of the most central group member. In mixed-incentive situations such as communications dilemmas, groups can be paralyzed if there is no undisputed central individual.

In such situations, the incentive to attain the collective outcome quickly may be overpowered by competition to maximize individual outcomes. For example, the collective goal of the intelligence agencies in the Flight 007 disaster was to assemble quickly the necessary information for prevention of an international incident. However, the competition

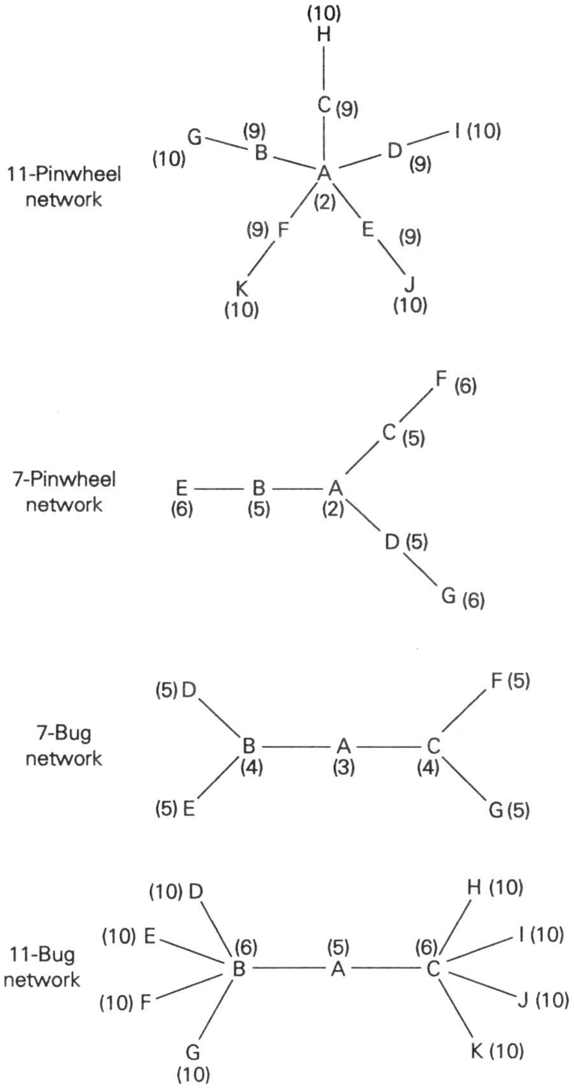

FIG. 14.1 Four communication networks.

between the agencies to be first to obtain the most important information interfered with the collective goal. In another example, in the race to determine the structure of DNA, collaboration between laboratories was slowed by each lab's individual quest for the Nobel Prize.

In the experiments described in this paper, subjects holding positions in communication networks are given incomplete sets of information.

They can communicate the information they possess only to those to whom they are connected, as in the classic restricted communication studies of Bavelas (1950) and Leavitt (1951). All members of a network are rewarded in proportion to the speed with which any one member of the network succeeds in possessing all or almost all of the network's information (this is the incentive members have to communicate with others), but the "winning" member receives an additional reward (this is the incentive to hoard information).

In the first two experiments described in this chapter, the four communication networks shown in Fig. 14.1 will be used.

These communication networks are arranged in order of centralization. In the top network, the "11-Pinwheel", there is little ambiguity concerning the most central position. If the network's task necessitates one position possessing all of the information, this will be most effectively accomplished if all network members forward their information to position A. In parentheses next to each position are the number of communication cycles the network would require to centralize its information at each position if one item of information could be communicated per cycle. All information could be centralized at position A in two cycles, whereas it would take four to five times as many cycles for information to be centralized at any other position.

The "7-Pinwheel" is less centralized because the advantage of centralizing information at position A is less pronounced. The "7-Bug" and "11-Bug" networks are still less centralized. In the "11-Bug" the three middle positions A, B and C have an almost equal claim to be the most central. Using Freeman's (1979) measure in which 1.00 is a network of maximal centralization, the centralization of the four networks in Fig. 14.1 is 0.83, 0.70, 0.47, and 0.47 respectively.

All the networks in Fig. 14.1 are "trees" in the language of graph theory; every pair of points are connected by a unique path (Harary, 1972, p. 32). We will distinguish between three kinds of positions in these tree networks. "Central" positions are the most central positions in the networks. According to the definition of a tree, every tree has either one most central point or two equally most central points adjacent to each other (Harary, 1972, p. 35). All four networks used in this study have unique centers. Additionally, every type of tree network has at *least* two endpoints (Harary, 1972, p. 34). These are "peripheral" positions. "Middle" positions are neither central nor peripheral. Trees need not have middle positions, but the four networks used in this study do.

For the peripheral positions in these networks, only the group reward should be salient. These positions can have no expectations of earning the individual prize. Moreover, even if the information were centralized at their position, the inefficiencies and group loss in so doing would offset the individual competitive reward. Therefore, peripheral positions should cooperate the most. For central positions, the individual reward should be more probable, and they should cooperate less.

We predict highly centralized networks will consist of one prominent central position plus a number of other positions that never accumulate much information and which are eager to forward their information to the central position. Therefore, the unwillingness of the central position to communicate should not interfere with the efficiency of these networks.

Moderately centralized networks, on the other hand, face three related problems. First, the central position enjoys a less clear cut and compelling advantage; other positions may be less willing to assume subordinate positions and sacrifice their chances for the individual reward. Second, unlike a peripheral position or a middle position in a highly centralized network (for example positions B, C, D, E and F in the 11-Pinwheel network), a middle or central position in a less than completely centralized network can effectively reduce the information available to others (potential competitors) substantially by not communicating.

The third exacerbating problem that moderately centralized networks such as "Bug" networks face is that middle positions enjoy a transitory advantage over the central position in the early stages of communication. For example, in the "11-Bug" network, if all positions were to communicate freely, after the first communication cycle position A, the most central, would have three units of information (their own plus what had been known initially by B and C) whereas B and C would each possess six items of information, more than half the network's total information. This transitory advantage might make the individual reward more salient to them. On the other hand, in a more centralized network, like the Pinwheel networks, centrality and the information possessed in early stages of communications are never discrepant. For example, if there were the maximum amount of communication in the 11-Pinwheel network, position A, the most central, would have six items of information after one cycle while the less central positions B, C, D, E and F would have only three.

The combination of these effects should make more centralized networks more effective (i.e., will experience less hoarding) than moderately centralized networks and, therefore, they will be faster in achieving collective goals. In centralized networks all positions except the most central ought to be oriented to the network goal, and whether the central position communicates or not should be irrelevant to the network's effectiveness. The self-interested behavior of intermediate positions in networks of moderate centrality should, on the other hand, be disruptive.

For these reasons, we hypothesize that communication rates in general will decrease with increasing centrality but that middle and central positions in relatively decentralized networks (for example, positions B and C in 7-Bug and 11-Bug) would be the most "selfish" members of their networks. Computer simulations (Bonacich, 1987) support these hypotheses.

Structure Based on Group Orientation

In addition to a linear hierarchy in which positions differ in their degree of centrality, organizations may also be grouped into subgroups or departments that cut vertically across levels (Porter & Roberts, 1976). The examples of communications dilemmas used at the beginning of this paper (the Korean Flight 007, the Challenger disaster, and scientific competition) were all dilemmas at the subgroup level. Differentiation of an organization that produces subunit orientation (such as NASA's space centers) produces an inherent potential for conflict and competition between subunits, and competition between departments can reduce communication between them (Blake, Shepard, & Mouton, 1964; Dutton & Walton, 1966).

Such subjective identification with a subgroup can transform individual motivations in social dilemmas such as the communications dilemma. In a series of studies employing a laboratory analogue of a social dilemma (Kramer & Brewer, 1984; Brewer & Kramer, 1986), subjects behaved more competitively when the collective was differentiated into subunits than when a common collective identity was made salient. However, when both subgroups and superordinate identity were present, individuals showed the highest amount of self restraint in the interests of collective welfare.

These experiments demonstrate that the subjective transformation from a collection of individuals to a social group can affect behavior dramatically even when the basis for social identity is a weakly induced laboratory manipulation and the opportunity for interpersonal interaction is absent (Turner, 1987). Group membership is an important variable in organizational settings as well. For example, Brown (1978) found that separate identities of the production and development branches of a factory became so strong, workers were more concerned with maintaining the relative differences between the salaries of the two groups, rather than increasing their absolute amounts.

In general, if the interdependent group is perceived merely as a collection of isolated individuals, choices will depend largely on the individuals' cooperative predispositions (Liebrand, 1984), or on the communication network structure, as hypothesized above. On the other hand, if group membership is made salient, either at the subgroup level or at the superordinate level, the communication dynamics may change such that communication between members of the salient group is increased.

In the first two experiments in this chapter, communication is hypothesized to be dependent on position in the network. Midpositions in networks of intermediate centrality are hypothesized to be the least cooperative, as they enjoy the biggest transitory advantage to reaching a solution first. Experiment 3 was designed to test two psychological manipulations based on group membership that should increase communication from the ordinarily least cooperative midpositions to the central position in a communications dilemma. A subgroup orientation based on network centrality (the two midpositions and the central position in the same subgroup) or a superordinate collective orientation were superimposed on the 7-Bug network of intermediate centrality. When group membership is stressed, the middle position's withholding of information should decrease. Group members will be more concerned with outcomes at the group or subgroup level than in maximizing individual gain, and will therefore communicate more within their group.

Hypotheses

In summary, we have the following four specific hypotheses:

1. In highly centralized networks, the more central a position, the less it should communicate.
2. In moderately centralized networks, however, the lowest communication rates should be found among middle (not peripheral and not central) positions.
3. In communications dilemmas, more centralized networks will be more effective (i.e., less overall hoarding of information should result in a speedier solution).
4. When group membership is stressed, the middle position's withholding of information should decrease.

Experiment 1

Method

Subjects

Participants in the experiment were 154 male and female Introductory Psychology students satisfying course requirements. Subjects participated in groups of seven, but they were placed in separate booths and were connected to each other only through computer terminals.

Procedure

Groups of seven subjects played a game in which each person was given a subset of the letters to a quotation too small to identify the quotation.

For example, for a quote with 80 letters, each subject might be given about half a dozen letters. Within each round of the game, subjects were offered opportunities both to guess the quote and to give to others some of the letters they had received from the experimenter or from other subjects.

There was a $3.50 group reward divided equally among all group members if any one member correctly identified the quotation, but this group reward declined $0.35 for each additional communication round it took for the group to identify the quote. The group reward for early identification of the quote provided a collective goal. This group goal was most effectively pursued when each individual communicated as many of his letters as possible to others in order to maximize the chance that some one would succeed.

There was an additional $2.00 reward for the first member or members to correctly identify the quote (and a $0.25 penalty for incorrect guesses). This competitive feature was an incentive to improve one's position in relationship to others by not sending to others while they continued to communicate. In the absence of an individual reward for being first, group members would have cooperated by sending the maximum number of letters to others. On the other hand, in the absence of a group reward there would have been little incentive to communicate with others. It is the simultaneous presence of both types of incentives that creates the social dilemma in which individual and group goals are at odds.

Subjects were in restricted communication networks; they could not send letters to all other positions. They were given a diagram of the structure of the communication network and their position in it. In each round they could choose to send nothing or up to a maximum of three letters to each of those group members to whom they were connected. The computer program allowed a player to send to another player only letters that he had not previously sent to or received from that player. They were told at the end of every round how many letters were possessed by each of the other members and how many letters had been sent to them by each of the others. A maximum of ten rounds was allowed for each quote. In order to keep the networks comparable to each other, data only on the first quote was used for those few groups that managed to identify more than one quote in their hour.

The measure of communicativeness should not be the sheer number of letters communicated by a subject. This number was inevitably affected by the number of letters that the subject had received from others and his/her position in the network. If a subject received few letters from others, the number of letters he/she could communicate to others would fall below the maximum of three letters per round. Players in peripheral positions connected to only one other player could send only the letters that they had at the beginning of the game.

Therefore, communicativeness was measured by a proportion sent in relation to the maximum that could be sent. For example, if the number of letters possessed by player A but not received from player B or previously sent by A to B was 6, 8, 10, 7, 4, 1, and 0 in the seven rounds before a puzzle was solved, then the maximum number of letters that could have been sent from A to B would have been 3 + 3 + 3 + 3 + 3 + 1 + 0 = 16. If player A had sent 2, 2, 3, 3, 3, 1, and 0 letters, then the rate at which A sent letters to B would be calculated as 14/16 = 0.875.

Ten and twelve sessions were run in the 7-Bug and 7-Pinwheel conditions respectively. After each session, each participant was debriefed and paid separately what he/she had earned.

Results

Table 14.1 reports the mean communicativeness by position in the two networks used in Experiment 1. The results only partly confirm the hypotheses. It was predicted that centrality would be negatively related to communicativeness in both networks, but that the lowest level of communicativeness in the less centralized Bug network would be by the middle positions.

TABLE 14.1 *Mean Communicativeness by Position Type in 7-Bug and 7-Pinwheel Networks*

	Position type			
Network	Peripheral	Middle	Central	[mean]
Bug (n = 10)	0.869	0.636	0.793	0.766
Pinwheel (n = 12)	0.763	0.601	0.686	0.680
[mean]	0.811	0.617	0.735	

Note: In a two-way analysis of variance with position type as a repeated factor, there were significant position effects ($F_{2,40} = 7.994$, $p < 0.01$), but insignificant network and interaction effects.

As can be seen from Table 14.1, there are significant positional differences in communicativeness; communication rates are highest in the peripheral positions. However, communication rates are lowest in the middle positions of both networks. There is a slight tendency for the middle positions to be relatively less communicative in the Bug network (the Central–Middle difference is 15 in the Bug networks and only 9 in the Pinwheel networks), but this difference in pattern is far from statistically significant.

Experiment 2

Design and Rationale

The principal reason for the failure to find the expected position-by-network interaction may have been that the two networks were not different enough in their degree of centralization. The 11-Bug network of Fig. 14.1 is more decentralized than the 7-Bug network; the "transitory advantage" enjoyed by the middle positions in relation to the central position is greater. The 11-Pinwheel network is more centralized than the 7-Pinwheel network because the central position is more central. The 11-Bug and 11-Pinwheel networks might show the anticipated difference because they are more extreme in degrees of centralization and decentralization. Therefore, in Experiment 2 these two networks were contrasted. The instructions and rewards were changed appropriately.

There was one additional change in Experiment 2. The behavior of the peripheral subjects in the first experiment seemed quite well-established; they typically gave at high levels until they had no more letters to give. Since the predicted cooperativeness of these subjects was no longer at issue, these subjects were simulated in Experiment 2. Subjects in Experiment 2 thought they were part of an 11-person experiment, but there were actually only three subjects in the 11-Bug and six subjects in the 11-Pinwheel networks. The simulated peripheral subjects were programed to follow the model peripheral strategy in Experiment 1; they gave letters to middle positions until they ran out of letters. This experiment, therefore, focuses on the middle and central positions.

Results

Eighteen and eight groups were run in the 11-Bug and 11-Pinwheel conditions respectively. Figures 14.2 and 14.3 show both the potential and actual accumulated information over the ten rounds for those in central and middle positions. The potential information is the maximum number of letters that a position could possess if all other positions communicated at the maximum rate. The actual information is based on the mean information by position of the (declining) number of groups that still had not identified the quote by that round. In these figures, the lines labeled PC and PM give the maximum number of letters that could potentially be possessed by central and middle positions respectively, while AC and AM give the actual mean number of letters possessed by central and middle positions.

Note that, in Fig. 14.2, in rounds one through seven it is possible that the middle positions (labeled PM) would have more information than the central position if all positions communicated maximally. It is only in the

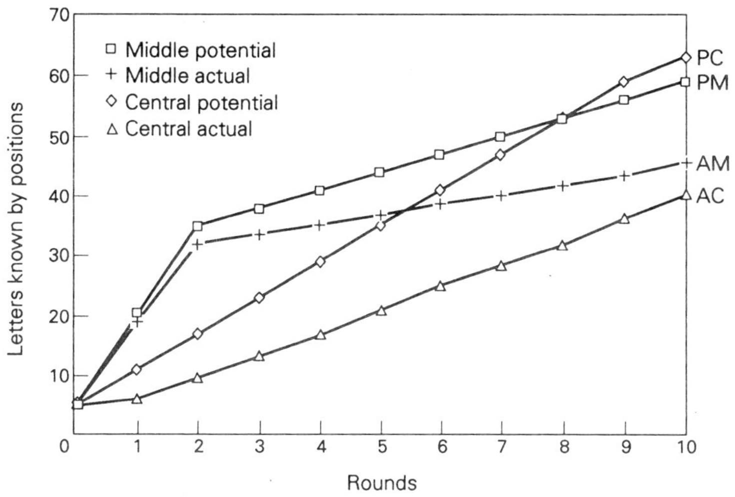

FIG. 14.2 Letters known by position and round in 11-Bug network.

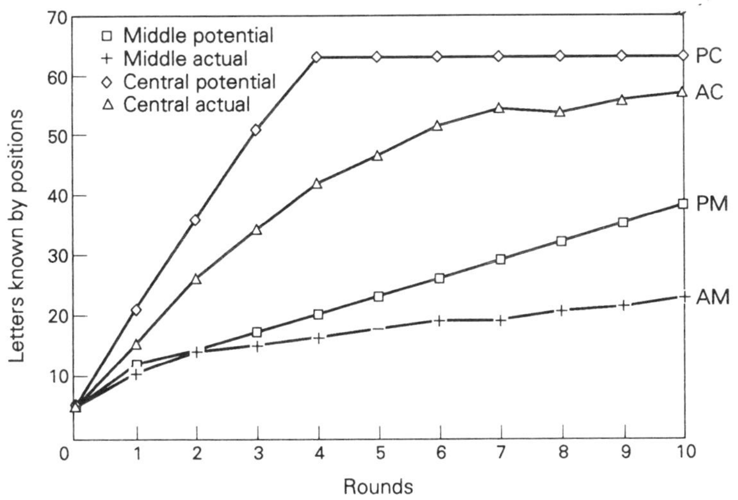

FIG. 14.3 Letters known by position and round in 11-Pinwheel network.

late rounds that the central position (labeled PC) would have an advantage in a fully cooperative group. This potential gap in the early rounds is one of the reasons why middle positions in these networks are expected to be less communicative. Looking at Fig. 14.3 for the 11-Pinwheel network, if all of the positions communicate maximally, the superiority of the central positions (labeled PC) is never challenged by the midpositions (labeled PM) in a cooperative group. It is the consistent superiority of the central positions that should lead to a high communication rate by the middle positions in these networks.

Table 14.2 shows the mean communication rates for the two eleven-person networks. The pattern is now consistent with Hypothesis 2. In the highly centralized 11-Pinwheel network the middle positions communicates more than the central positions, but in the less centralized 11-Bug network the middle positions communicate less. The lessor communicativeness of the middle positions accounts for why the central positions never do overtake the middle positions in total knowledge (see Fig. 14.2) despite their greater potential.

TABLE 14.2 *Mean Proportion of Available Letters Sent by Position in Two Networks*

	Position type		
Network	Peripheral (simulated)	Middle	Central
11-Bug (n = 18)	1.00	0.47	0.65
11-Pinwheel (n = 8)	1.00	0.64	0.36
[mean]		0.52	0.56

Note: In a two-way analysis of variance with position type as a repeated factor, there was a significant position by network type interaction ($F_{2,24} = 21.398$, $p < 0.01$).

There is an ambiguity, however. Subjects knew both their positions within the network and the number of letters known by other positions at the beginning of every round. Did middle positions in 11-Bug networks communicate less because they sensed their strategically advantageous position from the first, or did they instead simply respond in a more short-term manner to the growing "transitory advantage" they enjoyed in the early trials? The first hypothesis implies that the difference in communicativeness would exist from the first round, whereas the second implies that the two positions would start out with equal rates, but that there would be a growing gap.

Figure 14.4 shows the mean communication rates for each round in the central and peripheral positions of the 11-Bug network.

The means for the various rounds are not based on the same number of sessions because sessions ended when someone correctly identified the quote. However, the pattern is clear. The positions start out with equal rates in the first three rounds, then there is a growing gap in communication rates. Rather than making strategic assessments of their optimal long-range strategies, subjects in the middle positions of these decentralized networks appear to have been reacting to the greater knowledge they accumulated because of their connection to peripheral positions.

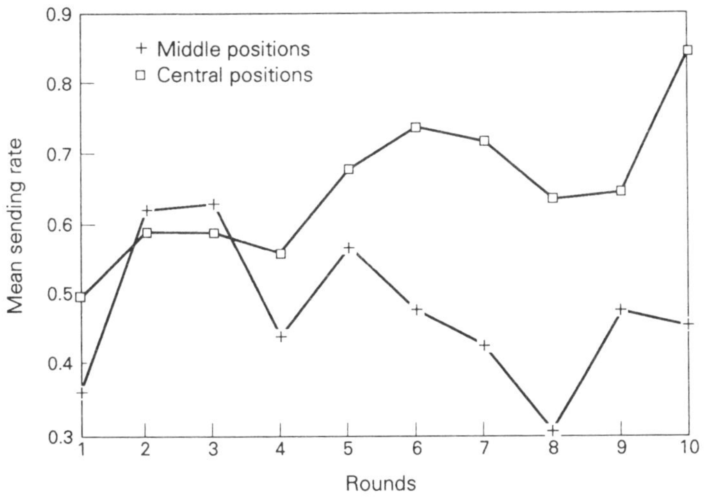

FIG. 14.4 Sending rate by position and round in 11-Bug network.

An analysis of variance was performed for the 16 of 18 groups that completed six rounds (after six rounds the number of remaining groups declined rapidly). The position by round interaction observed in Fig. 14.4 is highly significant, $F(5, 75) = 3.32$, $p < .01$. There is not a significant position effect because the largest positional differences occurred in the late trials that were omitted from these calculations.

The same analysis was performed on the first four trials of the 11-Pinwheel network with results that were different but consistent with the differences between the networks. The statistically significant difference in communication rates between the middle and central positions was constant across trials, instead of growing as in the Bug network. This is in agreement with the more pronounced early knowledge advantage of the central position in the Pinwheel network.

Hypothesis 3 is difficult to test. By the most straightforward criterion, the number of rounds to a solution, the 11-Pinwheel networks were somewhat more efficient; the median number of rounds before a solution was reached was 10 for the 11-Bug networks (only half of the networks identified the quote before the 10 round limit) and 7.5 for 11-Pinwheel networks, but this difference was not statistically significant. However, this measure may be biased against Pinwheel networks, in which there is only one position with a possible chance of solving the puzzle, in comparison to the 11-Bug, in which there are three.

The reasoning behind Hypothesis 3, the greater "selfishness" of middle positions in the Bug networks, can be tested directly. A *t*-test shows that difference in communicativeness of middle positions in the two networks

(.64 vs .47 in Table 14.2) is statistically significant, $t(21) = 3.1617$, $p < .01$.

Experiment 3

Design and Rationale

In Experiments 1 and 2, in networks of intermediate centrality, the midpositions did not communicate the optimum number of letters to the central positions that would have maximized the group's outcomes. Experiment 3 was designed to test two psychological manipulations based on group membership that should increase communication from the midpositions to the central position in a communications dilemma. This experiment compares the 7-Bug network with no subgroup divisions (identical to the network used in Experiment 1, which we will call the structural control) with a condition in which subgroup membership was based on position in the network (which included the two midpositions and the central position) and a condition in which a superordinate collective orientation was made salient.

Within our theoretical framework, subgroup orientation should increase the amount of communication the midpositions send to the central position because they now share an identity with that position. In addition, stressing the collective identity of the entire group has also been shown to be successful in increasing contributions in a social dilemma (Brewer & Kramer, 1984; Kramer & Brewer, 1986). It was hypothesized that adding collective identity to the network would also increase communication from the midpositions to the central positions.

Method

Subjects

Participants were 43 male and 50 female students enrolled in Introductory Psychology. Approximately a third (33) of the subjects served in the structural control condition, 29 served in the network-role condition and the remainder served in the collective condition.

The communication network

Since the focus of this experiment is on the midpositions, all subjects served in one of these two positions in the 7-Bug network. All remaining positions in the network were simulated by the computer. The peripheral group members were simulated in exactly the same manner as in

Experiment 2. The simulation of the network's central member was based on that position's behavior in Experiment 1. The mean number of letters the central position sent per round to the midposition was 1.5.

In addition, since the midposition was the only true group member, the simulated central position was programed to "solve" the first two quotes. Therefore, if the midposition communicated to the central position, it was a clear indication that they wanted to increase the probability of the group winning the group reward. Unless the midposition actually solved the quote first (as happened in a few cases), Quote 1 was solved by the central position on Round 6, and Quote 2 was solved on Round 9. Participants were given 90 minutes to solve a maximum of 3 quotes.

Procedure and Social Identity Manipulation

The procedure was similar to that used in Experiments 1 and 2, except identity in the subgroup condition was based on position in the network which was given meaning by labeling the peripheral positions as "Production" (those who give the letters to the central members) and the middle positions as "Development" (the central members who will develop the solution). Given the paradigm, Production and Development were thought to be meaningful distinctions, but were not such status-laden distinctions as "management" and "worker." To reinforce the Production/Development distinction, a network diagram of the Production and Development subgroups was placed next to each terminal, and additional instructions were added to beginning of the experiment that explained the "differences" between the two groups.

In the collective identity condition, an overall group identity was established by a shared-fate manipulation that had successfully increased cooperation in a social dilemma (Kramer & Brewer, 1986). A lottery was held at the beginning of the experiment to determine the group's shared rate of pay for each quote. Although the outcome was always fixed at $3.50 per quote, participants thought their group was unique in its ability to earn this amount.

Results and Discussion

Letters sent per round to the peripheral group members increased across quotes in all three conditions. On the other hand, letters sent to the central position decreased from Quote 1 to Quote 2, and then increased from Quote 2 to Quote 3 (see Table 14.3). However, letters sent in the undifferentiated structural control condition did not return to their Quote 1 level, while letters sent in the collective and prod/dev conditions were higher than their Quote 1 levels. This pattern accounted for the significant quote by

TABLE 14.3 *Letters Sent per Round from Middle Positions: Collective and Production/Development Orientation vs. Structural Control*

	Target	
Condition	Central	Peripheral
Quote 1		
Structural Control	2.0	1.7
Collective	2.0	1.8
Prod/Dev	2.0	1.8
Quote 2		
Structural Control	1.7	1.9
Collective	1.8	1.9
Prod/Dev	1.9	2.0
Quote 3		
Structural Control	1.8	2.0
Collective	2.2	2.2
Prod/Dev	2.1	2.2

target interaction when the structural control condition was compared to the two group membership conditions, $F(2, 180) = 3.17$, $p < .05$.

When the middle position's communication to the central position was examined separately (see Table 14.3), the condition effect was significant for Quote 3 only, $F(2, 90) = 3.08$, $p < .05$. It was hypothesized that any group identity, as long as it was inclusive of the central group members, would have greater communication compared to the structural control condition. The planned orthogonal contrast of group orientation versus structural control was also only significant for Quote 3, $F(1, 91) = 6.15$, $p < .05$. In Quote 3, the middle position sent more letters per round to the central position when group identity was made salient by either stressing communication role or the collective, and these two conditions did not differ significantly from one another.

That the effect is only shown in Quote 3 may denote some type of learning curve for the dilemma. In previous research on resource dilemmas (Brewer & Kramer, 1985; Kramer & Brewer, 1986), cooperative behavior based on group membership increased as the severity of the dilemma increased. Perhaps that is why we only see the divergence between conditions in the third quote, when participants were most likely to understand how communications dilemmas worked. Interesting supporting evidence for a learning effect is that letters per round increased to the peripheral members across quotes. This was an excellent strategy; increased communication to the peripheral members did not increase their chances of solving the quote, but may have prompted them to reciprocate with letters of their own (if they had been real group members, of course).

Conclusions

In the "real" world, competitive relationship between subunits of an organization can reduce communication between them (Dutton & Walton,

1966; Blake *et al.*, 1964). Coordination problems between subunits are known to be especially intense when the organization is decentralized and differentiated into somewhat independent subunits (Lawrence & Lorsch, 1967). On the other hand, subgroup loyalty can *increase* communication between members of any particular subunit, as it may decrease the salience of the individual rewards in favor of the subgroup's benefit (Brewer & Kramer, 1986; Kramer & Brewer, 1985; Schneider, 1989).

The present study is relevant to such organizational issues. It suggests that the relationship between differentiation and integration is not simple. An organization may be highly differentiated and yet no subunit may control enough information to effectively pursue its own goals. The most vulnerable organizational structure should be not a highly differentiated one with many somewhat independent units but one with a few nearly self sufficient subunits that can effectively compete with one another, even though such a structure might be less differentiated than one with more subunits. On the other hand, the organization that should be the least vulnerable should be a highly centralized[2] organization in which the importance of the superordinate goals of the organization are salient.

Reviews of bias in organizational communication tend to focus on distortions in upward communication; subordinates who are dependent on superiors for promotions and other rewards tell them what they want to hear (Athanassiades, 1973; O'Reilly, 1978). This study suggests that there are conditions under which bias is greater at the top. Those at the bottom of an organization may not have the resources to benefit from distortion or withholding information, whereas central individuals, particularly those in somewhat decentralized organizations whose subunits have a strong independent identity, may be able to do enough harm to their competitors to find it advantageous to withhold or distort information. In the Challenger disaster, it was the higher level managers of Morton-Thiokol and the Marshall Space Center who had the most invested in their organizational identity, and therefore had the greatest incentives to distort information. These upper level managers were, in fact, the most duplicitous. In the aftermath of the shooting down of KAL Flight 007, the withholding of information for competitive reasons occurred at high levels; according to Hersh's (1986) description, communication was more free at lower levels where competitive pressures for the organization to be first were less.

The factors studied here could be incorporated into all studies of the diffusion of innovation whenever there is a competitive aspect. Studies of the diffusion of innovation, from the most venerable (Coleman, Katz, & Menzel, 1966) to the most recent (Carley, 1988) have not attended to strategic aspects of communication. Two leading review books on communication networks (Rogers, 1983; Rogers & Kincaid, 1981) have not a single index reference to "conflict" or "competition." Studies of communication patterns among scientists have focused on collaboration within "invisible colleges" (Crane, 1972; Nelson & Pollack, 1970) and the diffusion of new discoveries among scientists, overlooking the important competitive and strategic aspects of communication. Many group researchers assume that if the option to communicate is present, it will be utilized. As the tragedy of the Challenger accident attests, this is not always the case.

References

Athanassiades, J. (1973). The distortion of upward communication in hierarchical organizations. *Academy of Management Journal*, **16**, 207–226.

Axelrod, Robert (1984). *The Evolution of Cooperation*. New York: Basic Books.

Bavelas, A. (1950). Communication patterns in task-oriented groups. *Journal of the Acoustical Society of America*, **22**, 725–730.

Blake, R. R., Shepard, H. A., & Mouton, J. S. (1964). *Managing Intergroup Conflict in Industry*. Houston: Gulf.

Bonacich, P. (1987). Communication networks and collective action. *Social Networks*, **9**, 389–396.

Brewer, M. B., & Kramer, R. M. (1986) Choice behavior in social dilemmas: Effects of social identity, group size, and decision framing. *Journal of Personality and Social Psychology*, **50**, 543–549.

Brown, R. (1978). Divided we shall fall: an analysis of relations between sections of a factory workforce. In *Differentiation Between Social Groups*. Edited by H. Tajfel. London: Academic Press.

Carley, Kathleen (in press). Structural constraints on communication: The diffusion of the homomorphic signal analysis technique through scientific fields. *Mathematical Sociology*.

Coleman, James S., Katz, Elihu, & Menzel, Herbert (1966). *Medical Innovation*. New York: Bobbs-Merrill.

Crane, Diana (1972). *Invisible Colleges: Diffusion of Knowledge in Scientific Communities*. Chicago: University of Chicago Press.

Dawes, Robyn M. (1980). Social dilemmas. In *Annual Review of Psychology*, vol. 31, pp. 169–193. Palo Alto, CA: Annual Reviews Inc.

Dutton, J., & Walton, R. (1965). Interdepartmental conflict and cooperation: Two contrasting studies. *Human Organizations*, **25**, 207–220.

Flament, C. (1963). *Application of Graph Theory to Group Structure*. Englewood Cliffs, N.J.: Prentice-Hall.

Freeman, Linton C. (1979). Centrality in social networks: Conceptual clarification. *Social Networks*, **1**, 215–239.

Harary, Frank (1972). *Graph Theory*. Reading, MA: Addison-Wesley

Hardin, G. (1968). The tragedy of the commons. *Science*, **162**, 1243–1248.

Hersh, Seymour M. (1986). *The Target is Destroyed*. New York: Random House.

Kramer, R. M., & Brewer, M. B. (1984). Effects of group identity on resource use in a simulated commons dilemma. *Journal of Personality and Social Psychology*, **46**, 1044–1056.

Kuhlman, D. M., & Marshello, A. (1975). Individual differences in game motivation as moderators of preprogrammed strategic effects in a prisoner's dilemma. *Journal of Personality and Social Psychology*, **32**, 922–931.

Lawrence, P. R., & Lorsch, J. W. (1967). *Organizations and Environment: Managing Differentiation and Integration*. Boston: Harvard University Press.

Leavitt, H. J. (1951). Some effects of certain communication patterns on group performance. *Journal of Abnormal and Social Psychology*, **46**, 38–50.

Liebrand, Wim B. G. (1984). The effect of social motives, communication, and group size

on behavior in an *N*-person multi-stage mixed-motive game. *European Journal of Social Psychology*, **14**, 239–264.
Liebrand, Wim B. G., & Van Run, G. J. (1985). The effects of social motives across two cultures on behavior in social dilemmas. *Journal of Experimental Social Psychology*, **21**, 86–102.
Liebrand, Wim B. G., Wilke, Henk A. M., Vogel, Rob, & Wolters, Fred J. M. (1986). Value orientation and conformity: A study of three types of social dilemma games. *Journal of Conflict Resolution*, **30**, 77–97.
Marwell, Gerald, & Ames, Ruth E. (1979). Experiments on the provision of public goods: I. Resources, interest, group size and the free-rider problem. *American Journal of Sociology*, **84**, 1335–1360.
McConnell, Malcolm (1987). *Challenger: A Major Malfunction*. Garden City, N.Y.: Doubleday.
Messick, D. M., & Brewer, M. B. (1983). Solving social dilemmas: A review. In L. Wheeler and P. Shaver (Eds), *Annual Review of Personality and Social Psychology*, vol. 3. Beverley Hills, CA: Sage.
Nelson, Carnot E., & Pollack, Donald K. (Eds) (1970). *Communication Among Scientists and Engineers*, Lexington, MA: Heath Lexington Books.
O'Reilly, C. A. III (1978). The intentional distortion of information in organizational communication: A laboratory and field investigation. *Human Relations*, **31**, 173–193.
Porter, L., & Roberts, K. H. (1976). In *Handbook of Industrial and Organizational Psychology*. Edited by Marvin D. Dunnette. Chicago: Rand McNally.
Presidential Commission on the Space Shuttle Challenger Accident (1986). *Report to the President by the Presidential Commission of the Space Shuttle Challenger Accident*, vol. I.
Rogers, Everett M. (1983). *Diffusion of Innovations*. New York: Free Press.
Rogers, Everett M., & Kincaid, D. Lawrence (1981). *Communication Networks*. New York: Free Press.
Schneider, Sherry (1989). Communication dilemmas: The effects of social categorization on communication networks. Unpublished Ph.D. dissertation.
Taubes, Gary (1986). *Nobel Dreams: Power, Deceit and the Ultimate Experiment*. New York: Random House.
Turner, J. C. (1987). *Rediscovering the Social Group: A Self-Categorization Theory*. London: Basil Blackwell.
Watson, James D. (1980). *The Double Helix*. New York: Atheneum.

Notes

1. Structural variables that affect contribution to a shared database such as contribution costs, asymmetries in quality of information between players, and group size are examined by Connolly *et al.* in Chapter 15.
2. Highly decentralized networks also may be less vulnerable to communications dilemmas because they contain fewer of the middle positions most likely to hoard information. However, this study cannot verify this hypothesis as only networks of high and intermediate centrality were tested.

15

Group Decision and Individual Choice in Intergroup Competition for Public Goods

GARY BORNSTEIN
The Hebrew University of Jerusalem
Israel

An intriguing class of collective action problems has been largely ignored by social dilemma researchers. Hardin (1982) observed that "It is often . . . the case that collective action is of interest to the group primarily because some other group has an ongoing interest that is being served to the detriment of the first group" (p. 15). However, little systematic research has been done to study social dilemmas in situations involving competition between groups.

A clash between opposing groups of demonstrators, elections, and even a war exemplify the class of social conflicts we have in mind. The *intergroup* conflict in these examples stems from the fact that the groups compete for "rewards" (political influence, strategically important territory) that can be gained in full by one group only. The group that wins the competition and, consequently, receives the rewards, is the one whose members' total contribution in terms of some relevant resource (effort, money, bravery) exceeds that of the competing group.

The *intragroup* conflict in these examples results from the fact that the rewards associated with winning the intergroup competition often constitute public goods since (1) they are jointly provided to the members of the winning group, and (2) individual group members cannot be excluded from sharing them regardless of their contribution to the group's success. The fundamental intragroup conflict in this class of intergroup conflicts and competitions is, thus, a problem of public goods provision (Rapoport & Bornstein, 1987). Since they can share the public good once it is provided, individual group members may be tempted to take a "free ride" by lowering or even eliminating their contribution to the group's effort. As a result, the group may fail to achieve the level of contribution it needs in order to win the competition and provide the public goods.

To study intergroup conflicts of this kind, Rapoport and Bornstein (1987) devised an n-person game, called the *intergroup public goods* (IPG) paradigm. The IPG game commences by randomly dividing a set of n players into two groups. Each player receives a monetary endowment of e units and has to decide privately and anonymously whether to keep the endowment or invest it. A reward of r units (the public good) is provided to all members of group A (B) if the number of investors in group A (B) exceeds that in group B (A). Members of group B (A) receive nothing but keep their endowment if they did not invest it. In case of an equal number of investors in both groups, each player receives a reduced bonus for a tie of $r/2$ ($r/2 > e$) units. The individual payoff matrix is illustrated in Table 15.1 with $e = 5$ and $r = 15$.

TABLE 15.1 *Individual Payoff Matrix for the IPG Paradigm*

Player i's decision	$m_{A\|i} < m_B - 1$	$m_{A\|i} = m_B - 1$	$m_{A\|i} = m_B$	$m_{A\|i} > m_B$
Invest	0	$r/2 = 7.5$	$r = 15$	$r = 15$
Not invest	$e = 5$	$e = 5$	$r/2 + e = 12.5$	$r + e = 20$

Note: $m_{A|i}$ denotes the number of contributors in group A excluding player i; m_B denotes the number of contributors in group B.

Preplay Communication

Problems of public goods provision are mixed-motive rather than strictly competitive games and as such they typically offer substantial gains for coordinated group action. Perhaps the most effective way to facilitate coordinated solutions is to allow group members to discuss the dilemma before making their individual choices. Several studies utilizing a variety of experimental paradigms have demonstrated that a short period of preplay communication enables subjects to achieve better collective outcome than subjects who are denied an opportunity to communicate (Jerdee & Rosen, 1974; Caldwell, 1976; Brechner, 1977; Dawes, McTavish, & Shaklee, 1977; Edney & Harper, 1978; van de Kragt, Orbell, & Dawes, 1983; Liebrand, 1984; van de Kragt, Dawes, & Orbell with Braver & Wilson, 1986). Whereas this empirical conclusion is by now generally accepted, the mechanism by which preplay communication affects individual choice has not been fully explored.

Communication in social dilemma studies is typically operationalized as an unstructured period of group discussion where group decisions (if made) are neither binding nor enforceable. This type of informal communication, or "cheap talk" (Farrell, 1987), has no direct bearing on the situation's reward structure. However, it can affect individual behavior in various ways. Group discussion may serve to clarify implications of available game choices, to exchange information about intended behavior, to enhance trust and establish social norms, to increase identification with the group, and, finally, to form agreements and make promises (Dawes, McTavish, & Shaklee, 1977; Messick & Brewer, 1983; Orbell, van de Kragt, & Dawes, 1989).

The difficulties in pinning down the effects of group discussion arise in part from the complex nature of this manipulation. One approach, therefore, is to use simpler, more structured, forms of communication where subjects are allowed to exchange only limited amounts of information (such as their intention to contribute or not) in a prespecified order (Palfrey & Rosenthal, 1988). Another approach is to allow unstructured, naturally occurring communication but to focus attention on a few key aspects of group discussion. Consistent with this latter approach, the present paper focuses primarily on one aspect of group discussion—the group decision concerning a coordinated strategy—and then examines its implications for the subsequent individual decision to contribute or not.

When deliberating the choice of a coordinated group strategy, all group members have a unitary interest to identify and pursue the collectively optimal strategy. In public goods problems where the outcome associated with any given number of contributors (or, alternatively, with the amount of contribution) is known, the group decision is rather simple. Thus, in problems of continuous public goods provision, as modeled by the n-person prisoner's dilemma (NPD) game, the optimal group strategy, the one maximizing collective payoff, is clearly to designate all group members as contributors. In problems of step-level public goods with binary contribution and a fixed provision point m (van de Kragt, Orbell, & Dawes, 1983), the optimal group strategy is to designate exactly m group members as contributors. In both of these paradigms, the group is faced with a decision under certainty (e.g., a riskless choice).

In other public goods problems, however, the level of contribution needed for provision is not known with certainty. When the source of this uncertainty is environmental (Messick, Allison & Samuelson, 1988; Suleiman & Rapoport, 1989), the group decision may be modeled as a decision under risk or uncertainty. When, as in the IPG game, the outcome of the group decision depends on the action taken by the rival group, each group is faced with a strategic decision.

When group decisions are neither binding nor enforceable (the case of "cheap talk" as referred to above), the impact of the group decision on the (private and anonymous) individual decisions may vary depending on the specific reward structure of the situation. For example, in the NPD game, a group decision to designate all group members as contributors does not change the fact that contribution is the dominated strategy for the individual player. In contrast, the decision to designate the exact number of contributors needed for provision in a step-level public goods game changes the structure of the game such that contribution (by designated contributors) becomes the rational individual choice.

This structural difference between the two games is of much theoretical importance in any attempt to explain the effects of preplay communication. Whereas in the NPD game increase in cooperation following preplay communication must necessarily be attributed to motivational changes or normative pressures created by group discussion, the designation of a minimal contributing set can explain contribution toward step-level goods without the necessity to assume that individuals contribute for reasons other than concern for their own interest or that additional payoffs have been introduced into the situation.

Effects of Communication in the IPG Game

In single-group social dilemmas all interdependent players participate in the discussion. In the IPG game other communication patterns are possible. In the first experiment reported below, communication was restricted to ingroup members. In the second experiment, subjects were allowed between-group communication (with or without an opportunity for separate within-group discussions).

Experiment 1. Within-group Communication (Rapoport & Bornstein, 1989)

When the players of each group are given an opportunity to discuss the game, they are hypothesized to reach an agreement to coordinate their individual strategies and act as a single team and, further, to believe that the members of the outgroup behave in a similar fashion. Thus, for the purpose of making a group decision, the IPG game is no longer framed as an *n*-person game but, rather, as a two-person game between groups A and B. In this derived matrix game, a pure strategy corresponds to the number of players each group designates as contributors.

Bornstein and Rapoport (1988) proposed a solution to the two-person IPG game. The solution is based on the observation that intergroup relations tend to be highly competitive (Tajfel, 1982; McCallum *et al.*, 1985; Insko *et al.*, 1987). Therefore, it is hypothesized that each group will act conservatively by choosing its maximin strategy—the one maximizing the minimum group payoff or security level.

The model consists of two stages. Whereas the first stage accounts for the group decision in terms of the maximin strategy, the second stage invokes the notion of criticalness to identify the conditions under which individual group members—who make their decisions privately and anonymously—are expected to adhere to the group decision.

The study used a factorial design with (within-group) communication vs. no communication defining one dimension and equal group size vs. unequal group size defining the other.

Table 15.2 presents the group payoff matrix for the equal group size condition (condition E) with $n_A = n_B = 5$, $e = 5$, and $r = 15$. It shows that the maximin strategy for each group is to designate all five members as contributors. Collective contribution is the only strategy that protects the group from the possibility of losing the competition (and, thus, guarantees each player a minimum payoff of $r/2 = 7.5$ units). What are the implications of this group decision for the subsequent individual choice? The individual payoff matrix in Table 15.1 shows that if all the other players contribute their endowments, player i cannot benefit from keeping his or her endowment. In other words, when the two groups are of equal size, collective contribution constitutes an equilibrium solution for the n-person IPG game. Collective contribution is the only equilibrium (in pure strategies) of the game. We contend that when the maximin solution (of the two-person game) coincides with the equilibrium point (of the n-person, noncooperative, game) the set of contributors designated by the group constitute *a minimal contributing set* (van de Kragt, Orbell, & Dawes, 1983). Designation of a minimal contributing set removes the option to take a free ride by rendering the contribution of each group member necessary or critical for provision.

TABLE 15.2 *Group Payoff Matrix for the Equal Group Size Condition*

	m_B					
m_A	0	1	2	3	4	5
0	62.5, 62.5	25, 95	25, 90	25, 85	25, 80	25, 75
1	95, 25	57.5, 57.5	20, 90	20, 85	20, 80	20, 75
2	90, 25	90, 20	52.5, 52.5	15, 85	15, 80	15, 75
3	85, 25	85, 20	85, 15	47.5, 47.5	10, 80	10, 75
4	80, 25	80, 20	80, 15	80, 10	42.5, 42.5	5, 75
5	75, 25	75, 20	75, 15	75, 10	75, 5	37.5, 37.5

It is important to note that the above explanation in terms of a minimal contributing set differs from the game-theoretic equilibrium solution in its assumptions concerning individual rationality. The game-theoretic analysis is based on the rather strong assumption of mutually expected rationality (Colman, 1982). According to this assumption, individual players adjust their expectations to arrive at an equilibrium solution and, therefore, the IPG game is predicted to result in the equilibrium solution of collective contribution regardless of whether or not communication is allowed. The mechanism of designating a minimal contributing set is based on a considerably weaker assumption of individual rationality. It assumes only that, following the group decision to designate all group members as contributors, each individual player realizes that he or she cannot benefit from unilateral defection and assumes that all other players also recognize that fact.

The group payoff matrix for the unequal size condition (condition UE) with $n_A = 3$, $n_B = 5$, $e = 5$, $r = 15$ appears in Table 15.3. The maximin criterion stipulates that the smaller group (group A) will reach an agreement to designate no contributors (thus securing each member's endowment) whereas the larger group (group B) will designate four of its five members as contributors (thereby ensuring a win). When the two groups are of unequal size, however, the group decision no longer renders individual decisions critical for provision. Assuming (as we do) that the small group will designate no contributors, designated contributors in the large group may be tempted to withhold their contributions. Anticipating this, members of the small group may contribute in an attempt to win or tie the game. Clearly, when $n_A = n_B$, the (noncooperative) IPG game has no equilibrium solution (in pure strategies). Therefore, the groups are no longer in a position to designate minimal contributing sets.

TABLE 15.3 *Group Payoff Matrix for the Unequal Group Size Condition*

				m_B		
m_A	0	1	2	3	4	5
0	37.5, 62.5	15, 95	15, 90	15, 85	15, 80	15, 75
1	55, 25	32.5, 57.5	10, 90	10, 85	10, 80	10, 75
2	50, 25	50, 20	27.5, 52.5	5, 85	5, 80	5, 75
3	45, 25	45, 20	45, 15	22.5, 47.5	0, 80	0, 75

Method

SUBJECTS

Two hundred and eight undergraduate students at the Hebrew University of Jerusalem participated in the experiment. The subjects were recruited by campus advertisements promising monetary reward for participation in a group decision making task. Subjects in sets of ten or eight (depending on the experimental condition) participated in a single session that lasted approximately 45 minutes. Subjects were paid between 0 and 20 IS (1.6 Israeli Shekels equals $1) contingent on their decisions and the decisions of the other members of their set.

PROCEDURE

Upon arrival at the laboratory, subjects were seated in a single room with arrangements to ensure their privacy. Each subject was handed an envelope containing a promissory note of 5 Shekels, a decision form, and a group membership card assigning him or her to one of two groups. In the equal group size (E) condition, five subjects were assigned to the "green" group and five to the "red" group. In the unequal group size (UE) condition, five subjects were assigned to the "green" group and three to the "red" group.

Following the identification of group membership, subjects were told that they could each choose to keep the 5 Shekels or to invest the money. Subjects were further told that members of the group with more investors would each receive a reward of 15 Shekels, whereas members of the other group would receive no payment. In case of a tie, all members of both groups would each receive a reward of 7.5 Shekels.

To indicate their decision, subjects had to check the appropriate box on their decision form. Subjects were told that in order to ensure the confidentiality of their decision they would receive their payment in sealed envelopes and leave the laboratory one at a time with no opportunity to meet the other participants. Subjects were also assured that the experiment involved no deception.

At this stage, subjects in the no communication condition made their decisions. Once all the decision forms were collected, one experimenter calculated the payoffs and prepared the payoff envelopes. A second experimenter debriefed the subjects on the rationale and purpose of the study.

In the communication condition, members of each group were allowed to discuss the situation for ten minutes before making their decisions. Within-group discussions were held in two separate rooms; they were monitored by the experimenters and audio-recorded with the explicit knowledge and consent of the subjects. In all other details the procedure in this condition was identical to that in the no communication condition.

Findings

GROUP DECISIONS

The recordings of the preplay group discussions were coded for a group decision by two independent judges. The two judges agreed on the outcome of 21 of the 24 discussions. In the three remaining cases, group discussions either did not result in a clear decision or the two judges did not agree on what the final group decision actually was. Thus, consistent with our assumption, within-group communication resulted

TABLE 15.4 *Group Decisions and Number of Contributors in Each Group by Group Type and Communication Condition*

Communication Condition

Group Type		Group 1	2	3	4	5	6	7	8	Mean Percent Contribution
S	GD	0	3	0	0	0	0	0	3	
	M	1	3	0	0	0	0	0	3	29.2
L	GD	4	4	4	4	5	*	*	4	
	M	4	4	4	4	5	4	3	4	80.0
E	GD	5	5	*	5	5	5	0	5	
	M	5	5	3	5	5	5	0	5	82.5

No Communication Condition

Group Type		Group 1	2	3	4	5	6	7	8	Mean Percent Contribution
S	GD	1	1	1	0	0	0	1	2	25.0
L	GD	3	3	0	1	4	2	4	3	50.0
E	GD	0	2	4	3	5	3	0	2	47.5

Note:
* No decision has been reached
GD Denotes the group decision
M Denotes the actual number of contributors.

in the restructuring of the IPG game with the members of each group coordinating their strategies and acting as a single team.

Group decisions are shown in the upper part of Table 15.4 for the small, large, and equal groups separately. The data support the hypothesis that groups choose to maximize their security level. In the unequal group size condition, six of the eight small groups designated no contributors, and five of the eight large groups designated four contributors. In the equal group size condition, six of the eight groups designated all five members as contributors. Overall, 17 of the 21 groups that reached a group decision designated a number of contributors corresponding to the maximin strategy.

INDIVIDUAL DECISIONS

Table 15.4 also shows the actual number of contributors in each group and the overall rate of contribution in each condition. We have contended that, when the competing groups are of equal size, the group decision to designate the maximin set of contributors renders the contribution of each designated contributor critical for provision. When the two groups are of unequal size this is no longer the case. Therefore, to the extent that criticalness determines individual choice, defection rate among designated contributors in condition UE was predicted to be higher than that in condition E. Whereas the finding that all designated contributors in condition E contributed their endowments is consistent with the minimal contributing set hypothesis, the fact that none of the designated contributors defected in condition UE suggests that criticalness (in the sense defined above) may not be necessary for explaining the adherence of individual players to the group decision.

There are two additional observations concerning the individual decisions that need to be emphasized. First, when no communication was allowed, the rate of contribution in the equal group size condition was only 47.5 percent. Clearly, the game-theoretic equilibrium solution does not account for the behavior of our subjects when the IPG game is played noncooperatively.[1]

Second, preplay communication does not necessarily increase contribution rates. Communication enhanced contribution in condition E ($Z = 3.67$, $p < .001$) and in the large groups in condition UE ($Z = 3.14$, $p < .001$), but not in the small groups in the latter condition.[2]

Experiment 2. Between-group Communication in the IPG Game (Bornstein, Rapoport, Kerpel, & Katz, 1989)

Table 15.2 shows that when all n players contribute their endowments in the IPG game, collective payoff is minimized. Thus, by promoting a solution to the intragroup conflict, within-group communication damages the interests of the wider collective. When the competing groups are of equal size, the Pareto optimal solution for the IPG game—the one maximizing collective rewards—is for all players to withhold their contributions.

To examine whether between-group communication can facilitate intergroup cooperation, Experiment 2 employed the IPG game with $n_A = n_B = 3$, $e = 5$, and $r = 15$. Each set of six subjects was randomly assigned to one of five communication conditions. The first condition, condition W, allowed subjects only within-group communication. The second condition, condition B, allowed all six subjects to discuss the situation jointly but denied them an opportunity for separate within-group discussions. Three additional conditions allowed subjects both within- and between-group communication. In condition WBW, groups first met separately for within-group discussions, then met together for a between group discussion, and finally conducted a second within-group discussion. In conditions WB and BW subjects were allowed only one opportunity for a within-group discussion before and after the between-group discussion, respectively.

Following Orbell, van de Kragt, & Dawes (1988), who argued that discussions are typically biased towards the collectively desirable solution, we hypothesized that subjects will use the opportunity for between-group discussion to reach a cooperative agreement between the two groups (rather than to coordinate ingroup strategies). Unlike an intragroup agreement of collective contribution, however, an intergroup agreement of collective non-contribution does not constitute a stable solution to the dilemma. The payoff matrix in Table 15.1 shows that when player i expects all the other players not to contribute, player i should, in fact, contribute his or her endowment. By contributing when all others do not, player i can increase both own and group outcomes. Of course, for the same reason, player i cannot trust the other players to keep the intergroup agreement. Thus, in the absence of ingroup coordination, the IPG game is constructed as an *n*-person rather than a two-person game.

Consider next conditions WBW, BW, and WB, which allow the subjects an opportunity for both within- and between-group communication. There are two reasons for expecting contribution rates in these mixed communication conditions to be lower than that in condition W. First, between-group discussions may reduce the proportion of competitive (or defensive) group decisions and, consequently, the number of contributors designated by the groups. Second, between-group communication may increase the rate of defection among designated contributors. As demonstrated earlier, the mechanism of minimal contributing set works because each individual contributor firmly believes that all other players will also contribute. This belief is likely to diminish as a result of a cooperative (non-contribution) agreement between the groups. This, in turn, is expected to reduce the individual's perception of his or her criticalness and, as a result, his or her willingness to contribute.

Method

Two hundred and forty male undergraduate students at the Hebrew University of Jerusalem participated in the experiment in sets of six. Except for the different communication patterns, the procedure was identical to that described above for Experiment 1. Following the game instructions, subjects were told that before making their decisions they would be allowed to discuss the situation with other participants and were informed of the planned sequence of discussions according to the experimental condition. Within-group discussions were held in two separate rooms and between-group discussions in the central experimental room. Each discussion lasted 7 minutes. Discussions were monitored by an experimenter and audio-recorded.

Findings

Table 15.5 reports the number of contributors agreed upon during the between-group discussion, the number of contributors designated during the within-group discussion(s), and the actual number of contributors by condition and group within condition.[3]

The mean number of contributors per set (of six subjects) was 5.250 in condition W, 2.750 in condition WBW, 2.625 in condition WB, 2.500 in condition BW, and 0.375 in condition B. Planned contrasts (using the set of six subjects as the unit of analysis) indicate that the number of contributors in condition W was significantly higher than that in conditions WBW, WB, and BW (t_{35} = 3.79, $p <$ .001), which, in turn, were significantly higher than that in condition B (t_{35} = 3.35, $p <$ .005). Differences among the three mixed communication conditions were not significant.

The effects of within-group discussion in condition W are practically identical to those obtained in Experiment 1 and in an earlier study by Bornstein and Rapoport (1988). In 14 of the 16 groups the decision was to designate all three members as contributors and only two players defected from the group's decision.

Except for two cases in which no agreement was reached, all between-group discussions resulted in the Pareto optimal agreement of collective non-contribution. Based on the analysis of the payoff matrix, we hypothesized that cooperative intergroup agreements would be unstable. Indeed, Table 15.5 shows that of 30 such agreements only 9 (30 percent) were kept by all six players.[4] However, Table 15.5 also shows that only 7 percent of the individual players violated the cooperative intergroup agreement in condition B as compared to 38, 42 and 46 percent who violated the agreement in conditions WB, BW and WBW, respectively.

Similar results were obtained with regard to violation of intragroup agreements. Table 15.5 shows that intragroup agreements of collective contribution were more likely to be violated in the mixed communication conditions than in condition W. When within-group discussions immediately preceded the individual decision (conditions WBW and BW), 16 of the 32 groups (all of which had agreed to cooperate with the other group) decided to designate three contributors. Out of the 48 designated contributors, however, 11 did not contribute—a defection rate of 23 percent as compared to less than 5 percent in condition W. In condition WB, where the only opportunity to coordinate ingroup strategies was before the between-group discussion, 10 of the 16 groups designated three contributors. Following intergroup discussions (in which all but one pair of groups reached a cooperative agreement), 15 of the 30 designated contributors decided not to contribute. This 50 percent defection rate is ten times higher than the defection rate in condition W.

TABLE 15.5 *Contribution Decisions in Each Set by Communication Condition, Type of Discussion, and Group*

Communication Condition	Discussion Type	Group A	Group B	Group A	Group B	Group A	Group B	Group A	Group B	Group A	Group B	Group A	Group B	Group A	Group B	Group A	Group B	Percent Contribution
W	W	3	*	3	3	3	3	3	0	3	3	3	3	3	3	3	3	
	M	3	2	2	3	2	3	3	0	3	3	3	3	3	3	3	3	67.5
	W	*	3	*	3	*	3	3	3	3	3	3	3	0	3	3	3	
WBW	B	0:0		0:0		0:0		0:0		0:0		0:0		0:0		0:0		
	W	3	*	3	3	0	0	0	0	3	3	3	0	0	3	3	3	
	M	3	1	3	3	0	0	0	0	2	3	0	0	0	2	2	3	45.8
	W	3	3	3	*	3	0	3	0	3	0	3	3	*	3	3	*	
WB	B	0:0		0:0		0:0		0:0		0:0		*		0:0		0:0		
	M	0	2	2	1	1	1	1	2	2	0	3	2	1	2	0	1	43.8
	B	0:0		0:0		0:0		0:0		0:0		0:0		0:0		0:0		
BW	W	3	0	0	0	*	3	*	3	*	*	3	3	3	*	3	0	
	M	1	0	0	0	0	3	2	3	0	0	3	2	3	2	1	0	41.7
B	B	0:0		*		0:0		0:0		0:0		0:0		0:0		0:0		
	M	0	0	0	0	1	0	0	0	0	0	0	1	0	1	0	0	6.3

Note:
* No decision was reached
W Denotes the group decision
B Denotes the intergroup agreement
M Denotes the actual number of contributors.

Discussion and Conclusions

In deriving predictions for the various communication patterns in the IPG game, we hypothesized that the subjects will use the opportunity for discussion to coordinate their individual actions and decide, as a team, on a strategy that best enhances their collective benefit. We then examined the conditions under which the group decision constitutes a structural solution to the dilemma confronting the discussing group.

Whereas the data concerning group decisions generally support our hypotheses, the effects of preplay communication on individual decisions are not fully accounted for by the reward structure of the IPG game. Specifically, narrow rationality cannot explain the fact that none of the designated contributors defected in condition UE of Experiment 1, nor can it explain the adherence of individual players to the intergroup agreement in condition B of Experiment 2.

"Extrarational" (Hardin, 1982) explanations for the individual choice behavior must, therefore, be considered. Two such explanations, recently proposed by Orbell, van de Kragt, and Dawes (1988), are compatible with our findings:

1. Discussion promotes cooperation by enhancing identification with the discussing group. When only within-group communication is allowed, discussion increases "subordinate" (Kramer & Brewer, 1984) group identity and group-regardingness. When subjects are allowed only between-group communication, discussion enhances the identification with the "superordinate" group, leading players to substitute concern for the larger society for subgroup interests as a value guiding their choice. The "social identity hypothesis" is also consistent with the data concerning individual behavior in the mixed communication conditions if one assumes that, following both within- and between-group discussions, subjects developed ambivalent identifications. Some of these subjects, motivated by group-regardingness, contributed their endowments, while others, for whom the collective level identity predominates, withheld their contributions.

2. Discussion promotes cooperation by providing the subjects with the opportunity to promise each other that they will act in accordance with the collective decision. Whereas promise-making behavior was not assessed in the present studies, an (intragroup and intergroup) agreement was operationalized as an explicit contract or understanding among all individuals participating in the discussion concerning a collective strategy. The "promise-making hypothesis" may account for the low rate of violations of intragroup agreements in conditions allowing only within-group communication as well as for the similarly low rate of violation of intergroup agreements in condition B. Individuals, it seems, tend to keep their promises.

Groups, however, do not! The data concerning group decisions in conditions WBW and BW (see Table 15.5) shows that groups were more likely to violate their agreement with the other group than to keep it. This finding may be attributed to the availability of a coordinated group strategy—the maximin strategy of collective contribution—which guarantees the group against losing the game. Whereas violation of the intergroup agreement by an individual group member is risky, coordinated violation of the agreement by all group members is not. However, as demonstrated by Table 15.5, when between- and within-group discussions resulted in conflicting agreements, both agreements were more likely to be violated. In other words, when keeping one's promise to the ingroup necessarily means breaking the promise made to the outgroup, promises are less likely to be kept.

Preplay communication, which proved to be highly effective in solving the intragroup conflict in condition W and the intergroup conflict in condition B, failed in solving either of these conflicts in the mixed communication conditions. Since restricting within-group communication is virtually impossible outside the laboratory, the finding that intergroup communication undermines solutions to the intragroup problem is especially relevant. Several interpretations of this finding are possible. As hypothesized earlier, a cooperative agreement between the groups may interfere with ingroup coordination by eroding the individual's sense of criticalness. Cooperative interaction in the collective setting may also reduce identification with the subgroups. Yet a third possibility is that the group decision to violate the intergroup agreement diminishes the trust in subsequent within-group promising. The present data do not distinguish between these interpretations. Our findings do suggest, however, that groups may benefit from restricting intergroup contact in times of conflict. Such restrictions will make each group more effective in solving its internal problem of "free riding." But society as a whole will have to pay the price of collectively deficient outcomes.

Directions for Future Research

Whereas our data do not support a strictly rational model of individual behavior, they fall short of demonstrating, unequivocally, that subjects behave in a purely altruistic manner. Contribution following within-group discussion may be an act of group allegiance, but can also (to the extent that other ingroup members are trusted) be motivated by the desire to avoid the (private) outcomes associated with losing the game. Similarly, withholding one's endowment following between-group discussion may reflect a concern for the collective interest or an intention to maximize security level.

The ambiguity of the individual choice in the IPG game stems from the fact that the rewards associated with the outcome of the game constitute step-level public goods. Thus, while there is an incentive for free riding (as each individual player prefers that others will supply the input necessary for the group's success), there is also an incentive to contribute (because the private benefit from the public good exceeds the cost of contribution).

Intergroup conflicts, however, are not necessarily resolved in a step-level manner. Many such conflicts result in a compromise between the parties rather than by a decisive victory of one side. This compromise reflects the relative amount of resources expended by the competing groups. When the rewards are divided between the groups based on the magnitude, rather than the direction, of the advantage, the intragroup conflict is more appropriately modeled as a continuous public goods problem.

To model intergroup competition over continuous public goods in the laboratory, a new game called the *intergroup prisoner's dilemma* (IPD) game has been proposed (Bornstein, 1989). The following example illustrates this paradigm. The game involves two groups with three members in each. Each of the six players receives a $5 endowment and has to decide between keeping the money and contributing it towards his or her group benefit. A reward of $18 is provided to each member of a group if all three members of that group contribute while none of the outgroup members contribute. Members of the losing group receive nothing but get to keep their endowments. If there are two more contributors in one group than in the other, each member of the winning group receives $15 and each member of the losing group receives $3. If a group has only one more contributor than the other group, each member of the winning group receives $12, whereas each member of the losing group receives $6. Finally, in case of a tie (an equal number of contributors in both groups) each player receives a reward of $9.

The payoff parameters of the IPD game are set such that the cost of contribution for player i exceeds his or her benefit from contributing. However, the total benefit to player i's group is higher than the contribution's cost.[5] These two requirements taken together render the intragroup reward structure a problem of continuous public good or a social dilemma (Dawes & Thaler, 1988). Whereas the dominant strategy for the individual player in the IPD game is not to contribute, the group's dominant strategy is for all group members to contribute. Collective contribution, in turn, is Pareto deficient as it minimizes the collective payoff.

Future research which compares the effects of communication in the IPG and the IPD games may help determine the relative importance of structural and motivational factors in resolving intragroup and intergroup conflicts in intergroup competition over public goods.

Acknowledgments

The research reported in this paper was supported by grants from the Israel Foundation Trustees and the Marshall Foundation.

References

Bornstein, G. Individual, group and collective interests in intergroup competitions over step-level and continuous public goods. Unpublished manuscript.

Bornstein, G., & Rapoport, A. (1988). Intergroup competition for the provision of step-level public goods: Effects of preplay communication. *European Journal of Social Psychology*, **18**, 125–142.

Bornstein, G., Rapoport, A., Kerpel, L., & Katz, T. (1989). Within and between group communication in intergroup competition for public goods. *Journal of Experimental Social Psychology* In press.

Brechner, K. C. (1977). An experimental analysis of social traps. *Journal of Experimental Social Psychology*, **13**, 552–564.

Caldwell, M. (1976). Communication and sex effects in a five-person prisoner's dilemma game. *Journal of Personality and Social Psychology*, **33**, 273–280.

Colman, A. (1982). *Game Theory and Experimental Games: The Study of Strategic Interaction.* Oxford: Pergamon Press.

Dawes, R. M., & Thaler, R. H. (1988). Anomalies: Cooperation. *Journal of Economic Perspective*, **3**, 187–197.

Dawes, R. M., McTavish, J., & Shaklee, H. (1977). Behavior, communication, and assumptions about other people's behavior in a commons dilemma game. *Journal of Personality and Social Psychology*, **35**, 1–11.

Edney, J. J., & Harper, C. S. (1978). Heroism in resource crisis: A simulation study. *Environmental Management*, **2**, 523–527.

Farrell, J. (1987). Cheap talk, coordination, and entry. *Rand Journal of Economics*, **18**, 34–39.

Hardin, R. (1982). *Collective Action*. Baltimore: Johns Hopkins University Press.

Insko, C. A., Pinkley, R. L., Hoyle, R. H., Dalton, B., Hong, G., Slim, R. M., Landry, P., Holtan, B., Ruffin, P. F., & Thibaut, J. (1987). Individual vs. group discontinuity: The role of intergroup contact. *Journal of Experimental Social Psychology*, **23**, 250–267.

Jerdee, T., & Rosen, B. (1974). Effects of opportunity to communicate and visibility of individual decisions on behavior in the common interest. *Journal of Applied Psychology*, **5**, 712–716.

Kramer, R. M., & Brewer, M. B. (1984). Effects of group identity on resource use in a simulated commons dilemma. *Journal of Personality and Social Psychology*, **46**, 1044–1057.

Kramer, R. M., & Brewer, M. B. (1986). Social group identity and the emergence of cooperation in resource conservation dilemma. In H. A. M. Wilke, D. M. Messick, & C. G. Rutte (Eds), *Experimental Social Dilemmas*. Frankfurt am Main: Lang GmbH.

Liebrand, W. B. G. (1984). The effect of social motives, communication and group size on behavior in an *n*-person multi-stage mixed-motive game. *European Journal of Social Psychology*, **14**, 239–264.

Messick, D. M., & Brewer, M. B. (1983). Solving social dilemmas: A review. In L. Wheeler and P. Shaver (Eds), *Review of Personality and Social Psychology*, vol. 4 pp 11–44. Beverly Hills, CA: Sage.

Messick, D. M., Allison, S. T., & Samuelson, C. D. (1988). Framing and communication effects on group members' responses to environmental and social uncertainty. In S. Maital (Ed.), *Applied Behavioral Economics*. Brighton: Wheatsheaf.

McCallum, D. M., Harring, K., Gilmore, R., Drenan, S., Chase, J., Insko, C. A., & Thibaut, J. (1985). Competition between groups and between individuals. *Journal of Experimental Social Psychology*, **21**, 301–320.

Orbell, J. M., van de Kragt, A. J. C., & Dawes, R. M. (1988). Explaining discussion induced cooperation. *Journal of Personality and Social Psychology*, **54**, 811–819.

Palfrey, T. R., & Rosenthal, H. (1988). Testing the effects of cheap talk in a public goods game with private information. Unpublished manuscript.

Rapoport, A., & Bornstein, G. (1987). Intergroup competition for the provision of binary public goods. *Psychological Review*, **94**, 291–299.

Rapoport, A., & Bornstein, G. (1989). Solving public good problems in competition between equal and unequal size groups. *Journal of Conflict Resolution*. In press.

Rapoport, A., Bornstein, G., & Erev, I. (1989). Intergroup competition for public goods: Effects of unequal resources and relative group size. *Journal of Personality and Social Psychology*, **56**, 748–756.

Suleiman, R., & Rapoport, A. (1989). Environmental and social uncertainty in single-trial resource dilemmas. *Acta Psychologica*, **68**, 99–112.

Tajfel, H. (1982). Social psychology of intergroup relations. *Annual Review of Psychology*, **33**, 1–39.

Van de Kragt, A. J. C., Orbell, J. M., & Dawes, R. M. (1983). The minimal contributing set as a solution to public goods problems. *American Political Science Review*, **77**, 112–122.

Van de Kragt, A. J. C., Dawes, R. M., Orbell, J. M., with Braver, S. R., & Wilson, L. A. II (1986). Doing well and doing good as ways of resolving social dilemmas. In H. A. M. Wilke, D. M. Messick, and C. G. Rutte (Eds), *Experimental Social Dilemmas*, pp. 177–202. Frankfurt am Main: Lang GmbH.

Notes

1. To account for individual decision making in the noncooperative IPG, Rapoport and Bornstein (1987) proposed an expected utility model in which player i's expectations are treated explicitly. Empirical tests of the expected utility model were performed by Bornstein and Rapoport (1988) and Rapoport, Bornstein, and Erev (1989).
2. Note that the rate of contribution following communication in the large group is a function of the task parameters. If, for example, there were three members in group A and ten in group B, the maximin model would have predicted contribution rates in group B to be 40 percent rather than 80 percent.
3. The procedure for coding group decisions and intergroup agreements was somewhat different from that described above for Experiment 1. One experimenter was present during the discussion and recorded the decision. Another experimenter independently coded decisions from the recordings of the discussions. The two judges reached an agreement concerning the outcome of 98 of the 112 discussions. The 15 cases (13.4 percent) in which no agreement was reached appear as missing data in Table 15.4.
4. To test whether some intergroup agreements were perceived as more sincere than others, we computed the correlation between the number of players violating the agreement in groups A and B across the 30 sessions in which a cooperative agreement was reached. The correlation was positive and significant ($r = .48$, $p < .005$).
5. Assume that player i is a member of group A. Denote by m_A the total number of contributors in group A and by m_B the number of contributors in group B. Denote by r the maximal value of the reward and by c the cost of contribution (in the example above $r = 18$ and $c = 5$). When $n_A = n_B = n$, player i's bonus payoff is given by $P_i = [1 + (m_A - m_B)/n]r/2$; $r/2 > c > r/2n$.

Part IV

Structural Solutions

16

Group Size and the Provision of a Sanctioning System in a Social Dilemma*

TOSHIO YAMAGISHI
Hokkaido University, Japan

Research on social dilemmas has proliferated since the mid-seventies as indicated by the recent reviews of the literature (Dawes, 1980; Edney & Harper, 1978; Messick & Brewer, 1983; Mitsui, 1983; Stroebe & Frey, 1982; Yamagishi & Iwamoto, 1985). Social dilemmas are characterized by the following features. (1) Actors involved have a behavioral choice on the level of cooperation (often the choice is binary between C, cooperation, and D, defection). (2) Each actor is better off for cooperating less (or choosing D instead of C), no matter what the choices of the other actors are. (3) However, each actor is worse off when the level of all actors' cooperation is the minimum (or all actors choose D) than when it is the maximum (or when all actors choose C). The tragedy of the commons discussed by Hardin (1968) is a classical example of a social dilemma. When villagers have free access to a common grazing ground, it is to each villager's advantage to raise more sheep there. However, if all or most villagers keep adding additional sheep to the common ground, the land will be overgrazed and eventually all villagers will suffer.

Despite the ubiquity of social dilemmas in our society, and despite the dismal logic they involve, human societies have somehow solved social dilemmas at least to some degree. Commonly held lands have been properly maintained in many societies over a long history; citizens of industrial nations have not all been destroyed by industrial pollution; and

* This research was supported by a grant from the National Science Foundation (BNS–8518939). I would like to thank Siok-Cheng Yeoh, Satomi Kurosu, Theresa Benson, and Barbara Andrews for their assistance, and Norbert Kerr and Paul van Lange for their comments on the earlier drafts of this chapter. Correspondence concerning this chapter should be sent to Toshio Yamagishi, Bungakubu, Hokkaido University, N10 W7 Kita-ku, Sapporo, Japan 060.

we still live in societies where at least a minimum level of social order is maintained. Our success, incomplete though it may be, in solving those social dilemmas may be partly attributed to the successful socialization of individuals into responsible citizens and to the long-term strategic decision-making style of the people. The success, however, mostly comes from organized efforts by the people involved to develop social systems designed to solve social dilemmas. For example, a set of rules are set up in a community to regulate the use of common land, and laws are enacted to penalize industries that pollute the environment. These rules and laws may be mutually enforced by the people involved themselves as in traditional villages, but it is often the case that agencies such as the police or the Environmental Protection Agency are established to enforce those rules and laws.

It is only very recently that social dilemma researchers started to pay attention to this important aspect of social dilemmas. In a typical social dilemma experiment, subjects are given a choice between C and D, but not an opportunity to change the system to provide a solution to the dilemma. To quote Buckley, Burns, and Meeker (1974), subjects in those experiments "have choices made available to them [by the experimenter] but the notion of human actors making choices available to themselves and, indeed, transforming game situations is missing" (p. 296). Partly as a response to this and a similar criticism by Edney and Harper (1978), several studies have been conducted in which subjects were given opportunities to alter the structure or the nature of the dilemma. Subjects in those studies were given an opportunity to organize themselves into a minimal contributing set (van de Kragt, Orbell, & Dawes, 1983), to elect a leader (Messick *et al.*, 1983; Rutte & Wilke, 1984; Samuelson *et al.*, 1984), to choose a rule to allocate the cost of maintaining a common good (Sato, 1987), or to contribute to the establishment/maintenance of a sanctioning system (Yamagishi, 1986a, 1988a, b). The study reported in this chapter is an effort to extend this emerging research tradition by providing further elaborations on the structural goal/expectation theory proposed by Yamagishi (1986b) to explain emergence/maintenance of collective action for changing the dilemma structure itself.

The distinction between two types of social dilemma, the original or the first-order dilemma and the second-order dilemma, is critical to Yamagishi's (1986b) structural goal/expectation theory.[1] The second-order dilemma exists in the provision of a social or collective solution to the original dilemma. For example, introduction of an effective monitoring–sanctioning system which rewards cooperators and punishes defectors alters the incentive structure of the original dilemma. However, the provision of such a system of monitoring and sanctioning may involve another social dilemma, a second-order social dilemma, since the benefit of such a system (an improved level of cooperation) is available to all actors regardless of whether or not he or she contributed to the provision of such a system. As in the original dilemma, it is more beneficial for each actor to free ride in the establishment/maintenance of such a system, but if not enough actors cooperate toward this end, such a system will not be provided. Yamagishi (1986a, b) calls cooperation in the second-order dilemma "instrumental cooperation" since it provides a means for encouraging cooperation in the original dilemma (called the "elementary cooperation").

The above distinction between the elementary and the instrumental forms of cooperation is important to the degree that these two forms of cooperation are affected by different factors and/or by the same factors but in different manners. Otherwise, we can simply generalize the findings involving elementary cooperation into the second-order dilemma situation involving instrumental cooperation. Yamagishi's structural goal/expectation theory specifies some of the factors that differentially affect these two forms of cooperation, and explains why those factors have differential effects. The theory is based on Pruitt and Kimmel's (1977) goal/expectation theory, which specifies conditions for elementary cooperation. According to the goal/expectation theory, cooperation results from long-range thinking that is directed "to achieve the goal of establishing and/or maintaining continued mutual cooperation" (p. 375). That is, emergence of cooperation requires that people realize (a) that individual pursuits of individuals' own self interest result in mutual defection, (b) so that the desirable outcome is obtained only through mutual cooperation. However, the development of the goal of attaining mutual cooperation is not sufficient for actual cooperation to emerge. Although people having developed this goal are willing to cooperate, they are afraid that their cooperation may be exploited by others. Using Arneson's (1982) terms, those who have adopted the goal of mutual cooperation are "nervous cooperators" or "reluctant cooperators" who are willing to cooperate but hesitate to do so due to their fear that their goodwill may be wasted or exploited. According to Pruitt and Kimmel (1977), actual cooperation emerges to the degree that those "nervous" or "reluctant" cooperators trust others that they would also cooperate. Unless people have this trust, they will feel that it is too risky to cooperate and actually defect in self-defense.

Yamagishi's (1986b) structural goal/expectation theory shares the first condition with Pruitt and Kimmel (1977). That is, emergence of cooperation, either elementary or instrumental, requires that people have adopted the goal of attaining mutual cooperation. On the other hand, Yamagishi (1986b) considers that the importance of the second factor, trust, declines as the group size increases. This is because strategic actions aimed at inducing others into mutual cooperation becomes less effective in larger groups. In large groups, whether one member cooperates or defects can hardly be noticed by others, and thus it hardly makes any difference in other members' choices. In other words, members of a large group cannot expect that their cooperation be reciprocated. In small groups, people who trust others and expect that their cooperation will be reciprocated by others will actually cooperate, feeling no fear of being exploited. In large groups, however, even those who generally trust others have no assurance that their cooperation will be reciprocated because their actions are hardly noticeable. It is thus predicted that even those who generally trust others will start defecting in larger groups, and this prediction is supported in Sato's (1988) experiment. High-trusters in Sato's (1988) experiment cooperated more than low-trusters in three-person groups, but the level of high-trusters' cooperation declined to that of low-trusters in seven-person groups.

Yamagishi (1986b) thus argues that emergence and maintenance of cooperation among "nervous" or "reluctant" cooperators in large groups requires that other members' cooperation be assured in some way other than strategically oriented elementary cooperation. This assurance, that cannot be provided through strategically oriented elementary cooperation, could be provided through instrumental cooperation for introducing a change in the dilemma structure. For example, fear of being exploited by others can be eliminated if a sanctioning system that discourages defection is introduced into the dilemma situation. Yamagishi (1986a, b, 1988a) argues that people facing a social dilemma will cooperate more toward a system change as a solution to the social dilemma problem they face to the degree that they realize (1) the importance of mutual cooperation *and* (2) the futility of strategically oriented elementary cooperation.

Yamagishi's argument outlined above may be considered as a social psychological version of Hobbes (1651) as interpreted by Taylor (1976). According to Taylor's (1976) interpretation, people facing a "war of all against all" are what Arneson (1982) calls "nervous cooperators," those who desire peace to war but are afraid of being exploited by others. What they lack is an assurance that they will not be exploited by others if they disarm themselves. As a result, they voluntarily cooperate to create a government that provides them with this assurance. What is important in the argument of Hobbes, as well as of Yamagishi, is the *indirect* effect of a sanctioning system rather than its direct effect. That is, the principal purpose of a sanctioning system is to provide this assurance rather than to force defectors into cooperation. In other words, such a sanctioning system (or any other system that provides such an assurance) makes it possible for the people involved to do what they desire to do (i.e., to engage in a cooperative action).[2]

Two of the predictions derived from the structural goal/expectation theory have been tested. The first prediction was that the subject's level of trust would be negatively related to the level of his/her instrumental cooperation; in particular, cooperation for the provision of a sanctioning system that punished defectors. High-trusters who expect a high level of voluntarily based cooperation by others would realize the need for sanctioning less seriously than would low-trusters, so that the high-trusters' level of instrumental cooperation would be lower than that of the low-trusters in the second-order dilemma. This prediction was supported by the results of Yamagishi's (1986a, 1988b) experiments. That is, high-trusters' level of elementary cooperation in the absence of sanctioning was higher than that of low-trusters, whereas their level of instrumental cooperation was lower than that of low-trusters when an opportunity to contribute to the establishment/maintenance of a sanctioning system existed.

Another prediction derived from the theory concerned the interaction effect between the gain of cooperation (how important cooperation was) and temptation to defect (how strong the incentive not to contribute) on instrumental cooperation. As stated earlier, the structural goal/expectation theory predicts that instrumental cooperation occurs to the degree that subjects realize the importance of mutual cooperation and the futility of strategically oriented elementary cooperation. It was expected that the importance of mutual cooperation would be more strongly realized by the subjects when the gain of cooperation was greater. It was also expected that subjects would consider voluntarily based mutual cooperation to be more difficult when temptation to defect was stronger. Thus, the need for a sanctioning system was expected to be more strongly felt, and as a result, subjects would cooperate more to the provision of a sanctioning system when mutual cooperation was more important (i.e., in the high gain of cooperation condition) *and* the voluntarily based elementary cooperation was less effective in inducing others into mutual cooperation (i.e., the stronger temptation condition). This prediction was also supported by another experiment by Yamagishi (1988a). In addition, Rutte and Wilke's chapter in this volume also reports a study in which group members voted to elect a leader when cooperation was important *and* other members did not cooperate.[3] Although voting to elect a leader in this study involved no cost (other than loss of freedom), the result is consistent with the structural goal/expectation theory in that group members' motivation to change the system was shown to be stronger when the "gain of cooperation" was high *and* other members did not cooperate.

The study reported in this paper deals with another set of predictions derived from the structural goal/expectation theory, predictions concerning the effects of group size. Previous research has shown that group size has a negative effect on elementary cooperation even when the incentive structure involved in the dilemma (such as the gain of cooperation and temptation to defect) does not change as a function of the group size (Bonacich, Shure, Kahan, & Meeker, 1976; Yamagishi, 1988b). One possible cause for this negative effect of group size is that strategic actions (such as "tit-for-tat") are less effective in inducing others into mutual cooperation in larger groups (Bonacich *et al.*, 1976; Dawes, 1980).[4] As discussed earlier, strategic actions aimed at inducing others into mutual cooperation become less effective as the group becomes larger, and then, even those who realize the importance of achieving and maintaining mutual cooperation and do not desire to free ride would be less willing to cooperate in large groups. Strategic actions become less effective in larger groups because (1) the target of the strategic action is harder to identify, and (2) even if the target of the strategic action is identified, the effect of the action is harder to be focused on the target.[5] This limitation of strategic actions in large groups can be removed if these two problems are effectively solved in large groups; that is, if an effective system of monitoring and sanctioning is provided which (1) identifies the target of strategic actions and (2) channels the consequences of such actions to become focused on that target. Given such a system, strategic actions should remain effective even in larger groups. For example, suppose that members are given an opportunity to cooperate to establish a system which identifies and punishes the defectors. Members' contributions to the system are used to maintain this system, so that the system is effective to the degree that they contribute to its establishment/maintenance. Their contributions to such a system are an example of instrumental cooperation. Their instrumental cooperation constitutes an effective strategic action, since the target of sanctioning is identified and only the target is sanctioned. *Under such a system, instrumental cooperation will not be affected by group size.*

Furthermore, there is a basis to expect that the level of instrumental cooperation will be even higher in larger groups because the need for sanctioning is expected to be greater in larger groups. The structural goal/expectation theory claims that instrumental cooperation occurs to the degree that mutual cooperation is important and mutual cooperation is hard to achieve based on strategically oriented elementary cooperation. If subjects expect that people would cooperate less in larger groups, as does Olson (1965) and as found in Yamagishi (1987), the larger group size is expected to play a role similar to that played by the stronger temptation to defect in the experiment conducted by Yamagishi (1988a). That is, both the higher level of temptation to defect and the larger group size will have an effect to reduce the subject's expectation about other members' elementary cooperation. Thus, we can expect a higher level of instrumental cooperation in larger groups, in the same way subjects confronted with the incentive structure involving a higher level of temptation exhibited a higher level of instrumental cooperation.

Whether or not group size has differential effects on elementary and instrumental cooperation is, however, an empirical question. No study has systematically investigated the differential effect of group size on the two types of cooperation. The main purpose of the current research is to demonstrate the predicted differential effects of group size on elementary and instrumental cooperation. The primary hypothesis to be tested in the following experiment, therefore, is:

Hypothesis 1: Group size will have differential effects on the two types of cooperation, such that

Hypothesis 1a: Group size will have a negative effect on elementary cooperation under no sanctioning, whereas

Hypothesis 1b: It will have a positive effect on the level of instrumental cooperation.

The primary hypotheses stated above are based on the assumption that subjects' expectations on the other members' voluntary cooperation (without sanctioning) will decline with group size.

In addition to the above primary hypotheses, the effects of trust on elementary and instrumental cooperation derived from the structural goal/expectation theory and supported in previous studies (Yamagishi, 1986a, 1988b) will be tested again. That is:

Hypothesis 2: Trust will have differential effects on elementary cooperation and instrumental cooperation, such that

Hypothesis 2a: Trust will have a positive effect on elementary cooperation when sanctioning does not exist.

Hypothesis 2b: Trust will have a negative effect on instrumental cooperation.

Another set of predictions derived from the structural goal/expectation theory and supported in previous studies (Yamagishi, 1986a, 1988b) is the differential effects of sanctioning opportunities on elementary cooperation among low-trusters and high-trusters. That is:

Hypothesis 3a: The level of elementary cooperation will be higher when a sanctioning system exists than when it does not.

Hypothesis 3b: The positive effect of a sanctioning system on elementary cooperation will be stronger among low-trusters than among high-trusters.

Furthermore, these predicted effects of trust are expected to be weaker in larger groups, since even high-trusters will not expect a high level of voluntary cooperation by the other members (cf. Sato, 1988). That is:

Hypothesis 4a: The positive effect of trust on elementary cooperation when sanctioning does not exist will be weaker in larger groups.

Hypothesis 4b: The negative effect of trust on instrumental cooperation will be weaker in larger groups.

Hypothesis 4c: The differential effects of sanctioning on elementary cooperation predicted in Hypothesis 3 will be weaker in larger groups.

These predicted interactions can also be interpreted from a different angle. That is, Hypotheses 4a and 4b also imply that the predicted effects of group size on elementary and instrumental cooperation (Hypotheses 1a and 1b) interact with trust. That is, the prediction of the differential effects of group size are based on a decline in the expectation of other members' cooperation levels in larger groups. Since this expectation is conceivably fairly low among low-trusters even in small groups, the decline in the expectation due to the larger group size will not be so salient among low-trusters as among high-trusters. In other words, there will be a floor effect among low-trusters which mitigates the predicted positive effect of group size on instrumental cooperation. That is,

Hypothesis 4aa: The negative effect of group size on elementary cooperation will be weaker among low-trusters than among high-trusters.

Hypothesis 4bb: The positive effect of group size on instrumental cooperation will be weaker among low-trusters than among high-trusters.

The Experiment

An experiment was conducted to test the above hypotheses. The basic features of the experiment were adopted from the previous experiments conducted by Yamagishi (1986a, 1988a, b). The experiment was run in four- or eight-person groups. Each member of the group was given resource money (50 cents per trial session) he or she could keep or contribute to the other members of the group. The money contributed by each member to the other members of the group was tripled and equally allocated to the other three or seven members. In this original or first-order dilemma, each member earned \$1.50 when all contributed 50 cents, and 50 cents when none contributed any, *regardless of the size of the group*. In addition, one-half of the groups of each group size were given an opportunity to contribute to the provision of a sanctioning system which penalized the least cooperative member (four-person groups) or the two least cooperative members (eight-person groups). (See the method section below for more details.) The level of penalty depended on the total amount of instrumental contribution made by the group members to the sanctioning system. The major difference of the current experiment from the previous ones by Yamagishi was the introduction of the group size condition (four-person groups versus eight-person groups). The other major difference was that computer print-outs rather than displays on computer terminals were used for instructions and feedbacks.

Method

Subjects

A total of 288 students were used as subjects. These subjects were run in 24 same-sex four-person groups and the same number of same-sex eight-person groups. These subjects were drawn from a subject pool for social psychology experiments in a large state university in the United States. The potential subjects in the pool were recruited from various classes in the university and through advertisements on campus. Monetary rewards were the only explicit incentive for the participants. The potential applicants were asked to fill out an eight-item trust scale designed to measure their general level of trust when they signed up for the experiment (two weeks to two months before the actual experiment). The pool was first divided into two groups, high-trusters and low-trusters, based on the median score of the trust scale. (The applicants whose scores were exactly the median score were not included in this experiment.) Four or eight applicants who indicated the same available time on the application form were contacted by the experimenter and scheduled for an experimental session. It was made sure, at the time of scheduling, that no mutual friends were included in the same session.

Design

The design consisted of three between-groups factors: (a) group size (4 vs. 8), (b) sanctioning (no-sanctioning vs. sanctioning), and (c) trust (low-trusters vs. high-trusters). In addition, each cell was counterbalanced by gender. Note that instrumental cooperation is relevant only in the sanctioning condition, so that analysis of instrumental cooperation involves only two factors, size and trust. Similarly, some of the hypotheses (1a, 2a, 4a, and 4aa) concerning elementary cooperation are relevant only in the no-sanctioning condition, and the tests of those predictions involve simple effects within the no-sanctioning condition.

Trust Scale

About 850 potential subjects in the pool were classified into high- (above average) or low- (below average) trusters based on their responses to the trust scale they filled out at the time of recruitment. The trust scale used in this study was a revised version of the trust scale successfully employed by Yamagishi and Sato (Yamagishi & Sato, 1986; Sato & Yamagishi,

1986) to predict Japanese subjects' behavior reflecting their trust levels. The current version, consisting of the following items, also successfully predicted subjects' cooperation levels among American subjects (cf. Yamagishi, 1988b). (1) In dealing with strangers, one is better off to be cautious until they have provided evidence that they are trustworthy. (2) In these competitive times, one has to be alert or someone is likely to take advantage of you. (3) Society will fall apart if the police power that counters criminal activities weakens. (4) One should not trust others until one knows them well. (5) Most people tell a lie when they can benefit by doing so. (6) When someone says something complimentary about you it's because they want to get something from you. (7) People will take advantage of you when you work with them. (8) Given the opportunity, people are dishonest. Yamagishi (1988b) analyzed responses of 852 students in the same subject pool as the one used in the present study and found two factors: Factor 1 (items 5 through 8) concerns the belief that people are honest-dishonest, and Factor 2 (items 1 through 4) concerns the belief that trusting others is risky. The same two factors were observed among 212 Japanese students (Yamagishi, 1988b). The reliability of the scale was moderately high (alpha = .77). The total score including all eight items was used for classifying subjects into low- and high-trusters.

Procedure

Subjects classified as having the same trust level (high- or low-trusters) were scheduled to an experimental session. As soon as each subject arrived at the laboratory, he or she was immediately led to a small isolation room so that he or she had no personal contact with other participants, and was asked to read and sign a consent form. Then printed instructions were provided to the subject. When the subject finished reading the instructions, he or she was asked to answer several questions designed to assess their understanding of the instructions. The experimenter provided further explanations if the subject's answers were not correct. The experiment started as soon as all four or eight subjects finished the questions and further questions were answered. The above process took place in each subject's isolation room.

The experiment consisted of 12 trial sessions. In each session, subjects were each given 50 cents as resource money, and was asked how much of the 50 cents they wanted to contribute to other members of the group. They could keep the rest to themselves. The amount contributed was then tripled in value and distributed equally among the other 3 or 7 members, depending on the group size condition. In each session, each subject was provided with an information sheet. This sheet in the no-sanctioning condition provided the following feedback about the subject's earnings in the previous period: (a) how much the subject contributed, (b) how much the subject received from the contributions of the other members, (c) how much the subject earned in total (i.e., 50 cents minus the subject's contribution plus the subject's share of the money generated by other members' contributions), and (d) the subject's cumulative earnings up to the period. Then the subject was asked to indicate the amount he or she wanted to contribute (any amount between 0 and 50 cents).

Subjects in the sanctioning condition were further asked to decide how much they wanted to contribute to the sanctioning system. They could contribute any amount between 0 and 50 cents *regardless of the amounts of their elementary contributions*. (When the total of the elementary and instrumental contributions exceeded the resource money of 50 cents, they paid the rest from their cumulative earnings. When they did not have enough money, they could "borrow" from the experimenter.) In the four-person groups, one-and-a-half times the total amount contributed to the sanctioning system (the total instrumental contribution) was then subtracted from the earnings of the member whose amount of elementary contribution (not including his or her instrumental contribution) was the lowest.[6] When there were two or more members whose elementary contributions were the same and the lowest, one subject was randomly chosen to be sanctioned. In the eight-person groups, 1.5 times the total instrumental cooperation was divided by two and assigned to the two lowest contributors (that is, each was punished by .75 times the total instrumental cooperation).[7] An average contribution of 8.3 cents to the sanctioning system was thus strong enough to cancel out the maximum savings of 50 cents. That is, when members contribute, on the average, 8.3 cents to the sanctioning system, the lowest contributor receives a penalty of 50 cents so that he/she gains nothing for his/her noncooperation. Subjects in the sanctioning condition were provided the following additional information on the information sheet: (e) how much the subject contributed to the sanctioning, (f) the total amount contributed to the sanctioning system, and (g) whether the subject received a sanction, and, if so, the amount of the sanction the subject received.

When the subjects made their decisions on the amount of elementary contribution and (in the case of the sanctioning condition) the instrumental contribution, they indicated these amounts on the information sheet and slipped it under the door. The experimenter collected the sheets and entered the amounts of contributions to a microcomputer. When all subjects' decisions were entered, the computer printed out the individualized information sheets. A new trial session started as the experimenter delivered the sheets to the subjects.

The experiment consisted of 12 sessions, but the subjects were not informed of the exact number of sessions they would have. They were told that there would be between 10 and 20 sessions. When 12 sessions were completed, subjects were asked to fill out a post-experimental questionnaire. Then, they were individually paid the amount they earned in the experiment. An extra effort was made so that two or more subjects did not leave the laboratory at the same time.

Results

In the following analyses, individual subjects are nested within groups so that the test of manipulated factors and their interactions required the use of group means as the unit of analysis. Gender was not used as a factor in the following analyses, since it was found to have no significant effects (including interactions effects) in a preliminary analysis.

Hypothesis 1a

As predicted, group size had a negative effect on elementary contribution when no sanctioning existed (the average of 23.82 cents per trial in four-person groups vs. 19.66 cents in eight-person groups); the simple main effect of group size in the size × sanctioning × trust ANOVA of elementary contribution was significant, $F(1, 40) = 4.70$, $p < .05$.

Hypothesis 1b

On the other hand, group size hardly had any effect on the level of instrumental cooperation (5.31 in four-person groups vs. 5.05 in eight-person groups); the main effect of group size in the size × trust ANOVA of instrumental cooperation was not significant, $F(1, 20) = 0.06$, ns.

In sum, group size did actually have differential effects on the two types of cooperation, as predicted by Hypothesis 1, and group size had a predicted negative effect on elementary cooperation in the no-sanctioning condition, but the predicted positive effect of group size on instrumental cooperation was not observed in the current experiment.

Hypothesis 2a

As predicted, the average level of elementary cooperation in the no-sanctioning condition was higher among high-trusters (25.02) than among low-trusters (18.46), and the simple main effect of trust in the no-sanctioning condition was significant, $F(1, 40) = 11.69$, $p < .01$.

Hypothesis 2b

The average level of instrumental cooperation tended to be lower among high-trusters (4.27) than among low-trusters (6.09) as predicted, but this effect of trust on instrumental cooperation did not reach the significance level, $F(1, 20) = 2.90$, ns.

HYPOTHESIS 3A

The predicted effect of the sanctioning system on elementary cooperation was highly significant, $F(1, 40) = 45.81$, $p < .01$. The average level of elementary cooperation was much higher in the sanctioning condition (30.93) than in the no-sanctioning condition (21.74).

HYPOTHESIS 3B

The positive effect of sanctioning on elementary cooperation tended to be stronger among low-trusters (28.44 vs. 18.46; a difference of 9.88) than among high-trusters (33.41 vs. 25.02; a difference of 8.39) as predicted, but the sanctioning × trust interaction did not reach the significance level, $F(1, 40) = 0.35$, ns.

HYPOTHESIS 4A

The positive effect of trust on elementary cooperation in the no-sanctioning condition tended to be stronger in four-person groups (27.57 vs. 20.07; a difference of 7.50) than in eight-person groups (22.47 vs. 16.85; a difference of 5.62) as predicted, but the trust × size interaction did not reach the significance level, $F(1, 40) = 0.24$, ns.

HYPOTHESIS 4AA

Although the trust × size interaction in the no-sanctioning condition was not significant as shown above, the negative effect of group size on elementary cooperation in the no-sanctioning condition tended to be stronger among high-trusters (22.47 vs. 27.57; a difference of −5.10) than among low-trusters (16.85 vs. 20.07; a difference of −3.22) as predicted.

HYPOTHESIS 4B

The negative effect of trust on instrumental cooperation was stronger in four-person groups (3.26 vs. 7.36; a difference of −4.10) than in eight-person groups (5.27 vs. 4.82; a difference of 0.55), as predicted, and the trust × size interaction was significant, $F(1, 20) = 4.54$, $p < .05$. The simple main effect of trust was significant in four-person groups, $F(1, 20) = 7.26$, $p < .05$, but not in eight-person groups, $F(1, 20) = 0.20$, ns.

HYPOTHESIS 4BB

The above interaction also indicates the differential effects of group size on instrumental cooperation. Actually the direction of the size effect was opposite in the two trust conditions. That is, the average level of high-trusters' instrumental cooperation tended to be higher in eight-person groups (5.27) than in four-person groups (3.26), whereas the average level of low-trusters' instrumental cooperation tended to be lower in eight-person groups (4.82) than in four-person groups (7.36). However, the simple main effect of size among high-trusters was not significant, $F(1, 20) = 1.77$, ns., and neither was the same simple main effect among low-trusters, $F(1, 20) = 2.82$, ns.

HYPOTHESIS 4C

The predicted sanctioning × trust × size interaction on elementary cooperation was significant, $F(1, 40) = 4.64, p < .05$, and the sanctioning × trust interaction was stronger in four-person groups than in eight-person groups as predicted. The sanctioning × trust interaction was significant in four-person groups, $F(1, 40) = 8.50, p < .01$; sanctioning did have a stronger effect on elementary cooperation among low-trusters (32.24 vs. 20.07; a difference of 12.17) than among high-trusters (32.29 vs. 27.57; a difference of 4.72) as predicted in Hypothesis 3b. This interaction was weaker in eight-person groups, as predicted; actually, the interaction effect did not reach the significance level, $F(1, 40) = 2.79$, ns. Although the interaction did not reach the significance level, the direction of the interaction was opposite to that predicted in Hypothesis 3b. That is, the effect of sanctioning on elementary cooperation was actually *weaker* among low-trusters (24.65 vs. 16.85; a difference of 7.80) than among high-trusters (34.53 vs. 22.47; a difference of 12.06).

Other Effects

The only other significant effect in the size × sanctioning × trust × trial block ANOVA of elementary cooperation was the main effect of trial blocks, $F(2, 80) = 33.15, p < .01$. (The twelve trials were aggregated into three trial blocks and was used as a repeated factor in this ANOVA.) As shown in Table 16.1, elementary cooperation generally declined over time. In addition, the sanctioning × trial block interaction, $F(2, 80) = 2.54, p < .10$, and the trust × trial block interaction, $F(2, 80) = 2.40, p < .10$, had marginal effects. The effect of sanctioning tended to become stronger, and the effect of trust tended to become weaker over time. No other effects were found to be significant in the analysis of simple effects (including interactions) on elementary cooperation in the no-sanctioning

TABLE 16.1 *Mean Elementary and Instrumental Contributions*

Trial Block	1	2	3	Overall
Elementary Cooperation				
Overall	29.58	26.93	22.49	26.33
N-sanctioning	26.02	21.41	17.79	21.74
Sanctioning	33.14	32.46	27.19	30.93
4-person	30.65	29.23	24.25	28.04
8-person	28.51	24.64	20.73	24.62
Low-trust	26.10	23.53	20.72	23.45
High-trust	33.05	30.33	24.26	29.22
4-person, Low-trust	27.37	27.12	23.98	26.15
High-trust	33.94	31.33	24.52	29.93
8-person, Low-trust	24.85	19.94	17.46	20.75
High-trust	32.17	29.33	24.00	28.50
No-sanctioning, 4-person	27.50	24.37	19.58	23.82
8-person	24.54	18.44	16.00	19.66
Low-trust	22.50	18.10	14.77	18.46
High-trust	29.54	24.71	20.81	25.02
4-person, L-T	23.37	21.04	15.79	20.07
H-T	31.62	27.71	23.37	27.57
8-person, L-T	21.62	15.17	13.75	16.85
H-T	27.46	21.71	18.25	22.47
Sanctioning, 4-person	33.79	34.08	28.92	32.26
8-person	32.48	30.83	25.46	29.59
Low-trust	29.71	28.96	26.67	28.44
High-trust	36.56	35.96	27.71	33.41
4-person, L-T	31.33	33.21	32.17	32.24
H-T	36.25	34.96	25.67	32.29
8-person, L-T	28.08	24.71	21.17	24.65
H-T	36.87	36.96	29.75	34.53
Instrumental Cooperation				
Overall	7.24	4.10	4.20	5.18
4-person	7.15	3.52	5.27	5.31
8-person	7.33	4.69	3.12	5.05
Low-trust	7.67	5.50	5.10	6.09
High-trust	6.81	2.71	3.29	4.27
4-person, Low-trust	8.58	6.12	7.37	7.36
High-trust	5.71	0.92	3.17	3.26
8-person, Low-trust	6.75	4.87	2.83	4.82
High-trust	7.92	4.50	3.41	5.27

condition, except the simple main effect of trial block, $F(1, 40) = 21.98$, $p < .01$. The other significant effects in the size × trust × trial block ANOVA of instrumental cooperation were the main effect of trial block, $F(2, 40) = 16.48$, $p < .01$, and the size × trial block interaction, $F(2, 40) = 3.76$, $p < .05$. As shown in Table 16.1, this interaction indicates that the effect of size on instrumental cooperation became more negative over time. The positive effect of size among high-trusters almost

TABLE 16.2 *ANOVA Tables*

		Size × Sanctioning × Trust × Trial Block ANOVA of elementary cooperation			Simple effects in the no-sanctioning condition			Size × Trust × Trial Block ANOVA of instrumental cooperation		
Factors	df	MS	F	*p*<	MS	F	*p*<	MS	F	*p*<
Size (SZ)	1	420.3	6.33	.05	311.5	4.70	.05	1.2	0.06	NS
Sanction (SC)	1	3038.8	45.81	.01						
Trust (TR)	1	1196.0	18.03	.01	775.2	11.69	.01	59.7	2.90	NS
SZ*SC	1	19.9	0.30	NS						
SZ*TR	1	142.0	2.14	NS	15.8	0.24	NS	93.3	4.53	.05
SC*TR	1	23.0	0.35	NS						
SZ*SC*TR	1	307.7	4.64	.05						
Group (SZ*TR)	20							20.6		
GP(SZ*SC*TR)	40	66.3			66.3					
Trial Block (TB)	2	615.9	33.15	.01	408.3	21.98	.01	76.4	16.48	.01
SZ*TB	2	18.2	0.98	NS	14.8	0.80	NS	17.4	3.76	.05
SC*TB	2	46.9	2.54	.10						
TR*TB	2	44.5	2.40	.10	1.5	0.08	NS	5.6	1.21	NS
SZ*SC*TB	2	5.0	0.27	NS						
SZ*TR*TB	2	24.2	1.30	NS	3.6	0.19	NS	0.3	0.06	NS
SC*TR*TB	2	26.3	1.42	NS						
SZ*SC*TR*TB	2	27.1	1.46	NS						
TB*GP(SZ*TR)	40							4.6		
TB*GP(SZ*SC*TR)	80	18.6			18.6					

disappeared by the third trial block, and the main effect of size became marginally significant in the third trial block, $F(1, 20) = 3.07, p < .10$. Full ANOVA tables for elementary and instrumental cooperation are shown in Table 16.2. The table also lists simple effects on elementary cooperation in the no-sanctioning condition.

Discussion

The results of the current experiment provide a positive answer to the fundamental question raised in this study: "Does group size affect elementary and instrumental cooperation differently?" On the other hand, the predicted positive effect of group size on instrumental cooperation did not emerge when both low- and high-trusters were pooled. The predicted positive effect did not emerge since group size had an unexpected negative effect among low-trusters. The results suggest an interesting and potentially very important role of trust in instrumental cooperation.

Actually, high-trusters' level of instrumental cooperation tended to be higher in eight-person groups than in four-person groups, as predicted. As a result, high-trusters maintained a high level of elementary cooperation even in eight-person groups when sanctioning existed. These results suggest that the structural goal/expectation solution to the social dilemma problem proposed by Yamagishi (1986a, b) is equally applicable to eight-person groups as to four-person groups *among high-trusters*. That is, high-trusters voluntarily cooperate in the provision/maintenance of a sanctioning system to solve a first-order dilemma even in the larger eight-person groups as in the smaller four-person groups. On the other hand, group size had a negative effect on instrumental cooperation as well as on elementary cooperation among low-trusters. This indicates that the voluntary cooperation for the provision/maintenance of a sanctioning system is not a viable solution in larger groups among low-trusters.

The question, then, is: Why did low-trusters' instrumental cooperation decline in larger groups? One possible answer to this is that trust has a non-linear effect on instrumental cooperation. When subjects think that others will voluntarily cooperate without sanctioning, their level of instrumental cooperation will be low because they do not feel that a sanctioning system is needed. As their level of trust declines, they start realizing the need for sanctioning and, as a result, their level of instrumental cooperation will increase. However, as their level of trust further declines, they might feel that others will not cooperate unless the level of sanctioning is extremely high. They will, then, give up their effort to force others to cooperate through sanctioning since they feel that it is futile (or the cost for sanctioning exceeds its intended effect). According to this explanation, self efficacy (cf. Kerr, in this volume) affects instrumental cooperation as well as elementary cooperation.

Another possible answer is that low- and high-trusters are different not only in their trust levels but also in other personal characteristics. Hypothesis 1 concerning the differential effects of group size on elementary and instrumental cooperation is based on the assumption that people are basically cooperative and the major disincentive for cooperation is the fear that unilateral cooperation may be exploited by others. Using Arneson's (1982) terms, the hypothesis is based on the assumption that people are either "nervous cooperators," who desire to cooperate but do not want to waste resources in support of a lost cause, or "reluctant cooperators," who desire to cooperate but are unwilling to allow themselves to be exploited by free riders. These are people who would willingly cooperate if they were assured that others also would, and for them the efficacy of their cooperation (either elementary of instrumental) related to group size does not matter insofar as they are assured of other members' cooperation. On the other hand, the rational–strategic actors, who cooperate insofar as it is strategically effective in inducing others into cooperation so that their cooperation "pays off" in the long-run, may instrumentally cooperate in small groups but not in large groups. This is because their instrumental cooperation is strategically more cost-effective (each member's instrumental cooperation is worth one-*N*th of the total amount of sanctioning). It is possible, and even likely, that low-trusters who have no confidence that others are cooperative are also "cold-calculators." Studies of social motivation indicate heterogeneity in social motivation between cooperators and defectors (e.g., Kelley & Stahelski, 1970; Liebrand *et al.*, 1986). Since high-trusters tend to be cooperators as well, some of the differences found between cooperators and defectors in the previous studies may also exist between high-trusters and low-trusters. In fact, the result of an additional questionnaire study of 167 Japanese student respondents (Yamashina, 1988) shows that the trust scale used in the present study correlates with Machiavellism scale ($r = .48$), suggesting that low-trusters are also "cold-calculators." If the ratio of rational–strategic actors to nervous and reluctant cooperators is higher among low-trusters than among high-trusters, this difference can explain the decline in instrumental cooperation among low-trusters in the larger group.

As a conclusion, the results of the current experiment clearly point to the fact that the structural goal/expectation theory of cooperation proposed by Yamagishi (1986a, b) is limited in its applicability. If the first answer to the above question is correct, even high-trusters would eventually stop making instrumental contributions in really large groups. The applicability may also be limited to the degree that the population consists of rational–strategic actors (and/or hard-core free riders who would always defect) rather than nervous or reluctant cooperators. These are important issues that need to be addressed in future research.

References

Arneson, R. J. (1982) The principle of fairness and the free-rider problem. *Ethics,* **92**, 616–633.
Bonacich, P., Shure, G. H., Kahan, J. P., & Meeker, R. J. (1976). Cooperation and group size in the *N*-person prisoner's dilemma. *Journal of Conflict Resolution,* **20**, 685–705.
Buckley, W., Burns, T., & Meeker, L. D. (1974). Structural resolutions of collective action problems. *Behavioral Science,* **19**, 277–297.
Cass, R. D., & Edney, J. J. (1978). The commons dilemma: a simulation testing the effect of resource visibility and territorial division. *Human Ecology,* **6**, 371–386.
Dawes, R. M. (1980) Social dilemmas. *Annual Review of Psychology,* **31**, 169–193.
Edney, J. J. (1980) The commons problem: alternative perspectives. *American Psychologist,* **35**, 131–150.
Edney, J. J., & Harper, C. S. (1978). The commons dilemma: A review of contributions from psychology. *Environmental Management,* **2**, 491–507.
Fleishman, J. A. (1980). Collective action as helping behavior: Effect of responsibility diffusion on contributions to a public good. *Journal of Personality and Social Psychology,* **38**, 629–637.
Fox, J., & Guyer, M. (1977). Group size and others' strategy in an *n*-person game. *Journal of Conflict Resolution,* **21**, 323–338.
Hardin, G. (1968). The tragedy of the commons. *Science,* **162**, 1243–1248.
Hechter, M. (1984). When actors comply: Monitoring costs and the production of social order. *Acta Sociologica,* **27**, 161–83.
Hobbes, T. (1909 [1651]). *Leviathan,* edited by W. G. P. Smith. Oxford: Clarendon Press.
Kelley, H. H., & Stahelski, A. J. (1970). Social interaction basis of cooperators' and competitors' benefits about others. *Journal of Personality and Social Psychology,* **16**, 66–91.
Kerr, N. L. (In this volume). Efficacy as a mediator and a moderator of cooperation in social dilemmas.
Liebrand, W. B. G., Jansen, R. W. T. L., Ruken, V. M., & Shure, C. J. M. (1986). Might over morality: social values and the perception of other players in experimental games. *Journal of Experimental Social Psychology,* **21**, 86–102.
Marwell, G., & Schmitt, D. R. (1972) Cooperation in a three-person prisoner's dilemma. *Journal of Personality and Social Psychology,* **12**, 158–163.
Messick, D. M., & Brewer, M. B. (1983). Solving social dilemmas: A review. In L. Wheeler (Ed.), *Review of Personality and Social Psychology,* vol. 4 pp. 11–44. Beverly Hills, California: Sage.
Messick, D. M., Wilke, H. A. M., Brewer, M. B., Kramer, R. M., Zemke, P. E., & Lui, L. (1983). Individual adaptations and structural change as solutions to social dilemmas. *Journal of Personality and Social Psychology,* **44**, 294–309.
Mitsui, H. (1983). Laboratory experiments on social dilemmas. *Japanese Journal of Experimental Social Psychology,* **23**, 53–59. (In Japanese).
Oliver, P. (1980). Rewards and punishments as selective incentives for collective action: Theoretical investigations. *American Journal of Sociology,* **85**, 1356–1375.
Olson, M. (1965). *The Logic of Collective Action.* Cambridge, Mass.: Harvard University Press.
Pruitt, D. G., & Kimmel, M. J. (1977). Twenty years of experimental gaming: critique, synthesis, and suggestions for the future. *Annual Review of Psychology,* **28**, 363–392.
Rutte, C. G., & Wilke, H. A. M. (1984). Social dilemmas and leadership. *European Journal of Social Psychology,* **14**, 105–121.
Rutte, C. G., & Wilke, H. A. M. (In this volume). Goals, expectations and behavior in a social dilemma situation.
Samuelson, C. D., Messick, D. M., Rutte, C. G., & Wilke, H. A. M. (1984). Individual and structural solutions to resource dilemmas in two cultures. *Journal of Personality and Social Psychology,* **47**, 94–104.
Sato, K. (1987). Distribution of the cost of maintaining common resources. *Journal of Experimental Social Psychology,* **23**, 19–31.
Sato, K. (1988). Trust and group size in a social dilemma. *Japanese Psychological Research,* **30**, 99–93.
Sato, K., & Yamagishi, T. (1986). Two psychological factors in the problem of public goods. *Japanese Journal of Experimental Social Psychology,* **26**, 89–95. (In Japanese).

Stroebe, W., & Frey, B. S. (1982). Self-interest and collective action: the economics and psychology of public goods. *British Journal of Social Psychology*, **21**, 121–137.
Taylor, M. (1976). *Anarchy and Cooperation.* London: Wiley.
Van de Kragt, A. J. C., Orbell, J. M., & Dawes, R. M. (1983). The minimal contributing set as a solution to public goods problems. *American Political Science Review*, **77**, 112–122.
Yamagishi, T. (1986a). The provision of a sanctioning system as a public good. *Journal of Personality and Social Psychology*, **51**, 110–116.
Yamagishi, T. (1986b). The structural goal/expectation theory of cooperation in social dilemmas. In E. J. Lawler (Ed.), *Advances in Group Processes*, vol. III pp. 51–87. Greenwich, CT: JAI Press.
Yamagishi, T. (1987). Efficacy of an altruistic action and expectations of other members' behavior in social dilemmas. Unpublished manuscript, Seattle: University of Washington.
Yamagishi, T. (1988a). Seriousness of social dilemmas and the provision of a sanctioning system. *Social Psychology Quarterly*, **51**, 32–42.
Yamagishi, T. (1988b). The provision of a sanctioning system in the United States and Japan. *Social Psychology Quarterly*, **51**, 264–270.
Yamagishi, T. (1989). Unintended consequences of some solutions to social dilemmas. *Sociological Theory and Method*, **4**, 21–37. (In Japanese)
Yamagishi, T., & Iwamoto, T. (1985). A review of research on social dilemmas. Pp. 15–26 in J. Hara & M. Umino (Eds), *The Current State of Mathematical Sociology*. Nishinomiya, Japan: Suuri Shakai Gaku Kenkyuukai. (In Japanese)
Yamagishi, T., & Sato, K. (1986). Motivational bases of the public goods problem. *Journal of Personality and Social Psychology*, **50**, 67–73.
Yamashina, S. (1988). The structure of trust. Unpublished bachelor's thesis. Hokkaido University, Sapporo, Japan. (In Japanese)

Notes

1. Oliver (1980) makes a similar distinction.
2. See Hechter (1984) for examples in which people voluntarily seek to be controlled.
3. The "low temptation" condition in Rutte and Wilke's study corresponds to the "high gain" condition in Yamagishi's (1988a) study. That is, gain of cooperation in the high-temptation condition in Rutte and Wilke's study was 1.0 and that in the low-temptation condition was 7.0. Mutual cooperation was much more important in the low-temptation condition than in the high-temptation condition.
4. Other possible reasons for the negative effect of group size are: expectations for other members' cooperation (Fox & Guyer, 1977; Sato, 1988; Yamagishi, 1986a), social incentives (Olson, 1965), "bad apple" effect (Bonacich *et al.*, 1976; Marwell & Schmitt, 1972), diffusion of responsibility (Cass & Edney, 1978; Edney, 1980; Fleishman, 1980; Stroebe & Frey, 1982).
5. Furthermore, the strategic action often has externality, that is, has "unintended" effects on people other than the target. This unintended consequence of the strategic action may cause a vicious cycle of mutual punishment (cf. Yamagishi, 1989).
6. The multiplication factor (1.5 times the total instrumental contribution) represents the middle of the low-sanctioning condition (1.0 times the total instrumental contribution) and the high-sanctioning condition (2.0 times the total instrumental contribution) used in the previous studies (Yamagishi, 1986a, 1988b).
7. If only the lowest contributor was punished in eight-person groups, he or she will receive twice as much punishment in eight-person groups as in four-person groups from the same level of average instrumental contribution (since the total amount of instrumental contribution is twice as much in eight-person groups as in four-person groups, given the same level of average instrumental contribution). Suppose that the average instrumental contribution is 10 cents. In four-person groups, the total instrumental contribution would then be 40 cents and the lowest contributor would receive a punishment of 60 cents. In eight-person groups, the total would be 80 cents and the amount of punishment would be a dollar and 20 cents. Since the maximum amount of savings from noncooperation is 50 cents, the level of punishment slightly

exceeding 50 cents would be effective enough. If the only-one-punishment rule is adopted, the average amount of instrumental cooperation in eight-person groups may be lower than that in four-person groups not because subjects in eight-person groups are less willing to make instrumental contributions but because the lower level of instrumental contribution provides strong enough sanctions in eight-person groups. The current rule that punishes the two lowest contributors was adopted to eliminate this potentially confounding factor of group size on instrumental contribution.

17

Goals, Expectations and Behavior in a Social Dilemma Situation

CHRISTEL G. RUTTE
Erasmus University, Nijmegen, The Netherlands

HENK A. M. WILKE
University of Leiden, The Netherlands

Introduction

Social dilemmas are group situations in which the rational choices of all group members result in a collective disaster (Messick & Brewer, 1983). Hardin (1968) for example describes a situation in which a number of herdsmen, sharing a common pasturage, must decide how many animals to graze on the commons. It is in the interest of each herdsman to increase the size of his herd, because the profit accrues to the herdsman; the cost, measured as damage to the commons, is shared equally by all. Thus, each herdsman has an incentive to increase the size of his herd and, yet, if all do so, the ultimate result is the destruction of the commons.

Dawes (1980) defined social dilemmas by two properties: (a) each individual receives a higher payoff for a socially defecting choice than for a socially cooperative choice, no matter what the other individuals do, but (b) all individuals are better off if all cooperate than if all defect. Wilke, Liebrand, and Messick (1983) give a number of examples of societal problems that can be understood as social dilemmas; those include tax evasion, energy waste, pollution and overpopulation.

Social dilemmas may be considered *N*-person versions of two-person Prisoner's Dilemmas (PDs). Reviewing the extensive literature on two-person PDs, Pruitt and Kimmel (1977) suggested that the conclusions they arrived at for two-person PDs can be easily extended to PDs involving more than two people. On the basis of their extensive literature review, Pruitt and Kimmel formulated the goal/expectation theory as a summarizing statement of the findings. The goal/expectation theory states that cooperative behavior in a two-person, multiplay PD game will only arise when a player has both a goal to achieve mutual cooperation and an expectation that the other player is ready to cooperate. The most distinctive prediction from the goal/expectation theory is a statistical interaction between goal and expectation, i.e., cooperation is assumed to be high only when both a goal to achieve mutual cooperation and an expectation that the other player is willing to cooperate are present. When the other player is not expected to cooperate, a player will defect himself. This defection can be seen as a sign that a player is not willing to be exploited by the other and thereby as an attempt to secure the other player's cooperation.

Pruitt and Kimmel's theory pertains to long-range thinking (1977, p. 375) of players who pursue a goal and infer expectations from the choice behavior of the other player in the two-person PD. In the following we will follow this distinction between goals and expectations, although the role of expectations is somewhat more complicated than supposed by Pruitt and Kimmel. From various experimental results it appears namely (see Dawes, McTavish, & Shaklee, 1977; Liebrand, Wilke, Vogel, & Wolters, 1986; Liebrand, Jansen, & Rijken, 1986; Dawes, 1989) that a subject's goal corresponds with initial expectations about the behavior of the other player from the outset of the game. These initial expectations should be distinguished from the expectations to which Pruitt and Kimmel refer, since the latter expectations are assumed to arise as a consequence of the other player's behavior.

Yamagishi (1986a) argues that the applicability of the goal/expectation theory to *N*-person PDs is limited because in groups as opposed to pairs a single member's action has low impact on other members. This leads to what Yamagishi calls a decreased sense of action interdependency. An individual action is hardly noticed by other members and therefore it is almost impossible to direct others' decisions, through one's own actions, into mutual cooperation. The result is that considerations of strategy are less relevant in groups than in dyads, and the larger the group the more this will be true. This will make the application of goal/expectation theory less appropriate in larger groups.

According to Yamagishi (1986a) people in groups will not simply engage in cooperative actions (he labels this *elementary* cooperation), but will rather cooperate for a structural change (he labels this *instrumental* cooperation). One possible structural change is administering selective incentives. The dilemma situation can be structurally altered for example by punishing defectors (Caldwell, 1976; Yamagishi, 1986b, 1988). Another possible structural change is the inauguration of a leader. The dilemma can be avoided if group members give up their freedom of choice and delegate the decision power to a leader who makes decisions for the group (Messick, Wilke, Brewer, Kramer, Zemke, & Lui, 1983; Rutte & Wilke, 1984; Samuelson, Messick, Rutte, & Wilke, 1984). The distinction between elementary and instrumental cooperation is also present in

Messick and Brewer's (1983) review, when they make a distinction between "solutions that derive from independent changes in individual behavior and solutions that come about through coordinated, organized group action on the other" (p. 22).

Although Yamagishi (1986a) argues that people in groups will engage mainly in instrumental cooperation rather than in elementary cooperation, evidence suggests that both forms of cooperation can be encountered in small groups. First we will discuss evidence concerning elementary cooperation and next evidence concerning instrumental cooperation. Several studies showed that people with cooperative goals engage more often in elementary cooperation than people with noncooperative goals (for example Kelley & Grzelak, 1972). Furthermore, several studies showed that people with induced cooperative expectations engage more often in elementary cooperation than people with noncooperative expectations (for example Schroeder, Jensen, Reed, Sullivan, & Schwab, 1983; Wilke & Braspenning, 1989).

Notably, Yamagishi demonstrated in three experiments that people in groups engage in elementary cooperation. In the first experiment, Yamagishi (1986b) measured trust with the help of a preexperimental questionnaire and compared the decisions of low trusters and high trusters. It was assumed that low trusters had noncooperative expectations and that high trusters had cooperative expectations. The results revealed that cooperative expectations led to higher levels of elementary cooperation than noncooperative expectations. The results of Yamagishi's second experiment (1988) revealed that the level of elementary cooperation declined as the dilemma became more serious (i.e., both temptation to defect and the gain for cooperation became greater). Elementary cooperation was also observed in the experiment that Yamagishi reports in this book. In this experiment high trusters and low trusters made choices in four-person or eight-person groups. It appeared that elementary cooperation was smaller in eight-person than in four-person groups, suggesting that indeed elementary cooperation is less likely to be a solution to social dilemmas when groups are larger.

In a recent study Wilke and Braspenning (1989) investigated the effects of goals and expectations on elementary cooperation. Goals were induced with the help of an unspecified bonus. Subjects in the competitive goal condition were informed that the group member who obtained most game outcomes would receive the bonus. Subjects in the cooperative goal condition were informed that all group members would receive the bonus, if one's own group would obtain more game outcomes than an outgroup. After the introduction of goals subjects were requested to make their first choice. It appeared that cooperative goal subjects made a more cooperative choice than competitive goal subjects. In agreement with previous findings, moreover, it was found that subjects' initial expectations about the choices of other group members correlated with their own choice. Before the second and third choice, expectations were induced by informing subjects of the choices of the other members of their group. In the cooperative expectation condition subjects received feedback that all others had made a cooperative choice, whereas in the competitive expectation condition subjects received feedback that all others had made a competitive choice. The results indicated that elementary cooperation was highest in the cooperative goal and cooperative expectation condition and lowest in the competitive goal and competitive expectation condition, whereas the level of elementary cooperation in the other two conditions (cooperative goal/competitive expectation and competitive goal/cooperative expectation) was in between. These results suggest that goals as well as expectations contribute to elementary cooperation.

Thus, there is evidence that elementary cooperation can be encountered in groups and that goals and expectations affect the level of elementary cooperation. This suggests that Pruitt and Kimmel's goal/expectation theory can be applied to social dilemma situations. In the present study both goals and expectations are part of a factorial design in order to study their combined effects. On the basis of Pruitt and Kimmel's theory (1977) one may predict an interaction effect, although the results obtained by Wilke and Braspenning (1989) suggest two main effects.

Let us turn now to instrumental cooperation. Several studies also demonstrate that instrumental cooperation can be encountered in groups. Yamagishi for example gave his subjects the opportunity to administer selective incentives, i.e., to punish the least cooperative group member. In one experiment (1986b) it was shown that low trusters engaged more in instrumental cooperation than high trusters. In a second experiment (1988) it was shown that the level of instrumental cooperation increased as the dilemma became more serious (i.e., both temptation to defect and the gain of cooperation became greater). In a third experiment (reported elsewhere in this book) it was shown that group size had a positive effect on high-trusters' level of instrumental cooperation but a negative effect on low-trusters' level of instrumental cooperation.

Messick *et al.* (1983), Rutte and Wilke (1984), and Samuelson *et al.* (1984) reported experiments in which subjects, acting in a resource dilemma game, were given the opportunity to give up freedom of choice and to delegate the decision power to a leader who makes decisions for the group. In these experiments subjects had received false feedback about other group members' behavior on a series of ten trials. One-third of the subjects had learned that the others were overusing a common resource, one-third that the others were optimally using it and the remaining third that the others were underusing it. This feedback may be interpreted, *post hoc*, as a manipulation of expectations inferred from the behavior of others. The experiments give evidence that expectations inferred from feedback influence the level of instrumental cooperation. When the others were overusing the resource, subjects engaged in higher levels of instrumental cooperation than when the others were optimally or underusing the resource.

The studies concerning instrumental cooperation suggest that Pruitt and Kimmel's goal/expectation theory could be extended even further, to encompass not only elementary, but also instrumental cooperation. Since there are no experiments in which both goals and expectations were included as independent variables in a factorial design to study their combined effects on the level of instrumental cooperation, it is unclear what predictions should be made.

Let us assume, however, that only people who want to achieve a situation of mutual cooperation have an interest to engage in cooperative behavior, whether elementary or instrumental. As long as others are expected to engage in elementary cooperation, there is no need to turn to instrumental cooperation, because simply engaging in elementary cooperation suffices to achieve one's goal. Only when others are not expected to engage in elementary cooperation, one's goal cannot be achieved by simply engaging in elementary cooperation and there is a need to turn to instrumental cooperation.

This rationale implies two interaction effects. Elementary cooperation is predicted to be highest when both a cooperative goal and cooperative expectations are present. Instrumental cooperation is predicted to be highest when both a cooperative goal and *non*cooperative expectations are present.

Method

General Overview

Five-person groups acted in a social dilemma situation. The design of the study was a 2 (temptation) × 5 (feedback) factorial one. The temptation to defect was either high or low. Subjects received feedback that zero, one, two, three or four (all) other group members intended to choose cooperatively. Subjects were randomly assigned to one of the ten experimental conditions. The main dependent variables were (a) whether subjects made a cooperative choice or not, and (b) whether subjects voted to elect a leader or not.

Subjects

Subjects were 147 male and female volunteers from a secondary school in Groningen, The Netherlands. Subjects were paid 10 dutch guilders per hour for their participation (one guilder is equivalent to about 50¢). The number of subjects per cell ranged from 14 to 16.

Procedure

Five-person groups arrived at the laboratory to participate in a computer-controlled experiment. Subjects were seated in private cubicles. With the help of video-screens and personal computers, instructions were given and responses recorded.

Subjects were instructed that in this investigation they were going to make one decision. The decision consisted of making one choice between C and D. The choice between C and D had financial consequences. It was stressed that subjects made their choices independently and anonymously, and that their monetary payoff depended upon their own decision and the decisions of the others jointly. Throughout the instructions no reference was given to the desirability of selecting either C or D.

The payoffs associated with a C or D choice were presented in a payoff matrix. Subjects were presented one of two payoff matrices, that differed with respect to the relative attractiveness of the defective option, which is, according to Pruitt and Kimmel (1977), a way to manipulate goals. Both payoff matrices had a social dilemma structure, i.e., each subject received a higher payoff for D than for C, no matter what the other group members did, but all group members were better off if all chose C than if all chose D. Half of the subjects were presented a payoff matrix in which the temptation to choose D was *low*, the other half of the subjects were presented a payoff matrix in which the temptation to choose D was *high*. In Table 17.1 the two payoff matrices can be found.

TABLE 17.1 *Payoff Matrices*

	Temptation for D High		Temptation for D Low	
Number of Cs	Payoff for C	Payoff for D	Payoff for C	Payoff for D
0		9		3
1	2	11	2	5
2	4	13	4	7
3	6	15	6	9
4	8	17	8	11
5	10		10	

Payoff in Dutch guilders (1 guilder is equivalent to about $0.50)

Subjects were told that they had to choose between C and D only once. After this one choice the experiment would be terminated and subjects would be paid according to the distribution of choices in their group given the payoff matrix. There was only one trial to avoid considerations of strategy. This was done because, as was told in the introduction, Yamagishi argues that considerations of strategy are less relevant in groups than in dyads, and the larger the group the more this will be true. To make considerations of strategy irrelevant in this experiment, we decided not to increase the group size but to have only one trial instead.

Before subjects made their choice, a quiz consisting of ten items was administered. All correct answers to these ten questions were displayed and explained to ensure a good understanding of the payoff matrix. After the quiz, questions were asked to check on the manipulation of goals. Next, subjects were asked what choice they intended to make.

After subjects indicated their choice intentions the console displayed: "You just indicated what choice you intend to make. The other group members answered this question too. We will show you now how everybody responded to this question." At this point in the experiment false feedback on the intentions of the other group members was displayed, which is, according to Pruitt and Kimmel (1977), a way to manipulate different expectations. One fifth of the subjects learned that zero others in their group intended to choose C, one fifth learned that *one* other intended to choose C, one fifth learned that *two* others intended to choose C, one fifth learned that *three* others intended to choose C, and, finally, one fifth learned that *four*, i.e., all others, intended to choose C. After the feedback, questions were asked to check on the manipulation of feedback. Subjects were randomly assigned to the experimental conditions.

Next, subjects were questioned about the attractiveness of the D-choice and their expectations about others' choices. After this, subjects were asked to indicate their choice intentions for the second time and they chose definitely between C and D. Then, subjects were asked to imagine that they had to do the same task again with the same group of people. They were asked whether in that case they would vote to elect one of the group members as a leader to make choices in the name of all group members, or whether they would like all members of the group to make their own choice again. Finally, subjects were debriefed and thanked and were paid 10 guilders.

Results

Manipulation Checks

Immediately after being presented with one of the two payoff matrices and after the quiz, a number of questions were asked to be answered on one-to-seven point scales, to check on the manipulation of goals. First, subjects were asked to what extent they thought the D-option was more attractive than the C-option. An analysis of variance revealed that when the temptation for D was high, subjects found D more attractive (M = 5.88) than when the temptation for D was low (M = 4.34), F (1,145) = 42.13, $p < .001$.

The second question concerned the desirability of all group members opting for C. An analysis of variance revealed that when the temptation for D was low, subjects considered "all C" more desirable (M = 1.86) than when the temptation for D was high ($M = 3.69$), $F(1,144) = 40.25$, $p < .001$.

In the third question subjects were asked how satisfied they would be if all group members would opt for C. An analysis of variance revealed that when the temptation for D was low, subjects would be more satisfied with "all C" ($M = 1.91$) than when the temptation for D was high ($M = 2.59$), $F(1,145) = 7.84$, $p < .006$.

In the fourth question subjects were asked to what extent they wanted to maximize the payoff for all group members together. An analysis of variance revealed that when the temptation for D was low, subjects wanted to maximize all group members' payoffs more ($M = 6.0$) than when the temptation for D was high ($M = 5.01$), $F(1,145) = 13.54$, $p < .001$.

At this point in the experiment subjects were asked whether they intended to make a C- or a D-choice. A chi-square analysis of the frequencies (Goodman, 1971) revealed two effects. First, there was an overall effect, reflecting that over all conditions more subjects intended to choose D (prop. = .69) than C (prop. = .31), chi-square = 21.09, df = 1, $p < .001$. Second, there was an effect for temptation, chi-square = 47.37, df = 1, $p < .001$. When the temptation for D was low, more subjects intended to choose C (prop. = .56) than when the temptation for D was high (prop. = .07).

Later on, after subjects were given false feedback on the intentions of the others in their group (ranging from 0 to 4 C-intentions) and before subjects made their choice, they were asked a number of questions, concerning (a) subjects' recollection of the purported choice-intentions of the other group members, (b) subjects' expectations about the choices of the other group members, and again (c) the attractiveness of choosing the D option. This last question was asked to check whether the feedback on the intentions of the other group members had influenced the attractiveness of the C- or D-option.

First, subjects were asked to indicate on a zero-to-four point scale how many of the other group members had indicated an intention to choose D. A 2 (temptation) × 5 (feedback) analysis of variance revealed only a significant effect for feedback, $F(4,137) = 121.87$, $p < .001$, reflecting that subjects generally reproduced correctly the purported intentions of the others (*M*s are respectively .57, 1.11, 2.07, 3.03 and 4.0).

Second, subjects were asked to indicate on a zero-to-four point scale how many other group members they expected to choose cooperatively in actuality. A 2 (temptation) × 5 (feedback) analysis of variance revealed two significant effects. First, there was a significant main effect for temptation, $F(1,136) = 77.26$, $p < .001$, reflecting that when the temptation for D was low, subjects expected more cooperative choices ($M = 2.54$) than when the temptation for D was high ($M = 1.15$). Second, there was a significant main effect for feedback, $F(4,136) = 18.24$, $p <$

.001. Subjects who had received feedback that *four* others intended to choose cooperatively expected more cooperative choices ($M = 2.93$) than subjects who had received feedback that *three* ($M = 2.15$) or *two* ($M = 1.80$) others intended to choose cooperatively ($p < .05$), and these subjects in turn expected more cooperative choices than subjects who had received feedback that *one* ($M = 1.20$) or *zero* ($M = 1.10$) others intended to choose cooperatively ($p < .05$). These results suggest that the more others purportedly indicated an intention to choose cooperatively, the more others were expected to choose cooperatively in actuality.

Third, subjects were asked to indicate on a one-to-seven point scale to what extent they found the D-option more attractive than the C-option. A 2 (temptation) × 5 (feedback) analysis of variance revealed only a significant effect for temptation, $F\ (1,137) = 54.19$, $p < .001$. When the temptation for D was high, subjects found D more attractive ($M = 5.95$) than when the temptation for D was low ($M = 4.33$).

We may conclude from these results that our manipulations of temptation and feedback were successful. When the temptation for D was low a goal of achieving mutual cooperation arose to a greater extent than when the temptation for D was high. Moreover, feedback on the intentions of the other group members significantly and independently influenced expectations about the other group members' choices. It seems, however, that temptation, or goals, also influenced expectations. We will comment on this last finding in the discussion.

Choice Behavior

Before subjects made their choice they were first asked to indicate on a one-to-seven point scale to what extent they felt inclined to choose D. A 2 (temptation) × 5 (feedback) analysis of variance revealed two significant effects. First, there was a main effect for temptation, $F\ (1,136) = 64.53$, $p < .001$, reflecting that when the temptation for D was high, subjects were more inclined to choose D ($M = 5.95$) than when the temptation for D was low ($M = 3.93$). Second, there was a main effect for feedback, $F\ (4,136) = 2.97$, $p < .02$. Subjects who had received feedback that *zero, one, two* or *three* others intended to choose cooperatively did not differ significantly in their inclination to choose D (Ms are respectively 5.14, 5.27, 4.93 and 5.26). Subjects who had received feedback that *four* others intended to choose cooperatively, however, were significantly less inclined to choose D ($M = 4.20$) than subjects in all the other feedback conditions (ps $< .05$). This result strongly suggests that the inclination to choose D is lowest when all others intend to choose C. The interaction of temptation and feedback was not significant, $F\ (4,136) = .65$.

At this point in the experiment subjects finally made a binding choice between C and D. A 2 (temptation) × 5 (feedback) chi-square analysis of the frequencies (Goodman, 1971) revealed three effects. First, over all conditions fewer subjects chose C (prop. = .29) than D (prop. = .71), chi-square = 26.99, df = 1, $p < .001$. Second, there was a main effect for temptation, indicating that when the temptation for D was low, more subjects chose C (prop. = .52) than when the temptation for D was high (prop. = .07), chi-square = 45.49, df = 1, $p < .001$. Third, there was a main effect for feedback, chi-square = 14.28, df = 4, $p < .01$. The proportions of C-choices for the subjects who had received feedback that *zero, one, two* or *three* others intended to choose cooperatively did not differ significantly. Subjects who had received feedback that *four* others intended to choose cooperatively, however, chose C more often than subjects in all the other feedback conditions. More specifically: subjects who had received feedback that *four* others intended to choose cooperatively chose C more often (prop. = .50) than subjects who had received feedback that *three* (prop. = .18, $p < .05$), *two* (prop. = .27, $p < .06$), *one* (prop. = .30, $p < .11$) or *zero* (prop. = .21, $p < .05$) others intended to choose cooperatively. Although not all of these differences are significant at the .05 level, these results strongly suggest that when all others intend to choose cooperatively, subjects choose cooperatively themselves more often than when fewer than all others intend to choose cooperatively. The interaction of temptation and feedback was not significant, chi-square = 3.59, df = 4.

There is as yet no evidence at all for the idea that temptation and feedback have an interaction effect on choice intentions or choice behavior. The results reveal two clear main effects of temptation and feedback.

Leader Votes

After subjects chose definitely between C and D, they were asked to imagine that they had to do the same task again with the same group of people. They were asked to indicate whether in that case they would vote to elect one of the group members as leader to make choices in the name of all group members, or whether they would like all members of the group to make their own choice again (cf. Messick *et al.*, 1983; Rutte & Wilke, 1984; Samuelson *et al.*, 1984).

A 2 (temptation) × 5 (feedback) chi-square analysis of the frequencies revealed two significant effects. First, there was a main effect for temptation, chi-square = 6.17, df = 1, $p < .025$, indicating that when the temptation for D was low, subjects voted more often to elect a leader (prop. = .62) than when the temptation for D was high (prop. = .41). Second, there was an interaction effect concerning temptation and feedback, chi-square = 18.46, df = 4, $p < .001$. Further analysis of this interaction effect revealed that the simple main effect of feedback was significant in the low temptation condition, chi-square = 17.99, df = 4, $p < .001$, and not significant in the high temptation condition, chi-square = 4.28, df = 4. The relevant proportions can be found in Table 17.2.

TABLE 17.2 *The Proportions of Votes for a Leader in Each of Ten Experimental Conditions*

	C-Feedback				
Temptation	0	1	2	3	4
Low	$.79^{a}$	$.94^{a}$	$.64^{ab}$	$.36^{b}$	$.31^{b}$
High	$.50^{a}$	$.21^{a}$	$.38^{a}$	$.57^{a}$	$.40^{a}$

[ab] Proportions with a different index within the same row differ significantly ($p < .05$).

It can be seen in Table 17.2 that subjects in the low temptation condition who received feedback that very few others intend to cooperate are especially willing to vote for a leader if they had to do the task again with the same group. In the high temptation condition the proportions in the various feedback conditions do not differ from each other.

Discussion

In the present experiment, goals and expectations were independently manipulated. Goals were manipulated by varying the temptation associated with the defective choice. Expectations were manipulated by varying the feedback about the purported intentions of the other group members. Predictions concerned both elementary and instrumental cooperation. For both forms of cooperation interactions between temptation and feedback were predicted. Not all the results of the experiment appear to be in agreement with these predictions.

The results show two clear main effects of temptation and feedback on elementary cooperation, implying that both these factors independently influence elementary cooperation on the part of a group member. Notable, moreover, is that feedback only seems to influence choice behavior when it implies that all other group members intend to choose cooperatively. This finding corroborates with one of Orbell, van de Kragt, and Dawes (1988). These investigators found that promises to cooperate were kept only when everyone in the group had promised to cooperate. Orbell *et al.* explained this result by speculating that people recognize universal promising as a condition that creates an ethical obligation to act on a promise, not only for others but also for themselves.

An alternative explanation can be given on the basis of conformity theory (Allen, 1965). The distinctive characteristic of the procedure used by Asch in his conformity experiments is that a single individual is opposed by an incorrect but unanimous majority. Asch also conducted experiments to determine the effect on conformity of a nonunanimous group by introducing a confederate who gave the correct answer throughout. Such a confederate decreased conformity drastically from about 35 to about 5 percent. Since in an *N*-person PD the noncooperative alternative is dominating (in the sense that an individual always receives a higher payoff for a noncooperative than for a cooperative choice no matter what the other individuals do), it may well be that the noncooperative alternative serves the same function as the correct alternative in Asch's conformity studies. This means that when a subject is confronted with a unanimous cooperative ("incorrect") majority he will be inclined to conform. But as soon as one other group member chooses the noncooperative ("correct") alternative, thereby serving as a partner for the subject, conformity decreases drastically.

The present finding that both goals and expectations affect elementary cooperation is also in agreement with findings collected by Wilke and Braspenning (1989). In the latter study a distinction was made between (a) goals, (b) initial expectations from the outset of the game after goals were induced and (c) expectations as a consequence of feedback about the choices of other group members. In the present study these initial expectations were not measured, but it seems safe to assume that low temptation to defect (cooperative goal) gave rise to cooperative initial expectations, whereas high temptation to defect (noncooperative goal) gave rise to competitive initial expectations (see, e.g., Dawes, 1989). That temptation gave rise to initial expectations may explain why in the present study the manipulation checks revealed that when the temptation for D was low, subjects expected more cooperative choices than when the temptation for D was high.

Wilke and Braspenning (1989) found that shifts in choice behavior took place when initial expectations about the behavior of others were violated. Subjects did not change their choice behavior when feedback on the behavior of others was in agreement with initial expectations and own choices. When the behavior of others was in disagreement with initial expectations and own choices, subjects tended to shift in the direction indicated by the feedback. According to Wilke and Braspenning their results suggest that their subjects pursued a matching strategy.

Assuming then that in the present study cooperative goal subjects held cooperative initial expectations and noncooperative goal subjects held noncooperative initial expectations, a similar interpretation as put forward by Wilke and Braspenning (1989) may explain the present result that only when all others choose C one is more inclined to make a C-choice than when less than all others make a C-choice. For cooperative goal subjects these initial expectations are confirmed when feedback shows that all others make a C-choice. For non-cooperative goal subjects the noncooperative initial expectations are clearly disconfirmed when all others make a C-choice and only then noncooperative goal subjects are apparently inclined to revise their initial expectations in the light of feedback. In other words, cooperative goal subjects make a C-choice, unless it appears that initial expectations are unjustified given feedback about choices of others. Noncooperative goal subjects make a D-choice, unless there is abundant evidence available that these initial expectations are unjustified, which is only the case when *all* others cooperate. Thus, noncooperative goal subjects emit their spontaneous response (D) as soon as one other does and only give it up when all others act in disagreement with initial expectations.

The present results further show a main effect of temptation and an interaction effect of temptation and feedback on leader votes. The main effect is qualified by the interaction effect, and therefore only the latter will be discussed. The interaction effect results from the fact that group members who were both in the low temptation and low cooperative feedback conditions voted most often for a leader. A possible explanation for this finding is, that after subjects in the low temptation condition had developed a goal to achieve mutual cooperation and learned via feedback that the other group members were not intending to cooperate, subjects felt frustrated. Because of the impossibility of securing others' cooperation through one's own strategic actions, the only way left to attain the goal was to change the structure of the situation by voting for a leader.

An alternative explanation has to do with the relative seriousness of the situation (Yamagishi, 1988). Yamagishi found in his experiment that the level of instrumental cooperation increased as the dilemma became more serious. In Yamagishi's experiment the dilemma became more serious when both the temptation to defect and the gain of cooperation became greater. In our experiment the dilemma is more serious in the low temptation condition than in the high temptation condition. In the high temptation condition (see Table 17.1) the payoff difference between All C and All D is small. If all group members choose C they all get 10 guilders and if they all choose D they all get 9 guilders. In the low temptation condition, however, the payoff difference between All C and All D is large. If all group members choose D they now all get only 3 guilders. This makes All D a more serious affair in the low temptation condition than in the high temptation condition, especially in conditions in which one gets to know that a majority in the group intends to make a noncooperative choice. So, when the difference between All C and All D has more financial consequences and when the likelihood that these consequences will come into being is large, group members could be more likely to vote for a leader.

Thus, the motive underlying the leader votes could be of a more emotional nature or of a more rational nature. The last explanation is corroborated by findings of Messick *et al.* (1983), Rutte and Wilke (1984) and Samuelson *et al.* (1984). These investigators used a resource dilemma game and in one of the experimental conditions group members witnessed an overuse of the resource. This overuse threatened to deplete the resource and to cut group members off from future incomes. Under those circumstances group members showed a great willingness to vote for a leader, up to 71 percent.

What are the implications of the results of the present experiment for our extended version of Pruitt and Kimmel's goal/expectation theory? Theoretically, the present results together with those collected by Wilke and Braspenning suggest that: (a) from the outset of the game, subjects with a cooperative goal prefer a cooperative choice and expect cooperative choices from other group members; conversely, subjects without a cooperative goal prefer a noncooperative choice for themselves and expect noncooperative choices from other group members; (b) when subjects with a cooperative goal receive feedback that all other group members indeed intend to make cooperative choices, they will maintain their preference to make a cooperative choice and in that case there is no need to prefer a leader; however, if not all others show a tendency to make a cooperative choice, then cooperative goal subjects' willingness to cooperate will be weakened and because achievement of their cooperative goal is frustrated by the choices of others, they will prefer a leader; (c) subjects without a cooperative goal, receiving feedback that at least one group member makes a noncooperative choice, will maintain their preference to make a noncooperative choice and since their goal is not frustrated their preference to elect a leader is relatively low; however, subjects without a cooperative goal, receiving feedback that all others will make a cooperative choice, will be inclined to revise their preference to make a noncooperative choice and since their goal is not frustrated their preference for a leader remains relatively low.

In sum, subjects' goals have a strong effect on elementary cooperation. Subjects revise their willingness to make a cooperative or a noncooperative choice when it appears that the others are more competitive or more cooperative respectively than expected from the outset of the game. When feedback indicates that feedback expectations are in agreement with initial expectations, subjects will not change their preference for a cooperative or a noncooperative choice. Instrumental cooperation arises only when cooperative goal subjects, initially expecting cooperative choices from the others, discover that the others show a preference to make a noncooperative choice. Instrumental cooperation seems to be a second chance to guarantee cooperation for cooperative goal subjects who encounter other group members who are not cooperatively oriented as expected from the outset of the game.

How do the present findings relate to the findings presented by

Yamagishi in this book? As for elementary cooperation, Yamagishi found that contributions were higher in four-person than in eight-person groups, a result which is in agreement with earlier findings (see, e.g., Liebrand, 1982). This result suggests indeed that in larger groups elementary cooperation is rather problematic, since the larger the group the smaller the likelihood of elementary cooperation. Yamagishi's results for instrumental cooperation are somewhat more complicated. Yamagishi found that in small groups high trusters contributed less to a sanctioning system than low trusters, whereas in large groups high trusters contributed more to a sanctioning system than low trusters. Yamagishi assumes that his subjects are basically cooperative (in other words: have cooperative goals), and that trust and group size affect the expectations subjects have about other group members' behavior, whereby high trust and small group size lead to more cooperative expectations than low trust and large group size. If we follow his reasoning for a moment and assume that high trusters in small groups had more cooperative expectations than low trusters in small groups and that all subjects had cooperative goals, then Yamagishi's result that in small groups low trusters engaged more often in instrumental cooperation than high trusters may be consistent with the finding of the present study that instrumental cooperation was highest for cooperative goal subjects faced with a majority of noncooperative choices from other group members. However, such an interpretation could not explain why in large groups low trusters would engage less often in instrumental cooperation than high trusters.

Like Yamagishi, we may conclude that our theoretical notion may be limited in its applicability to small groups. It should be noted on the other hand that the comparability of the present study to the one reported by Yamagishi is low for several reasons. A first point of difference is the nature of the instrumental cooperation variable: where our subjects could elect a leader, Yamagishi's subjects could contribute points to a sanctioning fund. Second, where our subjects engaged in elementary cooperation and thereafter in instrumental cooperation in a one-trial game, Yamagishi's subjects could simultaneously contribute points to a fund of elementary cooperation and to a sanctioning fund of instrumental cooperation at each trial of a multi-trial game. Third, where we gave systematic feedback about the (intended) choices of other group members, Yamagishi gave real feedback (which was not under the control of the investigator), which may bias the results. A last point is that Yamagishi assumes cooperative goals on the part of subjects and infers expectation levels on the basis of trust measures and manipulations of group size, whereas we tried to independently manipulate goals and expectations with the help of variations in temptation to defect and feedback about other group members' choice-intentions.

All in all we consider our approach to the goal/expectation theory somewhat more convincing. A strong point in favor of Yamagishi is that his subjects were exposed to a multi-trial game, which allows generalization to long range decision making. It should be noted however that the present data are rather similar to the data reported by Wilke and Braspenning (1989), who also employed a multi-trial game.

What are the practical implications? Yamagishi (1986a) has pointed out that elementary cooperation is not a practical solution for social dilemmas, because in large groups individual actions are hardly noticed. In view of the data described by Yamagishi in this book which show that elementary cooperation is smaller in large groups than in small groups, this position seems to be tenable. If we assume, however, that society is built up through hierarchically linked small groups, it may be argued that elementary cooperation may be promoted by cooperative goals and cooperative expectations of individual group members.

Instrumental cooperation seems to be fostered by cooperative goals and noncooperative expectations, which means that cooperative goal subjects tend to favor the inauguration of a leader when other group members are not assumed to act in a cooperative way. Assuming that in large groups there is a high likelihood of noncooperative expectations, our results suggest that in these groups cooperative goal subjects are likely to promote instrumental cooperation.

References

Allen, V. L. (1965). Situational factors in conformity. In: Berkowitz, L. (Ed.), *Advances in Experimental Social Psychology*, vol. 2. New York: Academic Press.

Caldwell, M. D. (1976). Communication and sex effects in a five-person prisoner's dilemma. *Journal of Personality and Social Psychology*, **33**, 273–281.

Dawes, R. M. (1980). Social dilemmas. *Annual Review of Psychology*, **31**, 169–193.

Dawes, R. M. (1989). Statistical criteria for establishing a truly false consensus effect. *Journal of Experimental Social Psychology*, **25**, 1–17.

Dawes, R. M., McTavish, J., & Shaklee, H. (1977). Behavior, communication and assumptions about other people's behavior in a commons dilemma situation. *Journal of Personality and Social Psychology*, **35**, 1–11.

Goodman, A. (1971). The analysis of multidimensional contingency tables: stepwise procedures and direct estimation methods for building models for multiple classification. *Technometrics*, **13**, 33–62.

Hardin, G. J. (1968). The tragedy of the commons. *Science*, **162**, 1243–1248.

Kelley, H. H., & Grzelak, J. (1972). Conflict between individual and common interest in a *n*-person relationship. *Journal of Personality and Social Psychology*, **21**, 190–197.

Liebrand, W. B. G. (1982). *Interpersonal Differences in Social Dilemmas; a Game Theoretical Approach*. Meppel: Krips.

Liebrand, W. B. G., Jansen, R. W. T. L., & Rijken, V. M. (1986). Might over morality: social values and the perception of other players in experimental games. *Journal of Experimental Social Psychology*, **22**, 203–215.

Liebrand, W. B. G., Wilke, H. A. M., Vogel, R., & Wolters, F. J. M. (1986). Value orientation and conformity: a study using three types of social dilemma games. *Journal of Conflict Resolution*, **30**, 77–97.

Messick, D. M., Wilke, H., Brewer, M. B., Kramer, R. M., Zemke, P. E., & Lui, L. (1983). Individual adaptations and structural change as solutions to social dilemmas. *Journal of Personality and Social Psychology*, **44**, 294–309.

Messick, D. M., & Brewer, M. B. (1983). Solving social dilemmas: a review. In: Wheeler, L. and Shaver, P. (Eds), *Review of Personality and Social Psychology*, vol. **4**, Beverly Hills: Sage.

Orbell, J. M., van de Kragt, A., & Dawes, R. M. (1988). *Covenants without the sword. When promises don't work, and when they do.* Paper delivered to the Annual Meeting of the Public Choice Society and the Economic Science Association.

Pruitt, D. G., & Kimmel, M. J. (1977). Twenty years of experimental gaming: critique, synthesis, and suggestions for the future. *Annual Review of Psychology,* **28**, 363–392.

Rutte, C. G., & Wilke, H. A. M. (1984). Social dilemmas and leadership. *European Journal of Social Psychology,* **14**, 105–121.

Samuelson, C. D., Messick, D. M., Rutte, C. G., & Wilke, H. A. M. (1984). Individual and structural solutions to resource dilemmas in two cultures. *Journal of Personality and Social Psychology,* **47**, 94–104.

Schroeder, D. A., Jensen, T. D., Reed, A. J., Sullivan, D. K., & Schwab, M. (1983). The actions of others as determinants of behavior in social dilemma situations. *Journal of Experimental Social Psychology,* **19**, 522–539.

Wilke, H. A. M., & Braspenning, J. (1989). Reciprocity: Choice shift in a social trap. *European Journal of Social Psychology,* **19**, 317–326.

Wilke, H., Liebrand, W., & Messick, D. M. (1983). Sociale dilemma's, een overzicht. *Nederlands Tijdschrift voor de Psychologie,* **38**, 463–480.

Yamagishi, T. (1986a). The structural goal/expectation theory of cooperation in social dilemmas. In: Lawler, E. L. (Ed.), *Advances in Group Processes*, vol. **3**. Greenwich, JAI.

Yamagishi, T. (1986b). The provision of a sanctioning system as a public good. *Journal of Personality and Social Psychology,* **51**, 110–116.

Yamagishi, T. (1988). Seriousness of social dilemmas and the provision of a sanctioning system. *Social Psychology Quarterly,* **51**, 32–42.

18

Persuasive Communication: Measures to Overcome Real-life Social Dilemmas

BERT KLANDERMANS
Free University, Amsterdam, The Netherlands

Industrialized countries face a growing number of large-scale social problems, among them, environmental pollution, traffic congestion, crime, unhealthy eating and living habits, the depletion of natural resources, and overpopulation. Because the solution to such problems may require thousands or even millions of people to change their habits, governments and policy makers must determine how to alter the behavior of large numbers of individuals. We know quite a bit about strategies to control individual behavior, but the problem of controlling behavior on this large a scale raises different kinds of questions. For example, rewarding desirable behavior and punishing undesirable behavior is a classic means of modifying an individual's behavior (Gergen & Gergen, 1986), but how can we reward or punish the behavior of millions of people? Who has the resources to reward so many people, and who is prepared to mete out punishments on such a scale? Moreover, how can we know which rewards and punishments will be effective, and how are we going to make sure that offenders are caught? And what about privacy? Do we deem it acceptable to monitor people in their daily lives? Further, in a democracy public rewards and punishments are regulated by law, and we all know that many wonderful dreams have been killed in the lawmaking process.

Constrained by these difficulties, policy makers often choose to wage a persuasive campaign that attempts to change the citizens' behavior by influencing their attitudes and beliefs. The advantages are evident: you do not need to pass new laws; such a campaign is relatively cheap; it fits nicely into the model of the enlightened citizen, who makes his or her own decisions; it is highly visible and demonstrates that the administration is attending to the problem. It has only one disadvantage: too often it does not work. In the Netherlands, for example, despite large-scale campaigns to reduce energy consumption, such consumption is primarily determined by energy prices. Despite intensive anti-speeding campaigns, car drivers continue to exceed speed limits; despite forceful persuasion, fishermen ignored regulations issued to prevent overexploitation of the North Sea.

The power of persuasion to solve societal problems is at the very least questionable. Consequently, we must look to other strategies, strategies that attack the undesirable behaviors more directly. Rather than try to influence the choices people make, we should try to change the alternatives available to them by, for example, removing phosphates from detergents or ensuring that all gas is unleaded. Not every problem, however, can be solved in this way. I can assume that people will be willing to buy phosphate free detergents or unleaded gas, that, indeed, they might even be willing to accept enforcement. But would we allow our governments to turn off the central heating after 11 o'clock p.m. or to prohibit us from living more than ten miles from our workplace? Presumably not, yet these two measures would help solve major environmental problems.

In many situations, then, we may have no other option than to try to persuade people to change their behavior. Consequently, despite its perhaps dubious success rate, persuasion will always remain a possible alternative for anyone who wishes to influence large numbers of people. Therefore, it is worth investigating the use of persuasive campaigns in attempts to solve social problems.

The Motivational Dynamics of Individual Behavior in Real-life Social Dilemmas

Those groups or people who set out to persuade individuals to change their behavior must know the motivational dynamics of the behavior they want to influence. Knowledge of these dynamics is vital when one wants to develop campaign strategies, define one's targets, and set one's goals. Two bodies of literature are relevant to this subject—the social dilemma literature and the literature on collective behavior. Both attribute a central role to rational-choice theory—a theory that defines human beings as rational actors whose behavior is controlled by the perceived costs and benefits of available alternatives. Reformulated in terms of rational-choice theory, the essence of the social problems we are concerned with is: uncertain risks and costs and benefits to the collective in a distant future must be measured against certain costs and benefits to the individual in the present; and as long as the certain benefits to the individual outweigh the uncertain costs to the collective we can predict what individuals will favor in their own short-term interests. Accordingly, the basic principle underlying any strategy for influencing individual choices in such circumstances is to try to change the cost-benefit structure of the situation.

Unlike the cost-benefit structure of hypothetical social dilemmas made up in the laboratory, the cost-benefit structure of real-life social dilemmas is neither objectively given nor explained to the individual subject. In real life, costs and benefits are perceived—that is, they are subjective and are often unclear to the individual. Consequently, individual perceptions of cost-benefit structures of specific situations often vary greatly. It is thus strategically important for campaigners to know precisely how those individuals involved in the situation perceive its costs and benefits. For no matter how diverse the perceptions are, they share, analytically, a number of elements. In the course of my research on one particular type of real-life dilemma—individual decisions to take part in collective action—I developed a model for predicting individual behavior (Klandermans, 1984). Presumably, we can apply this model to other real-life social dilemmas.

The model combines value-expectancy theory (Feather & Norman, 1982) and collective behavior theory (Olson, 1968; Oberschall, 1973). According to value-expectancy theory, an individual's behavior is a function of the value of the expected outcomes of behavioral choices. The more likely it is that a specific behavior will produce a specific set of outcomes and the more valued these outcomes are to a person, the more likely it is that he or she will engage in that behavior. Although the value-expectancy assumption may hold in general, when the situation involves the individual's contribution to the production of a collective good, the motivational dynamics are more complex. To account for the increased complexity, we incorporated collective action theory in the model.

The core of the theory of collective action is the distinction between collective and selective incentives. The factor that distinguishes the two is excludability (Olson, 1968; Oliver, 1980). Collective incentives are all-inclusive—that is, once they have been provided, everyone profits, even people who never contributed to their realization. Selective incentives, in contrast, distinguish between those who cooperate in a collective action and those who do not. Typically, the incentives germane to solutions of the large-scale social problems I am concerned with here (e.g., air pollution, water pollution, energy consumption and traffic congestion, and so on) are collective incentives. Some relevant incentives, however, are selective, rewarding only those who actively help to solve the social problem (one may save money, receive an award, gain prestige, improve his or her health, and so on).

Of key importance for our topic—how to persuade individuals to contribute to the solution of a social problem—is the distinct functional relation of collective and selective incentives to individual behavior. Whereas selective incentives are directly contingent on an individual's behavior, collective incentives are only indirectly related to the individual's behavior; the mediator between individual behavior and collective incentives is the behavior of others. Whether you benefit financially by insulating your house depends on *your decision*; whether the nation's energy consumption goes down substantially depends on how many *other* people decide to insulate their houses. The same relation holds for other collective incentives. This dependence on other people's decisions would not be a problem if each person knew what everyone else would do. But, at the time that an individual must decide what to do, he or she does not know what other people will do. This uncertainty is exactly what generates the dilemma. Nevertheless, each individual will certainly have *expectations* about the behavior of others. And in the absence of factual information about the behavior of others, it is these expectations that, supposedly, influence the individual to decide for or against helping to solve a social problem. Expectations about the behavior of others are one element in a set of three distinguishable expectations that together determine an individual's expectation that a problem will be solved. The two other expectations are: that one's own behavior contributes to the solution of the problem; and that the problem can be solved if enough people contribute.

Figure 18.1 summarizes the argument developed thus far: Whether an individual is willing to contribute to the solution of a social problem depends in the first place, of course, on the value the social problem has for that individual. We would not expect someone who does not care about a social problem to contribute to its solution, unless he were persuaded to do so by the threat of severe punishment or the promise of generous rewards. But, no matter how much a person cares about a problem, its presupposed solution can be an incentive only if the person believes that the problem will be solved.

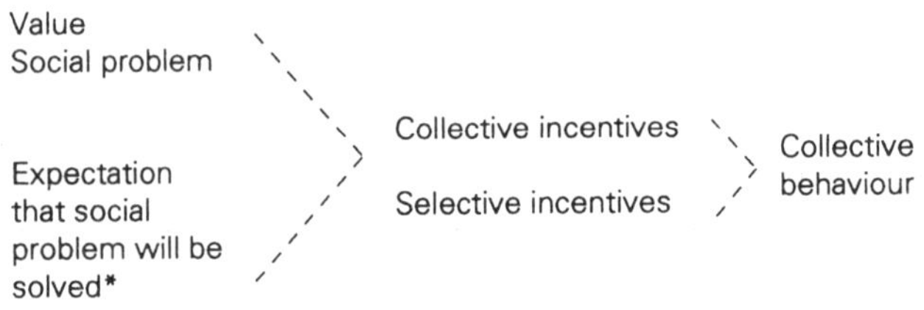

* Expectation that social problem will be solved:
- Expectations about the behaviour of others
- Expectations about one's own contribution
- Expectations about success

FIG. 18.1 A model for the prediction of behavior in real-life social dilemmas.

Persuasion in Social Dilemma Situations

Having analyzed the motivational dynamics of behavior in dilemma situations we can proceed to the next important question: What kinds of leverage are available to persuasive campaigns, according to this model?

First, one can try to influence the perceived value of the social problem. This strategy involves the attempt to influence attitudes toward the problem. It seems reasonable to assume that the greater a population's concern about a problem, the greater their willingness to help to solve it. But a look at the model quickly reveals the weaknesses of this strategy. If we cannot take for granted that the other determinants suggested by the model are under control, we have no guarantee that an increase in the value of the collective good will have any positive effect. More precisely, as long as people lack a guarantee that the problem will be solved, a campaign that aims at increasing the value of the social problem will not be very successful in motivating them to behave in the interest of the collective. Stressing the problem without specifying its solutions might even be counterproductive.

Second, one can try to control selective incentives. The basic idea underlying this strategy is simple. If people prefer choices in their individual interest because these choices are more profitable, why not change priorities and make choices that contribute to the collective interest more attractive? In other words, we can try to enhance the selective incentives for acting in the collective interest. Oliver (1980) has pointed to the limitations of this strategy, particularly its failure to answer one fundamental question: which strategy is preferable, increasing the costs of choices that favor the individual's interests (punishment) or increasing the benefits of choices that favor the collective interest (rewards)? Psychologists have always argued that rewards are more effective than punishment (Gergen and Gergen 1986; see Komorita and Barth, 1985, for additional support for the effectiveness of rewards rather than punishments in a social dilemma context). This assertion may be valid in the case of a single individual, but will it hold as well when the subject whose behavior we wish to influence is a mass population? Do we really have the resources to reward every citizen who acts in the collective interest? A real-life example demonstrates that this question is not simply hypothetical: The Dutch government subsidizes home insulation, but regularly before the fiscal year is over, the insulation fund runs out of money and so must disappoint some people.

Precisely because resources are scarce, a government can, alternatively, decide to punish people who fail to act in the collective interest. This strategy seems reasonable as long as the majority of the population behaves in the preferred way. But what if a substantial proportion of the population violates the rules, deems the particular collective good at issue irrelevant, or does not accept the government's punishment for violaters. Punishment presupposes that a government has convinced its citizens of the value of the collective good, but even if it has tried to do so, people will not always feel that punishment is a legitimate means of modifying behavior. True, we are willing to accept a fine for exceeding a speed limit, but are we as willing to accept fines for exceeding some specified limit of energy consumption or for failing to insulate our homes? A government that does not determine whether the population will accept punishment as a means of modifying a certain behavior runs the risk of losing legitimacy when it uses punishment as its means of control.

The third strategy, which is related to that described above, is to form and activate social networks to reward people who cooperate and to punish those who do not. The basic idea behind this strategy too is simple: to try to make use of social bonds so that they foster behavior in the collective interest. Social psychologists tell us that significant others (e.g., peers and primary groups) play an important role in shaping an individual's behavior. This approach has been used, for instance, in Dutch campaigns against drink and driving: television spots dramatize situations in which a person's friends restrain him from drinking because later he will have to drive.

A serious disadvantage of all three strategies is that they can tell the individual whether the social problem will be solved. Consequently, they cannot know whether it is worthwhile for them to abandon their individual interests. Sometimes this consideration is not important. Selective incentives may be rewarding enough to outweigh the costs (for example, some insulation measures save so much energy that they are profitable independent of the collective incentives). But very often selective incentives are not so rewarding, and one cannot be certain that the question of whether the problem will be solved. As we have seen, solutions to large-scale social problems do not depend solely on the choices a single individual makes; they depend on the choices other people are making as well. Laboratory dilemma experiments strongly support this importance of others' choices (Messick *et al.*, 1983; Schroeder *et al.*, 1983; Yamagishi & Sato, 1986). Therefore, a campaign that aims at persuading people to choose in the collective interest must not only stress the value of the social problem at issue and—wherever possible—control selective incentives, it must convince the individual that enough other people will choose in the collective interest to effect the desired change. Persuasive campaigns that fail to convince large numbers of people inevitably get stuck with those few people for whom the cost-benefit structure of the situation is favorable and with the true believers who value the social problem so much that they contribute regardless of costs and benefits. In most cases such a response will be inadequate to solve the social problem the campaign was designed to rectify.

Social psychological literature on attitude change and persuasion shows hardly any awareness of this collective aspect of the dynamics of individual behavior in real-life social dilemmas. Although the model of Fishbein and Ajzen (1975) does encompass social pressure as a factor distinct from the individual's attitude toward the behavior concerned, this factor is more closely related to selective incentives and to collective ones. Their model does not include any category such as the perceived behavior of others, nor does it include any other variable that takes into account the specifics of collective behavior. Researchers on change and persuasion, like those on attitude and behavior in general, assume that the costs and the benefits involved are directly contingent on the individual's behavior. But as I have argued, their assumption does not hold for behavior in dilemma situations in which the realization of a collective good is dependent on the behavior of other people. If we assume that people are aware of this situation, we may expect them to take into account the available information about the choices others plan to make. We can hypothesize that if they learn that only a few people plan to contribute to solve the problem, it is unlikely that they themselves will contribute.

Influencing Expectations about the Behavior of Others

Expectations about the behavior of others function as self-fulfilling prophecies. If a person believes that no one else will cooperate, he himself will not be highly motivated to cooperate. Thus predictions about the insolubility of the social problem will be proven true. By the same token, campaigns that can convince an individual that his/her fellow citizens are cooperating will win his/her cooperation as well. And the more people who are thus convinced, the more likely it is that predictions of success will be proven true. Transforming expectations about the behavior of others, however, is a sensitive matter; too much optimism reduces motivation, but so does too much pessimism. A campaign that stresses the number of other people that have already joined or how much they have contributed may easily end up encouraging free riders. Alternatively, a campaign that repeatedly stresses how many more participants it needs before the problem can be solved may lead people to conclude that their individual contributions will not make any difference because so few people plan to contribute and chances are the problem will never be solved anyway. No wonder that in practice we often see campaigners painfully trying to convince people that their contribution is crucial.

Although our expectations about the behavior of others are rooted in our objective experiences and observations, several studies have indicated that these expectations have subjective aspects as well. Granberg (1983), discussing voting behavior, demonstrated that people tend to overestimate the number of votes they expect their preferred party to win. Opp (1986) showed that although collective behavior theory asserts that the actual impact of individual contributions on mass collective action is insignificant, many individuals *feel* their effect on collective action is far from negligible. Kerr (forthcoming) demonstrated in an experimental setting that if the size of a group increases, its members become more doubtful that it will produce a collective good. As long as size is the only parameter we are considering, the members' judgments will prove correct, an outcome confirmed by every dilemma experiment in which group size is the dependent variable. More importantly, Kerr found that the respondents in this study continued to predict a diminishing efficacy for large groups even when they knew (according to the rules of the experiment) that the opposite was true. In his study Kerr used Kahneman and Tversky's work on the operation of the representativeness heuristic in judgments of subjective probability (1972). These authors demonstrated that individuals may be insensitive to sample size when making judgments about subjective sampling distributions. In short, then, expectations about the behavior of others have a complex relationship to reality. It is this complexity that can be and is exploited in attempts to convince people that a collective good is attainable; that, chances are, enough other people will contribute to attain it; but that each individual's contribution is crucial nonetheless.

One can accomplish these goals in several ways, as the routine practice of campaign organizers illustrates:

– Make a contract, that specifies conditions for contribution in such a way that contributors can withdraw if not enough other people contribute. Usually such contracts specify a goal in terms of the number of people to be recruited or the amount of money to be collected. The individual pledges to contribute provided that the campaign reaches its goal. If the campaign does reach its goal each individual fulfills his or her pledge; if the campaign does not succeed, all provisional contributors are free to withdraw. This approach is common in money collecting campaigns.

– Divide the goal into smaller subgoals. If a campaign frames its goals in terms of some grand end result, it may make individual contributions seem insignificant, and it may cause people to doubt its ability to achieve that end. By establishing subgoals (for, e.g., a region, a sector, or a time period), a campaign can eliminate these barriers to participation. The mobilization of the large peace demonstrations in the Netherlands illustrates how effective this approach can be. Throughout the country local peace groups mobilized participants and sold bus or train tickets to get people to the large peace demonstrations. These local groups formulated their goals in terms of the number of tickets they hoped to sell. The mobilization of three busloads of demonstrators in a community of 5,000 people seems much more attainable than the mobilization of 500,000 participants in the Dutch population as a whole, even though, proportionally, the two figures are the same. Further, in a small-scale campaign (i.e., in the small communities) individual decisions to participate affect turnout much more directly than it does in large-scale campaigns, related to the turnout in this community.

– Break the population down into subpopulations. This strategy is akin to establishing subgoals. The strengths of this approach, in fact, are nicely illustrated by the findings of Kerr (forthcoming), who concludes that when a problem involving a collective good of a large group is reframed as a problem pertaining to several smaller groups, it is more likely that the collective good will eventually be achieved.

– Conduct small-scale experiments to demonstrate that success is achievable. One way to convince individuals that other people will participate is to point to successful experiments. Small-scale experiments are easier to control than large campaigns, and they can take advantage of the small-goal and small-group mechanisms described above. The protest meetings organized by a union to determine whether it can mobilize enough workers (Klandermans, 1982) is one example of a small-scale experiment; energy saving innovations in selected communities is another (De Rooij, 1987). This strategy, of course, does present one serious risk: the experiment might fail. If it does, organizers of future campaigns will obviously have a hard time convincing individuals that other people will participate.

– Point to past successes. This strategy, while related to the previous one, may be less risky. Waddington (1986) provides an example of how a movement can extrapolate from the successes of the past: recent strikes in the Ansell Brewery led the workers to assume that the vast majority of the work force would join a current industrial action. Of course, this strategy works only if a campaign has some past successes to point to. As I have already indicated, past failures can be devastating, since they fatally undermine a campaign's ability to persuade potential contributors.

– Persuasive communication. If a campaign has no previous experiences to draw on to demonstrate its effectiveness, it can try to persuade people to believe that others will participate and that success is possible. Persuasive communication of this kind typically includes the following arguments: more and more people are becoming concerned; something should be done soon; a substantial proportion of those who are concerned already contribute; the campaign can successfully attack the problem if enough people contribute; and each individual can make a significant contribution (Godwin, 1984). This strategy will be used only once. If it succeeds, its success provides more convincing arguments in future campaigns; if it fails, the original arguments will no longer work.

All these strategies attempt to influence expectations about the behavior of others; all attempt to make the individual believe that enough people will cooperate to ensure that the proposed action will succeed. To convince people, however, is not necessarily to mislead them. Basically, campaign organizers try to reframe reality in such a way that the need to choose between the collective and the individual interest no longer presents a social dilemma. The more certain we are about the behaviors of others, the less likely we are to find ourselves in a dilemma. Thus the relevance of my last topic: framing and persuasive communication in dilemma situations.

Framing and Persuasion

In reframing a social problem so that it no longer creates a dilemma for the individual, a campaign must guarantee the individual that other people will participate. If a campaign focuses too much on the social problem itself or on the importance of its solution without guaranteeing such participation, it intensifies the dilemma rather than resolve it. Hence, the success of a persuasive campaign depends to a great extent on the way a social problem is framed. Accordingly, we must learn much more about the determinants of framing. We may assume that the process involves personality traits (Liebrand, 1982) and situational and contextual factors (Kerr, forthcoming). And what is particularly important for our topic, we know that persuasive campaigns themselves attempt to frame the social problem at issue.

In several publications Snow and his colleagues (1986, 1988, 1990) have analyzed (a) the task of framing itself—that is, defining social problems so that individuals are motivated to contribute to a solution rather than discouraged from doing anything; and (b) the task of frame alignment—linking the interpretive orientations of the individual and the campaigner to make them congruent or complementary. In their discussion of framing, Snow *et al.* distinguish between diagnostic framing (identifying problems and attributing causality), prognostic framing (suggesting solutions and strategies), and motivational framing (providing a rationale for action) (1988). They argue that, to mobilize individuals, it is not enough to identify problems and suggest solutions. Their discussion of frame alignment is based on the assumption that everyone adheres to some frame of reference (belief system) which may be more or less distinct from those advocated by would-be campaigners. Within an individual's frame of reference, some opinions are obvious and others are completely out of order. For most part, people act according to the opinions that are obvious to them, given their particular frame of reference. Those who want to change behavior must recognize that they will have to transform pre-existing frames of reference. This process is much more difficult than it appears to be: even dramatic events usually do not divert people from what they are used to doing—which is usually nothing.

Depending on the frame of reference to which a population or subpopulation adheres, the problems that persuasive communication must solve differ widely. Snow *et al.* (1986) developed a typology of framing processes based on the difference between the campaigner's frame of reference and that of the campaign's targeted population. These four processes (in ascending order of complexity) are: (a) frame bridging, required if the two frames are congruent and need only to be connected; (b) frame amplification, appropriate if campaigners can argue that the behavior they propose is in line with the population's existing values and opinions; (c) frame extension, appropriate if points of view that are of considerable salience to potential supporters are added to the campaign's frame; and (d) frame transformation, necessary if the two frames are completely different and campaigners need to redefine activities, events, and biographies. Presumably, the more complex a framing process a campaign must engage in, the more difficult and time-consuming its task of persuasion will be.

Using Snow's typology, we can devise the following strategy for persuasion. First, of course, the public must be made aware of the problem. (Anyone who does not even recognize that a particular social problem exists will certainly not be troubled by a social dilemma.) To rectify lack of awareness, a campaign must undertake frame transformation. If the target population demonstrates some awareness of a social problem, campaigners then have to deal with individual expectations about the behavior of others. Snow's typology suggests that strategies for persuasion can take advantage of the snowball effect. It seems reasonable for a campaign to look first to those individuals who can be reached by frame bridging. Once these people have been persuaded to participate, the fact that they are cooperating can be used to convince others who are more difficult to approach. This strategy, however, will not work unless a population contains enough people eligible for frame bridging. If it does not, even the few people who can be reached through frame bridging may begin to doubt whether the collective good can be produced at all.

Summary and Scope

Many social problems have the characteristics of social dilemmas. Therefore campaigns to solve social problems find it difficult to persuade people to contribute, even when they are aware that the problems exist. A campaign's success depends to a great extent on the way it frames a social problem. Persuasive campaigns that concentrate on the gravity of the problem without solving the dilemma run the risk of discouraging rather than encouraging participation.

The ideas presented in this paper must be understood as hypotheses that need to be tested in future research. This research should analyze the dilemma characteristics of social problems, investigate the framing of social problems in the general population and by campaigners, and examine campaign strategies to solve the dilemmas.

References

De Rooij, G. M. (1987). Milieu—en energiegedrag. In P. G. Klandermans & E. Seydel (Eds), *Overtuigen en activeren. Publieksbeïnvloeding in theorie en praktijk*. Assen: Van Gorcum.

Feather, N. T., & Norman, T. (Eds) (1982). *Expectations and Actions: Expectancy-Value Models in Psychology*. Hillsdale, N.J.: Lawrence Erlbaum Associates.

Fishbein, M., & Ajzen, I. (1975). *Belief, Attitude, Intention and Behaviour*. Reading, Mass.: Addison-Wesley.

Gergen, K. J., & Gergen, M. M. (1986). *Social Psychology*, 2nd ed. New York: Springer-Verlag.

Godwin, R. K. (1984). Direct mail appeals and the mass society. Paper presented at the 79th Annual Meeting of the American Sociological Association, San Antonio.

Granberg, D. (1983). Preferences, expectations and placement judgments: Some evidence from Sweden. *Social Psychology Quarterly*, **46**, 363–368.

Kahneman, D., & Tversky, A. (1972). Subjective probability: A judgment of representativeness. *Cognitive Psychology*, **3**, 430–454.

Kerr, N. (forthcoming). Illusions of efficacy: The effects of group size on perceived efficacy in social dilemmas. *Journal of Experimental Social Psychology*.

Klandermans, P. G. (1982). Arbeidsplaatsenovereenkomsten: Waarom de mobilisatiecampagne voor een vernieuwing mislukte. *Tijdschrift voor Agologie*, **11**, 23–36.

Klandermans, P. G. (1984). Mobilization and participation: Social psychological expansions of resource mobilization theory. *American Sociological Review*, **49**, 583–600.

Komorita, S. S., & Barth, J. M. (1985). Components of reward in social dilemmas. *Journal of Personality and Social Psychology*, **48**, 364–373.

Liebrand, W. B. G. (1982). Interpersonal differences in social dilemmas: a game theoretical approach. Unpublished Dissertation, Rijksuniversiteit Groningen.

Liebrand, W. B. G., Jansen, R. W. T. L., Rijken, V. M., & Suhre, C. J. M. (1986). Might over morality: Social values and the perception of other players in experimental games. *Journal of Experimental Social Psychology*, **22**, 203–215.

Messick, D. A., Wilke, H., Brewer, M. B., Kramer, R. M., Zemke, P. E., & Lui, L. (1983). Individual adaptations and structural change as solutions to social dilemmas. *Journal of Personality and Social Psychology*, **44**, 294–309.

Oberschall, A. (1973). *Social Conflict and Social Movements*. Englewood Cliffs, N.J.: Prentice Hall.

Oliver, P. (1980). Rewards and punishments as selective incentives for collective action: Theoretical investigations. *American Journal of Sociology*, **85**, 1356–1375.

Olson, M. (1968). *The Logic of Collective Action: Public Goods and the Theory of Groups*. Cambridge, Mass.: Harvard University Press.

Opp, K.-D. (1986). Soft incentives and collective action: participation in the anti-nuclear movement. *British Journal of Political Science*, **16**, 87–112.

Snow, D. A., & Benford, R. D. (1988). Ideology, frame resonance, and participant mobilization. In B. Klandermans, H. Kriesi, and S. Tarrow (Eds), *From Structure to Action: Comparing Movement Participation Across Cultures*. Greenwich, Conn.: JAI Press.

Snow, D. A., & Benford, R. D. (1990). Master frames and the cycle of protest. In A. Morris & C. Mueller (Eds), *Frontiers in Social Movement Theory*. New Haven, Conn.: Yale University Press.

Snow, D. A., Rochford, E. B. Jr., Worden, S., & Benford, R. D. (1986). Frame alignment processes, micro-mobilization and movement participation. *American Sociological Review*, **51**, 464–481.

Waddington, D. P. (1986). The Ansell Brewery dispute: A social–cognitive approach to the study of strikes. *Journal of Occupational Psychology*, **59**, 231–246.

Yamagishi, T., & Sato, K. (1986). Motivational bases of the public goods problem. *Journal of Personality and Social Psychology*, **50**, 67–73.

Name Index

Subject Index